JEAN-CLAUDE KILLY'S
Guide to
Skiing

JEAN-CLAUDE KILLY
HONORÉ BONNET

JEAN-CLAUDE KILLY
HONORÉ BONNET

JEAN-CLAUDE KILLY'S
Guide to
Skiing

THE PROVEN
TECHNIQUES OF
AN OLYMPIC
GOLD MEDAL WINNER

BARRON'S

foreword

It would be difficult to imagine more ideal collaborators for a book on skiing than Jean-Claude Killy and Honoré Bonnet. Killy, of course, is the greatest skier of our time. He was gifted with every talent necessary to make him a champion; and, thanks to his extraordinary determination and intelligence, he was able to make optimum use of those talents. Honoré Bonnet was the coach whose skill assured an uninterrupted series of victories for French ski teams from 1960 to 1968.

It may be said without exaggeration that Killy and Bonnet re-invented the art of ski racing. Far from being satisfied merely to work within the framework of what had been done in the past, they dared to push past the frontier of accepted techniques and to replace standard formulas with the genius of improvisation.

Skiers everywhere have long waited for this book. But Killy and Bonnet—perhaps wiser than we, and certainly more patient—insisted on working at their own pace, being certain to communicate their discoveries in a way that would enable as many people as possible to profit from them.

For this is a book for every skier. The reader will discover the secrets that gave Bonnet's ski teams the edge on their competitors. And the casual skier will discover that there is a spontaneous and joyful way of skiing, an approach free of inflexible techniques and inviolable rules. What Jean-Claude Killy demonstrates, and what he teaches us here, is that the art of skiing consists of establishing a harmony among one's body, one's skills, and the terrain. Those things that are natural and simple to the skier—these are the elements on which Bonnet and Killy build.

Perhaps, to those elements we must add love of sport and joy of skiing.

Finally, let us say that this is the very first book on skiing that is, in every sense of the word, inspired.

Michel Clare

All inquiries should be address to
Barron's Educational Series, Inc.
113 Crossways Park Drive
Woodbury, New York 11797

Library of Congress Catalog Card No. 77-15023
International Standard Book No. 0-8120-5198-X

Library of Congress Cataloging in Publication Data
Killy, Jean-Claude.
  Ski.
    1. Skis and skiing. 1. Bonnet, Honoré, 1919-
joint author. II, Title.
GC854.K49713   1977   796.9'3   77-15023
ISBN 0-8120-5198-X

PRINTED IN THE UNITED STATES OF AMERICA

contents

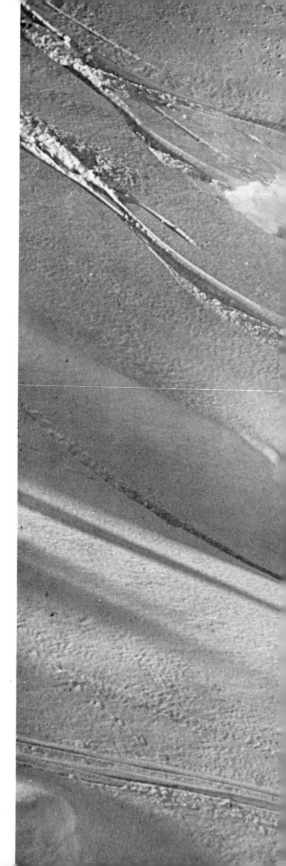

A skier's greatest delight is
soft, virgin snow.

introduction: pretensions & aspirations

Why would a former champion, Jean-Claude Killy, and a former coach, Honoré Bonnet, work together to help skiers enjoy the snow and its pleasures? Why would two men, both of them veterans of the Olympics, want to show vacation skiers how to ski more easily, more safely, more enjoyably and more happily, so that they may gain the maximum benefit from a brief stay in the mountains?

It is all the more curious when you consider that Killy tortured himself for years to become the fastest skier in the world. He himself was able to give up everything and anything to become the ski virtuoso of the 'sixties, the man who often surpassed the (theoretical) limits of the laws of nature to become the most dexterous skier of them all. It goes without saying that his sureness of eye, his hair-trigger reflexes, were not acquired overnight. They required an incredible amount of relentless training in which there was no room for weakness.

If Killy suffered to become a champion, then Bonnet was one of those who made others suffer for the same purpose. Young men and women came to him by the dozen, and he subjected them to an unbelievably severe regimen of training, in the hope that a few of them might one day be admitted to the rarefied circle of champions, of gold medals and titles. . . .

For both men, the process of training was a life of sacrifice, a kind of hell on earth. Killy, as a trainee, embraced that life and those sacrifices for himself. Bonnet, as a coach, imposed them on others. Now, they tell us that there is such a thing as skiing-made-easy; and they offer to teach us how. Is this some kind of heresy?

Both men, of course, are certified ski instructors, and both are familiar with all of the great ski resorts of the world as well as with many of the smaller ones. They've given lessons to vacation skiers everywhere; in their leisure hours, they've often skied with them and among them. Killy worked for years to rationalize and simplify his every movement on skis and to make it as effective as possible. Bonnet, an utter realist, has made a practice of adapting "technique" to each of his athletes—to the trainee's physique and aptitudes; that is, to his personality.

Both have always sought ways to realize the maximum return for the energy expended by the skier, and they have therefore always excluded those superfluous frills which, in skiing, are by no means a necessary luxury.

Through the years, they have participated in the selection of those techniques best suited to instruction, and their elaboration of those techniques constitutes a very substantial contribution to the art of instruction.

At the same time, they have remained acutely conscious that skiing is more than a matter of technique, and they have both been in the forefront of the battle for more functional equipment of higher quality, for the modification, remodeling, and widening of ski trails, for various safety measures, and for better-prepared and better-maintained snow.

Neither Killy nor Bonnet are any longer involved in active competition—even though Jean-Claude, four years after his retirement from the ranks of amateurs, skied professionally just long enough to capture a World Championship title. Bonnet currently is president of the Alpine Committee of the International Ski Federation, an organization involved both in ski competitions and in vacation skiing. Skiing, therefore, remains a daily preoccupation with both men.

Jean-Claude Killy is now involved in the winter sports industry, and particularly in the area of his particular expertise: equipment. Bonnet is manager of a winter sports resort, where he participates enthusiastically in the daily life of thousands of skiers.

The purpose of this book, therefore, is not to impose Killy's and Bonnet's ideas on men and women who ski for pleasure. Rather, it is to pass on to skiers the benefit of their experience. The authors hope to demonstrate that everyone—beginners as well as advanced skiers—can share in the joys and satisfactions of the sport. Consequently, the reader who is accustomed to finding doctrines and dogmas in books on skiing will be pleasantly surprised to find none in this particular work. The intention of the authors is simply to advise, to guide, and, finally, to issue an invitation to everyone to claim his or her fair share of the joys and pleasures of the snow.

Jean-Claude Killy and
Honoré Bonnet: an
association of concepts,
ideas, and effort.

1
the
snow
and
its
pleasures

the mountains

Snow! There is nothing quite like it. It gentles everything, cleans everything, purifies everything. And it has given birth to an activity that is at once the most beautiful and the most human of sports: skiing.

In an era when emphasis is on the social aspects of human activity, it is obvious that skiing, by its very nature and because of the conditions in which the sport is undertaken, is the social sport *par excellence,* in that it is, more than any other athletic activity, within the reach of everyone.

That is not a paradox. Even less is it an attempt at humor. There are no social barriers at ski resorts. There are no private or restricted trails. Everyone, from the austere Boston millionaire to the clerk from Macy's, waits his or her turn on line at the ski lift. When there is a pileup and everyone is covered with snow, with arms, legs, poles, and skis in an indiscriminate heap, who can tell the difference? All one hears is a roar of laughter—laughter from the heart, from the spirit. It is a liberating, uninhibited sound: the spontaneous and joyful sound that, somehow, is peculiar to skiers.

This kind of laughter, so frequent on the slopes, is symptomatic of skiing as a unique, ideal, and unrestrained and universal pleasure. For skiing is unquestionably a source of gaiety and joy for everyone, regardless of the contents of the pocketbook. This is not to say that skiing is inexpensive; but it is not, and should never become, a sport only for the rich. There are numerous "plans" available that put the sport within the reach of everyone.

By the same token, there is no such thing, and there never should be any such thing, as a resort exclusively for the rich—any more than there should be "cheap" resorts, with everything that that word implies of limited and unsatisfactory facilities. At a modern ski resort, there is room for the skier who does not count the cost, as well as for the skier on a stringent budget. No one is made to feel inferior, for everyone goes home from the slopes equally aching and exhausted, but happy, to the accommodations suitable to his or her purse.

You arrive at a ski resort. You have a place to stay. What should you wear? Anything. Everything. There is no such word as *ridiculous* at a resort. Whatever you wear, you can be sure that you'll be fashionable; and sometimes you'll be ahead of the fashions. You'll see millionaires skiing in blue jeans, and you'll see typists who've blown a week's salary on the finest ski pants.

Having settled in, you sign up for instruction. Be ready to suffer though the technique in vogue at the moment—realizing that it has little or no relationship to what you learned last year, and perhaps even less to what you'll be taught next year. Smile, and don't complain. If you don't learn to ski as well as "the great one" does—the great one, of course, being the great champion of the moment—at least you'll learn to navigate, more or less easily, on the great white slopes, to weave in and out among the other skiers. And—why not?—perhaps even to impress some of the latter. The day may even come when, intoxicated by success, you will feel enough confidence to ski fast, perhaps too fast; that is, faster than your skill actually permits; and then—but that is another story.

Finally, you will venture out onto the slopes alone to experience that extraordinary sense of freedom that solo skiing allows today. I say *extraordinary* because there are very few places in this crowded, possessive, and suffocating world that a person can actually be alone and left to one's own resources. You make a couple of turns. Perhaps five or six turns. It's nobody's business but yours. You ski slow. You ski fast. Faster. Then *really* fast; or at least it seems really fast to you. You feel light-headed. You can stop wherever you want, for as long as you want, to contemplate the unearthly beauty of the snowy landscape. Why not? There is no one here to tell you to move on.

You can, if you are strong enough and daring enough, if you don't mind the effort, and if you're willing to make do only with a sandwich for lunch, get one of the best bargains available today: a day of freedom for the price of train fare. So enjoy it. Ski to your heart's content. Talk to yourself if you like. Stop and rest. Sit down and relax in the warm, comforting rays of the mountain sun.

Then, at night, when you're tired, but filled with a sense of well-being, let yourself go. Relax in front of the fireplace. And dream. For it is truly a dream—a dream that can be dreamed only when you have tasted, at least once, the pleasures of skiing.

The important thing is to keep trying.

The skier's evening: pleasant fatigue, a roaring fire, and the company of one's friends.

1. The snow and its pleasures

Where? what? how?

Skiing is snow-covered mountains. It is ski resorts and lodges with facilities proportionate to their means and aspirations. But, above all, it is snow—be it domestic snow or "wild" snow; natural snow or artificial snow; even plastic snow.

Mountains, of course, are the natural habitat of the skier, so long as they are covered with snow. But not all mountains are suitable for skiing. Some mountains have snow too rarely. Some are too low. Some are inaccessible. Some are so high, and the air so thin, that physical activity requires an extraordinary effort. Some are so steep that they are impractical for skiing. And some are located in places where the daylight hours are too short. The ideal ski mountain, at least for the moment, seems to be situated in a temperate climate and to be between, say, 5,000 and 10,000 feet high.

Some mountains are steep; some slope gently. Some are heavily wooded; others, totally without trees. Each type has special qualities of which the skier must be aware.

Generally speaking, a self-respecting resort will be located in a spot where slopes of about 2,500 feet, minimum, are available. However, there are exceptions to this rule. The topography of the area dictates the location of the ski lifts; and so, in some cases, heavy-duty lifts are used to transport skiers up much higher slopes. There are also small lifts that are designed to serve a wide variety of terrain.

Although it is true that not all mountains are suitable for skiing, it is also true that some mountains can be remodeled in such a way as to make them suitable. Thus, under pressure from ski competitions—and, certainly, lured by the prospects of a steadily growing clientele—resorts have been persuaded to revise their ideas of ski slopes. For many years, a slope was "designed" by cutting down a tree here, and by removing a rock there. Now, things are changing. The speed of skiers has increased because of new techniques and new equipment; and greater speed, of course, means greater danger. In the late 'sixties, instructors and coaches campaigned vigorously for wider slopes and for a thorough remodeling so as to insure the safety of the skier—a factor which the natural lay of the land did not satisfy. At the same time, the fact that crowds of skiers were flooding into the resorts during the same season of the year, made it necessary for the managers of the resorts to redesign their slopes so as to assure an easy flow of traffic—not only during competitions, but also during everyday skiing. This resulted also in greater safety on the slopes and in greater durability of the snow.

Thus, bulldozers, jackhammers, and explosives began to appear on the slopes. At every resort, hundreds of trees were cut down. Acres of soil were shifted. The profile of the slopes was changed. Anti-avalanche safeguards were created. And, of course, it was all very bare and ugly.

Fortunately, the assault on the skier's aesthetic sense was of short duration. Stretches of bare earth were soon converted, thanks to new

methods of planting, into handsome meadows. In areas where the topsoil had virtually disappeared, new plantings were undertaken. Some of these plantings were long-rooted, so as to hold the soil in place. Others were plants known for their hardiness. And all plantings were done on a scale calculated to insure the survival of a sufficient number of plants to achieve the intended effect.

Once these seeds were planted, straw was spread over the ground, about one pound of straw for every square yard of earth, which served to retain humidity in the soil and, later, when the straw decomposed, as a humus. This was sufficient, in one season, to achieve the refoliation of any area at an altitude of less than 7,500 feet. After that, all that was required was regular maintenance.

Under the impact of such loving care, the ugliness began to disappear, and—an important practical side effect—it was observed that, since snow is more resistant to the sun and to heat when it lies on grass than on bare ground, it lasted longer. Also, because of the embankments, it became much easier for the rollers to move about the slopes, and therefore it was easier and faster to prepare the snow for skiers.

Below: Cutting down trees, terracing,
bulldozing—it's necessary, but ugly.
Fortunately, it's only temporary.
Right: Jim Hunter, the Canadian skier, takes
off at over 90 miles per hour.

the resorts

What is a resort? It is the oyster within which is found the pearl of winter sports: skiing.

There are an astonishing number of resorts throughout the world: over 14,300 of them, ranging from the great resort which, gradually, has developed its facilities as well as its clientele, to the isolated and primitive lift installed by some enterprising farmer on his land. Thus, resort skiing, through the efforts of entrepreneurs, has been transformed, within a short time, into an important industry—the felicitous complement of a summer resort industry of long standing.

The development of this industry gave birth, in turn, to a flourishing business; or, rather, to a gold mine. The beginnings of skiing as a popular sport were slow and somewhat laborious, but the sport began to develop more rapidly after World War II. Its most extraordinary growth came during the 'sixties, when ski resorts began to spring up everywhere, like mushrooms—and with as much variety. Nowadays, they are everywhere: at high, medium, and low altitudes indiscriminately. They have been established by small private developers, by huge corporations, by banks, and (more recently) in certain areas by townships and municipalities.

It goes without saying that no two resorts are exactly alike with respect to size, location, extent, approach, quality of terrain and slopes, lifts, accommodations, and—of course—price.

This ever-growing number of facilities, limited only by the good business sense of the developers, has resulted in a competitiveness which requires that resorts constantly improve and expand their facilities and that they lower their rates—at least in theory. So long as we remain in the theoretical domain, this is all very nice. At the practical level, however, the reality of the situation is often something else. For some, the dream is turning into a nightmare. Many of the developers, the corporations, and banks, and the private investors rushed into this new industry with a full supply of illusions. They seemed to believe that they had finally discovered the goose that lays the golden egg.

Very few of them paused long enough to consider the utter unpredictability of that material of the industry: snow. And even fewer, perhaps, tried to understand the market for the commercial products and equipment that they were developing. No one seemed to recall that the entire booming industry depended on nature's cooperation in the form of abundant snow which, at best, is a very fragile foundation. Some years, there is too much snow and the mountains become dangerous, the slopes are blocked, the lifts function erratically, if at all, and so the customers are very unhappy. Other years, there is no snow to speak of. Skiing is limited to a few dangerous stretches of white here and there. The resort takes on the appearance of a ghost town. And usually the disappointed customers hold the management responsible for their ruined vacations.

Curiously enough, it seems that the snow is less regular than it used to be, and that there is less of it. Nature *is* unpredictable, and resorts require large investments, heavy maintenance costs, and enormous overhead—while the season for winter sports is relatively short. It is not surprising, therefore, that many resorts are trying to establish a summer season of sorts. Sometimes this is a relatively simple matter if, for example, the resort's location permits summer skiing. Most resorts, however, have to think in terms of adding swimming pools, tennis courts, handball courts, and children's playgrounds. And the presence of such facilities, in turn, means a larger investment and increased maintenance costs.

At first glance, it would appear that the last area to suffer from a recession or depression would be the winter sports industry. The number of skiers, we are told, increases by fifteen percent every year. We are too seldom reminded, however, that some three to five percent of this year's skiers will, for various reasons, have abandoned skiing by next year. Thus, the growth of the industry is not really as spectacular as some public relations people would have us believe.

One of the more inviting illusions of the industry is that conjured up by college midterm vacations. During such periods, it does not matter whether the resort is elegant or shabby, well maintained or dilapidated. Everywhere, the

Since 1960, ski resorts and lodges have sprung up everywhere. They exhibit a wide range of aesthetic qualities. The ski industry is entirely dependent upon Nature, which means that its foundations are very fragile indeed.

16

Skiing is joy and celebration.

lodges are full—and even full to overflowing. Extra beds are added to rooms, and superfluous furniture (chairs and tables!) are moved out to accommodate more people. Rooms, studios, apartments designed to accommodate one or two people in comfort are suddenly sleeping four, six, or eight. It is not hard to imagine why. Skiing is not an inexpensive sport, and students generally vacation on tight budgets. They do not live in apartments and hotel rooms so much as camp out in them. But the inconvenience and discomfort is worthwhile because it makes it possible for them to ski.

The period of student vacations in all resorts is a time of madness. There are people everywhere, shouting, laughing—a wild party that begins with the first day of vacation and ends with the last. It is not, perhaps, the ideal time to ski, simply because there are too many people waiting on line for the lifts and too many on the slopes. Nonetheless, student vacations are a happy phenomenon, both for the student themselves and for the resorts. But they are not enough to pull a resort through the whole season, and it is obvious that, outside of student vacations, many resorts are virtually empty and deserted.

The lifeblood of any resort is a steady repeat clientele and this is a need that the various tourist organizations do their best to satisfy. At some resorts, the problem is not very serious. There, generally, are the older, well-known resorts where hotel facilities are still plentiful. At the newer resorts, however, where perhaps ninety percent of the available accommodations

are rental apartments or studios, the question of a steady clientele returning annually is one that is not easily resolved. The utilization of the motel concept in accommodations is one possible solution, with its mass production rooms and furnishings, but this is certainly less inviting than a full-service hotel as far as attracting a desirable clientele is concerned.

It is possible that there are rough times ahead for the winter sports industry if these sports remain as expensive as they are at present. The ideal, of course, would be to structure prices in such a way as to make resort skiing available to the greatest possible number of people and especially to spread the clientele out over the entire season. If resorts were assured of a steady flow of customers from December to April, prices could be lowered substantially and the pleasures of skiing would then be available to more people. For the moment, however, the winter resort industry, with few exceptions, exists in a nightmare world of feast or famine—a nightmare aggravated by the always imminent possibility that, even when every room, apartment, or studio is jammed with eager skiers, the snow may simply not come. . . .

There are, predictably, almost as many kinds of resorts as there are skiers, ranging from the sumptuous super-resorts made fasionable by a steady flow of "beautiful people" (some of them, skiers), to the isolated mountain lodge with one lift and accommodations for only a handful of people. Here are a few of the representative types in the United States, selected more or less at random for the sake of diversity.

Vail, Colorado

When thinking of large, self-contained super-resorts, the name of Vail is one of those that springs naturally to mind. It claims to be the largest and is certainly one of the best known ski complexes in the Western hemisphere. Its fame rests not only upon presidential (nor ex-presidential) patronage, but upon two factors in which nature and technology combine to optimum results: a good, reliable snowfall and advanced slope-grooming techniques.

In addition, Vail has the advantage of having something for everybody, from experts to beginning skiers, from powder-snow fanatics to camp followers who grow dizzy at the sight of snow. There are shops galore; approximately seventy-five restaurants and lounges, some of them quite good; a nursery school (ages 2 to 9) and a "Bratskeller" (ages 5 to 9), featuring lessons for children. There are saunas, movies, sleigh rides, heated swimming pools and, wonder of wonders, a system of free public transportation so good that automobiles are blessedly superfluous. In fact, in the central shopping areas of Vail Village and Lionshead, it is strictly "pedestrians only."

Vail ski facilities are extraordinary. Its 14 major lifts are capable of transporting 18,000 skiers uphill every hour—an astonishing capability which does not prevent some of the chair lifts from being so crowded that lines form for late morning and early afternoon skiing. The less-crowded part of Vail Mountain is usually Lionshead (which is also the newest area). Moreover, at the top of Lionshead, there is a new Beginners' Bowl, reached by a double chair lift. Also less congested is the Northeast Bowl section, served by Vail's first triple chair lift. Both the Bowl and Lionshead feature the same facilities as Vail Village itself: instructors, child-care centers, equipment rental, food, drink, etc.

Generally speaking, Vail is the kind of place you think of if you're looking for excellent skiing in combination with glamorous skiing. It has a vast variety of terrain, the famous Rocky Mountain powder snow, challenging runs, and effective instruction for both adults and children. It also boasts mobs of beautiful people, fine (if occa-

Snowmass at Aspen, Colorado.

sionally pretentious) shops and restaurants, high prices, and a festive, let's-make-whoopee atmosphere that compensates in part for the crowds, the noise, and the relentless, sometimes overwhelming, gaiety.

Vail, like the equally celebrated Aspen, is the prototype of the American super-resort, a community founded wholly on the skiing industry and dependent entirely upon it for its survival. It is a self-contained community in which a skier can be born, marry, have children, die, and be buried, all without ever leaving the complex. There are worse ways to live and die. If one can afford it.

Information on all accommodations and facilities, as well as reservations, are available from the Vail Resort Association, P.O. Box 1368, Vail, Colorado 81657.

Jackson Hole, Wyoming

Off in the northwestern corner of Wyoming is a spot justly famed for its beauty: Jackson Hole. It is also a skier's dream. Two exceptional mountains (Giant Rendezvous and Apres Vous) tower over the Snake River and a sprinkling of silvery lakes below in the valley. Giant Rendezvous has the greatest vertical of any ski mountain in the U.S.; and Apres Vous is not far behind as far as resorts are concerned. The two mountains are connected by Casper Bowl, which has its own triple chair lift, and by a network of cross trails. In Jackson Hole's several thousand acres of ski country the beginner as well as the intermediate and advanced skier will find a virtually unlimited variety of terrain. All one has to do is choose the area that suits one's own personality best.

Teton Village, at the base of the two mountains, is jammed during the winter with skiers attracted by the resort's fabulous deep powder—almost 500 inches of it every year. Even nature seems to conspire with the Jackson Hole Ski Corporation: meterological conditions assure that snow usually falls at night, and that the days are clear, sunny, and windless.

During the summer months, the area is transformed into a complete summer resort, and its condominiums, lodges, restaurants, bars, and shops are filled to overflowing with vacationers coming to enjoy the white waters of the Snake, camping, and, of course, the Grand Teton Music Festival, an annual event which does its share for the economy of Teton Village. It doesn't hurt much, either, that Jackson Hole is next door to Yellowstone National Park. . . .

Sugarloaf, Maine

Thirty years ago, Sugarloaf Mountain was already popular with a hardy race of skiers—pioneers, really—who dutifully and laboriously climbed the mountain for the sheer pleasure of being able to ski down its slopes. Today, when skiing has become a popular sport among the general public, Sugarloaf has lost none of its allure. In fact, in the opinion of many knowledgeable skiers, it offers the best skiing in the eastern United States.

The first thing that strikes the newcomer to Sugarloaf is its sheer size: a single mountain, with a 2,600-foot continuous vertical drop, 11 lifts, 39 miles of trails and slopes. The abundance of snow matches the mountain: an average snowfall of 15 feet a year! And, of course, the length of the season is in proportion to the availability of snow, running from mid-November to the end of April or the beginning of May.

Sugarloaf's steep trails and backside snowfields make it a favorable haunt of competition skiers and racers. It was the site of the 1971 World Cup Downhill. It is also very popular with freestyle (acrobatic) skiers. Medal-winners, both amateur and professional, abound at Sugarloaf. But so do beginning and intermediate skiers, who delight in the immaculately maintained and serviced lower trails and slopes, and in the superior ski instruction.

One of the big attractions of Sugarloaf—in addition, obviously, to the super snow and the great facilities and the fresh air of the Maine mountains—is the diversity, financial and otherwise, of the resort's accommodations. There are one hundred condominium units, for example, which are all situated along the trails themselves. Therefore, there is no problem with transportation from lodging to skiing and—for clubs and large groups—no irksome "rendezvous times." These apartments rent out for between $10 and $15 per day per person—which is something of a bargain.

Sugarloaf also has a hostel-style Ski Dorm, divided into six bunkrooms, with cafeteria dining. With two meals, accommodations in the Dorm run to $10 or $12 per person per night. The Dorm is especially popular with ski clubs and student groups, and has a capacity of about 200 persons.

There are, of course, a number of lodges, including Sugarloaf Inn, located at the foot of the slopes and equipped with its own lift. All told, the valley can provide sleeping accommodations for over 2,000 skiers.

Sugarloaf has a talent for festivals and fun—witness the Easter parades for children, canoe racing on snow, the Spring Festival, New Years Eve ski jumps, World Heavyweight Ski race, and so forth—all of which make Sugarloaf a place to remember when you think about skiing in Maine.

Taos Ski Valley, New Mexico

Taos Ski Valley, situated some 19 miles from the town of Taos, New Mexico, has the reputation of being a resort for experts. That reputation is partly, but not entirely, deserved. The fact is that many, many experts do ski there; but so do many beginners and intermediate skiers.

Taos' principal attraction for expert skiers is its superabundance of soft snow, the light, powdery stuff so dear to the accomplished skier's heart. It is the same wet, heavy snow that falls in California—except that it dries and cools as it moves across the desert into New Mexico. Then it falls at Taos—as much as 36 inches of it in a single night!

Taos Ski Valley has 26 runs covered with this deep powder, which is about half of the total ski terrain. These are steep runs; too steep, in fact, to be packed by machines. Taos, therefore, is one of the few major resorts where some of the snowpacking is still done by ski patrols on foot. But then, once the snow is packed, the powder no longer flies. . . .

Taos has a total of 52 runs. Twenty-seven of these are for experts only—and the signs really mean what they say. Thirteen trails are for intermediate skiers; and the remaining 12, for beginners, are classified as "Easiest." So, despite its reputation for exclusiveness, Taos does attract a good number of beginners as well as more advanced skiers—a fact with which the excellent instruction available at the Taos Ski School no doubt has a lot to do. Even expert skiers at Taos play it safe by seeking guidance before attacking some of the steeper, more avalanche-prone runs. Everyone finds the instructors affable, capable, and solicitous.

There is even a Kinder Kafig, as its called: a ski program for children between the ages of three and eight, offering not only ski instruction but also games and arts and crafts.

In addition to the soft snow and the superior instruction, there are a number of factors that draw skiers to this relatively isolated resort. One of them is that there is an abundance of lifts and, consequently, no long wait on line for the lifts.

Another factor is service: everyone, from the instructors to the waiters in the restaurants, seems to knock himself out to be accommodating to guests.

Finally, we should mention the weather. Taos has about three hundred days of sunshine a year, at the high (and dry) altitude of 12,000 feet. The sky is incredibly blue; the temperature, relatively mild. And the snow stays on the top of the mountain until June—although the lifts close down on Easter weekend.

Waterville Valley, New Hampshire

The state of New Hampshire has a number of outstanding resorts. The largest—comprising two ski areas with a ski village between them—is Waterville Valley. It is also one of the most popular resorts in the area, and with good reason.

The Valley is situated within the limits of the White Mountain National Forest, and practically all of the ski facilities are located on the slopes of White Mountain. The resort was built to be, and actually is, totally self-contained. The ski village has shops, restaurants, bars—just about everything that a skier could look for in the line either of equipment or of entertainment. The accommodations, like the other facilities, run the gamut of price in such a way as to provide for both the millionaire sportsman and for the student on a budget.

The ski facilities reflect the management's determination that Waterville should be all things to all people. It is a family-oriented ski community, which means that the ski requirements of children are as carefully tended to as those of adults. It also means that skiing and ski facilities, which are uniformly of top quality, are provided for beginners as well as for intermediates and experts, even though the majority of skiers at Waterville belong to the two latter categories.

The basic reason for Waterville Valley's popularity is that it has received more than its share of Nature's blessings. The Valley itself is surrounded by a ring of 4,000 peaks, which serve both to draw snow into the Valley and to keep it there by protecting the slopes from winds. The consequent reliability of snow enables the Valley to operate from late November to late April—at least the equivalent of most resorts in the West.

The two ski areas are actually two different mountains, Snow's Mountain and Mt. Tecumseh. And, on those occasions when Nature does not supply adequate snow, the slopes of Mt. Tecumseh are equipped with snow-cannon of sufficient capacity to supply snow for the trails serviced by four lifts. Since these trails have been selected on a representative basis, beginners as well as intermediates and experts can take advantage of this man-made snow.

Mt. Tecumseh is, in fact, the larger and more popular of the two ski areas. It has seven lifts, 32 trails, and a vertical drop of some 2,000 feet. The lifts vary according to the level of ability that they are intended to service, from first-day beginners (a J-bar) to a T-bar for transporting the experts to the resort's slalom hill.

In the unlikely event that the Valley does not sate the skier's passion for variety, there are five additional ski areas nearby, all open to Waterville Valley's patrons at a nominal charge.

Left, top: The unbroken field of deep powder in Taos Ski Valley. Left, bottom: Spectacular scenery in Jackson Hole. Below: The slopes at Waterville Valley.

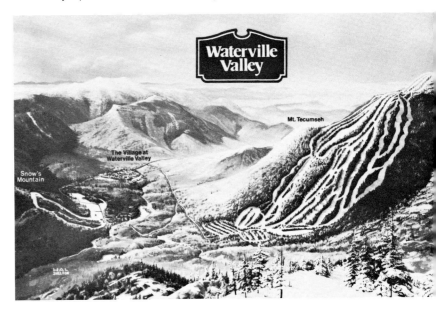

domesticated snow

Time was, before the first mechanized ski lift made its appearance, that the ski trail as we know it did not exist.

Skiers were comparatively rare, and skiing took place in surroundings quite different from what they are now. The skier was a sort of adventurer, a maverick who thrived on difficulty and isolation.

The fact is that a skier in those days actually skied very little, for it was a difficult sport to practice. The skier, of course, had to climb the mountain before he could ski down its slopes through relatively small clearings, down trails of unpredictable width. It was only at high altitudes—where the air was too thin for vegetation—that a skier could let himself go.

Later, as skiers became more numerous, trails—or what were then regarded as trails—began to make their appearance. But even then, the skier was left pretty much to his own resources, for there was no ski industry to support him and no functioning commercial interests to make the sport less onerous or more accessible.

In our own time—and this was not very long ago—a few of the larger resorts began to realize that their mechanical lifts were good investments only if the trails and slopes they serviced were of relatively high quality. Snow, after all, varies greatly in quality and therefore in ski-ability; not everyone is able to ski on any kind of snow. The solution seemed to be to "domesticate" the snow. The first step was to hire "trailblazers"—skiers whose job it was to go through a trail, one after the other, in order to open it up for a resort's clientele. In this way, it was hoped, the customers would be encouraged to use the lifts more frequently.

This sort of undertaking was, by its nature, very limited—particularly since the trailblazers were also expected to be responsible for security on the slopes. It was part of their job, too, to do repair work on the trails from time to time, and, for this function, they were armed with shovels. It goes without saying that the benefits of this primitive sort of maintenance were fleeting indeed, and that it was largely a wasted effort.

Such situations belong, so to speak, to the prehistoric period skiing. When public interest in skiing began to increase by leaps and bounds and the number of skiers multiplied proportionately, the owners of resorts and lodges quickly had to come to grips with the realities of the problem. The trailblazers, whose job it had been to open up the trails, quickly disappeared in the larger resorts. The primitive, rather haphazard trails were replaced by carefully measured and cleared trails from 100 to 125 feet wide. These trails, in a resort of respectable size, represented a skiing terrain of tens—and perhaps of hundreds—of square acres, all of which had to be maintained in such a way as to provide maximum usability for hundreds of skiers. Obviously, an entire regiment of trailblazers would have been necessary for such an undertaking. And, even then, they would not have been able to achieve the quality of maintenance that was necessary. Their replacement, therefore, was the machine—the snowplow or bulldozer. These were of different makes and types, but all have become the indispensable accoutrement of the ski slopes.

By commonly accepted international convention, the various ski trails are flagged according to their degree of difficulty. A green flag marks an easy trail; blue, less easy; red, difficult; and black, most difficult of all. Actually, this system of flagging, useful as it may be in theory, in practice is often misleading. A green trail at one resort may be the equivalent of a blue trail elsewhere, leaving the skiers hopelessly confused. And, of course, there is no way to compel a skier to stick to the trails that are commensurate with his expertise. A beginner, through pride or false confidence, will risk life and limb by launching himself down a red trail; or an expert will spread havoc and terror by cavorting on a blue trail among the beginners.

Perhaps the most useful function of the flagging system, along with the system of numbering trails, is to make the work of the rescue teams easier: it makes the site of an accident easier to identify. These rescue teams are connected by radio to the resort's office, which gives all in-

1. A solitary pioneer.
2. Packing snow by foot–or rather, by ski. It is an outdated technique.
3. Trail teams now spend their time evacuating the injured and leave snowpacking to the machines; that is, to tractors with special accessories.
4. Modern skiing, in fact, would be impossible without the mechanical means of preparing and maintaining the snow properly.
5. Tractors, equipped with enormous blades, repair and smooth snow on the trails.
6 & 7. The ascent trails are not forgotten. They require the same sort of maintenance as the descent trails.

1

5

2

3

6

7

1. The snow and its pleasures

The prudent skier exercises caution in virgin snow. Avalanches are an ever-present danger.

structions for intervention or evacuation by the team.

The snow itself, of course, must be packed. Well-packed snow not only pleases the skier, but also lasts the longest. Packing is a never-ending task—as is obvious when one considers what happens to the snow on a slope after several hundred skiers have had a few runs on it.

Actually, the work of packing begins (or should begin) early in the season, with the first snow-falls of November. At that point, the snow should be packed as hard as possible, so that it will become a solid foundation for later snows. If, as sometimes happens nowadays, there is no more snow for a month or so, then it also becomes the snow for the early-bird skiers.

The most desirable thing would be for all trails to be packed simultaneously, but this is impossible. Therefore, as soon as the snow begins to fall, a choice has to be made. Those trails have to be selected for packing which will provide the early arrivals with a terrain proportionate to their skill. Once these trails have been designated, the plows go out and work all night, with the operators periodically relieving one another.

When the mechanical lifts open in the morning —generally at nine o'clock—it is absolutely essential that the pedestrian trails be ready, as well as all trails for beginners, the green trails of whatever length, several of the wider blue trails, and the ascent trails. And, since advanced skiers often like deep snow, two or three trails are usually left unpacked for several days for their use. The unpacked trails deteriorate rapidly, however, and after a short time they must be packed from one end to the other.

Snow, even packed snow, is easily disturbed. After considerable use or because of certain climactic phenomena, trails quickly become a series of bumps, known as "moguls." As enjoyable as these may be for a time, they rapidly become difficult to maneuver and are often dangerous for the skier.

At that point, the machines are brought into play once more, and the snowplows, equipped with enormous blades or trailing a planer behind, are dispatched to trim rises which have become dangerous, to fill holes that are too deep, and generally to restore the trails to their original condition.

In the evening, as soon as the mechanical lifts have closed down, other machines begin restoring the ascent trails. This is done early so that the snow will pack and harden during the night. By the next morning, the trail will be easier for the skiers to climb, the vehicles will strain less, and there will be less wear and tear on the equipment.

All of this restoration and maintenance becomes even more critical toward the end of the season. Particularly in those areas that are most used, patches of earth or grass may begin to appear.

In the month of March, when the ground begins to warm up, these patches are apt to be troublesome because they tend to spread very quickly. They must be covered with the least possible delay, otherwise they soon become too large to be repaired.

This painstaking work of protecting and renewing snow is particularly important in the area surrounding the mechanical lifts at relatively low altitudes and on the most frequently used trails. Keeping in mind that nature can sometimes be very stingy with her gifts, many resorts have found it useful to stockpile snow in some out of the way area for use around the lifts.

All of this may seem like a great deal of hard work. It is. It is also absolutely necessary if a resort is to keep its customers and attract new ones. Today's skiers are no longer adventurers. The spirit of the skier has changed. Skiers are now customers who are willing to pay for the pleasure of skiing. They do not expect, or want, problems and hardship in return for their money. They want to learn quickly to ski, to ski well—and not to exhaust themselves in the process. They know that accidents are possible, but they want to reduce that possibility to an absolute minimum. From this, it follows that only well-designed, well-maintained ski trails can satisfy them.

This holds true for the great majority of skiers. There are still a few, however, who like skiing in the wilds; that is, in virgin snow untouched by plows or other forms of human intervention. These skiers are looking for the same kind of adventure that their predecessors, the pioneers of skiing, enjoyed. They want skiing without restraints. There is certainly something to be said for this approach. Prudence requires, however, that these skiers exercise the greatest care in their choice of slopes, depth of snow, exposure, and climactic conditions. It is certainly understandable that a skier may want to seek out difficulty and "go it alone"; but it is less understandable that he or she should risk his or her life to do so, to say nothing of the lives of others.

Today's skier is not an adventurer or a daredevil. He has a different kind of motivation. He wants to become a good skier in the shortest possible time.

two remedies for lack of snow

Artificial snow

In the skiing world, two separate phenomena have become noticeable in recent years. First, interest in skiing has increased enormously, as has the number of skiers. Second, nature, it seems, has simultaneously gone into a sulk and has become parsimonious with the *sine qua non* of skiing: snow.

To these two considerations, we might add a third. In certain areas of the world which, although very cold, are generally devoid of snow, there are imaginative businessmen who would like a share in the skiing industry's boom.

These factors have all contributed to the invention of a substitute for that snow which either does not exist, or does not exist dependably at certain times of the year, at certain altitudes, and in certain climates. Thus, we now have artificial snow.

The concept of artificial snow is simple enough. Natural snow, when it melts, forms water. Conversely, water, when subjected to certain pressures at certain temperatures, may be transformed into ice or snow. All that one needs is a supply of water, a compressor, an apparatus known as a "snow cannon," and a temperature of no more than 3°C (37°F). The cannon shoots a spray of water into the cold air and, *voilà*, snow. This is an extreme simplification of the procedure by which it is possible to manufacture snow sufficient to cover several hundred square yards of terrain. In some countries—the United States, France, Finland—the manufacture of artificial snow is a fairly well developed branch of the ski industry. It requires a substantial investment, but it is one which will surely return a profit. In a few years, we can expect to see more and more resorts making use of snowmaking installations, particularly in the lower areas of their ski complexes where snow is less abundant and where there is heavy traffic. Without new snow, whether natural or artificial, these areas now become almost unusable after a relatively short time.

It should be added that artificial snow is of exceptionally good quality because it is very compact—which means that it has increased

durability. To give an idea of what is involved, let us note that, in order to cover about 5,000 square yards of earth to a depth adequate for skiing, a cannon must operate for approximately twelve hours. This means that one cannon is generally sufficient to provide major trails with enough snow to attract skiers.

Above: a snow-cannon in action. Below: The compressors used to power snow-cannons.

Plastic snow

Given the tremendous growth of the ski industry in practically every part of the world, it was inevitable that some enterprising businessman would turn his attention to the possibility of providing ski areas in cities or in resort areas that are generally devoid of snow and without mountains. The obvious solution to the problem lay in the creation of a durable man-made substance that has the most important properties of snow.

Several plastic products have been tried which are generally satisfactory in that one can actually ski on them. It is true that skiing is more difficult on plastic than on snow, but plastic, nonetheless, provides much the same pleasure as skiing on snow.

In England, there are about sixty plastic ski trails which, for the most part, are used for beginners' classes. One of the largest plastic trails is in France, at Lyon. Many skiers have learned their craft on that trail, and it is also used regularly for competition skiing.

Skiing on plastic snow does not require special equipment, and it involves no special danger. In fact, there is an advantage in learning to ski on plastic snow: since it is more difficult than skiing on real snow, the beginner, when transferring to the latter, will be surprised at how proficient he or she actually is. Beginners will also be delighted at the feeling of space and openness in the mountains as compared to a plastic trail. Since plastic snow represents a large investment, it is always used on relatively small areas.

Plastic snow at a ski area in Lyon, France. A great many people have learned to ski on this man-made substitute.

2

the
skier

What is a skier?
A physical being of any age and any shape.
A motivation.
A bit of muscle.
And decent equipment.
A certain technique.
A minimum of logic.
That is, an ensemble of factors,
interdependent and, in fact, inseparable,
necessary for the attainment of
the purpose of skiing: lasting pleasure.

a physical being

A physical being of any age and any shape.
A skier can be . . .
A slightly overweight gentleman;
A long-limbed girl;
An elderly gentleman, probably retired;
An elegantly handsome woman;
A sun-bronzed lad;
A child;
A handsome athlete;
A knobby-kneed little girl, a future champion;
A mountain climber;
A traffic cop,
or a sailor on leave.
So why not you?

It is true that many people love skiing. It is equally true that many more people don't dare to try skiing.

Some don't try because they think it is difficult—perhaps impossible—to learn. Others don't learn because they "can't afford to have an accident": businessmen, executives, professional people, the self-employed, and so forth. All of these people refuse to take advantage of the marvelous relaxation that results from skiing. The purpose of this book is to show, first, that, following the technique we describe, anyone can very easily learn to ski in a very short time (no more than three days); second, that skiing is not dangerous for any reasonable person who makes use of the proper equipment.

We promise that anyone who follows our system and our advice will survive to get home, under their own power, every single night, without a single broken bone.

a motivated being

Motivation is the specific difference in every skier.

There are the young athletes whose whole lives are skiing. They ski with wholehearted concentration, and sometimes without discrimination. They often reach the saturation point, but without knowing it, for they know only that, in order to become better skiers, they must ski, always ski. They ski as spontaneously as they breathe. They know that, one day, if they are good enough, a trainer will imprison them in a training camp and, little by little, through incredible work and discipline, polish the rough edges until the time comes for trophies, titles, and glory.

There are the bargain, or budget skiers. You see them standing, not in front of the ticket window, but in front of the list of prices, figuring mightily, calculating the number of possible climbs against the cost of a ticket on the lift. . . . Suddenly, the computations are over. They take a deep breath of bracing air, push their way to the window, buy their tickets, take their place on the lift. They go up the mountain and come down the mountain. Up, down. Up, down. As rapidly as possible, so as to amortize the cost of their tickets. A couple of hours later, we see them again. But what a transformation. They are no longer frantic. They are skiing calmly, happily, as though they had not a care in the world. And the don't. They have already completed what they consider the number of trips required to offset the price of their tickets. From now on, according to their calculations, they are skiing "free."

There are the sun gods and goddesses, candidates for the title of The Most Perfect Tan in the World. They learned to ski for one reason: to go where they could satisfy their single ambition in life, to have skin of a satisfactory color.

There are the comparative skiers. They ski often, and well. They work at it. They regularly test their progress in the small competitions organized by their instructors—all so that they can compare themselves constantly to their "ideal" skiers.

There are the loners. They set out very early, sometimes dressed in sealskin, almost always carrying a bag of one kind of another, their equipment hopelessly out of date. They climb to the summit—and they are back at the lodge long before the invasion of trail skiers begin.

There are the braggarts who, at night in the bars, spin with tales that no one can verify but which impress the gallery. The next morning, one can see them going off alone to some remote spot, where, if one peeked, one could see them laboriously practicing their turns.

Opposite page: The chair lift is one of the most usual (and one of the chilliest) kinds of mechanical lifts.

The first day at a ski school marks the beginning of a special kind of happiness that, sooner or later, everyone is eager to experience.

There are the purists who, *a priori,* reject such sissy stuff as packed trails. They regard themselves as mountaineers and adventurers, and they know how to equip themselves for their long wanderings in the snow. Their pleasure? The virgin, difficult stretches of white.

There are the contemplatives. They are calm, unruffled, arriving at any time, quickly buying their tickets. They ski alone, often pausing for considerable periods to admire the landscape. They make a few turns, then stop once more to study a certain view or a certain color. Nothing hurries them. They ski in order to move about, to breathe, to fill their eyes, their minds, their hearts.

There are the artists who always seek out snow with designs in it; that is, snow with ski tracks. They make two or three turns, stop, study their own tracks and eventually admire them. They are purists whose goal it is to emulate the best in order to perfect their own performances.

There are the salon skiers, whose boast it is that they never ski alone. They ski a bit, then talk; make a couple of turns, then talk. For them, time has no meaning. The longer the line at the lift, the better, for it gives them more time to talk.

There are the make-out skiers (usually male), recognizable by their magnificent plumage in all the colors of the rainbow. They ski in order to seek out their prey, an impressionable young thing who, unless she is aware of the game, will eventually be seduced by a few soft words and a neatly executed inclinated turn. . . . These fellows are no less adept on the dance floor than on the slopes.

And finally, there are the skiers just-passing-through; they are usually hurried and harried executives. They love to ski, but their time is precious. All they need is a few moments of relaxation. They are not too concerned about their equipment, and they are satisfied if they get a bit of exercise and a few gulps of fresh air.

a bit of muscle

There is no comparison to speak of between a winter ski vacation and a summer vacation. In the latter case, the most violent effort one is required to make consists of rotating one's body on the beach so as to obtain an even tan. A ski vacation is something else again. It involves a physical commitment at every level—a commitment which the skier cannot afford to neglect. It would be a mistake to believe that the pull of gravity alone is responsible for the skier's movement in the snow. Muscular effort is always involved—more intense effort, perhaps for the beginner, but also for every skier, no matter what his or her degree of expertise.

It goes without saying that comparatively few people are able to ski regularly, every day, in accordance with a progressive rhythm of training. Generally, what happens is that one goes directly from work to skiing, for a few hours or for a few days. Often, a part of those precious hours or days is spoiled by sore or strained muscles. How much more pleasurable ski vacations could be—and how many accidents would be avoided—if vacation skiers could be persuaded to devote a little time, before their vacations, to preparing themselves physically for skiing.

We are not talking about an onerous method of "working out," but about a few minutes a day for, say, three weeks before a winter ski vacation or daily if one skies every weekend.

The equipment and material you need is negligible: a chair, and a sweatshirt, and the sweatshirt is optional.

Anybody who is about to learn to ski must implant one immutable fact firmly in his or her mind: *you are going to fall*.

That having been said, it follows that, from the very first day (even before setting foot on a slope) the learner must know how to get up when he or she falls. This skill is learned, not on the slopes, but in the privacy of one's own room. It is not hard to learn.

Take a chair. Sit on the floor next to the chair, with your legs together alongside your body. Place one hand on the back of the chair and the other on the seat. Then, raise yourself by pushing upward with your legs and, at the same time, pulling with—and finally supporting yourself on—your arms. (See illustrations below.)

Repeat this exercise five times on the left side of the chair, then five times on the right side.

Learning to get up

Falls are inevitable.

Balance — limbering up the arms

The arms play an important role in balance, and the skier should dress in such a way as to have as much freedom of movement as possible in every direction.

Standing position: rotate the arms from front to back and from back to front. Repeat five to ten times.

Still standing, arms outstretched to the side, move your arms as far back as you can, then return them to beginning position. Do three sets of five to ten exercises.

Another standing exercise: the windmill. Swing each arm from front to back, or from back to front, windmill fashion. Repeat five to ten times.

Building up the arms

Whatever you wear should be very supple because skiing requires use of the arms—even
though the effort required of the arms may be of
brief duration, as in use of the poles.

*Front push-ups with body
rigid (five times).*

*Back push-ups, arms
slightly to the rear and
about level with the
shoulders (three times).*

In order to maintain balance, we must build up
our abdominal and dorsal muscles and make
them more supple.

The abdominal muscles

Sitting position, legs spread: Try to touch your outstretched leg with your forehead, once to the right and once to the left. Repeat five times.

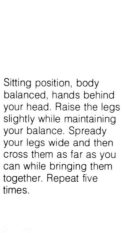

Sitting position, body balanced, hands behind your head. Raise the legs slightly while maintaining your balance. Spready your legs wide and then cross them as far as you can while bringing them together. Repeat five times.

The torso

Standing position, legs spread slightly, hands on thighs: Rotate the body as shown in the illustration, from right to left and then from left to right. Repeat ten times.

Standing position, one leg out, hands on hips: Rotate the body, using the arms, as you turn, in order to draw your head as far down toward your knees as possible. Repeat three times.

Developing the leg muscles

The condition of the legs is obviously of great importance in skiing. The musles must be strong and supple and capable of effort in any direction.

Standing position, legs straight, feet turned slightly: Lift one leg sideways and outward as though kicking, and then, without pausing, bring the leg back and swing it out on the other side of your body. Repeat five times for each leg.

Loosening up the legs and ankles

From a semi-stooped position, jump sideways from one leg to the other without straightening up. Repeat ten times.

This is the same kind of exercise as the above, but it begins with the feet joined. Jump from side to side, while holding the torso as motionless as possible. In both exercises, the feet do most of the work. This is preparation for edging—an important technique to be described.

Another exercise: Standing on the balls of your feet, rest your hands lightly on the back of a chair so as to help you retain your balance. Then, do ten deep knee-bends, keeping your torso straight. This exercise is very important indeed because our technique requires that the body always remain perpendicular to the skis.

a bit on equipment

The role of equipment is much more important than many skiers realize. It is certainly not 100 percent of skiing. But it is often 60 percent responsible—and almost always 50 percent responsible—for skiing accidents.

We have no intention of giving price lists or of pushing any particular brand of equipment. In choosing equipment, the decisive factor usually is the weight of the skier's pocketbook. However, you should look at the purchase of equipment more as a long-term investment in pleasure than as a simple purchase. If you are going to ski only once, almost any kind of equipment will last that long (or almost that long). But skiing does not usually stop there. There is almost always a next time, and then a next. . . .

What sort of advice can we give you?

If money is no object, then there is no problem. There are always instructors and merchants who will orient you toward equipment of superior quality in accordance with your means, your skill, your preferences, and the amount of time that you can devote to skiing.

If you merely want a tan, they will insist more on lotions and sunglasses than on skis. If you are a real skier, they will discuss the virtues of this or that make of boots or skis.

Most people who ski have neither an inexhaustible supply of money nor a complete lack of it. They stand somewhere in the middle. And it is a middle course that we would like to suggest. As a general rule, in buying equipment do not choose the cheapest thing in the shop. It is usually too cheap to be worth even what you pay for it. There are medium-priced items in every kind of equipment.

This advice holds particularly true when buying boots, which are the skier's prime piece of equipment. They must be comfortable. They must protect the feet against cold and humidity. They must be solid and firm, while soft enough next to the feet to allow the freedom of movement that skiing requires. Do not skimp on boots. They are your most important skiing investment.

We intend to say very little about the clothing that you wear for winter sports. Clothing, after all, is largely a matter of personal taste in color,

style, and so forth. The only stipulation is that what you wear should be warm; that is, it should be able to retain the heat that your muscles store while you are indoors so as to protect you from the cold out of doors.

Gloves should be rather loose around the fingers so as to allow the blood to circulate. They should also protect the upper part of the hand, by meeting and overlapping the sleeves of your jacket. The best kind of glove is probably a fairly new product on the market: an electronic glove, which promises an end to frostbitten fingers.

Goggles are very important to the skier. These are generally of two kinds: the wraparound or panoramic type, which protect your eyes from the cold and provide unobstructed visibility, and the regular sunglass type. Sunglasses should be equipped with quality lenses that will protect your eyes not only from the sun, but also from the ultraviolet rays which are quite strong in the mountains.

Boots, whether simple or sophisticated, must meet two criteria which are, in principle, contradictory: they must combine the qualities of both bedroom slippers and plaster casts.

Bedroom slippers? Of course. The skier's feet must be both warm and comfortable. Otherwise the enjoyment of skiing will be spoiled. All boots worth buying should have a removeable inner liner—or "bladder"—that is filled with pliable material that can mold around the shape of the foot. This material within the bladder is like the Silly Putty children play with. When it is warmed by the skier's foot, this soft substance flows around the foot, providing a close, yet forgiving fit.

A plastic cast? Well, in a sense the foot and ankle of the skier should be strengthened and supported uniformly by the boot's outer shell, which is normally made of plastic. The boot must provide lateral support, but still allow the ankle to flex forward naturally. This forward freedom of the ankle is vital to the skier's balance and to his or her ability to control the skis.

Too often skiers choose boots that are too stiff and rigid or ones that cannot hinge forward. The result is that they are forced to stand in an awkward or contorted position on their skis, and

Good equipment is, above all, comfortable equipment. This means warm clothing and gloves, perfectly fitted boots, and protective sunglasses. It also means special equipment necessary to your progress as a skier, such as properly adjusted bindings, skis suitable to your height, and well-balanced poles.

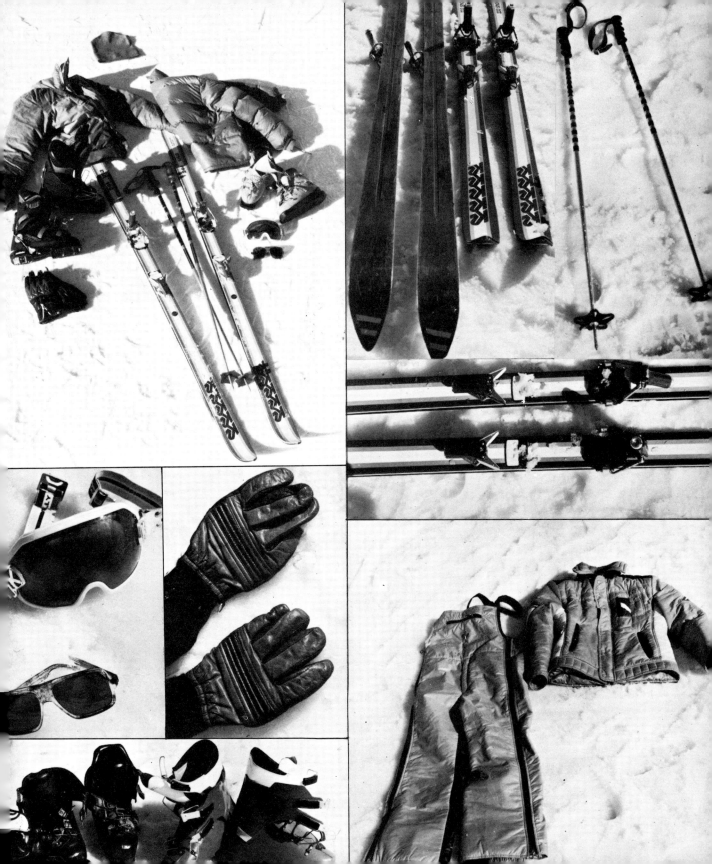

One of your greatest pleasures will be soft, powdery snow. You'll plunge into it and emerge in a swirling cloud of the most beautiful and purest white imaginable.

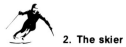

2. The skier

must make all kinds of unnatural compensations in their skiing.

It is also a mistake to select boots that come up too high on the leg, that somehow tilt the foot too far forward or too far backward, or that have some sort of buckling system that restricts the blood circulation. When these conditions exist, it is almost impossible to ski well.

Great care should be taken in selecting and fitting boots. In many cases, it is a process that takes several hours. The boot should have enough room for toe movement, should have proper arch support, should not pinch or bind anywhere, and should not allow the heel of the foot to lift off the sole. In the end, the skier should walk out of the shop with a boot that is supportive enough to suit his or her skiing ability, comfortable, yet still permits a good feel for the skis.

There are certain boots on the market known as "seven league boots," which claim to facilitate balancing. As far as we are concerned, these are useless since they sometimes seem to throw one out of balance. We do not recommend them.

Bindings are one of the most useful inventions of the industry, provided they are properly adjusted. This is rarely done, mainly because skiers neglect to do so. Every responsible skier should have his or her bindings adjusted in relation to the snow that he or she is skiing and to the degree of fatigue. If this were the case, many accidents would be avoided. Parents should adjust their children's bindings themselves in certain conditions; for example, in wet snow.

Poles should be lightweight, well balanced, equipped with straps, and high enough to reach the middle of the skier's rib cage.

Finally—*the skis. We recommend, without reservation, the compact ski.*

Evolution and changing concepts have resulted over the years, in improbable fluctuations in the length of skis, from the 220 centimeter ski of the beginner in the 'fifties to the "sawed-off" skis of the freestyles, passing through a certain classical rigidity in the period from 1960 to 1975 which resulted in lengths from 203 centimeters to 215 centimeters, depending on the height of the skier.

Many technicians have taken great pains to demonstrate, in the past few decades, that the short ski was as effective as the long ski. Thus, the Austrians, shortly before and during World War II, tried to introduce a ski only 160 to 170 centimeters in length. The trouble with it was that the ski's width was exaggerated—a feature which, in theory, was supposed to compensate for the lack of supporting surface which resulted from the ski's reduced length. It also had the effect, however, of handicapping a skier who was edging or executing a traverse. Nonetheless, at the time the short ski was more or less acceptable, since the trails were not packed as they are today.

One avant-garde skier, an acrobat of the slopes, Jojo Tournier, used very short skis with which he was able to do nearly anything on any sort of slope. The tails of his skis were turned up just like the tips. There was much to be learned from Tournier. Howver, since he was an acrobat gifted with an extraordinary sense of balance who could ski equally well on short skis or on a single very long ski—or on stilts, for that matter—no one took him seriously.

The Olympic champion of 1948, Henri Oreiller, as much a nonconformist in his own way as Tournier was, scandalized the purists one day by taking to the slopes of Val-d'Isère with a pair of short skis also. He, too, was ignored.

Gaston Cathiard, president of the then Syndicate of French Ski Instructors—a man as concerned with the teaching of skiing as with practical application of improvements—had also tried to popularize a short ski, which, like the Austrian short ski, was disproportionately wide. By then, however, ski trails were beginning to be well packed, and the width of the ski made edging and turning difficult. For the moment, short skis disappeared from the market.

Then, one day, they were back—very short skis, a bit wide, and once more presenting problems in edging and turning. They also necessitated a change in equipment, since the length of skis had been steadily growing apace with technical progress.

Now, since trails everywhere are firmly packed, the problem of support is no longer of any importance, and we prefer a "compact" ski—from 160 to 195 centimeters in length, depending upon the height of the skier. The compact ski has the same shape as the classic ski and allows for rapid learning since it combines ease of handling with security—preoccupations of all skiers—and allows a beginner to enjoy skiing immediately. *Best of all, the compact ski does not disturb longitudinal balance in the slightest.* Moreover, beginners do not tire nearly so easily when using compacts; as soon as a certain amount of progress has been made in technique, they will find that these skis are very practical for use in any kind of snow.

All these things taken into consideration, it seems to us that the compact ski is the logical one to use, and we recommend it for that reason.

Compact skis originally were the gift, so to speak, of American acrobatic skiers called "Hot Doggers" or freestylers, who made use of these skis in their own incredibly difficult kind of skiing. Another type of short ski also came to us out of the recent past, from those slalom champions, the Goitschel sisters who were outstanding not only for their ability but also for their size. The Goitschels always used skis 180 to 185 centimeters in length while slaloming. The great slalomers of the moment, the Italians, Austrians, and Swedes, have reduced the length of their skis to achieve greater maneuverability in competition. In setting forth our technique, which rests upon use of the compact ski, we allow a beginner to climb the ladder of technique very rapidly while diminishing considerably the risk of accidents. This guarantee, obviously, holds good only for skiers who recognize that masochism and suicide have no place in winter sports and who are innocent of the illusion that, as soon as they put on their first pair of skis, they are champions of the slopes. In other words, our guarantee holds good only for reasonable skiers.

For advanced skiers, incidentally, we advise the use of longer skis for hard snow. The ideal, it goes without saying, is to have two pairs of skis.

We said that boots are the skier's "prime" piece of equipment. Does this mean that skis are secondary? Not at all. It does mean, however, that you do not have to buy skis immediately. You can rent them until you are ready to undertake the more or less major commercial transaction that is involved in buying a good pair of skis that will satisfy you in every respect.

When you do get ready to purchase your own skis, the selection of makes, models, and materials may seem overwhelming. You will do well to seek the advice of a knowledgeable and impartial ski shop clerk or a ski instructor who is familiar with your skiing.

Most modern skis are not made of wood exclusively. Instead they are combinations of laminated wood, reinforced polyester (fiberglass), synthetic foam, plastic, and even rubber. Different manufacturers use these components in different ways, but often the results are similar. Some American companies have done wonders making skis out of the type of honeycomb aluminum used in aircraft parts. Others are doing astonishing things with molded plastic prisms that run the entire length of the ski.

Other important considerations for ski selection are the "cut" or shape of the ski, as well as its bending pattern. Most recreational skiers will not want to choose a ski with either a highly specialized sidecut or flex. A ski will probably turn most comfortably if it bends more or less

LENGTH OF SKIS IN RELATION TO SKIER'S HEIGHT

Turning Skis

32" 40" 54" 62" 67" 72"-76" 62" to 76" or 78"

WIDE COMPACT SKIS   SHORT SKIS

evenly from its tip to its tail. Also check to see that both skis match. Occasionally one ski will be softer, wider, or more flexible than the other, and mismatched skis like this should be avoided.

As important as it is to buy good skis, that is not the end of it. Skis must be maintained if they are to perform well. The steel edges must be kept square, sharp, and smooth by using a metal file or sharpening stone, and the bottoms should be kept perfectly flat. Any nicks, scratches, or gouges in the ski base, caused by rocks, stones, or other foreign matter in the snow, should be filled with melted plastic and then smoothed. Blemishes in the base can misdirect a ski uncontrollably.

In certain kinds of snow, our "mistakes" are often attributable to equipment that we have neglected to maintain properly. Ski "tuning," or maintenance, sounds complicated, but it is a process that any skier can learn in a matter of a few minutes.

What about bindings? They are the next important consideration. But let us say from the start that you don't have to buy the most expensive ones available to get some that will be one hundred percent satisfactory.

First of all, a binding should be adjustable in several different ways: It must adjust upward and downward to accommodate your boots, and the release-tension spring should be easy to set, according to snow conditions and the skier's ability level. These adjustments are best made by a well-informed ski shop mechanic.

Today's bindings require very little effort to take off and put on. In most cases, the skier need not even bend over! We have come a long way from the complicated clamps and straps of years

Ski clothing is a matter of fashion but also of personal taste. Boots, whether simple or sophisticated, must be as comfortable as slippers but as supportive as braces. This is the paradox of ski boots. Progress in materials over a ten-year span: Leather, 1968; Polyurethane, 1977. How to transport your equipment: get a ski rack for your car. Patrick Russel at the starting gate: a maximum of concentration.

past. Most so-called step-in bindings have separate toe and heel units. On the other hand, some have a one-piece plate that attaches to both the sole of the boot and the ski. The plate binding has two disadvantages as we see it: it elevates the foot off the ski more than seems necessary, and it can interfere with the natural flexing of the ski in some cases.

A properly adjusted release binding should be reasonably safe, even though most manufacturers are no longer willing to call their products "safety bindings." A good binding is engineered to be sensitive to slow rotating falls as well as to sudden twists. Those bindings that are designed for competitors and advanced skiers usually have stronger springs and an "elastic" quality, which permits the release mechanism to absorb impact shocks without actually releasing the foot.

All release bindings should be kept well lubricated and free of dirt or road salt. They should be examined closely and the tension checked regularly during the skiing season. One critical element in many bindings is the anti-friction pad located under the instep of the boot. This thin plastic device allows the boot to slide out of the binding in the event of a serious fall. Whenever this Teflon pad becomes scratched with use or filled with grit, it is no longer slippery and is therefore potentially dangerous. A new pair costs next to nothing, so replace worn anti-friction pads immediately.

Also, don't forget about retaining leashes. These are no more than straps that loosely attach to both the boot and the binding. The strap is meant to hold the ski loosely to the foot after the binding has released in a fall. The leash prevents the freed ski from being lost in the snow or from running uncontrollably down the slope to endanger other skiers below.

But there are times when it is far better and less dangerous to have the ski fall off completely. Many experienced skiers object to retaining leashes because they fear being hit by a "windmilling" ski that is still attached to their leg. "Ski stoppers" are small spring-loaded brakes that allow the ski to fall off—if for example you fall—but prevent it from sliding too far away for

you to be able to recover it easily. The brake digs into the snow, stopping the ski quickly at a safe distance from the body, and then holds the ski in place while you put it back on. Many consider ski brakes to be worth the additional expense.

Boots, skis, bindings—these three are the indispensable components of "good skiing," whether we're talking about skiing for pleasure or in competition.

Poles should be of a comfortable length; that is, they should reach just below the skier's armpits. Make sure that the poles you buy are well balanced, have good straps, and soft baskets that will not ricochet off hard snow.

Another important accessory: sunglasses. This is something that it would be foolish to scrimp on, and we feel that you can never pay too much for a good pair. The reflection of sun off the snow, the ultraviolet rays in the mountains—these are things to be wary of. Those who don't know what the sun's rays can do often pay for their ignorance.

These are just a few of the things that the skier has to be aware of. The list is by no means exhaustive.

What clothing looks like is much less important than how warm it is. When it's very cold, don't hesitate to wear long underwear. We don't mean necessarily the kind that our grandfathers wore. Long underwear today can be quite attractive, even elegant. And there's no denying that it makes a lot of difference in cold weather.

Ski clothes, and sport clothes generally, seem to be dominated today by the use of nylon. Often nylon jackets or pants are lined or quilted with poly-something-or-other. From the standpoint of protection against the cold, quilted nylon is quite effective. The only complaint we've heard about it is that it does tend to make one look—well —voluminous, if that is important to you.

If we had our druthers, we'd suggest to the manufacturers that they do something about the *slipperiness* of nylon. There are times and places that, when skiers fall, they should be able to stop themselves from sliding as quickly as possible. If they are wearing nylon clothes, that becomes very difficult.

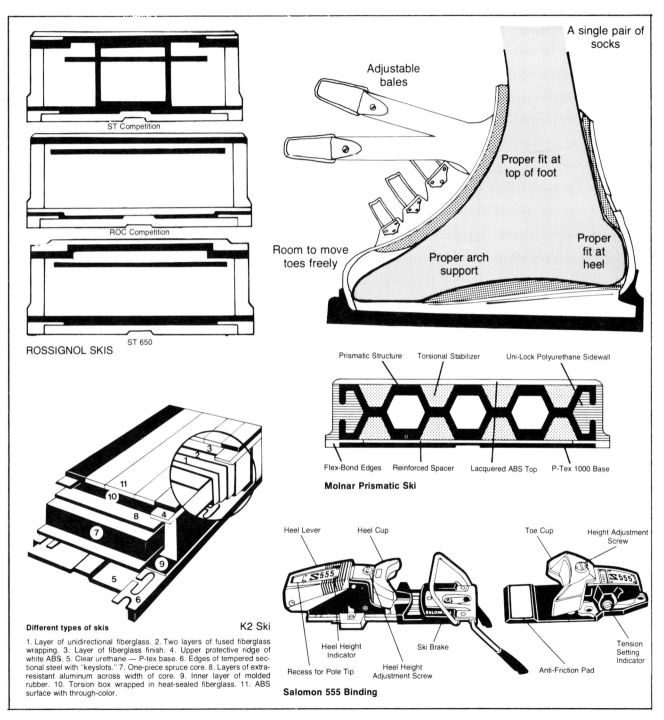

ST Competition

ROC Competition

ST 650

ROSSIGNOL SKIS

Adjustable bales

A single pair of socks

Proper fit at top of foot

Room to move toes freely

Proper arch support

Proper fit at heel

Prismatic Structure   Torsional Stabilizer   Uni-Lock Polyurethane Sidewall

Flex-Bond Edges   Reinforced Spacer   Lacquered ABS Top   P-Tex 1000 Base

Molnar Prismatic Ski

Different types of skis   K2 Ski

1. Layer of unidirectional fiberglass. 2. Two layers of fused fiberglass wrapping. 3. Layer of fiberglass finish. 4. Upper protective ridge of white ABS. 5. Clear urethane — P-tex base. 6. Edges of tempered sectional steel with "keyslots." 7. One-piece spruce core. 8. Layers of extra-resistant aluminum across width of core. 9. Inner layer of molded rubber. 10. Torsion box wrapped in heat-sealed fiberglass. 11. ABS surface with through-color.

Heel Lever   Heel Cup   Toe Cup   Height Adjustment Screw

Heel Height Indicator   Ski Brake   Tension Setting Indicator

Recess for Pole Tip   Heel Height Adjustment Screw   Anti-Friction Pad

Salomon 555 Binding

3
a
certain
technique

Learn to ski in three days

Our technique for learning to ski is first of all a matter of balance. You must have *longitudinal balance:* your legs planted squarely on your skies and perpendicular to them. You must maintain this balance whenever you ski.

You must also have *lateral balance*—a factor which, in turns, involves a sort of controlled leaning.

And, finally, for the third element of balance, you must learn the art of *edge control*. This is something that you will learn more or less by yourself, as you make progress. Edging, essentially, consists of tilting the skis onto their uphill edges—about which there will be more later. One of the important elements in successful edge control is having a pair of high quality boots.

If you follow directions scrupulously, you'll find that you become able very quickly to keep your balance, to move in the direction that you want to move, and to keep from falling when you stop; that is, you'll soon begin to taste the unalloyed pleasure of skiing.

We give you, the beginner, this guarantee: in three days, you'll be able to ski. You will make steady progress, and you will have no serious worries about having an accident.

As far as readers are concerned who already know how to ski, it's our purpose to give them access to more balanced and functional skiing. We have no intention of imposing this or that way of doing things on anyone. We offer a spectrum of possibilities. It's up to you to choose the stage at which you feel you don't need any more instruction.

And you can stop anywhere that you want. After all, no one but you knows at what point you feel that you are happy with the way you ski.

first day, first slide

You've just put on your skis for the first time. You already know—and if you don't, you're about to discover—that almost the first thing a beginner does is to fall.

Let us give you a word of advice about falling. When you fall, your fall will be "soft" if you relax your muscles as much as possible and try to fall in a ball or crouch. Even before you fall, let's see how you will go about getting up as effortlessly as possible so as to conserve your strength—which you'll need later on.

Wearing your skis, and holding your poles firmly in your hands, sit down in the snow. Once you are sitting, disengage your hands from the pole-straps. Put the two poles together and place them in front of you with the points alongside your body. With one hand, grasp the poles toward the top, just under the straps. With the other hand, hold the poles at the bottom, slightly above the basket. Then bring your body and the poles close together. Pull yourself up with the hand at the top of the poles, pushing with the hand at the bottom, and supporting yourself on the angled edges of your skis. (It also develops your legs.)

Do this exercise three or four times on the left side, then three or four times on the right.

When you fall on a slope of no matter what degree, before trying to get up make sure that you skis are downhill from your body and perpendicular to the line of the slope. The poles, which you'll use to pull yourself upright, will then be uphill in relation to your body.

Later on, when you've learned to ski, you'll discover that you can rise quickly by simply pulling yourself up on your poles in a normal position. By then, your legs will be strong enough for you to do this without tiring yourself unduly.

Now, since you know how to get up after you fall, the next thing to do is to learn how to move on your skis.

Skis are, in a sense, like shoes. When you're wearing them, your skis *are* your feet. And so, for practical purposes, when you're skiing, your feet are five or six times longer than when you're just walking down the street. Keep that in mind when you begin to move around in the snow.

The first run

Even before sliding on your skis, plant your poles solidly in the snow and, while remaining in the same spot, slide your skis back and forth under you. Then, let go of your poles and do the same exercise without them.

68

On a perfectly flat stretch of snow, plant your poles firmly in the snow. Raise one ski and pivot it first to the right and then to the left. Do the same exercise with the other ski.

Without moving from where you are standing, make a few small changes in direction by spreading the tips of your skis, bringing them together, spreading them. . . . Be careful that the back part of one ski does not come to rest on the other ski.

Now, give yourself a little push with your poles and move forward without bending either your torso or your legs too much.

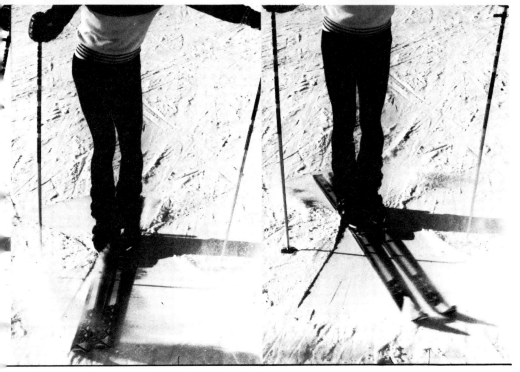

Plant your poles firmly in the snow and pivot both
skis simultaneously.

Move forward, without your poles, by sliding one
ski forward and then the other.

71

The first downhill run

Let's take a few moments to prepare for *balance*—an indispensable element once you go out on the slopes.

So far, the movements you've practiced have been on flat terrain. Now let's orient ourselves toward the first downhill run. First, you'll have to climb a small slope.

We've already mentioned *edging*. Now is the time to edge. It is something like building a staircase for yourself by making a small angle between the downhill edge of your skis and the snow, and then moving upward or downward on the slope. First, put your weight on the downhill ski and raise the uphill ski, moving it 20 or 30 centimeters toward the crest of the slope. Put your foot down, being careful to keep an angle between the ski and the snow, and rest your weight on that foot. Then, using the same procedure, raise your downhill ski and bring it up next to the uphill ski. Keeping your body in a natural position, climb two or three meters uphill, and then two or three meters downhill.

It's possible that, at first, you will have some slight difficulty in maintaining the angle between your skis and the snow. If so, don't hesitate to bend your knees toward the uphill side. You'll find that this does a lot to facilitate edging.

Now—finally—we're ready to try a run downhill. For this, of course, you'll have to climb up a slope. It should be a relatively gentle slope—but a slope nonetheless.

Sidestepping

Following the principle we've just explained, you're now ready to climb the slope by side-stepping.

Plant your two poles firmly in the snow, with the uphill pole a bit further away from your body than the downhill pole. Now, raise the uphill ski and move it about eight inches uphill. Put it down—and don't forget to edge it. Rest your weight on the uphill ski and raise the downhill ski, bringing it up next to the uphill one. Adjust your poles to the proper position. Then repeat until you are as far up the slope as you want to go.

The herringbone climb

Another way of walking is through what we call the herringbone, which is particularly easy with compact skis. Face uphill, with the tips of your skis spread apart and your poles firmly planted behind your feet. Put all your weight on one ski, then raise the other ski and move it uphill. (Be careful to hold the ski out far enough so as not to put it down on the other ski.) Now shift your weight onto the forward ski and bring up the rear ski.

This method is more tiring than the sidestep, but it does allow you to move more quickly than the latter.

Facing downhill

Now that you know how to sidestep, you can easily get into position for your first run.

Let us say that you have climbed as far up the slope as you want to be. Your skis are perpendicular to the slope and you now have to turn and face downhill.

Use the following method for turning: plant both your poles downhill, one of them forward of the tips of your skis, the other level with your feet. Supporting yourself on the poles, move your skis uphill sideways by spreading them apart in the back and bringing the tips into position between your poles. You are now facing the fall line, as it's called.

This is going to be your first downhill run—at a very slow speed and on a slope gentle enough for you to be able to stop whenever you want. So, don't worry about accidents.

Let yourself slide forward naturally through your initial pole placement. Your body is perpendicular to your skis, your knees slightly bent in a natural position. Your skis are parallel—not too close, not too far apart. Above all, avoid leaning too far forward or too far to the rear.

Wrong

Right

Traversing

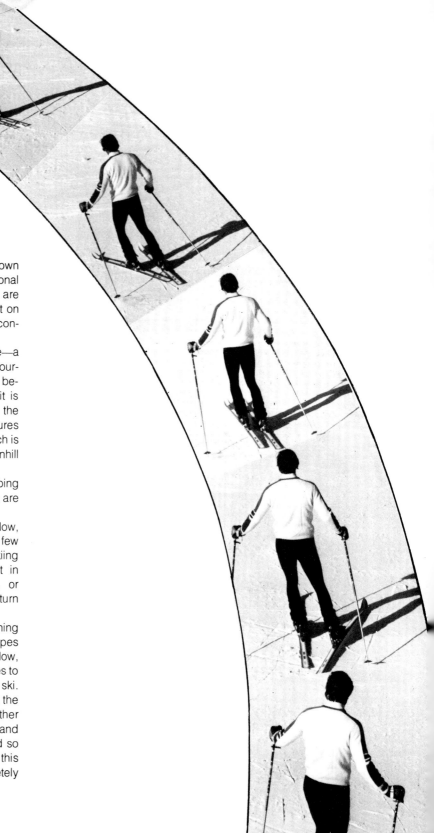

Your first forward run on skis is not straight down the slope, but across the slope. These diagonal runs are called traverses. So, what we are talking about is not skiing with your skis flat on the snow, but with them tilted uphill (edge control).

You begin by sidestepping up the slope—a gentle slope, as we said before. Then, let yourself slide forward, maintaining the angle between your skis and the snow. Note that it is essential that the uphill ski be forward of the downhill ski. The reason for this is that it assures the freedom of movement of both legs—which is impossible if the uphill ski is behind the downhill ski.

The two elements mentioned above—climbing and sliding—are the two basic factors which are indispensable to progress in skiing.

We've already talked about balance. Now, complement your concept of balance by a few maneuvers that will introduce you to what skiing is really about: *turning*. This is important in traversing because after each traverse, or diagonal run across a slope, the skier has to turn so as to be able to make another traverse.

For the moment, concentrate on a small turning step on a very gentle slope—but one that slopes enough, nonetheless, to allow you to slide. Now, put all your weight on one ski—use your poles to keep yourself steady—and raise the other ski. Move the latter slightly forward while turning the tip outward so that the ski fans out from the other ski. Put the ski down, rest your weight on it, and then immediately bring the other ski around so that it rests parallel to the first ski. Repeat this exercise until you have turned completely around.

Skating

You've now practiced the preceding exercise—with turns both to the right and to the left—to the point where you've mastered it. The next step is to set yourself in motion on the snow by a maneuver that is known—somewhat pretentiously, perhaps—as skating.

Plant your poles firmly in the snow. Raise one ski. Turn the tip outward and move it forward. Put it down. Bend the knee of the other leg and give yourself a slight push while, at the same time, giving yourself a push with your poles. This will move you forward in the direction in which you've placed the first ski. Bring the second ski around, positioning it forward of the first ski, with its tip angled outward. Now, give yourself a push with the first ski and your poles.

The purpose of this exercise is to give you a certain stability on your skis. You're going to need it, since the whole technique of skiing rests on balance.

Practice skating with great patience—a whole day should be devoted to it. It's not wasted time, as you will discover.

79

Flexing and rising

Here's another exercise for you: while sliding forward, do a series of half knee-bends and rises, bringing your arms and poles forward to maintain your balance.

The pivot turn

Now for one last exercise. This one is obviously very practical since it teaches you how to turn—that is, how to change your direction while standing in place. The pivot turn is particularly easy with compact skis.

Put your weight on one ski and position your two poles to the rear of that ski, with one pole on either side of your foot. Raise the other ski and pivot it outward, bringing it down parallel to and behind the first ski. Rest your weight on the ski you've just moved and bring the first ski around until it is parallel to the other ski: that is, until both skis are facing in the same direction. Now, increase the edge of that ski by moving your knee inward as far as you can comfortably. This will give you the change in direction that you want. After moving forward for a few yards, do the same thing on the other side. That is, shift your weight to the other ski.

You've now made your first sure, controlled turns.

You can use the same maneuver to bring yourself to a halt. All you have to do is pretend that you are making a much sharper turn.

the second day: the wedge or snowplow

The snowplow

The snowplow is indispensable simply because it is irreplaceable. Jean-Claude is not embarrassed to admit that he uses it ten or twelve times a day—on obstacles, dangerous terrain, and so forth.

It will allow you to move at your own pace, at the speed you think best—and only on the kind of slope that you, with all prudence and reasonableness, should be using at this stage.

The snowplow does not require any particular exertion on your part, and it is not merely a temporary expedient for beginners. On the contrary, it will prove to be the necessary link between the straight-line skiing of the beginner and the elegantly coordinated turns that you'll begin making as you progress.

The second day, therefore, will be well spent with the snowplow.

To begin, face the fall line and spread your skis apart slightly. Gently—that is, without straining your muscles—bring the tips of your skis close together. This, of course, means that your skis will spread apart in the back—but not too far. Your skis now form a (small) angle to the snow, and your (slow) movement forward will thus be braked and controlled.

By a slight bend of the knees and angles, shift your weight onto the ski which corresponds to the direction in which you want to move. Your body should be turned toward that direction.

Two classic mistakes

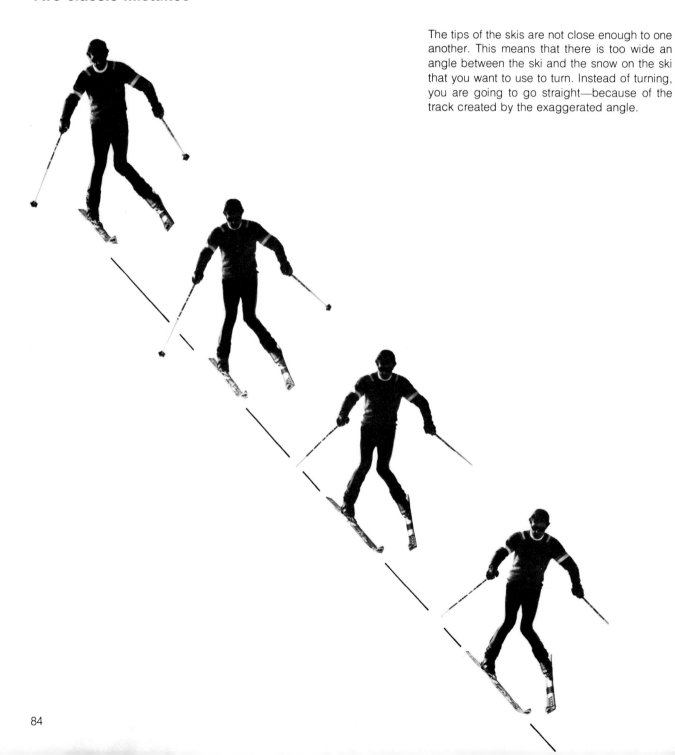

The tips of the skis are not close enough to one another. This means that there is too wide an angle between the ski and the snow on the ski that you want to use to turn. Instead of turning, you are going to go straight—because of the track created by the exaggerated angle.

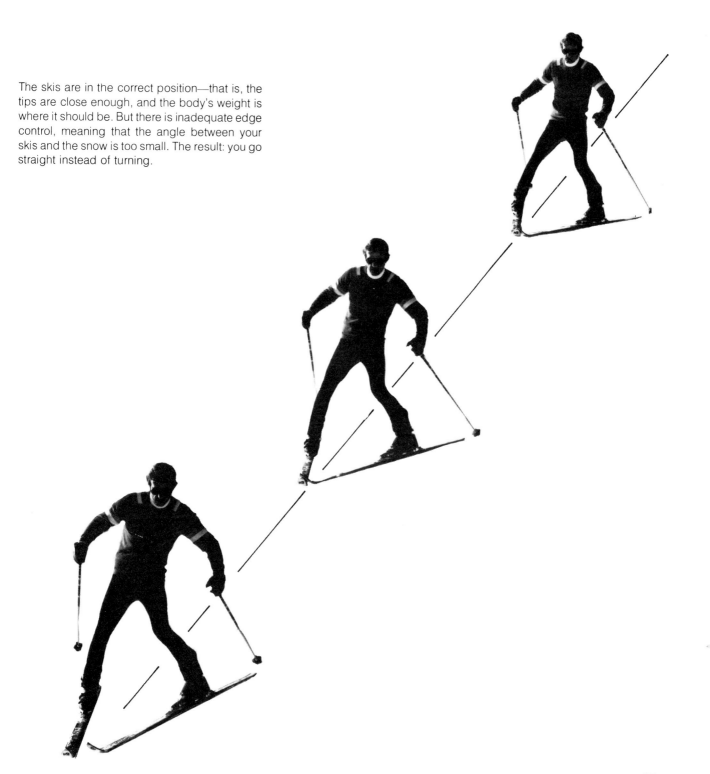

The skis are in the correct position—that is, the tips are close enough, and the body's weight is where it should be. But there is inadequate edge control, meaning that the angle between your skis and the snow is too small. The result: you go straight instead of turning.

Your first wedeln

We're now on the second day of your three-day course and already you have control over where you go on your skis. If you feel that you're already almost a skier—well, you're not all that far from the truth. Actually, if you're careful in choosing your terrain, you can anticipate what's to come by doing your first wedelns right now. That is, by undertaking a series of very slight changes in direction.

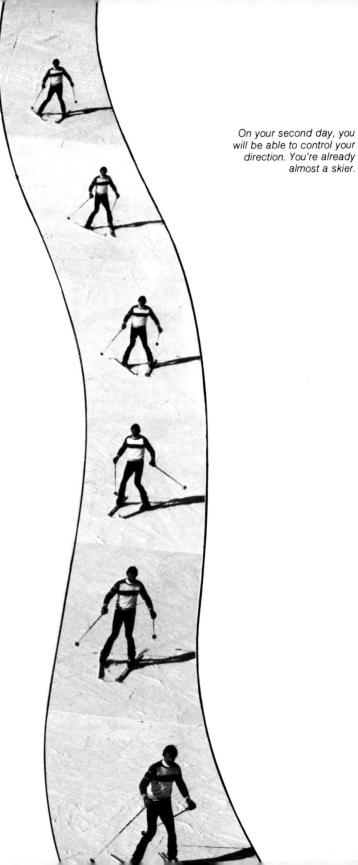

On your second day, you will be able to control your direction. You're already almost a skier.

the third day

Now that you've learned the snowplow (which will also be the lesson for the first part of the third day), don't keep your skis in that uncomfortable position. Instead, as soon as you've made a slight turn, bring the ski on the inside of the turn to a position parallel to the other one and continue your traverse run.

Although you are still on a comparatively slight slope, you'll notice that changing direction, or turning, is now rather easy for you. Continue to do the same exercises on the opposite side; that is, resume the snowplow position and then bring your skis parallel after the turn.

By now, you're a full-fledged apprentice skier.

If you want to progress further and faster, practice—intense practice—is absolutely indispensable. Progress in skiing consists of doing an exercise over and over again, with a slight improvement each time.

Now that you're going to practice seriously, don't go up the slope on foot any more. Don't even use the sidestep or the herringbone step. Learn to economize your strength. Keep it for use in coming down rather than in going up the slopes. Instead, use the mechanical lift to the slopes which are proportionate to your abilities. Don't let the lift make you nervous. While waiting for the lift, slip the straps of both your poles over the wrist that corresponds to the side from which you are going to mount the left. (In the illustration, it's the left side.) Let yourself slide forward and take hold of the lift with both hands. Place it between your legs, keeping your knees slightly bent and supporting yourself with your arms, while letting the bar—which is going to be your seat—slide through your hands.

As soon as you are seated—or rather, supported—take the slight shock of the moving lift with your arms. Be careful not to stiffen your legs too much and not to bend them too much. Try to keep your skis in a parallel position.

You are now on your way to faster progress in skiing.

A few moments of exercise

It's highly advisable, after a trip on a ski lift—especially if it's quite cold—to limber up before you do any skiing. A few easy exercises will do a lot to loosen up your joints and warm your muscles.

Stand with your skis flat on the snow. Raise your arms to a 90° angle to your body and turn your torso to the right and to the left three to five times—energetically!

Plant your poles in the snow and walk in place, taking giant steps and sliding your skis under you with each step. Do this three to six times.

With your poles firmly planted, raise each leg alternately as high as you can while bending your knees. (Three to five times for each leg.)

Finally, supporting yourself on your poles, bend both legs simultaneously and squat, as though you were going to sit on your heels. Repeat two to four times.

Now that you've completed your warm-up exercises, you can head for the slopes knowing that you're ready for almost anything.

Edge control

Let's see what we've accomplished so far.
You can now control your (low) speed, change
direction to the right and to the left—and even
turn and make successive traverses across the
slope. This means that you are already a skier.
Within the framework of the three days that
we've allowed ourselves for you to learn to ski,
we are going to concentrate now on two maneuvers that are eminently useful in being able to
better control your movements.

We are talking about lateral sideslipping and
oblique sideslipping.

Since edge control is the key to these
maneuvers—as, indeed, it is in all turns—we
had better begin by going into a bit of detail. As
we've already said, edge control consists of the
taking of an angle between your skis and the
snow. The size of this angle will vary infinitely
according to the degree of the slope, the condition of the snow, the speed at which you're
moving, and the width of your turn. In the final
analysis, you are the only one who can decide
and control your edging.

Holding the angle that you've established requires a physical effort, but one that is facilitated
by today's boots, which give firm support to the
skier's ankles. In order to partially release your
edges, all you have to do is decrease the
amount of energy you are expending to hold the
angle. In order to release the edges fully, simply
let your skis go flat on the snow. You will then
begin to slide downhill. Please note, however,
that skiing *on the flat* is just a figure of speech.
There must always be an angle, however small it
may be, between your skis and the
snow—otherwise you'll probably lose your balance very quickly and, if you encounter the
slightest irregularity in the snow, you'll fall to the
downhill side.

Having released your edges you will begin
sliding sideways—that is, sideslipping down the
slope. In order to stop sideslipping, simply re-
set your edges—eventually exaggerating the
angle somewhat by leaning your knees uphill.

Setting and releasing edges have taken the form of the two maneuvers mentioned above, both of which are extremely useful in skiing. They give you the means for going through passages that are narrow, difficult, or otherwise dangerous—or for easily losing altitude.

Lateral sideslipping

Your skis are perpendicular to the fall line and your edges are set into the hill. Now, gradually release your edges—that is, narrow the angle between your skis and the snow until you begin to slide down the slope.

While you're learning to do this, support your weight on your uphill pole and perform only short, gentle sideslips. Avoid planting your downhill pole at all.

Generally speaking, your skis will be close together. Later, however, when you use steeper slopes, avoid having them too close together; otherwise, the uphill foot will brush the snow and, almost inevitably, cause you to fall.

This will be also true in certain turns on steep slopes where leaning will cause a very tight angle between your skis and the snow—a situation in which it is advisable to keep your skis rather far apart.

Oblique sideslipping

Oblique sideslipping is, in essence, the end of a turn without going completely around. It allows the skier to brake his or her speed or to easily reach a certain point downhill and in front of him or her.

You begin with a traverse.

Then, at the proper moment, you release your edges to a certain extent—just enough for the degree of slope—keeping your body perpendicular to your skis. Your skis will remain perpendicular to the fall line and will sideslip in the direction you choose—under the push of your initial momentum.

Obviously, the thing for you to learn to do is to calculate and control your edging.

The snowplow turn

This maneuver should be the climax and the high point of our three days. It is somewhat delicate—which is to say, difficult—with long skis but easy and comfortable with compacts. It will serve you long and well in your career as a skier.

It requires no particular effort, and it is a happy medium between the snowplow stop, which you practiced on the second day, and the stem turn, which we'll get to later on.

Here is the way the snowplow turn is done:

While traversing, move your uphill ski out to the side while making the tips of your skis converge. Shift your weight onto the uphill ski, and pay particular attention to your edging, so that the angle between skis and snow is adequate.

The ski is going to begin changing direction, just as it does in the snowplow.

As soon as the uphill ski has passed the fall line, quickly bring the other ski forward, either by raising it or by sliding it, until your skis are parallel, which will enable you to continue your turn.

There is a little psychological trap in the snowplow turn which you should be aware of beforehand. When your uphill ski passes the fall line, there may be a slight increase in your speed. So, just grit your teeth and don't panic. Note that the snowplow turn can be practiced on slopes somewhat steeper than those that you've used up to now, and that it requires a bit more alacrity in bringing the downhill ski forward into a parallel position with the uphill ski.

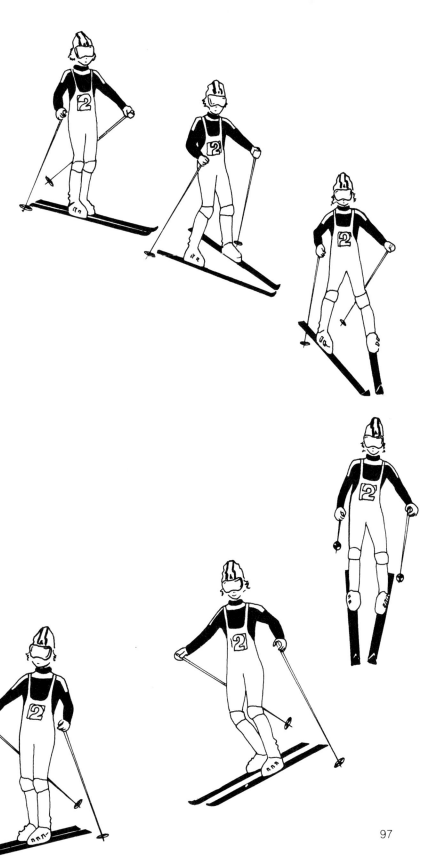

and now . . .

Planting the poles

Your poles are not only for use in moving forward, in maintaining your balance, or in getting up if you've fallen. They also play a very important role in, and serve to simplify, your turns. You can use a single pole, either on the right or on the left, or both poles simultaneously. They are not used at all at very high speeds or in certain types of maneuvers that are outside the capabilities of every skier.

Until now, your turns have been executed with a certain amount of what we might call "passivity." Now, we're going to talk about a technique that requires a bit more activity on your part because it is practiced on slightly steeper slopes at somewhat greater speeds—and also because you've now had some experience in maintaining your balance.

However, before getting into this new technique, which involves use of your poles, let's reflect a bit on the role of the latter.

In every kind of dynamic turn—that is, as soon as a skier has passed the snowplow stage—the use of poles is absolutely indispensable. When the skier makes the move that effectuates a turn, the pole provides a third point of support; the other two, of course, being the skier's feet.

Planting the two poles

The ski pole, in a way, is the pivot point around which you make your turn, and it helps you to maintain your balance. The shifting of your weight toward the inside of the turn, combined with the momentum given by the bending of the knee (or knees) and your speed at the moment that you change direction, make it possible for you to begin moving down the slope in a curve which becomes the beginning of a turn.

When you use both poles simultaneously, they eventually enable you to regain your balance, but, essentially, their function is to make a change in direction easier and more stable.

It may be hard to believe at this stage, but "pole plants" are going to be extremely useful in your future as a skier. Remember that the faster you ski, the easier it is to maneuver.

This is the paradox of skiing: everything is hard when you ski slowly, and everything is easy when you ski fast. The only problem is that, for a skier to ski simply and painlessly, he or she must be a pretty good skier. . . .

For the moment, remember that your pole is planted (or your poles are planted) at the tips of your skis, but that they become effective only when your feet draw level with them.

The stem christie

This having been said, let's study the stem christie—a technique that you can use throughout your skiing career without either offending a sense of purity and elegance of style or impeding your effectiveness.

At the beginning, it will seem that the stem christie requires a distinct separation of your movements, but, as your practice, you will see that the stem christie often blends into the parallel turn—unless it's the parallel turn that often blends into the stem christie. . . .

Here is how to do a stem-christie:

You are in a traverse.

Now, push out the tail of your uphill ski, while keeping the tips of your skis close together.

Bring your downhill pole level with the tip of your downhill ski by bending the corresponding ankle and knee.

Quickly and firmly set your edge on the downhill ski—that is, shift your weight to it and immediately push your bent knee in, support yourself on your pole, and keep your body perpendicular to your skis.

Because of your pole, your speed (you're sliding, remember) and your bent knee, the position
of your body will release the edge on your uphill
ski which, now "on the flat," will start moving
down the slope.

What you have to do now is to bring your
downhill ski up to the uphill ski by raising it
slightly or by sliding it.

When your skis are parallel and even, you can
turn according to the way that you've set your
edges and to your whim. The skis themselves,
by their shape, will do most of the work. Remember that careful edging will give you a
graceful curve. By the same token, careless
edging will cause you to sideslip too much and
result in a "square turn."

Initially, it's important that you perform each
movement distinctly and separately: sideslipping with the downhill ski, planting of the pole,
moving of the bent knee inward, and balancing
of the body.

Closing the tails of your skis

Later, when you're skiing faster and are surer of your balance, you will be able to do stem christies without keeping the tails of your skis so far apart.
In fact, once you've learned and assimilated the parallel turn, you'll find out that you often do the stem christie without realizing it.

some other fundamentals

Sudden stops

It may happen that you want to—or must—stop suddenly.

Let's say you're skiing straight down the fall line of a slope (*schussing,* it's called), and you want to stop. With as much force as you can muster, drive in the tails of your skis. This will cause the skis to swing around and position themselves perpendicular to the fall line.

No less energetically, set your edges, according to the steepness of the slope, in order to brake yourself.

Remember that the degree to which your body leans uphill may be important. But, to neutralize the imbalance that will result from the sudden slipping of your skis from under you, turn your torso downhill and angulate—that is, lean away from the hill so as to keep weight on your uphill edges. And then, as soon as you come to a stop, plant your downhill pole.

The degree of slope will determine whether your skis should be close together or slightly spread apart.

Isolated moguls

A mogul is simply a bump in the snow. Bumps are pretty much everywhere—individual bumps and veritable fields of bumps. In neither case are moguls a special problem, either for the beginner or the experienced skier. All that's necessary is to adapt your skiing technique to the speed at which you hit a mogul.

As a learner, you are still skiing slowly, just as the tips of your skis reach the mogul, be ready to shift your weight forward to adjust to the change that your skis will make because of the change in slope. Thus, when you reach the mogul itself, you will stay perpendicular to your skis and you'll pass over the mogul without losing your balance.

If you are an intermediate skier, you are able to ski faster than a beginner. Even so, you don't want to be thrown into the air when you encounter a mogul. So, as soon as you reach the bump, absorb the change in terrain by flexing your knees, ankles, and waist. Also, press down with your toes—which will make your skis continue to adhere to the snow and thus follow the mogul better.

If you are already a somewhat experienced skier, you are steady on your skis and sure of your balance. Certainly, you are able to ski faster than before and you may even want to experience the thrill of "flying" off the mogul. This experience presents no particular problem—not even a psychological problem.

Remain upright on your skis. When your skis reach the top of the mogul, your momentum will carry you off the snow and into the air. Spread your arms slightly so as to keep your balance.

When you touch ground, absorb the small "shock" of landing by flexing your ankles, knees, and waist.

Straighten up as soon as you feel you can do so without losing your balance.

107

A series of moguls

When you encounter a series of moguls, don't be alarmed. They're not going to throw you off balance, let alone make you fall. A little flexibility, a little relaxation, and the moguls will be crossed without mishap.

When you reach the depression preceding the mogul, make sure that you're in an upright position. As your skis climb the uphill side of the bump, move your weight forward and let your body "unhinge" loosely at ankles, knees and hips, allowing your knees to act as shock absorbers.

When your skis and feet reach the crest of the mogul, quickly straighten your legs so that your skis will maintain contact with the snow, at least partially. (Here, your legs are acting as springs.) In any event, be sure to remain perpendicular to your skis.

When you've become a thoroughly experienced skier, you may want to adopt a technique a bit more, shall we say, airborne? For that, all you'll have to do will be to calculate your speed and judge your distances correctly.

The parallel turn

The parallel turn—or christie, as it's called—is a logical, but not an indispensable, goal for effective and well-equilibrated skiing.
It is the aesthetic aim of your career as a skier; but it is also a means of better controlling your skis.

Finally, it is a simplification of turning, and, since we should always use the simplest way of doing things, we would strongly urge you to master the parallel turn. The mechanics of it are far from difficult:
— Begin a traverse, with your skis in a parallel position.
— Move your downhill pole forward, while bending your ankles and knees.

The christie

When your feet have drawn even with the down-hill pole, relax your legs and shift your weight to them—or to only the downhill leg, is you prefer—and keep them perpendicular to your skis. Now, with support from your pole, lean your body toward the inside of the turn. Your speed, the bend in your legs, the releasing of your edges by your body leaning into the turn—these factors, in combination, will cause your skis to start down the slope and will give you the beginning of the turn that you want.

The rest of the turn depends on your personal preferences and on the way in which you re-set your edges.

At the beginning, practice this kind of turn on relatively easy terrain.

The counter-turn

Relaxing the legs and leaning the body often involves lifting one ski—or even both skis—off the snow, particularly on steep or undulating slopes.

You can also make a christie by prefacing it with what is called a "counter-turn." The counter-turn is essentially a releasing of your edges, followed by a very forceful and sudden re-setting of the edges. The latter results in a kind of muscular compression which, when it is relaxed, makes for a relatively effortless beginning of a turn, even if the counter-turn results in a change in direction more pronounced than seems called for.

It's possible that, in certain cases and on certain trails, your downhill ski will get away from you. However, if this gives you better stability, it's not important. In such cases, the weight of the body is distributed as follows: 60% on the downhill ski, 40% on the uphill ski.

The freedom of movement of the legs is immeasurably more important in skiing than a purity of style.

tips

Skiing in soft snow

You're now well equipped to venture forth and confront—happily and, we hope, fearlessly—all the problems that you might encounter on packed snow on any slope.

We'd like to invite you to sample another of the pleasures of skiing—in soft snow. (Also called deep snow or "powder," it rarely falls in the eastern part of the United States.)

We can tell you that, if you use your parallel turns, you'll enjoy it and be pleased with your performance, no matter what kind of snow it is. It's not difficult. The biggest effort you'll have to make, in fact, will be at the psychological level.

Soft snow varies greatly, both in quality and in depth. You may choose to ski, for example, on a trail that has been packed and then covered with anywhere from 10 to 40 centimeters (4 to 18 inches) of powder—a light and relatively easy-to-manage layer. You'll find that the powder flies (pleasantly) around you as you ski and presents not the least impediment to your customary technique. It also allows you, when you come to a stop, to admire the graceful curves of your turns in the snow.

In fact, one of the advantages of soft snow—and this is by no means an advantage to be despised—is that it affords you a visual appreciation of the quality of your turns, your sideslipping, and the harmonious linking of your wedelns. In its way, therefore, soft snow can be an excellent teacher.

Skiing in soft snow is not quite so simple when, instead of a light layer of powder, we are talking about a fresh, damp "heavy" snow. This calls for more concentration on your part. Grit your teeth—and keep your skis together. This is really "soft snow," and it's the way to go if you want to experience a rare pleasure in skiing. In any case, if you really love the sport, it's an experience that you won't be able to resist: soft snow, without an underlying base of packed snow.

The supreme pleasure is to be found in very deep snow, but of a light, powdery quality in which you'll twist and turn in billowing clouds and in a trail of "smoke" of incredible beauty and purity.

Skiing in soft snow: here, the skier's greatest effort often must be at the psychological level.

Skiing in powder has the added advantage of giving the skier a visual appreciation of the quality of his turns.

You'll find yourself covered with white from head to toe; and you'll become part of the snow while dominating it and delighting in it.

It's worth repeating again what we said earlier: the effort required in this kind of soft snow is essentially of a psychlogical nature.

It is somewhat different when the snow is heavy, irregular, and crusty. In that case, we are talking about a technical and athletic adjustment as well as a psychological one.

Contrary to what you may be told elsewhere, the use of compact skis will simplify considerably the application in soft snow of the technique that you've learned; this holds true of soft snow of any kind.

In the accompanying illustration, we've used the most difficult kind of soft snow: crusty and rutted. The technique remains essentially the

same as on a packed slope—but with this difference: lean back slightly in order to raise the tips of your skis from the snow. (Pretend that you're waterskiing.) Also, you'll find that your movements in soft snow will have to be a bit more brusque and energetic than on a packed trail.

The more "difficult" the snow, the closer together you should keep your skis. But we must add that, sometimes, in certain kinds of snow (heavy snow, for example) when you'll have to make closed turns, a good stem christie, or a snowplow turn with an uphill opening, will allow you to make an effective (though possibly inelegant) turn.

Remember that it's better to carve curves in the snow than to have your tracks look like some sort of elementary Morse code; i.e., a dash (your tracks) followed by a dot (where you fall).

Opposite page, above: A few inches of powder do not require any appreciable change in the skier's technique. Below: For experienced skiers: making "figure eights" in virgin snow.

New tracks in the snow are the only clue to the skier's presence. They will last until obliterated by fresh snow or by the sun.

to ski even better

With the technical knowledge that you've now acquired, you should be able to ski with complete pleasure. You have our guarantee: you can do whatever you want, wherever you want, with complete security.

It's now up to you to decide if you want to acquire techniques beyond those that you've learned—and to practice those techniques.

We're willing to gamble that you'll want to go forward. And so, we're going to describe a few more techniques that you may find both useful and amusing.

A necessary trick: turning on the moguls

Moguls, as we mentioned earlier, arc bumps in the snow. When these bumps are of the proper shape, they will make it much easier for you to turn. In fact, if you make judicious use of moguls, pivoting your skis only very slightly at the summit of the mogul, you'll find that the bump is a blessing in disguise.

As you approach the mogul, raise your pole to the same height as the bump. When the tips of your skis reach the mogul, bend your knees and, as soon as your feet reach the crest of the mogul, simultaneously straighten up and pivot on the crest. This will enable you to achieve a painless turn.

Three kinds of skiing: on a rock-strewn trail, for the love of adventure; in soft snow, for the skier's own enjoyment; in a slalom event – for the sake of being the best, as Franz Klammer is doing here.

Having fun: avalement

Avalement is from a French word meaning "to swallow," and it refers to the technique by which a skier "swallows" a mogul by retracting his knees and feet at its crest.

In the title of this section, we talked of "having fun" with avalement because, as a technique, it is amusing to master and practice while not being altogether necessary to the skier.

The technique consists essentially in crossing over a series of moguls. In the depression preceding the moguls, your body is erect. Then, retract your knees and body to absorb the shock of contact with the mogul.

When your ski tips reach the crest of the mogul, pivot your skis and lean toward the inside of your turn as you quickly relax your legs so that your skis remain in contact with the snow.

A finishing touch: turning with two poles

In certain cases, we recommend that you use both poles simultaneously for support in turning. You'll find this technique very convenient when skiing on a steep slope, when you've almost lost your balance and want to recover, and, above all, when you're carrying extra weight.

In order to turn with both poles, simply plant the poles forward on either side of your ski tips. Take advantage of the momentary support gained from your poles (and from a slight extension of your arms) to lift your skis above the snow and turn them in the desired direction without, of course, attempting too radical a change of direction.

As soon as you're facing in the direction you want, shift more of your weight onto the interior pole in order to obtain the proper angulation.

Don't worry about the outside pole. Your skis won't ever touch it since, by the time your skis reach the spot where it was planted, the pole won't be there anymore.

A useful maneuver: the wedeln

The *wedeln* is a maneuver that can be used on all slopes. It is useful both in breaking your speed and in controlling it. Essentially, it consists of a series of short turns.

To do a wedeln, move your pole forward and plant it. Flex your body joints. Lean on the pole and spring up and forward to your original tall downhill running position. Lean slightly into the turn so as to facilitate sideslipping, but remain perpendicular to your skis. After a few inches—or more, depending on what you want to do—re-set your edges so as to stop sideslipping.

Immediately plant your pole forward, flex your joints, etc., and you'll begin a short turn in the opposite direction.

You can use both poles in executing the wedeln. If you do, plant them simultaneously.

With a touch of pride: jumping

When you've become a really good skier—which is not necessarily the same thing as *thinking* that you're a really good skier—and when you've become quite good at estimating speed and distance, you'll probably find it's fun to "take off" from one mogul and land behind another by turning and leaning in the air just as you would on the snow.

A hint of competition

Competition skiing is both stimulating and fun. We're talking about competition skiing, of course, at your own level.

Competition can serve as a point of reference, a yardstick by which to measure your progress as a skier toward that mastery of technique which must always be your goal. Which is another way of saying that competition skiing has the immense advantage of compelling you to make your skis do what they *should* do rather than letting them do whatever they want to do.

In your case, of course, competition does not require any technical expertise, any skiing at improbable speeds, any impossible tricks of balance; most of all, it does not require any period of strenuous training.

Nonetheless, you'll have to do a certain amount of practicing in order to be able to ski through the flags without reducing your speed below what it should be.

Skiing among markers or flags is, for most people, a means of measuring their progress as skiers. For competition skiers, however, it is the result of years of work and perseverance, as demonstrated (above) by Jim Hunter, a Canadian and (below) by Franz Klammer, an Austrian skier.

a few final comments

We've just exposed you to a whole spectrum of possibilities with respect to the technique of skiing.

If you take advantage of them, and if you stick with them until you've mastered them, you will become what is called a "good skier;" that is, a skier who can go anywhere and do pretty much anything with ease and safety.

What then?

That's up to you. You may want to go on, learning new things—including a number of useless and superfluous things—as long as you ski.

There's no reason why you shouldn't indulge even in freestyle and "trick" skiing if you want to. However, at this point, we should remind you that there is still something missing in your education as a skier. Something small, but indispensable, that we alluded to earlier: *A minimum of logic.*

Freestyle or acrobatic skiing, the newest of disciplines, is a recent export of American skiers.

On a gentle slope: You're an expert skier – you can shoot down like a meteor in quest of ever more speed.

A minimum of logic

Skiing, as all skiers know, is a world of absolute freedom.

But, within the framework of that freedom, the skier must exercise prudent judgment in keeping with his abilities and experience.

On a gentle slope: You're a good skier – not an expert. Ski downhill in a high downhill position.

On a steep slope: You're a really good skier – so, you can wedeln down the fall line.

On a gentle slope: You're an advanced beginner – using the snowplow, wedeln down the slope.

On a gentle slope: You're a skier at the intermediate level – execute a gentle wedeln, thus braking your speed.

On a steep slope: You're good, but all that good – ma your turns wide.

On a steep slope: You're a very good skier – you can use a series of controlled wedelns.

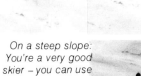 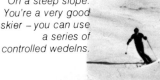  

On a steep slope: You're not too sure of yourself – so do some traverses connected by turns.

You're a bit wobbly on your turns, so do some sideslipping.

You're not really good enough even to be sure of your sideslipping, so do a traverse slightly downhill, and then do a pivot turn.

You really don't feel up to trying anything at all. Walk down the slope, carrying your skis over your shoulder.

To attempt more than you're capable of doing, to be unable to decide what to do, to take chances– you're going to fall, with all that that implies!

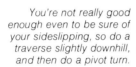

Skiing is a source of enormous pleasure and of unequalled joy. Don't spoil it by attempting to do more than you're capable of doing at any given stage. Be logical and reasonable in the demands you make on yourself.

Be patient. And, if you want truly to master your technique, never unconsciously anticipate by trying to do today what you should only be doing tomorrow. Make haste—but slowly!

If you do otherwise, you may find yourself being carried down the slope on a stretcher—and it will be your last downhill run for a long while.

It's much better to make it down under your own power, on your own two feet—happy and joyous!

4

the world of skiing

equipment on the slopes

The mechanical lifts

The first mechanical lifts were used, for the most part, in the summer to carry tourists up into the mountains. These visitors were not there to ski, but to enjoy the scenery, and the lifts they used were cable cars.

Rack railways were also much used, and had been popular for a long time in Switzerland and in several other countries.

These means of transport helped establish skiing in those countries. The early skiers were quick to realize that, while hiking up the mountains might have a certain charm, it would not appeal greatly to people who were interested in downhill skiing.

As soon as alpine skiing began to be popular, the problem of getting skiers up the slopes came under study. In a short time, tractor-drawn toboggans and ski lifts were introduced.

The ski "boom" encouraged a number of companies to specialize in equipment designed to satisfy both the manufacturers of mechanical lifts and their customers, regardless of the particular topography involved or the (ever increasing) number of skiers to be transported.

There is a wide choice of the kind of lift equipment available, depending upon the buyer's technical requirements and, of course, upon budget: rack rail, chair lift, cabin lift, etc.

The worth of a lift of any kind depends entirely upon the trails that it serves.

It must be capable of carrying the largest possible number of skiers.

And it must be suitable to the kind of skier who is going to use it; that is, an experienced skier, a beginner, a child, etc.

Lifts in all countries are subject to government safety regulations, and periodic inspections against very exacting standards assure complete security for users of the lifts.

The tendency, far from relaxing these regulations, is to tighten them. Every year, new equipment is required and new measures implemented for the safety of the skiers using these lifts. It goes without saying that these improvements represent a large investment on the part of the operators of the lifts.

It is no exaggeration to say that, almost as soon as a new lift is installed, it is made obsolete by technical improvements and by the never-ending quest for greater passenger capacity. It should be noted, however, that government approval for such improvements is slow in coming and is accorded only after extensive testing, in which the primary consideration is the safety of the passenger.

Nowhere in the world are lifts used to their maximum capacity throughout the winter. Nonetheless, they must be designed and constructed so as to handle traffic during the peak periods of the year: weekends, college vacations, etc., depending upon the country.

The number of people that a lift can transport is (after cost, of course) the chief consideration of the buyer. A cabin lift of from four to six places, or a three-place chair lift, can carry from 1,400 to 1,800 persons per hour. The cost of a cabin lift of this kind, not counting delivery charges and taxes, depends upon its length and upon the elevation which it will have to ascend. A lift costing two or three million dollars is not extraordinary, and additional expenses of all kinds can raise that price by twenty or thirty percent. Chair lifts generally are of two kinds. The fixed-seat chair lift, as the name suggests, remains in place all year long—with all that that implies for the landscape and the environment. A lift of this kind, let's say 1,200 yards in length and three or four hundred yards in elevation, costs about $250,000. A removable chair lift of approximately the same length and elevation will cost twice that amount; but it can handle more traffic than the fixed-seat lift.

Chair lifts of all kinds are all automatic nowadays and are all more or less capable of handling heavy traffic. They realize their maximum potential when used by beginners or by children who have to be helped onto the lift.

Even beginners' and children's lifts have a large theoretical capacity, but, in practice, they travel

Mechanical ski lifts represent a substantial investment. The gondola lift shown on the opposite page can carry from 1,400 to 1,800 skiers per hour—but it may cost as much as $2-3 million.

at much less speed than lifts in use by skilled skiers.

The automation of lifts has had several peripheral advantages. It requires the physical cooperation only of the individual who is using the lift—thus avoiding the possibility of incidents which were once not uncommon on the slopes.

A small lift for beginners, 200 yards long and with an elevation of about 125 feet, costs between $40,000 and $50,000. A long lift— from 1,200 to 1,600 yards long and between 400 and 500 yards elevation—runs from $150,000 to $200,000. All these prices, of course, are before taxes and do not include installation costs.

All told, a ski resort of medium size that opened, let us say, in 1976, would have had to spend around five or six million dollars for lifts alone—between twenty-five and thirty of them being required.

The location of lifts varies according to the topography of the area. There are two factors to consider in laying out the lifts. The first, obviously, is their convenience to the trails; the second, the most logical connections between lifts. There will be two or three lifts to the most popular areas.

The lifts to the most used trails turn a good profit, but those to the more difficult trails do not do nearly as well, since they are used only by expert skiers who, needless to say, are far rarer than intermediate skiers.

The summer maintenance of these lifts is as much a financial burden as the original purchase. Seats have to be repaired or replaced, cabins have to be renovated or replaced after a certain number of years, cables must be inspected regularly and replaced every five or six or ten years—and more often for the cables of chair lifts and cabin lifts.

The rack railway is the most expensive of all the means of transportation to the slopes. For that reason—notwithstanding the fact that the rack can carry a very large number of skiers per hour—the more adaptable cabin lifts are often preferred to the railway. The rack railway, in fact, is ordinarily used now only for long distances and on very dangerous terrain.

Packing the snow

Another very large and indispensable investment for every self-respecting resort is snowpacking equipment.

A medium-sized resort normally needs five or six
tractors; a large resort, from eight to twelve.

The smallest of these Caterpillar-treaded monsters capable of doing the work costs between
$25,000 and $30,000; and the larger machines
(the most efficient ones) sell for $50,000 to
$75,000.

If, as optional equipment, the buyer wants a
hydraulic plow for maintaining the snow, he
must pay an additional $5,000 or $6,000.

It goes without saying that tractors of this kind
are extremely powerful and capable of very
heavy work. They have, in fact, become irreplaceable in the preparation and maintenance
of snow for skiers.

Despite their power, the machines are surpris-
ingly delicate, taking into account the use to
which they're put, and they require extremely
painstaking care and maintenance.

*Opposite page: Chair lifts
are very pleasant when the
sun is shining, while
gondolas provide more
protection from wind and
cold.*

*Snow is no longer packed
by men on skis. Nowadays,
every respectable resort or
lodge has several of these
Caterpillar monsters to
maintain its ski areas.*

ski organizations

The International Ski Federation

The International Ski Federation now includes 46 member nations. The last candidate to be admitted was Israel—a welcome addition to the group, but one whose membership may well create problems.

The headquarters of the F.I.S. is at Berne, Switzerland, where resides the federation's president, Marc Hodler. Mr. Hodler's performance as president is so extraordinary that he is re-elected, year after year, by unanimous acclamation at annual federation meetings.

To aid the president in his work, there is a council comprising two vice-presidents and 15 members from various countries who are elected at local conferences.

In order to implement the policies established by the president and the council, a complex system of international committees has been organized which handle the two major divisions of the federation: the Nordic disciplines (biathlon, jumping, etc.), and the Alpine disciplines.

The carrying out of decisions and instructions emanating from the committees is undertaken at the Berne headquarters by professionals employed for that purpose. The following committees deal with the Alpine disciplines:

– *The Alpine Committee,* chaired by Honoré Bonnet, a Frenchman. Bonnet is assisted by the chairmen of the other major committees and by five representatives selected on a geographic basis. This committee is in charge of everything that has to do with competition Alpine skiing. It proposes reforms, changes in regulations, and new regulations.

Generally, the only time that regulations can be changed is at the so-called Rules Conference, which is held every four years. (The last one was in 1975, at San Francisco.) This conference alternates with one known as By-laws Conference.

The committee has succeeded in having a resolution adopted by virtue of which any change or innovation can be required to undergo a series of "tests," the results of which are considered by the Rules Conference in due course. Even though skiing is a comparatively new sport, it is a very traditionalist one. And as one can imagine, it is not always easy to introduce changes.

– *The Competition Rules and Control Committee,* with the chairman of this committee also a Frenchman, Robert Faure. The committee is responsible for the enforcement of rules, the consideration of proposed changes and adaptations of rules and the training of the technical representatives who are, in a sense, the arbiters of skiing. Through the intermediary of these representatives, the committee exercises control over all competition meets.

– *The Classification Committee,* chaired by Sepp Sulzberger, an Austrian. This group is responsible for analyzing and expressing the results of competitive meets by I.S.F. points, for scoring, for penalties, and for classification (three times yearly) of the participants.

– *The Trails Committee,* presided over by an Austrian, Hubert Spiess. As its name indicates, it is charged with regulating the quality and physical characteristics of descent trails in particular, with special attention to safety factors. Only members of this committee are authorized to exercise any control over, and to classify, international trails.

– *The Ladies Committee,* under the aegis of a Swiss woman, Odette Perret. This committee was established to protect female skiers from the more brutal aspects of skiing by opposing any change in rules and regulations that would place males and females on an equal footing.

– *The World Cup and European Cup Committee,* with its chairman, a Frenchman, Serge Lang. This committee is responsible for the enforcement of the special rules and regulations that pertain to the World Cup competition and for the working out of schedules some two years before the actual meet. It is also responsible for the organization of the European Cup competition, for its location, and—since not even the I.S.F. can dictate to Nature—for finding a substitute location in case its first choice turns out to be unsuitable because of lack of snow.

There are several other committees whose responsibilities are less well defined but, nonetheless, essential:
– *The Committee on Citizen Skiing,* chaired by Helen Tomkinson of Great Britain, is concerned with skiing and ski competition for city-dwellers.
– *The Legal Committee* is presided over by Paul Moranne, a French lawyer.
– *The Medical Committee,* with its chairman, Bud Little, an American.
– *The Qualification Committee* is chaired by a Norwegian, Dag Bergegrav.
– *The Training and Instruction Committee,* whose job it is above all to make information available to new skiers.
In addition, there are three "mixed committees" who work on behalf of both Alpine and Nordic disciplines:
– *The Agenda Committee,* which must try to find time for all the expressed needs of the organization.
– *The Scoring Committee,* which has a role in all changes in F.I.S. scoring procedures for jumping, etc.
– *The Publishing Committee,* which edits and publishes a quarterly magazine.

A few years ago, a technical corps, known as the *Alpine Bureau,* was set up. Its function is to see to the proper execution of the technical directives of the various committees, to the collation of all reports from technical representatives, and to preparations for international meetings. In addition, representatives of the bureau are on hand, before all major competitive meets, to assure that adequate preparation has been made—both technically and logistically—for the meet.
The International Ski Federation, as is obvious from the above, requires financial support in order to operate properly and to pay its employees. The national federations contribute to its support in proportion to their respective number of members.
In addition, the resorts hosting the major competitions (World Championships, World Cup, European Cup) must pay a certain amount to the federation for the privilege of organizing the competitions.
The federation's largest source of income, however, is derived from the sale of television rights to the World Championships and the Olympic games.

Roger Staub,
World Champion in the
Austrian Alps.

4. The world of skiing

ski instructors

Training

Everywhere, in every country that boasts at least a few skiers, the profession of ski instructor is tightly controlled, either by the national federation (as in Italy) or by a Minister of Sports (France, Austria, Switzerland, etc.) or, as in the United States, by a self-regulating organization of the instructors themselves (the Professional Ski Instructors of America). In each case, schools or training courses have been established to train and certify ski instructors. The kind of teaching—or rather, the emphasis in teaching—varies, of course, from country to country. In one area, the school's orientation may be scholastic; in another, commercial.

In France, for example, the training school for ski instructors, located at Chamonix, is controlled by the government—specifically by the Secretary of State for Youth and Sports. The National Ski and Alpinism School, as it is known officially, is responsible for supplying examiners to the various resorts, where the initial test for certification is given to aspiring instructors. Its overall responsibility is for the training of instructors at

all levels, and it alone is able to grant diplomas; i.e., to certify qualified ski instructors.

The Professional Ski Instructors of America

The nearest equivalent that the United States has to the Ecole Nationale of France, and to similar governmental training courses in other European countries, is the organization known as Professional Ski Instructors of America. The P.S.I.A., however, has no government affiliation. It is a national association of professional ski instructors who, to qualify for admittance, subject themselves to rigorous examinations. The badge of the association, reading "Professional Ski Instructors of America," is exhibited with pride by members and regarded with envy by instructors who have either been unable to qualify or not chosen to do so. In any event, it is regarded among American instructors as symbolizing a high standard of competence and

Ski instructors often meet to compete among themselves and to keep abreast of the latest techniques.

effectiveness in both skiing and the teaching of skiing.

When skiing began to "take hold" in the United States, members of the industry became acutely aware of a number of problems which could be resolved only by a national organization of professionals. Some of these problems were technical in nature; others had to do with the necessity for standardization in the certification of ski instructors and with practices used in the training of these instructors. In 1961, at a meeting at Whitefish, Montana, the P.S.I.A. was formed to deal with these problems.

The P.S.I.A. has eight geographic divisions which enjoy a certain degree of autonomy, but all of which certify instructors in the American Teaching Method. The requirements for becoming a certified instructor vary from one division to the other, at least with respect to procedure. Generally, an applicant must have not only skiing skills, but also prior teaching experience. He is required to undergo approximately one week of intensive training preparatory to the certification examination. Despite differences among divisions as far as training procedure is concerned, all applicants, regardless of division, must perform according to similar requirements and standards in order to be certified as an instructor. A candidate does not "compete" against other candidate–instructors, but only against the standards established by the Technical Coordinating Committee of the P.S.I.A.

Once a candidate has passed the examination—approximately fifty percent of the candidates do pass—and becomes a certified instructor, he does not rest on his laurels. All divisions require its instructors to attend regular refresher courses in order to keep abreast of developments in technique and teaching methodology.

It should be obvious that the P.S.I.A., like its European equivalents, is not a "ski school." It prepares instructors for certification, and, when the instructor is able to perform according to the standards set by the association, it certifies that he is a capable and competent instructor.

The certified instructor may himself aspire to become an examiner of other candidates—once he has had sufficient experience as an instructor, exhibited proper dedication to his profession, and, of course, passed another examination.

Ski competitions are festive occasions.

Skiing, like other sports, requires its future champions to begin training at a very early age.

151

1 2

3 4

5

1. Jim Hunter, one of the
leading Canadians.
2. Danièle Debernard, who
saved France's honor twice
at the Olympics: once in
1972, at Sapporo; and
again at Innsbruck in 1976.
3. S. Strand doing his
thing . . .
4. Soederin, a Swedish
skier, is out to win. But does
he have a chance?
5. Jean-Claude Killy. Four
years after his triumph at
Grenoble, he hasn't lost his
know-how.

Gustavo Thoeni
specializes in the Slalom,
but he became an
outstanding Downhill man
and won his fourth World
Cup.

competition

There is not a real skier anywhere, male or female, whose secret dream is not to participate in one (or two, or all three) of the great ski competitions: the Olympics, the World Championship, or the World Cup.

The Olympic Games

The Olympics take place every four years, alternating with the World Championship. Only three ski events are recognized by the Olympic Committee: the downhill, the giant slalom, and the special slalom.

However, combining these events is not allowed; and the only recompense awarded to a team is the title "World Champion," bestowed by the International Ski Federation.

Thus far, no one has been able to give a rational explanation for this discrimination. And certainly no one can deny that combined teams are allowed in certain other events—decathlon, for example, or swimming.

A maximum of four participants per country is allowed to compete in each event; but the total number of representatives of any country cannot (at this time) exceed fourteen. It is therefore up to each country to decide precisely how they are going to deploy their athletes.

The atmosphere—the *ambiance*—of the Olympics is unique. Perhaps it is because of the overwhelming importance attached to the games.

Certainly, from the standpoint of pure athletics, the games are a source of unexpected (sometimes astonishing) performances, victories, and defeats. Favorites must have nerves of steel to win—which happens rarely.

Unlike the participants in the summer games, those who take part in the winter Olympics meet every winter, at one resort or another and in one country or another. The games themselves, however, are subject to the same general rules for both summer and winter.

For better or worse, it seems that the status—we might almost say "the aureole"—attached to Olympic titles has a noticeable impact on the behavior of certain participants in the games.

This effect is difficult, and perhaps impossible, to analyze.

Two outstanding events have characterized the Winter Olympics:

(a) The three Gold Medals won by Toni Sailer, of Austria, in 1956;

(b) The three First Places won by the Austrian team in 1964;

(c) The three Gold Medals won by a Frenchman, Jean-Claude Killy, in 1968.

The winter Games have also suffered a major scandal: in 1972, at Sapporo, a great Austrian champion, Karl Schranz, was expelled from the games and sacrificed on the holy altar of amateurism—all for an "offense" of which he was no more guilty than any other participant in the games.

The World Championships

The World Championship takes place every two years under the sponsorship of the International Ski Federation, in a relaxed, informal atmospere. (Prior to World War II, this competition was held yearly.)

The Downhill at Lauberhorn.

The World Championships coincide with the Olympics every four years. Only four participants are allowed to compete in each event: downhill, giant slalom, and special slalom. In the Championship, however, the use of three-event teams is recognized—which requires coaches and trainers to develop appropriate tactics.

Here are a few memorable statistics from the World Championships:

In 1962, the Austrians won 15 of the 24 medals, of which 5 were Gold Medals; but, in 1966, the French team established a new record by winning 16 medals (including 6 Gold Medals).

It would be impossible to talk about the Olympics or the World Championships without mentioning the extraordinary triumphs of a French skier, Marielle Goitschel:

1962 — World Championship, Combined; Silver Medal, Special Slalom
1964 — Olympic championship, Giant Slalom (just ahead of her sister, Christine); Silver Medal, Special Slalom (behind her sister, Christine); World Championship, Combined
1966 — World Championship, Giant Slalom; World Championship, Combined; Silver Medal, Special Slalom (behind another Frenchwoman, Annie Famose); Silver Medal, Downhill (behind a female Austrian skier who, a few months later, became a male)
1968 — Olympic champion, Special Slalom; Combined Silver Medal

In 1966, the World Championship in giant slalom was, for the first time, contested in two heats. The winner of the first heat was Jean-Claude Killy; the second was won by another Frenchman, Georges Mauduit. The holder of the World Championship title is yet another Frenchman, Guy Périllat.

When the giant slalom was being run in a single heat, the Austrians succeeded twice in placing three of their men in the first three places.

The World Cup

The World Cup was born in the summer of 1966,

during the World Championship meet taking place that year at Portillo, Chile. Its parents, so to speak, were a not undistinguished lot: Serge Lang, the eminent sports journalist; three coaches of major teams, Bob Beattie (American), Sepp Suzberger (Austrian), and Honoré Bonnet (French) along with the latter's trainers, René Sulpice and Jean Béranger. A few participants in the meet also had a hand in it; Karl Schranz, the great Austrian skier, and three Frenchmen, Leo Lacroix, Guy Périllat, and Jean-Claude Killy.

Unlike the Olympic games and the World Championship, the World Cup competition does not take place all at once in one fell swoop. It is spread out over the winter. The three basic competitions (as well as a few team competitions) are the same as in the other games. The participants must therefore try to accumulate as many points as possible in each of the two meets.

In the first few years of this new competition, the winners of the Cup were skiers who performed equally well in the downhill, the giant slalom, and the special slalom. Thus, Jean-Claude Killy in 1967-68; Karl Schranz, 1969-70; Nancy Greene (a Canadian), 1967-68; and Gertrud Gabl (Austrian) and Michele Jacot (French).

Then, overall skill began to give way to very specialized skill, particularly among male skiers. There were now participants who took part only in the downhill, and others who raced only in the slalom events, giant or special.

The latter are at a distinct advantage in the competition for the World Cup. The two types of slalom competition are similar in many ways, while the downhill requires a special and specifically different skill.

Since the number of events in each discipline is approximately the same, it has happened in the past few years (regrettably) that the Cup has been won by skiers who are no doubt great champions, but who, nonetheless, were able to win without having been obliged to participate in a single downhill event. An exception was Gustavo Thoeni, an Italian, four times winner of the Cup, who had the courage—and the good manners—to compete in the downhill.

4. The world of skiing

From the above, it is evident that, under the present system, skiers specializing in the downhill event have absolutely no chance ever of winning the Cup.

The number of events figuring in the World Cup varies from year to year, but generally it is organized as follows:

— Downhill, six to nine events
— Giant slalom, seven or eight
— Special slalom, seven or eight

There has been only one five-time winner of the Cup, and this occurred in the Women's Division, where general skill has been intelligently prized and maintained. Anne-Marie Proell, an Austrian, holds this record—which she set, however, by winning in both the Special and the Giant Slalom events.

We should make special mention, also, of 1966-1967—"the unparalleled year" of Jean-Claude Killy, winner of the very first World Cup. Here are the events of that winter:

Val'd'Isere:
— Downhill, fourth place. Ahead of him were three other Frenchmen; and the winner was Leo Lacroix
— Special Slalom, second place, behind a Swedish participant, A. Grahn
— Giant Slalom, first place

Berchtesgaden (January, 1967):
— Special Slalom, Third Place (First Place went to Messner, an Austrian)
— Giant Slalom, Third Place (A Frenchman, Georges Manduit was first)

From then until April; except for the Special at Megevè where Killy took Second Place to his teammate, Guy Périllat, he won all the events: downhill, giant slalom, special slalom, and combined, for a total of 28 victories out of a possible 33. (A few years earlier, in 1961, when international skiing competition recognized only the traditional events, Guy Périllat had won all of the classic events.)

Killy's exploits were unique in the annals of the ski world. And they still are. No one has come near his record—let alone surpassed it.

There were other noteworthy events in the Cup competitions: Karl Schranz's performances, for example, and those of the brilliant Austrian

downhiller, Klammer, who won eight downhill events in a single winter (still one less than Jean-Claude Killy in 1967).

It goes without saying that the World Cup competition is not, and cannot possibly be, open to every skier who would like to participate. Participants are selected, individually and by national teams, on the basis of the International Ski Federation's point system. A candidate must accumulate a certain minimal number of points in a single discipline in order to qualify for all the events.

It was therefore necessary to organize other, comparable meets. The European Cup, for instance, after somewhat laborious beginnings, was established. It permits a wider variety of events than the World Cup, and its organization allows for competition among all kinds of skiers and all levels of skill. It often happens that champion skiers compete in the European Cup meets.

One of the major problems in organizing winter games is that of setting up geographic "circuits" in such a way as to avoid both exhausting participants by zig-zag journeys from one end of Europe to the other and ruining organizers and federations by travel costs.

One way in which this problem was solved, at least partially, was by establishing an American equivalent to the European cups: the North American Cup, for the United States and Canada.

Most countries, especially in a World Championship or an Olympic year, participate in the cup competitions according to their geographic situation—the North American Cup, the European Cup, the World Cup.

In addition to these competitions, there are many regional-international competitions—e.g., in the Scandinavian countries, the Balkans, the Near East, etc. By the same token, some of the Southern Hemisphere countries (New Zealand, Australia, Chile, and Argentina) have their own competitions. European skiers take part in these meets as a means of testing new equipment or as an expression of friendly solidarity, or for reasons of prestige.

Since 1974, there has been a new addition to

the official list of events approved for amateur competition: the Parallel Slalom. Its inclusion was rather hesitant and controversial, despite the fact that the Parallel Slalom has enjoyed great success among professional skiers.

The Parallel Slalom, as its name indicates, consists of two tracks parallel to a single marker, with simultaneous departure. Since it is impossible to maintain strict parallels in the snow, the competitors race against one another twice, while changing tracks. The differences in arrival time serve either to eliminate a participant or to qualify him for the next run—and so until the finals.

When professional skiers compete in the Parallel Slalom, the tracks are embellished with relatively high artificial moguls. These allow the spectators to see who is winning—and they also serve as the ideal spot for billboards advertising the products of the firm sponsoring the meet.

A new kind of downhill event, which as been long in gestation and slow in acceptance, may well become established in the future despite the strong opposition of purists and traditionalists. This new event is the downhill in two heats.

Nothing could be more logical. Certain areas simply do not have the topology necessary for the classic downhill. And, even where topology does permit the downhill, it often happens that lack of snow makes it necessary to shorten it beyond what regulations permit.

Skiing demands a willingness to accept reality, and a sense of what is practical—even though there are still some who are blind to both reality and practicality. Here, as in all else that has to do with skiing, patience is a virtue that we must cultivate religiously.

The "International Ski Federation Competition"

These international competitions were created—or, more accurately, are tolerated—in order to satisfy certain countries and federations in their scramble for F.I.S. points.

There are often a very large number of participants in these meets. And the organizers always manage to "arrange" to have several well-known skiers on hand to harvest a good crop of F.I.S. points for the rest of the team.

At the regional level in all countries, for a mass event of between one hundred and two hundred and fifty participants, preference is given to the Giant Slalom over both the Downhill and the Special Slalom.

The problem with the Downhill, at a meet of this kind, is that it monopolizes one of the trails for several days, with all that this implies in the line of personnel, supervision, and security. As for the Special Slalom, it requires a very painstaking set-up, a large number of personnel in attendance, and it lasts for an indeterminate period.

The ski schools, rather astutely, have created both competitions tailored to their own requirements, although derived from the classic disciplines, and tests which they give regularly for the enjoyment (or the frustration) of children (or their parents), adolescents, and adults.

Thus, during their winter vacations, skiers of every age, size and quality can—without having to submit to a painful period of training—examine themselves, compare themselves to their instructors, and make a proper judgment regarding their progress or lack of progress.

The popularity of these tests is enormous. The most elementary of them is designed for children, who take great delight in passing them (and who dissolve in tears when they fail).

It should be added that the tests are administered by judges who take their work seriously. They maintain a high level of objectivity; and they are pitiless in their decisions. When a candidate passes a test, he or she is awarded a badge.

The first of these badges is the Snowflake, which is perhaps the grammar-school diploma of skiing.

Next come the Stars—one, two, or three, depending on the technical difficulties to be overcome in the tests, which range from skiing a straight track to doing a little slaloming.

The best known of these tests is that which leads

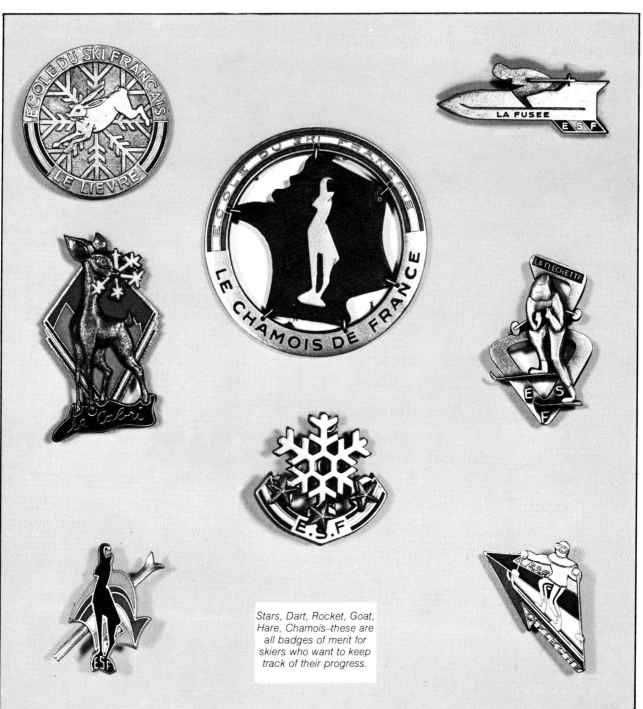

Stars, Dart, Rocket, Goat, Hare, Chamois–these are all badges of merit for skiers who want to keep track of their progress.

Betsy Clifford, a Canadian
(above), and Monika
Kaserer, an Austrian
(below), in the Downhill.
Generally, women do not
ski as fast as men, but they
are the equals of any male
in technical proficiency.

to the much-desired Chamois badge. This stage has become more or less universal and is particularly popular in the United States. The test consists in a kind of slalom, the base-time of which is set by a specialized instructor. The Gold Chamois (which is relatively rare) is awarded for coming within 5% of the instructor's time; the Enamel Chamois, for 12%; the Silver Chamois, for 20%; and the Bronze Chamois, for 50%. Finally, so as not to offend anyone or to discourage future champions, a Goat Badge is awarded for 66%.

Given the popularity of these competitions and the attractive features of the Giant Slalom, it was to be expected that a special test would be conceived for this event. This test leads to the award of the following badges: Golden Arrow, Enamel Arrow, Silver Arrow, Bronze Arrow. (In this series, there is an equivalent to the Goat Badge, which is the Dart (given for coming within 70% of the base-time.)

Every skier talks, and hears talk, about the fantastic speeds attained by skiers in major competitions: average speeds of 100 kilometers per hour (65 mph), peak speeds of 140 kilometers per hour (85 mph). . . .And it is common knowledge that the world's record is slightly in excess of 194 kilometers per hour (121 mph). Obviously, it was necessary to devise a test for speed on a typical, short downhill run, as well as a series of corresponding badges: Gold Rocket, Enamel Rocket, Silver Rocket, Bronze Rocket.

David Murray of Canada: "During the Downhill, I don't even have time to think about being afraid."

the competitors

Amateurs

Amateur status is governed by national and international rules and regulations, and amateurs compete in contests of all kinds organized at ski resorts throughout the world.

When talking about skiers, we should note that there are amateurs and *amateurs*. The first kind of amateur, numbering in the hundreds of thousands, love to compete against the stopwatch, against certain other participants—but, most of all, against themselves. They compete, essentially, for the love of competition. Some of these amateurs remain forever at a certain level of expertise; others make enormous progress.

When referring to the second kind of amateur in skiing—the skier with amateur status who competes in the great ski meets of the world—we may as well forget the dictionary definition of *amateur*.

We do not mean to imply that these skiers do not love competition. They do. What we do mean is that they devote their lives to skiing. They submit to rigorous training, and they expect certain compensations for the sacrifices they make for the sport.

At the present time (and with rare exceptions) the amateur who participates in these meets must give up any idea of simultaneously following a trade or profession, or of pursuing serious studies. Instead, he must embrace an improbable life-style which includes rigorous training in the summer and fall, followed by week after week of travel from one country to the next in pursuit of medals and titles, with only short intervals of rest. And this schedule does not last merely for one year, or two. It goes on for many, many years.

It goes without saying that, if a skier really wants to become a "star" and to remain one, he must be willing to give up many of the pleasures that other young people enjoy.

How, then, do they support themselves? In those countries lucky enough to have such skiers (or in those who want to develop some), ways have been devised to give financial aid to young men and women who want to (and who must) devote themselves exclusively to the sport. The hope of everyone concerned is that this will bear fruit in the form of national prestige, or company profits, or political advantage, or—let's not forget the skier himself—fame and fortune.

The International Olympic Committee has set out the essential requirements for amateur status among participants in the games. Each country, according to its political and ideological bent, its administrative peculiarities, and its concept of society, has adopted those statutes and devised their own methods of subsidizing amateurs.

In the West, particularly in the United States and Canada, athletes with amateur status are given generous (sometimes very generous) scholarships. In the East, an exceptional performer is designated an "Athlete of the State." In some countries, the athlete is a member of the armed forces; or, if he has performed brilliantly, he is given a lifetime pension.

In those countries where the ski industry is particularly prosperous, the industry, through its national association of manufacturers, has worked out a system of remuneration which is, on the one hand, a guarantee of security for the amateur (usually, a guarantee of employment in case of disability), and, on the other, proportionate to the skill and success of the athlete.

A few malicious gossips, and some athletes from other sports, believe, or at least say, that amateur skiers do not pay taxes on such income. That, of course, is nonsense. Skiers pay taxes like everyone else. And they do it with as little enthusiasm as the next man.

All the national Olympic committees, and the International Olympic Committee itself, have gone to great lengths to work out a formula which would preserve the concept of "amateur status" while taking into account the exigencies of society as it exists today and respecting that rather nebulous code of ethics which, it seems, reasonable men have an increasingly difficult time accepting.

From time immemorial, poets, writers, artists —all have had sponsors who provided subsidies; and the world smiled approvingly. But the idea that an athlete—who, after all, has brains as well as muscles—should have a sponsor, still excites opposition in some countries.

Professionals

Not unexpectedly, professional skiing appeared first in the United States. In 1962-1963, an organization was created the purpose of which was to organize professional ski meets; i.e., competitions in which the participants would be paid.

The first hero of the meets was a Frenchman, Adrien Duvillard.

The events offered by the association were similar to those in the amateur meets: giant slalom and special slalom.

Sometimes, in the special slalom event, two juxtaposed tracks were in use simultaneously, though of different types and duration. On rare—very rare—occasions, well-known skiers were the stars of these competitions, and "extras" were used for padding so as to make the most of sufficiently long duration to satisfy the spectators and, eventually, the television audience.

With this kind of organization, it was obvious that professional skiing was doomed to die a lingering, but nonetheless certain, death.

Then Bob Beattie, a ski coach of the American team from 1963 to 1968, appeared on the scene and took charge. Under Beattie, professional skiing took on new life through the introduction of an event of which Beattie himself was initially skeptical: the parallel slalom.

The idea actually was that of Honoré Bonnet, who was then coach of the French ski team. Bonnet had been experimenting with the parallel slalom for some time, and he had hopes eventually of having it accepted as a recognized discipline by the International Ski Federation. Beattie's reservations soon gave way to unbridled enthusiasm; and, from that time, professional skiing's success was assured. It has

since become extremely popular, particularly in the United States and Canada. The foremost stars are Jean-Claude Killy, and more recently, Henri Duvillard.

The life-style of professional skiers is determined by the champions themselves, although it includes some commitments of which the skier must always be aware since his livelihood depends on these obligations. The skiers' salaries are paid by sponsoring firms—manufacturers of skis and skiing equipment, certain American ski resorts, or large corporations such as airlines. Naturally, these salaries are structured according to a skier's success and fame.

The parallel slalom event is extremely difficult and demanding. It requires the skier to be in top physical shape; and it demands nerves of steel. The winners in these competitions are paid very handsomely, even by American standards. The losers—well, they are compensated by participating in a unique experience.

Robert Barron competing in a national contest in Stowe, Vermont.

careers in skiing

The ski industry in many countries is flourishing, even booming. Thanks to the emergency of this industry, countries which were once abandoned and incapable of supporting human inhabitants have been reborn and are now throbbing with life.

Millions of people are employed in the industry in a great variety of capacities, not all of them on the slopes. There are manufacturers of special ski clothing and underwear, skis, boots, poles, bindings, lifts, snowplows, tools, fuel pumps, etc.

In the mountains themselves, however, there are careers for those who enjoy the snow. Unfortunately, such positions tend to be as seasonal as skiing itself. Nonetheless, here is a list of the jobs usually associated with ski lodges and resorts. (The job titles themselves, of course, vary from area to area, but the functions described exist in virtually every ski complex.)

Resort director: This is the manager—a title signifying that he is generally in charge of keeping everything running as it should. Depending upon the resort and its particular stage of development, the director or manager may be the developer himself, a professional administrator, a management agent, a specialist in mechanical lifts, a mayor (if the complex is an incorporated village)—or a ski star.

The function of a manager is ill defined. He must strive to be the glue that holds everything together: the lifts, the accommodations, the transportation, the entertainment, and so forth. If one of the component parts of the complex falters, the whole is in danger of grinding to a halt.

Director of Tourism (or Manager of the Resort Association): Regardless of the title by which he is known, this person's job is to get skiers to come to the resort. He is in charge of advertising and public relations, a critical area in the success or failure of a resort. Sometimes this director or manager or supervisor is also in charge of preparing the snow for skiers, for security on the slopes, and for organizing competitions. He has several assistants and secretaries, and one or more hostesses depending upon the size of the resort.

Planning Manager: Also known by a diversity of titles, this person is basically responsible for getting the resort "off the ground"; that is, of dividing the land into lodging areas, entertainment areas, ski areas, etc. He is also responsible for the location of the lifts and the laying out of the trails.

Real Estate Developer: This is the industrial or commercial agent who builds (or converts) accommodations—studios, rooms, apartments—and who is generally in charge of marketing these accommodations.

Managing Agent: This is a real estate agent who is responsible for selling and renting accommodations, for their maintenance, etc. Generally, the managing agent has a large number of employees, from salesmen to janitors and chambermaids.

Lift Supervisor: This position entails responsibility for the mechanical lifts, for the various items of machinery used at the resort, and for the operators of the lifts and the machines. One of the qualifications for these operators is the ability to maintain cordial relations with the resort's customers.

At some resorts, the Lift Supervisor is also in charge of preparing and maintaining the trails, and for evacuating any injured skiers. (In many resort areas, the latter responsibility rests with the local municipal officials.)

Maintenance Supervisor: The specific responsibility of the Maintenance Supervisor—a combination mechanic and electrician—is to keep the lifts in good working order.

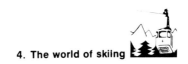

Maintenance Electrician and Mechanic: This employee must be a good skier capable of getting to the site of a breakdown and of making necessary repairs when the on-the-spot employee assigned to a lift is unable to make those repairs.

Trail Chief: This person is in charge of the snow. He sees that it is prepared and maintained. He takes special care to assure that the snow is of first-class quality and that the trails comply with all security rules and regulations. He is also in charge of preparing the trails for competitive meets, of security, and of installing all the necessary equipment for those meets.

Trailmaster-Medic: This is usually an expert skier and all-around athlete who works under the Trail Chief, or under a Supervising Trailmaster-Medic. He is responsible for the maintenance of certain critical areas of the trails and for the proper installation of all warning markers. His primary responsibility, however, is to give first-aid to injured skiers and to evacuate them as safely and as rapidly as possible.

Tractor Operator: The tractor operator drives the various pieces of heavy equipment used in preparing "commercial" snow—that is, packed snow—which must be constantly maintained and renewed regularly. This work is often done at night, so that the snow will be ready when the lifts begin operating in the morning.

Tractor Mechanic: He is specially responsible for maintenance and repairs on snow equipment.

Lift Personnel: There are a number of jobs connected with the operation of mechanical lifts, ranging from a lift manager to the ticket sellers. The number and functions of these employees vary according to the number and kind of lifts used, and also according to the number of hours and shifts worked by employees in a

given area. Generally speaking, the smallest lift requires no less than two or three on-site employees; and the heavy aerial lifts—even the automated ones—have as many as six to ten.

Secretary of the Resort Club: This functionary is in charge of club membership and of the administrative aspects of the resort's teams as well as of the competitive meets of any kind, local or international, sponsored by the resort.

Ski Instructors: Of course, they are the gods of the snow and of the resort. Usually, they are supervised by the resort manager in conjunction with a committee of instructors selected by the instructors themselves.
Instructors are available for both private and collective instruction. As well as being teachers, they also play an important role in the life of the resort as catalyzers, public relations people, and salespeople (who sell good skiing). In incorporated ski complexes, they will often devote one or two afternoons a week, without pay, to the instruction of children from the local school.
They also are responsible, in collaboration with the Trail Chief and the Trailmasters, for organizing the technical aspects of competitive meets. Frankly, it is not easy to find a job as a ski instructor. It is simply a matter of there being too few openings for far too many applicants. It goes without saying, of course, that an applicant for a job as an instructor is far ahead in the game if he has been certified by the Professional Ski Instructors of America (P.S.I.A.).
There are, in addition to the above, many auxiliary occupations open to qualified personnel at any resort: hotel management, specialists in the building trades, maintenance people, sales personnel for the shops (clothing, sporting gear, etc.), restaurant and bar personnel, medical personnel, therapists, travel agents, postal employees, security guards, baby-sitters, and so on. Altogether, the number of employees necessary to the smooth operation of a medium-sized resort is between four and five hundred.

On page following:

1. In the heart of the Berne Oberland: Gstaad, the rendezvous of the jet set, is one of the most popular resorts in the world.
2. Grindelwald, also in the Oberland, is the Mecca of purists and of those who thrive on dizzying slopes. The Wetterhorn is in the background.
3. At Villars-Bretaye, near Lake Leman, skiers reach the trails by train.
4. Switzerland offers the Downhill skier uncounted opportunities to exercise his art.

1

3

2

4

5

some top skiing spots in the world

*The joys of soft snow are
the culmination of
adequate preparation on
the trails.*

skiing in Canada

It was during the World Cup meet of 1975 that we all discovered (or rediscovered) skiing in Canada.

Ironically, the meet was being held, not in Canada, but at Val d'Isère. From the moment of the first Downhill, everyone expected the winner to be either Collombin of Switzerland or Klammer of Austria. Instead, a group of Canadian champions emerged: Ken Read, twenty years old, took first place, followed closely by David Irwin. Two weeks later, at Schladming, Irwin won first place, and Read second place. In addition, two other Canadians were among the top five winners. It was a more than ample demonstration of Canadian superiority.

No doubt in 1967 and 1968, when Nancy Greene won the first two World Cups from under the noses of the legendary French time of those years, everyone suddenly became aware that Alpine skiing was something of a national sport in Canada—second to ice hockey, of course, but thriving nonetheless. The Europeans had not yet come to grips with the fact that skiing in Canada is practiced on a scale unfamiliar to them; that is, on the scale of the New World.

All European skiers who were lucky enough to make the trip to Canada came back convinced that they had at last found the skier's paradise, and that they had at last found the skier's paradise, and that it was located in western Canada on the border between Alberta and British Columbia, to the east of the formidable Rocky Mountains. (The Rockies, of course, already had the reputation of being the breeding ground for a generation of Ken Reads.)

From Calgary, the capital of Alberta, it is one hour's drive to Banff, situated in the heart of one of the two great national parks of the province. (The other is Jasper, further to the north, at the foot of the Rockies.) From Banff, the skier can wander in search of the lodges established by Hans Gmoser, an Austrian who migrated to Canada in 1950, and of the Bugaboos, Cariboos, and Monashees. In so doing, he'll discover a new kind of skiing: skiing via helicopter, which seems to have little in common with the beginnings of helicopter transport for skiers

as it is now, in its initial stages, being practiced in Europe.

To begin with, everything in Canada is undertaken on a scale proportionate to the size of the country; which is to say, a vast scale. The helicopters are huge, able to carry fifteen skiers and all their equipment. But that is not the end of the helicopter's work. Once the skiers are on the slopes, the aircraft hovers constantly over the trails, acting at once as a track railway and as a visual point of assemblage for the skiers. This is an essential function, for one of the peculiarities of Gmoser's stations is that there is no access road to the lodge and no mechanical lift. Skiers get from the valley to the lodge by helicopter; and the same means of transport is used in going from the lodge to the trails on the surrounding mountains.

Another peculiarity that characterizes the resorts and lodges in Jasper Park, Lake Louise, Sunshine and Kananaskis is the quality of the snow. The soft snow here is unequalled anywhere in the world. It is *deep*—over a man's head; but, at the same time, it presents not the slightest difficulty to a skier making turns. Which is not to say that there is no danger. There is indeed: the avalanche. To be careless about avalanches is to make a mistake which you may never have a chance to correct.

The opposite slopes of the Rockies also have some pleasant surprises for the skier. At Vancouver, on the Pacific coast, the landscape changes with startling suddenness. There is a ski lodge on Mt. Grouse, less than ten minutes away from the center of the city, overlooking the strait and its incessant nautical traffic. Skiing here has an unreal quality. The trails are illuminated, and the snow, hardened by cold, crunches beneath your skis. The only other sound is that of the boat whistles below. . . .

There are resorts other than the Mt. Grouse Skyride to the Canadian far West. Garibaldi Park, about sixty miles north of Vancouver, is one of the best known of these, since several of the World Cup contests have been held there, but especially because it has the biggest trails in North America. In addition to the usual lifts,

In the Rocky Mountains,
altitude and trail skiing go
hand in hand.

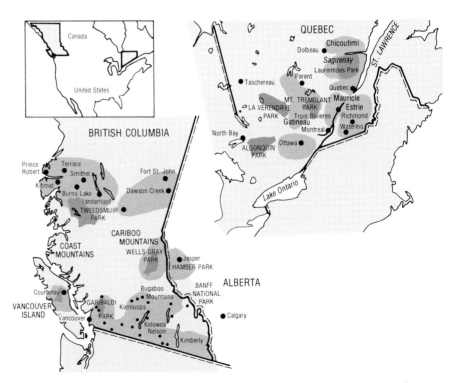

Peaks like these are a common sight to skiers in Canada.

Garibaldi Park is equipped with helicopters, which makes it possible to land skiers on the glacier. There is also Mt. Seymour, less than a half hour from Vancouver, with its extraordinarily long trails. Some of the other well-known resorts are Rossland, at Mt. Red, those in the Okanagan Valley, and, finally, to the southwest of Penticton, the Apex-Alpine resort which is known for its unusually difficult trails.

The diversity of the resorts of western Canada, whether they are family resorts (Big White near Kelowna, Silver Star near Vernon), bucolic (Mt. Grouse Skyride), or reserved for champions (Garibaldi, Lake Louise, Marmot Basin), may well explain why young Canadians are so successful in the Downhill. It also serves to demonstrate that Europe certainly has no monopoly on Alpine skiing.

Skiing is as popular in eastern Canada as in the western part of the country, and especially in French Canada, even though the topography is quite different. In the West, the mountains generally average around 12,000 feet in height; in the East, around 3,000 feet. Therefore, Alpine skiing thrives in the West and is practiced much less in the East. In fact, skiing in the Province of Quebec does not necessarily involve long trips by automobile or train. You can ski in the outskirts of Montreal and Quebec. If the trails of eastern Canada cannot match those of the West in altitude, they are always remarkably well laid out and there is always an abundance of snow. The reason for the latter is simple. If nature

defaults in providing snow, the snow cannons go to work to make up for this deficiency.

It would be beyond the scope of this book for us to list all of the resorts and lodges in the East. Instead, we'll divide them into four major categories, by location: Quebec City, north of Montreal (with its spectacular Laurentians), the southern or eastern townships of Quebec Province, and the northwestern part of the province of Ontario.

Very near the U.S. border, there are six areas with trails of over a thousand yards; but the trails and the lodges closer to Quebec (Mount Sainte-Anne, twenty-five miles from the city, Lake Beauport, about fifteen miles from Quebec, and Stoneham, about twenty miles) are just as good.

In the Laurentian Mountains, less than one hour from Montreal, it would be more accurate to speak, not of lodges and resorts, but of motels lost in the mountains or of isolated inns. It is a paradise for skiers; and even expert Alpine skiers take advantage of Mt. Tremblant. The Laurentians, in fact, represent Canada as we Europeans have always imagined it to be.

We should mention one of the specialities of skiers in eastern Canada: freestyle, or acrobatic skiing—impossible jumps, ballets on skis, unbelievable downhills through fields of moguls, etc. Finally, we must say that skiing in Canada offers skiers something that is rare—and cannot be found in Europe at all—an incredible vastness of virgin snow which few have the opportunity to experience.

Dave Irwin (in red) and Ken Read, currently two of the best Downhill men in the game. Their "rodeo" technique consists essentially in giving free rein to their skis and trying to be still on them when they cross the finish line . . .

173

Above: The Rockies, as seen from a helicopter, are a sea of foam-covered waves.
Below: Helicopter skiing originated in western Canada. It's so well organized in that part of the country that a skier has virtually unlimited possibilities for satisfying his love of the sport.

skiing in Switzerland

Since tourism is Switzerland's chief natural resource, it is to be expected that skiing receives a lot of attention from the Swiss government. Once we accept that premise, it is easier to understand the seriousness with which the Swiss regard everything having to do even remotely with skiing, from the instruction of beginners to the organization of major competitions. And this includes promenading on skis, which, as a discipline, is more important than we might think. It is a discipline practiced by those who have passed the age for regular skiing and by those (even more numerous) whose social, economic, or political responsibilities make it foolish for them to take the slightest risk on the slopes.

The Swiss are, in effect, caught between the devil and the deep blue sea. Since tourism is their major industry, the almost irresistible temptation is for them to attract as many skiers as possible. This, however, would be to the detriment of competition skiing, which has some decided disadvantages from the standpoint of the physical facilities available. A trail reserved for training purposes is used by no more than a few dozen skiers. If the same trail were open to the public, it would attract thousands of tourists. By the same token, skiers-in-training for a meet are dispensed from the necessity of waiting their turn for the use of lifts; they go to the head of the line—to the irritation and inconvenience of skiers who are waiting patiently in line, shivering, encumbered by skies and loaded with equipment. On the other hand, the fact remains that, in skiing as in winter sports generally, the "stars" are the spark plugs of tourism. When a skier wins a medal or a title, the sports pages of all major newspapers give substantial coverage to the event—all of which is excellent advertising for the country, the resort, and the training conditions at the resort. There are photographs in the newspapers and in magazines, not only of the champion himself, but of his family, his house, his surroundings, the facilities at his disposal—in other words, there is a windfall of publicity that mere money could not buy.

This being the case, skiing in Switzerland has only a few elements in common with skiing elsewhere. The main reason for this difference is that tourism was a major industry in Switzerland before leisure skiing made its appearance. The famous Swiss resorts like Saint-Moritz and Davos were already known all over the world as summer resorts long before they became popular as winter resorts. The only wintertime inhabitants then were a few intrepid souls addicted to bobsledding and tobogganing who took their ease in the evening around loaded tables presided over by hearty Englishmen who were in Switzerland on a "bachelor's holiday."

In most cases, winter sports resorts were built around a village or, occasionally, around a farm. The most celebrated resorts, however, were developed in the heart of tourist centers already equipped with adequate accommodations, stores, restaurants, bars and, above all, facility of access by road as well as by railway.

Certainly, there is no lack of "lodges," where a skier wears his skis to the very door of the chalet. But these are not what one has in mind when speaking of skiing in Switzerland. What one does have in mind are the great resorts of the Engadine, such as Saint-Moritz where the Olympic Games were held in 1928 and 1948, the World Championship in 1974, and an uncounted number of lesser but still important international competitions. There are other resorts in the Graubünden area, such as Davos—one of the best known of Swiss resorts—and Arosa, which has produced some World Champions for Switzerland. There are also the resorts of the Bern-Oberland which are the center of international skiing along with Grindelwald, Wengen, Mürren, Adelboden, Gstaad, whose histories are intimately connected with that of skiing in Switzerland. Mürren, we might add, is one of the five resorts where the "Kandahar" contests are held. Along with Saint-Anton, Mürren was also one of the two cradles of the most famous of Alpine-ski competitions. Opposite Mürren is Wengen and the Lauberhorn, where one of the best known of the Downhills is held. A short distance away, at the foot of the Eiger glacier, with the Jungfrau as a backdrop, is Grindelwald —one of the most popular centers of international skiing. (Adelboden is now well on its way

An isolated lodge in the mountains offers welcome shelter to passing skiers.

The Matterhorn, seen from Stockhorn, has one of the highest lifts in Europe.

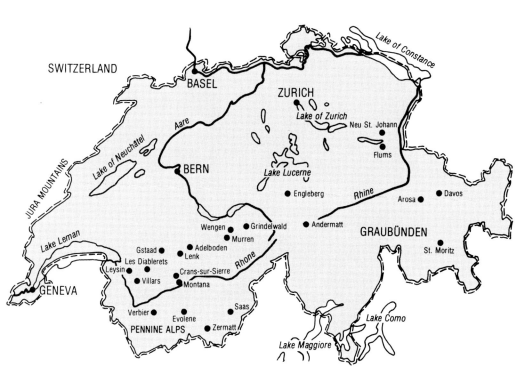

SWITZERLAND

BASEL

ZURICH

Lake of Constance

Lake of Zurich

Neu St. Johann

Flums

Aare

Lake of Neuchâtel

BERN

Lake Lucerne

● Engleberg

Rhine

Arosa ●

● Davos

JURA MOUNTAINS

Lake Leman

Wengen ● ● Grindelwald

● Andermatt

GRAUBÜNDEN

● Murren

Gstaad ● ● Adelboden

Les Diablerets ● Lenk

Rhone

St. Moritz

Leysin ●

Crans-sur-Sierre

● Villars

Montana

● Saas

Verbier ●

Evolene

PENNINE ALPS

● Zermatt

Lake Como

Lake Maggiore

GENEVA

to becoming Grindelwald's rival in the latter respect.)

Engelberg, where the World Championship of 1938 was held; Andermatt in central Switzerland; Flums and Saint-Johann toward the east; Les Diablerets and Leysin in the Vaudois Alps; Crans-sur-Sierre, Montana, Verbier and Zermatt in the Pennine Alps—all are tourist centers which have become ski resorts without losing anything of their charm or their interest for tourists.

It must be said that, in Switzerland, the facilities for skiers, the quality of the snow, and the care and maintenance of the ski trails are all unsurpassed anywhere in the world. These factors are, of course, of primary importance in the eyes of serious skiers. We might add that the concept of "service" is one which the Swiss take very seriously indeed. The Swiss know that visitors must be able to find in Switzerland what they want to find. And if a visitor cannot find something, there is always a Swiss ready to find it for him.

In keeping with this attitude, the Swiss are at great pains especially to insure the safety and

security of skiers. And this holds true not only in actual skiing itself, but also with respect to the transportation of skiers by lift. Swiss governmental requirements for bindings, for example, set the standard for the entire industry. No manufacturer would dare put on the world market a product that does not bear the stamp of approval of the Bureau d'Etudes sur la Securité. It is also in Switzerland, at Davos, that the most intensive research is being carried out in avalanche-control, detection, protection, and rescue. It is certainly true that Davos' Institut de Nivologie has already saved hundreds of lives, either by avalanche-prevention or by the methods of rescue developed by its staff.

To sum it up, let us say that Switzerland is the country of comfortable skiing because the tourist is king; the country of leisure skiing because there is an unlimited number of trails of every conceivable kind; the country of sport skiing because champions flourish there; and, finally, the country of safe skiing because everything possible is done to avoid accidents which are, in the first place, avoidable.

skiing in Austria

A mere glance at a map of Austria will show why Austria has played, and continues to play, such an important role in the world of skiing. The entire western part of the country, which fits like a wedge between Germany and Italy and abuts against Switzerland, is one huge ski area littered with famous resorts the names of which are associated with champions who have done so much to establish the renown of Austrian skiing. The Austrians were quick to take cognizance of the booming popularity of skiing throughout the world and had the foresight both to define and codify the teaching methods worked out by their ski instructors and then to diffuse those methods throughout the world. The purpose of this procedure, of course, was to attract to Austria the neophytes who wished to be initiated into the mysteries of this novel sport.

Thus was born the so-called Arlberg School, whose godparents were Hannes Schneider and Mathias Zdarsky. The school is actually a synthesis of all the theories and methods developed until then but not yet incorporated into any manual.

Later, comparable efforts were made in France and in Switzerland; but the methods and theories formulated by those schools were studied only in comparison with those already enunciated by Hannes Schneider.

It is undeniable that, as far as teaching is concerned, Austria has not relaxed its efforts for a moment. The Austrians work constantly at perfecting their methods. Predictably, therefore, these efforts have led to widespread adoption of Austrian methods and to an increase of Austrian influence in ski schools throughout the world. And, in fact, Austria has long been the chief exporter of ski instructors to other countries.

In many of the schools associated with resorts in Canada, the United States, Chile, Argentina, Brazil, Australia, New Zealand, and Japan, there is always at least one Austrian instructor to begin with. Usually, after the first Austrian has been hired, he is shortly followed by a second, then a third, and so on. Later, an Austrian will become chief instructor. Austrians will arrive to open sporting goods stores which import Austrian equipment. There will be a travel agency, run by Austrians who will orient skiers toward Austria. The overall effect, thanks as much to the amazing technical qualities of Austrian instructors as to their carrying back-breaking workloads, is an overwhelming propaganda effort to attract ski-tourists to their homeland. The success of that effort is manifest in the prosperity of Austrian resorts, which have become the headquarters of international skiing.

The success of these resorts, however, is due not only to the work of the hundreds (or perhaps thousands) of Austrian ski instructors throughout the world, but also to a series of factors which make a visit to Austria such an attractive and enjoyable experience. No matter where one stays—Arlberg, Vorarlberg, the Tyrol, Styria, Carinthia, Montafon, or Salzberg, you can be certain of a warm welcome in surroundings of the highest and most carefully maintained quality—marvelous houses with painted facades, wooden balconies, and flowering window boxes, which seem to appear always in the depths of forests, against snow-covered slopes, or against a startlingly blue sky.

Moreover, the valleys in the Austrian mountain ranges seem to allow miraculously for the laying of railway tracks everywhere, so that Austrian ski resorts are practically all accessible by train. This, obviously, represents an enormous advantage for Austrian resorts. In other countries, there are marvelous resorts and lodges which are so isolated and difficult of access that it is very difficult for them to build up a steady clientele. This is not the case in Austria. Austrian resorts have a far higher record of repeat-business than any other national resorts in the Alps.

However difficult it may be to single out one or another resort in Austria, we should mention something special that has been done at Kitzbühel, which is one of the most likely (if not actually the loveliest) and the best designed. This innovation consists in the creation of a resort for children in the very heart of international skiing, at the foot of the celebrated Hahnenkamm on which Toni Sailer, himself a child of Kitzbühel, won his first great victories. This children's resort is actually a sort of skier's

Igls-Patscherkofel: Austria, like Switzerland, is the heaven of Downhill experts. The Downhill trail (male) for the Olympics is 3,145 meters in length (3,500 yards) and has a drop of 870 meters (965 yards).

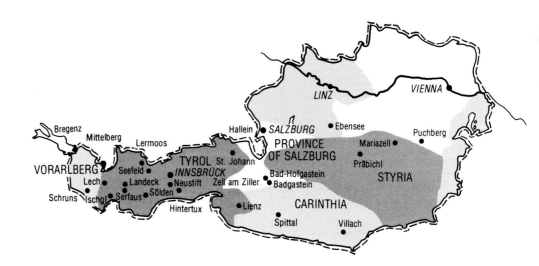

Disneyland where children can do, at their own level, what their elders are doing in the other resorts. One of the main attractions is a free-wheeling teaching method in which a group of devoted and perceptive instructors lead the children to "do what comes naturally" rather than explain to them what must be done.

Austrian skiing, therefore, consists first of all in an unending search for better techniques and better teaching methods at all levels; for the happiness and well-being of tourists, whether or not they are skiers; and, finally—and perhaps most important—it consists in an intense respect, almost a religious zeal, for the beauties of nature. And, God knows, Austria occupies a privileged position with respect to those beauties!

An added factor, of course, is the preoccupation of teachers and instructors, and indeed of everyone connected with the Austrian school of skiing, with the formation of good skiers regardless of the raw material with which the instructors have to work.

It is no accident that the International Olympic Committee has twice, within the past twelve years, designated Austria as the site for the Winter Games. For Austria is a synthesis of everything that a superior resort must have: ease of access, adequate accommodations, quality and variety of trails, organizational know-how, etc.

It is well known that what is called the *après-ski* is, in Austria, reduced to its simplest expression. But the skiers who go year after year to Saint-Anton, Schruns, Kitzbühel, Seefeld, Saalbach, Zell-am-See, and the other resorts, are not there for the pleasures of *après-ski*. They know that there will be a train, on time, to take them wherever they want to go. They know that, if they choose to drive, the roads will have been thoroughly cleared of snow. They know that, when they arrive, they will find the trails in first-class condition, and that, no matter where they stop, they will be received with warmth and courtesy.

The Tyrol is a glorious
opportunity for the
beginner as well as for the
expert who loves virgin
snow. There are high
mountains everywhere, for
everyone.

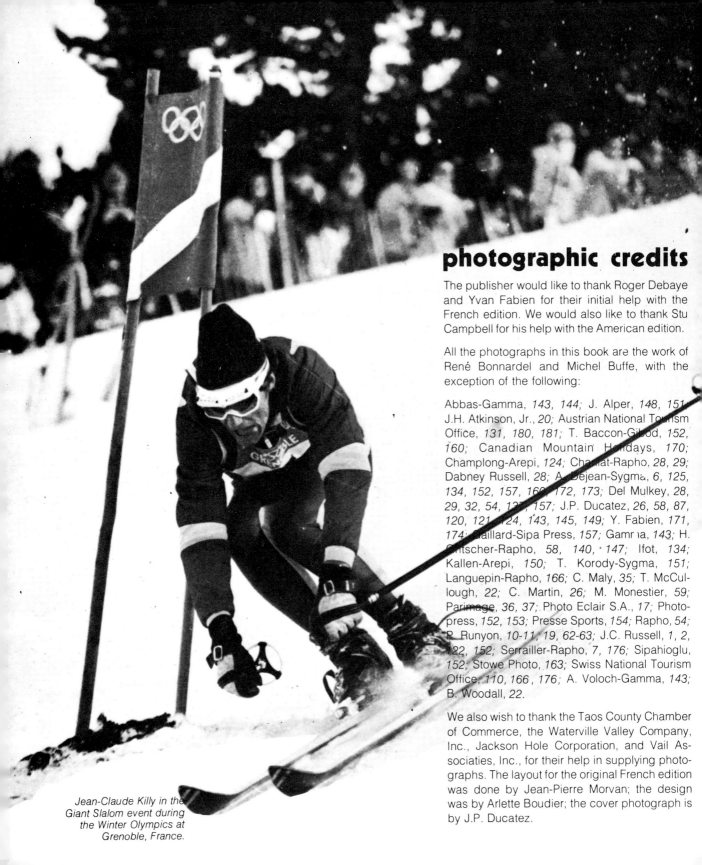

Jean-Claude Killy in the Giant Slalom event during the Winter Olympics at Grenoble, France.

photographic credits

The publisher would like to thank Roger Debaye and Yvan Fabien for their initial help with the French edition. We would also like to thank Stu Campbell for his help with the American edition.

All the photographs in this book are the work of René Bonnardel and Michel Buffe, with the exception of the following:

Abbas-Gamma, 143, 144; J. Alper, 148, 151; J.H. Atkinson, Jr., 20; Austrian National Tourism Office, 131, 180, 181; T. Baccon-Gibod, 152, 160; Canadian Mountain Holidays, 170; Champlong-Arepi, 124; Charliat-Rapho, 28, 29; Dabney Russell, 28; A. Dejean-Sygma, 6, 125, 134, 152, 157, 160, 172, 173; Del Mulkey, 28, 29, 32, 54, 135, 157; J.P. Ducatez, 26, 58, 87, 120, 121, 124, 143, 145, 149; Y. Fabien, 171, 174; Gaillard-Sipa Press, 157; Gamma, 143; H. Gritscher-Rapho, 58, 140, 147; Ifot, 134; Kallen-Arepi, 150; T. Korody-Sygma, 151; Languepin-Rapho, 166; C. Maly, 35; T. McCullough, 22; C. Martin, 26; M. Monestier, 59; Parimage, 36, 37; Photo Eclair S.A., 17; Photopress, 152, 153; Presse Sports, 154; Rapho, 54; R. Runyon, 10-11, 19, 62-63; J.C. Russell, 1, 2, 122, 152; Serrailler-Rapho, 7, 176; Sipahioglu, 152; Stowe Photo, 163; Swiss National Tourism Office, 110, 166, 176; A. Voloch-Gamma, 143; B. Woodall, 22.

We also wish to thank the Taos County Chamber of Commerce, the Waterville Valley Company, Inc., Jackson Hole Corporation, and Vail Associates, Inc., for their help in supplying photographs. The layout for the original French edition was done by Jean-Pierre Morvan; the design was by Arlette Boudier; the cover photograph is by J.P. Ducatez.

The goal of this handbook is to explain that waxing is not so complicated, tedious, and difficult to manage successfully, and that any skier can learn to wax well.
$1.95 paper

Style is the subject of this book. It begins where most ski books leave off — with parallel skiing — and teaches the techniques that make a competent skier into a very good skier. $5.95 paper

Chester Barnes' object in writing this book was to describe methods of play as he has come to understand them as a champion, and to encourage newcomers to try their hand at this exhilarating game. $4.95 hardcover

Expert Celia Brackenridge shares her knowledge and skills in this fast-paced game. Intended to teach an effective way of playing lacrosse, this book looks at all aspects of the sport in relation to the game and game situations, rather than isolation.
$4.95 hardcover

An international team of 12 boating authorities wrote this book that takes in all aspects of sail and power boating including history, theory, navigation, safety, construction, and more.
$29.95 cloth

A champion and an experienced coach with knowledge of all aspects of field hockey, Rachael Heyhoe Flint gives sound advice on the techniques and method of play, which is enhanced by excellent action photos.
$4.95 hardcover

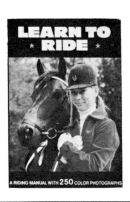

In association with:

UK Trade
& Investment

The Investors' Guide to the United Kingdom 2015/2016

Edited by
Jonathan Reuvid

WATSON FARLEY
&
WILLIAMS

CONSULTING
TECHNOLOGY
INNOVATION

M MAZARS

Legend Business

Independent Book Publisher

Legend Business Ltd,

175-185 Gray's Inn Road, London WC1X 8UE

info@legend-paperbooks.co.uk | www.legendpress.co.uk

Contents © Legend Business, Jonathan Reuvid and Individual Contributors 2015

The right of the above authors to be identified as the authors of this work has been asserted in accordance with the Copyright, Designs and Patents Act 1988. British Library Cataloguing in Publication Data available.

Print ISBN 978-1-7850795-3-5

Set in Times. Printed in the United Kingdom by Clays Ltd.

Cover design by Simon Levy www.simonlevyassociates.co.uk

Publishers Note

CONTENTS

Contents

PREFACE

The contents of *The Investors' Guide to the United Kingdom 2015/16* are arranged somewhat differently from previous editions in order to be more reader friendly. Companies and their advisers in the early stages of considering investment in the UK and those who are at more advanced stages in planning their entry will find that the chapters of most interest are grouped more conveniently in the separate parts of the book.

As before, after the introduction by Michael Boyd, Managing Director, Investment, UK Trade & Investment (UKTI), Part One comprises overviews of the UK economy and business environment for inward investors with chapters identifying the multiple services and offerings of UKTI; grants and incentives available for new investment; and the science parks and business incubators where accommodation on favourable terms are on offer.

Part Two, authored by the law firm Watson Farley & Williams and accountants Mazars, both sponsors of the book, focuses exclusively on the regulatory environment to which inward investors will need to pay attention.

Similarly, Part Three authored by the same two professional firms provides essential information for businesses operating in the UK on financial reporting and accounting, taxation and employment, pensions and employee benefits and incentives.

Thereafter, the focus of the book moves to investment overviews of the Energy and Regeneration sector (Part Four) and in Part Five to the UK's advanced manufacturing industries: automotive, life sciences and agricultural science with its supporting technologies. The authors of these chapters are drawn from UKTI and its associated industry organisations with issues for investors in the upstream oil and gas sector explored in detail by Watson Farley & Williams.

Part Six turns to the banking, financial services and commercial property sectors with chapters elaborating on mergers, acquisitions and joint ventures, the AIM market of the London Stock Exchange, the setting up of a financial services institution and commercial property in the UK. These chapters are provided by Mazars, Watson

Farley & Williams and UKTI's Financial Services Organisation.

The final section of the book, Part Seven, highlights the emergent opportunities of investing in the UK as a launchpad for scaling up into a global business, as an export hub in light of the UK's current re-shoring trend and for long-term success in digital healthcare. These insights are given by authors from PA Consulting Group, the book's third sponsor, and UKTI's Investment Group.

As usual, the contact details for authors are listed in Appendix I and readers seeking further information and advice are welcome to be in direct touch.

Jonathan Reuvid,
Editor

Note: Addressing the requirements of readers whose interest is confined to one or two parts of the book only, digital versions of individual chapters and parts of this edition or the whole book may be ordered online at
http://www.legendtimesgroup.co.uk/legend-business

FOREWORD

It is once again my pleasure to introduce the Investors' Guide to the United Kingdom.

Why is the UK such a great place to do business? Global business leaders clearly believe that it is, and prove it by voting with their feet - In 2014-15 the UK was once again the leading destination in Europe for Foreign Direct Investment (FDI), and once again second in the world only to the United States. In successive years the UK has seen record numbers of FDI projects coming to the UK, creating and safeguarding jobs in the UK economy and bringing the best of the world's innovation, creativity and business acumen to the UK's shores.

Internationalising CEOs see something in the UK's business environment that makes them want to come here and, as it is my day job to help international companies land successfully in the UK, I am keen to understand

Michael Boyd
Managing Director,
Investment,
UK Trade & Investment

what that is. I speak to senior business leaders on a daily basis, and it is clear from my conversations that the drivers which lead global companies to these shores cut across sectors or industry boundaries, and reflect aspects of the UK which are of fundamental importance in business decision-making.

I am convinced companies make these decisions based on a combination of three factors. Firstly, it is the opportunity. The UK provides extraordinary business opportunities across all sectors of the economy. Whether that be 'shovel ready' infrastructure projects, retail opportunities for the household names of the far east seeking to bring already successful businesses here, or research and development collaborations to create new and disruptive technologies, there are endless opportunities for global businesses to make their mark. One of the world's leading markets in our own right, doing business in the UK also gives access to European markets, with

500m consumers on your doorstep. The UK is opportunity rich for investors with the eyes to see it.

Secondly, it is the environment. The UK leads the world in our approach to supporting business and providing the right environment for businesses to prosper. Britain is highly competitive in the factors which drive business decisions. Our rock-solid stability as an economy and long history of fairness and rule-of-law mean that companies can have absolute confidence that they can come here, set up and compete on a level playing field. We have a highly skilled workforce, and support international leaders to come here to lead their businesses. And we have a robust national infrastructure and logistics base, providing the core requirements for businesses to thrive. So business can have confidence that, when they bring the companies to the UK, they will be able to concentrate on growing their business without distraction.

Thirdly, we have the right attitude. Successive Governments have developed policies which make clear that Britain is truly open for business. We have the lowest corporation tax in the G20 and a route map for further reductions in the future. And we take investors seriously, and act on their concerns – because we believe that globalising businesses are a force for good in the UK economy, driving competitiveness and profitability and creating good jobs and lasting economic value.

It is these three things – the opportunity to succeed, the right environment to do so, and the right attitude from the British Government and British people, which influences more and more companies each year to come to the UK. This independent guide sets out the information you need to decide whether to become one of them. It gives you key facts about the UK and its legal and policy framework which, considered with your expansion strategy, will give a rich understanding of the benefits of coming to the UK. I hope that after reading it you will join the many companies which have done so.

Michael Boyd
Managing Director, Investment
UK Trade & Investment

CONTRIBUTORS

Watson Farley & Williams LLP

Corporate

Christina Howard is a partner of Watson Farley & Williams LLP, dealing with a wide range of corporate and commercial work, including corporate finance transactions, mergers and acquisitions, joint ventures and restructurings.

Tanvir Dhanoa is an associate in the International Corporate Group of Watson Farley & Williams LLP. Tanvir's areas of practice include public and private mergers and acquisitions, equity capital markets and joint ventures, as well as general corporate and commercial work across a range of sectors.

Ravinder Sandhu is an associate in the International Corporate Group of Watson Farley & Williams LLP specialising in a broad range of domestic and international general corporate and corporate finance transactions, including mergers and acquisitions, equity fundraisings, group reorganisations, joint ventures and regulatory matters.

Sarah Williamson is an associate in the International Corporate Group at Watson Farley & Williams LLP specialising in a broad range of corporate work, including corporate finance, group reorganisations, mergers and acquisitions and commercial transactions.

Energy and Project

Heike Trischmann is a senior associate in the International Corporate Group of Watson Farley & Williams LLP. She specialises in all aspects of oil and gas law, but has also been involved in electricity and water projects. Heike has advised governments, national oil companies as well as junior and major oil and gas companies, banks, energy trading companies, regulators and individual investors world-wide on a broad range of international and domestic corporate, commercial, regulatory and projects work. Through her work, she has developed an in-depth knowledge of various energy regulatory regimes in the UK, Continental Europe, Latin America and Africa, including in relation to upstream E&P, LNG, gas storage and various energy infrastructure projects.

Victoria Barkas is an associate in the Energy and Projects group at Watson Farley & Williams LLP specialising in transactions in the energy sector with a particular focus on renewable energy. She advises on project financing, the corporate and commercial aspects of energy transactions and the development, construction and operation of energy projects.

Employment

Liz Buchan is a partner of Watson Farley & Williams LLP specialising in employment law and employee incentives. She heads Watson Farley & Williams LLP's Employment Group and is a former member of the Law Society's Employment Law Committee.

Asha Kumar is a partner of Watson Farley & Williams LLP specialising in employment law and advises on a range of employment law issues affecting inward investors.

Rhodri Thomas is an associate at Watson Farley & Williams LLP. Rhodri specialises in employment law and employment benefits, regularly preparing and advising on share incentive and option plans, as well as handling a wide range of contentious and non-contentious employment law matters.

Property

Gary Ritter is a partner of Watson Farley & Williams LLP. Gary specialises in advising on a broad range of residential and commercial property matters, including development, investment and landlord and tenant. He acts for substantial companies as well as for individual investors.

Felicity Jones is a partner of Watson Farley & Williams LLP. Felicity is head of Watson Farley & Williams LLP's Hotel and Leisure Group and specialises in sales, purchases, funding, shareholders agreements and management structures in the hotel, leisure and technology sectors.

Competition & Regulatory Law

Emanuela Lecchi is a partner of Watson Farley & Williams LLP. She focuses, in particular, on competition law and regulation of communications and utilities. Emanuela has a Masters in International and Comparative Business Law, a Masters in Information Technology and Telecommunications Law, and a MSc in Economic Regulation and Competition.

Kristina Cavanna is an associate in the Competition, Regulatory & Networks group at Watson Farley & Williams LLP. Kristina specialises in competition law and regulation and has experience across several industry sectors, such as telecoms, energy and the healthcare market.

Immigration

Angharad Harris is a partner of Watson Farley & Williams LLP specialising in all aspects of employment and immigration law. She is currently the Chair of the Law Society's Employment Law Committee.

Devan Khagram is an associate at Watson Farley & Williams LLP specialising in employment and immigration law. His immigration practice includes advising on all aspects of the Points-Based Immigration System, including investors, entrepreneurs and Tier 2 and also applications for settlement and naturalisation.

Intellectual Property

Mark Tooke is a partner of Watson Farley & Williams LLP. Mark is head of Watson Farley & Williams LLP's London intellectual property department, and has a particular focus on the corporate and commercial aspects of IP, including assisting clients in the communications, media and technology sectors.

Mazars

Mazars is an international, integrated and independent organisation, specialising in audit, advisory, accounting and tax services. The group operates in 72 countries and draws on the expertise of 13,800 professionals to assist major international groups, SMEs, private investors and public bodies at every stage of their development. In the UK, Mazars LLP has over 1500 partners and staff serving clients from 20 offices, and is ranked as the ninth largest firm nationally.

Financial Report & Accounting

Stephen Brown is a Partner at Mazars specialising in Audit and Assurance services. His client base ranges from owner-managed businesses, charities and not for profit organisations to international groups, either based in the UK or reporting to overseas parent companies.

Business Tax and Business Tax Planning

Andrew Ross is a Tax Director at Mazars with extensive experience of both UK and non-UK/cross-border tax issues, including tax efficient corporate restructuring and transaction planning (for both acquisitions and disposals/exits). He advises a range of clients, ranging from multinational corporate groups to owner-managed businesses.

Company Formation

Mark Jackson is a Director in the Company Secretarial Department of Mazars and a Fellow of the Institute Chartered Secretaries and Administrators. Mark has over 25 years' experience of advising all types of UK companies in all areas of concern to the Company Secretary. He is also currently the company secretary of a listed asset management business.

undation, and is a Chartered Surveyor. Nick leads the the Carter Jonas Technology Team, which specializes in the development and marketing of Science Parks and Innovation Centres. Carter Jonas is one of the leading property consultants in the Science Park sector. The Technology Team offers a broad spectrum of services to both public and private sector clients, including feasibility studies, demands and needs studies, development agreements, marketing strategy reports, lettings and acquisitions of incubators, laboratory and/or R&D buildings.

Jonathan Reuvid is an editor and author of business books and a partner in Legend Business. He has edited all six editions of 'The Investors' Guide to the United Kingdom' and has more than 80 editions of over 30 titles to his name as editor and part-author, including 'The Handbook of International Trade', 'The Handbook of World Trade', 'Managing Business Risk' and business guides to China, the 10 countries that joined the EU in 2004, South Africa and, more recently, Morocco. Before taking up a second career in business publishing, Jonathan was Director of European Operations of the manufacturing subsidiaries of a Fortune 500 multinational. From 1984 to 2005, he engaged in joint venture development and start-ups in China. He is also a founder director of IPR Connections, the quality conference organiser.

Olaf Swanzy is the PNO Group UK sector specialist for innovation with close working relationships with all principal funding bodies in this sector. He joined the PNO Group in 2004 to help establish the UK operation with an initial focus on technology development within the Environmental Sector. Over the past 8 years Olaf has worked with an extensive range of SMEs and large companies across all industry sectors and academia to advance research and innovation activities through the procurement of government funding from national and EU sources. Since 2008, he has been involved in the delivery of training to SMEs in the areas of government funding for innovation investment activities. In 2009 alone, he secured in excess of £15 million of grant support for clients.

Part One

Investment in the
United Kingdom:
The Current Environment

16

1.1 THE UK ECONOMY AND INVESTMENT ENVIRONMENT

Jonathan Reuvid Legend Business

During the past year the UK economy has consolidated its recovery from the last decade's recession. With a new majority government pledged to continue the previous coalition government's policies of deficit reduction, a firm control of public spending, infrastructure investment and a fresh commitment to growth, stability is assured through to 2020.

Nevertheless, there are challenges ahead both from the possible impact of the downturn in China's economy and more sluggish recovery of some of the UK's major EU trading partners. At home, productivity improvement is recognized as a prerequisite for sustained economic strength and the government is applying fiscal adjustments and further incentives to assist businesses in achieving this goal.

Securing a broad base from which foreign investments are generated is critical to the UK retaining its position as the leading destination for FDI in Europe. During 2014/15 investments were received from a record number of countries and territories, notably emerging markets of which India became the third largest source of all investments. The effectiveness of the UK offering is being enhanced through UK Trade & Investment (UKTI) joint trade and investment sector teams in order to create more export-led inward investment opportunities.

MACRO-ECONOMIC INDICATORS

Forecasts for 2015/16

Composite forecasts for the basics of the UK economy published by HM Treasury are highlighted in Table 1.1.1.

Table 1.1.1 Macro-economic indicators August 2015

	2016			2015		
	Lowest	Highest	Average	Lowest	Highest	Average
GDP growth (%)	2.3	3.0	2.6	1.4	3.0	2.4
Inflation Q4 (%)						
- CPI	-0.2	1.0	0.4	1.2	2.7	1.7
- RPI	-0.4	1.6	1.2	1.3	3.5	2.8
Unemployment (Q4%)	4.9	5.6	5.3	3.8	5.8	5.1
Current Account (£bn)	-110.7	118.0	-69.6	-122.8	109.0	-63.5
PSNB (2015-2016:£bn)	62.1	85.0	72.2	29.7	79.6	51.3

Source: Economic Assurance Team, HM Treasury No. 340, 19 August 2015

The highest and lowest and forecasts are extracted and the averages calculated from the forecasts made during the previous month by 22 city banks and investment firms, and 17 non-City research institutions and forecasters including the OECD, IMF, EC, Economist Intelligence Unit (EIU) and Confederation of British Industry (CBI).

Prospects for the UK are compared with those of other major advanced economies and the emerging and developing economies in Table 1.1.2 by reference to recent IMF growth forecasts, indicating a steadily improving outlook for the UK in the near-term, second only to the US among the developed economies.

Table 1.1.2 2016 forecast GDP growth vs 2015

	2015 %	2016 %
Advanced economies		
UK	2.4	2.7
US	2.5	3.0
Canada	1.5	2.1
Japan	0.1	1.2
Germany	1.6	1.7
France	1.2	1.5
Italy	0.7	1.2
Spain	3.1	2.5
Euro area	1.5	1.7
Emerging and developing economies		
Europe	2.9	2.9
Asia	6.6	6.4
China	6.8	6.3
India	7.5	7.5
World	3.3	3.8

Source: IMF forecasts June/July 2015

The growth prospects for Asian economies, notably China and India exceed the UK GDP forecasts and underline the renewed focus on these markets for trade and investment.

The UK Population

The population stands at an estimated 64.6 million, with a growth of 491,000 over the previous year and a forecast annual growth rate of 0.7% through to 2021. The population has aged since 2004 with the proportion of those aged 16-64 decreasing marginally from 65% to 64% and those aged 65 and over increasing from 16% to 18% (*Source: Office of National Statistics, June 2015*).

As of May 2015, 30.98 million were in work, 265,000 more than a year earlier. As of July the jobless rate stands at 5.6% (*www.tradingeonomics.com*) Applying the international "standardised" measurement, the UK's rate of unemployment compares favourably with the EU average of 9.7% (*source: Eurostat, 2015*) although higher than the US (5.3%) and Germany (4.7%).

According to the 2011 census, 83.9% of the population are resident in England, 8.4% in Scotland, 4.9% in Wales and 2.8 % in Northern Ireland. Of those living in

England and Wales, 7.5 million (13%) were born abroad of which almost half (3.4 million) held a UK passport.

Some of those born abroad have since become British citizens. Of the 694,000 born in India, 379,000 had taken British citizenship. By contrast, of the 579,000 residents born in Poland, 558,000 remained Polish nationals having acquired the right to live and work in the UK since Poland joined the EU in 2004. The other top 10 countries of birth of UK residents were: Pakistan, Republic of Ireland, Bangladesh, Nigeria, South Africa, US and Jamaica and China. Immigration has risen sharply and continues to rise since the millennium.

UK INWARD INVESTMENT

The UK stock of inward foreign investment is valued at US$1.7 trillion (£1.0 trillion), an increase of more than 9% during 2014 and advanced by almost 50% since 2010, according to the OECD 2015 report. The UK continues to rank third as the largest global recipient of FDI stock after the USA and China and foremost in the EU. In 2014 the UK attracted FDI inflows of $35 billion representing 28% of all capital investment flows into greater Europe against a share of 10% into Russia, 7% into Spain and 5% each into Germany and Poland, while France, Netherlands Ireland, Turkey and Romania scored 4% each. The FT fDi report (2015) records that the UK received FDI for 909 projects in 2014, 8 % more than the previous year and significantly more than Germany (378), Spain (252) and France (237).

As Michael Boyd, Managing Director, Investment, at UK Trade & Investment (UKTI) concludes in his introduction to the UKTI Inward Investment Report 2014/15 "These results show once again that the UK is a world-beater in attracting foreign direct investment." The Ernst & Young attractiveness survey 2015 confirms that the UK received a record number of new FDI projects (887) excluding mergers and acquisitions in 2014, an increase of 11 per cent over 2013 which raised its market share in Europe to 20.4%, the highest share since 2009. In terms of employment, FDI generated 84,603 new jobs in 2014 (source: UKTI), 12% more than in the previous year, 70 per cent more than in Russia and almost 2.5 times more than in Germany. In addition, FDI activity also safeguarded a further 23,055 UK jobs in 2014.

Sources of FDI
According to the same Ernst & Young report, investor sentiment towards Europe has strengthened and Western Europe is now judged the most attractive region by 50% of investors followed by the US (39%) and China (38%). However, the 2015 AT Kearney FDI Confidence Index continues to rank the US first and China second among the top 10 countries for FDI with the UK now ranked a further place up in third. Analysing the investments of the top 10 countries of origin in 2014, we can see that the UK was the leading destination for US, French and Japanese investors. For

most of those countries where Germany or France was the preferred destination, the UK also received significant shares of FDI: China (19%); Netherlands (18%); and Italy (17%).

The investment contribution over the past five years of the top 9 geographical sources of FDI towards the total of 1,988 new projects which generated 84,603 new jobs and safeguarding 23,055 jobs in 2014/15 is displayed in Table 1.1.3.

Table 1.1.3 Top nine sources of investment 2010/11 to 2014/15

| | Projects | | | | | New and Safeguarded Jobs | | | | |
	2010/11	2011/12	2012/13	2013/14	2014/15	2010/11	2011/12	2012/13	2013/14	2014/15
USA	388	366	396	501	564	34,424	37,525	48,802	32,488	36,778
France	69	65	65	110	124	5,902	12,038	16,001	19,077	8,198
India	97	91	89	74	122	6,096	5,454	7,255	4,563	9,350
China	59	92	70	88	112	1,471	2,116	3,409	5,450	5,927
Japan	105	88	114	116	107	5,508	7,818	7,442	5,049	3,873
Germany	71	66	78	102	97	4,360	4,994	14,589	8,805	9.727
Italy	53	98	93	70	91	2,940	1,763	6,892	3,807	2,193
Australia	53	51	61	68	81	4,344	1,500	1,297	2,687	4,012
Canada	68	59	63	89	72	1,947	1,342	21,208	2,857	3,762
FDI (Top 9)	963	976	1,029	1,218	1,370	66,992	74,550	126,895	84,783	83,820

Source: UK Inward Investment Reports: 2010/11 to 2014/15

As in the previous four years, the US remains by far the biggest source of FDI with 564 projects, accounting for 28% of the new project total and 34% of created and safeguarded jobs. This corresponds to the FDI stock figures which also confirm that the USA is the continuous largest source of inward FDI. The two largest European sources of FDI in 2014/15 were France and Germany, together contributing more than 220 projects. However, while France remains in second place, German's contribution was surpassed by India, China and Japan, in that order, each investing in more than 100 projects. Italy regained its level of 2011/12 and 2012/13 with 91 projects while Australia and Canada reversed their positions with 81 and 72 projects, up and down 19% respectively on their 2013/14 investment activities. Of the 112 Chinese projects, 13 investments originated from Hong Kong.

Overall, the almost 2,000 FDI projects were gained from a record number of more than 70 countries and territories. In addition to the nine sources detailed above, projects were secured from Spain (59), Ireland (51) and Switzerland (42) with 24 projects from the rest of the Americas, 342 from other EMEA countries and 103 from the rest of

APAC territories. In addition, UKTI reports that its drive in emerging markets had yielded a combined pipeline of over 500 registered opportunities by mid-year 2015.

COMPOSITION OF INVESTMENT PROJECTS
Inward investment by category

The proportions of 2014/15 FDI recorded between completely new investments, expansions of previous investments and mergers and acquisition (M&As) including joint ventures (JVs) are compared with the proportions of the previous four years in Table 1.1.4 below.

Table 1.1.4 Types of investment

	2010/11	2011/12	2012/13	2013/14	2014/15
New investments	724	752	777	820	1,058
Expansions (incl. retention)	544	506	577	677	740
M & A and JVs	166	148	205	276	90
Total	1,434	1,406	1,569	1,773	1,988

Source: UK Inward Investment Report: 2014/15

The overall growth rate of 12% in investment projects in 2014/15 more than matched the previous year's growth of 11%. In 2014/15 growth was driven primarily by new investments, an increase of 238 (29%) in absolute numbers, whereas the primary growth element in 2013/14 was expansions. This year expansions increased in numbers by 67, rather less than the 100 recorded in the previous year while the number of M&A and JV Investments declined by 86 below the level for 2012/13.

Inward Investment by Industry Group and Sector
The dispersion of FDI by primary business sector in 2013/2014 and jobs created or safeguarded is detailed in Table 1.1.5; project numbers are compared with 2012/13.

Table 1.1.5 UK inward investment projects by primary industry group

Industry group	Projects			Total jobs
	2012/13	**2013/14**	**2014/15**	**2014/15**
Advanced Manufacturing	380	418	468	33,288
Energy and Infrastructure	250	310	241	14,738
Finance and Professional	309	385	515	34,921
Creative industries and ICT	369	400	486	13,590
Life Sciences	142	156	168	6,583
Electronics and Telecom	109	104	110	4,538
TOTAL	1,559	1,773	1,988	107,658

Source: UKTI Inward Investment reports 2012/13 to 2014/15

As in the previous two years, FDI in advanced manufacturing delivered 12% more projects than in 2013/14 but 11% less jobs. Foreign investments continue to perform an important role in strengthening many of the key sectors and industries across the UK economy including the advanced manufacturing group in which automotive and advanced engineering (117 projects), aerospace (43 projects) and chemicals (36 projects) sectors are prominent. Almost 17,000 jobs were created or safeguarded in the automotive industry alone.

In 2014/15 financial and professional services together generated both the most projects, 34% more than the previous year, and most jobs (up 61%). Of this total, financial services contributed 222 new investment projects and 11,843 new and safeguarded jobs.

In terms of job creation and safeguarding, the energy and infrastructure sector generated 22% less projects and less than half the number jobs than in 2013/14. However, UKTI secured £10.4 billion in capital investment commitment for infrastructure involving institutional and corporate investors in 30 projects and the creation of 3,000 jobs. The oil and gas sub-sector recorded investments in 48 projects involving 2,961 new and safeguarded jobs.

The creative industries and ICT sector again contributes strongly with project numbers up 21% and jobs created and safeguarded up 12%. Within the sector, creative industries accounted for 124 recorded projects and 2,915 new and safeguarded jobs. The information economy group, including ICT, software electronics and communications services, chalked up 454 projects with 14,871 new and safeguarded jobs. Other individual sectors which performed strongly were life sciences (161 projects and 6,583 jobs) and the food and drink industry, the UK's largest manufacturing sub-sector with a turnover of £90 billion for which 104 FDI projects 6,072 jobs were recorded.

The Nature of Investment

In 2014/15 R&D was an important element in 345 FDI projects, an 11% improvement on 2013/14. In addition UKTI has promoted and secured 34 R&D collaborations and partnerships between UK-based research centres and foreign investors which may lead to major FDI investment and long-term relationships.

Likewise 370 foreign investments in 2014/15 involve responsibility for some headquarters function in the UK. According to the Ernst & Young attractiveness survey 2015, the UK attracted 35% of HQ-based investments in Europe.

THE ROLE OF UK TRADE AND INVESTMENT

In Chapter 1.2 UK Trade and Investment (UKTI) describes its work in supporting foreign owned companies to do business in the UK. UKTI works closely with its investment partners throughout the UK to ensure that all investment promotion activities contribute to wider economic policies and strategies. How this work is organised and the current status of key investment industries and investment opportunities is detailed in the remainder of Part One and in Parts Four to Seven of the book.

Note: Much of the content for this chapter is derived from the Great Britain and Northern Ireland Inward Investment 2014/2015 Report published July 2015 by UK Trade & Investment.

1.2 UK TRADE & INVESTMENT – SUPPORTING FOREIGN-OWNED COMPANIES TO DO BUSINESS IN THE UK

Rodney Berkeley, Director Global Accounts, UKTI Investment Group

The UK is the place to be for overseas businesses seeking to drive up their profitability and competitiveness. The World Bank reports that it's easier to do business here than any other major European economy, and it rates the UK as the eighth most business-friendly country in the world. We achieve this position through our commitment to making the UK the most open, welcoming and business-friendly country in the world. Our low corporate taxes and competitive rules for taxing the profits of multinationals attract the biggest global enterprises. We are the sixth biggest exporter in the world, with global trade supported by a record investment in infrastructure and sophisticated supply chains. The UK's dynamic economy is acknowledged as Europe's best location from which to succeed in global business, and investors are showing their confidence in the UK's long-term economic plan.

Investors choose the UK because of the breadth of skills across multiple industry sectors in a very large workforce. With four of the top six universities in Europe, and the highest percentage of adults with tertiary education in Western Europe, businesses have access to highly-skilled pool of workers. In fact, according to the Global Talent Competitiveness Index, the UK is second only to the US for "availability of labour and vocational skills" and "global knowledge skills" among the world's major economies.

Skills are central to the UK's Industrial Strategy. The government is committed to creating 3 million apprenticeship starts during the five-year term (2015-2020) and is putting employers in the driving seat of apprenticeship design, funding and standards to ensure they deliver the skills business needs.

UK Trade & Investment (UKTI) has been at the heart of achieving the UK's position as the number one destination for international business in Europe. UKTI is the government department that helps UK-based companies succeed in the global economy. It also helps overseas companies bring investment to the UK, and once established here, continues to support them to expand and export from the UK. UKTI offers flexible support packages and bespoke advice to investors of all sizes, from start-ups to institutional investors. UKTI's support for inward investors is free of charge and commercial-in-confidence, and can be accessed through the Investment Services Team: +44 (0)207 333 5442 or enquiries@ukti-invest.com. UK Embassies, High Commission and Consulates around the world can also put businesses in touch with the Investment Services Team.

UKTI has offices in 107 markets around the world - 51 with dedicated investment teams - and UKTI staff and partners in every part of the UK. Its advisers and account managers have expertise in all aspects of setting up a business in the UK and using the UK as a base for export or expansion. The organisation's nationwide and global reach gives businesses easy access to its expertise and services, both in their home country and in the UK. Once businesses are established in the UK, account management teams stay in regular contact with businesses to help them overcome any challenges they may encounter.

UKTI also works to ensure that the concerns of inward investors are heard across government, and is central to the cross-government approach to tackling the issues and challenges faced by these key contributors to the UK economy.

UKTI bases its service on building an understanding of businesses' long-term strategic objectives, and helping businesses achieve them. It can do this thanks to its global and nationwide networks of advisers and account managers, pools of specialist advisers, access to information, influence within Government, big business, and analytical tools. Businesses which choose to invest in the UK have a dedicated UKTI account manager, who acts as a single point of contact and provides access to this network of specialist advisers and policy influencers.

Crucially, once a business is established in the UK it can benefit from all the services and support to help it succeed in overseas markets that UK businesses have access to.

SUPPORT THROUGHOUT THE BUSINESS LIFE-CYCLE

UKTI offers businesses support at all stages of locating in the UK, from choosing an investment location, through setting up and eventually expanding.

For businesses which aren't sure which country is the best location for their investment, UKTI will explain the business environment in the UK and benchmark this against competitor countries. Through its unique financial analysis tool, UKTI can provide detailed cost information, profit comparisons and financial benchmarking insights tailored to individual projects, to help them compare different potential investment locations. This will enable investors to draw meaningful and cost effective conclusions about the UK's competitiveness as compared with other possible locations.

For businesses which have already decided to bring their operations to the UK,

UKTI will provide the support they need to get set up quickly and efficiently. Guidance and support on the essential steps – such as choosing the right location, finding premises, recruiting staff, obtaining visas, and connecting with the value chain – can save businesses valuable time and money and enable them to start doing business sooner.

For businesses already established in the UK and wanting to expand, UKTI can help them develop the relationships necessary to do so. Typically, this could be connecting businesses with innovation support for new products and services, with UKTI's overseas network to increase exports or expand to new markets, with organisations and funds which can help finance expansion plans, or with the UK's skills programme to support training and recruitment issues.

Specialist Expertise

UKTI has a network of specialists, who can provide expert support at every stage of an investment or expansion. They offer straightforward, informed advice to investors when they need it. There are six policy specialists covering the major cross-cutting areas for investors: tax, visas, skills, planning, finance and opening bank accounts. There are also sector specialists who have extensive experience in and understanding of their particular industry. UKTI's specialists have up-to-date information on market opportunities and developments, and wide-ranging contacts in their fields.

Support across the UK

UKTI works closely with the English regions to link them to teams in the centre of government. These regional teams provide expert insight into UK opportunities through the Local Enterprise Partnerships (LEPs) network: partnerships between local authorities and businesses. Regional teams can also address barriers to local growth and answer questions from investors and potential investors, from visas and export licence queries to recruitment and Regional Growth Fund questions. UKTI can also link businesses to opportunities in the rest of the UK in a similar way, through its close relationships with the Devolved Administrations of Scotland, Wales and Northern Ireland. Visit the Local Investment Showcase to explore which LEP or Developed Adminsistration could provide the best match for your sector.[1]

Access to Finance

A crucial area for many businesses thinking of setting up in a new location is availability of finance. UKTI can provide information and insight into a wide range of government and non-government funding streams, including state-aid funding options like Regional and Local Growth Funds, EU funds, business angels and many others. UKTI also provides support for businesses to access finance through UK

---

1 www.localinvestuk.com

Export Finance[1], the British Business Bank[2] and the Green Investment Bank[3]. UKTI's Finance Specialists can support businesses to identify and access sources of funding, and understand and navigate the process for opening a UK bank account.

Support for Innovators

UKTI can help innovative businesses find commercial UK innovation projects and companies to work with. Its **Innovation Gateway** team works to raise UK innovation, attract investment from international funds and secure increased R&D presence from large corporates. It can support investors to access an exclusive pool of commercial innovation projects and companies, make introductions to large international funds and corporate enterprises, and navigate UK Research Councils and universities. innovation@ukti.gsi.gov.uk

Overseas entrepreneurs, leading early-stage technology companies, who want to scale up and internationalise their business from the UK can take advantage of the Global Entrepreneur Programme (GEP). This programme is supported by 22 "dealmakers" – internationally successful entrepreneurs with the expertise and networks to help entrepreneurs make the move to the UK and grow once here. Support is free and includes continued help once entrepreneurs have relocated to the UK. The programme so far has helped over 300 businesses relocate to the UK, and raised over £1 billion of private investment for companies (info@entrepreneurs.gov.uk).

UKTI can also broker access to innovation expertise through **Innovate UK**, which supports businesses to access research & development facilities and expertise and bring products and services more quickly to market. Its seven Catapult Centres bring together the best of the UK's businesses, scientists and engineers to work side by side on late-stage research and development, and can enable businesses to access advice and cutting-edge facilities which might otherwise be out of reach. www.innovateuk.org.

Support for High Value Investments

With foreign ownership standing at about 40 percent, and published plans for over £375 billion worth of projects and programmes over the next 20 years, UK infrastructure is an attractive market for global investors. UKTI publishes a "pipeline" of major infrastructure and regeneration investment opportunities, setting out the value and development stages of major projects throughout the country.

UKTI offers specific types of support for the biggest investment opportunities through its High Value Opportunities programme. This provides information and

---

[1]https://www.gov.uk/government/organisations/uk-export-finance

[2]http://british-business-bank.co.uk/

[3]http://www.greeninvestmentbank.com/

support to help UK-based businesses win large scale overseas procurement project contracts by identifying, researching and validating opportunities as they become available, and informing businesses at an early stage. https://www.gov.uk/high-value-opportunities.

Sector-focused investment organisations (IOs) support the promotion of priorities under the UK's Industrial Strategy[1]. The IOs are chaired and staffed by business people with wide experience in their industry, who work closely with UKTI staff. The IOs provide comprehensive, hands-on support to investors in the Automotive, Financial Services, Life Sciences (including Agricultural Technologies), Offshore Wind, and Regeneration sectors.

Support for Foreign Investors Exporting from the UK
The UK is the sixth-largest exporter in the world. UKTI, through its UK and global networks, supports businesses to export to international markets. Its support is available equally to both UK and foreign businesses, regardless of company size, whether they are new exporters or experienced exporters wishing to explore new markets. Some of UKTI's most popular export services include:

- Bespoke research into specific markets and/or sectors.
- Information on new business opportunities via email alerts tailored to suit specific interests, sectors, markets or type of opportunity.
- Assistance with winning major contracts overseas through the High Value Opportunities Programme.
- Advice and support delivered locally across the UK by regional international trade advisers.
- Access to regular overseas trade missions, visits and trade shows, to help businesses build relationships with overseas companies, governments and other essential contacts.
- Investors in the UK can also receive support from UK Export Finance, which can provide credit insurance policies, political risk insurance on overseas

  investments and guarantees on bank loans, including in markets where private insurers and banks are less willing to take on the risks.

Businesses can contact UKTI's Investment Services Team for information on any of UKTI's services: enquiries@ukti-invest.com, phone +44 (0)207 333 5442, or via any UK Embassy, High Commission or Consulate.

[1]https://www.gov.uk/government/publications/industrial-strategy-explained

1.3 OVERVIEW FOR UK INWARD INVESTORS

Christina Howard, Watson Farley & Williams LLP

INTRODUCTION

The UK is one of Europe's most favoured jurisdictions for inward investment[1], that is, the investment of money from an external source into a region. Despite continuing global economic uncertainty, inflows of foreign direct investment (FDI) into the UK reached a little over US$72 billion in 2014[2]. Once established in the UK, foreign-owned companies are treated no differently from UK companies. London is seen to be a particularly attractive place to invest and has been voted the number one destination in Europe for FDI[3], attracting 48% of the UK's FDI[4].

There are many reasons for investors and businesses to choose to invest or establish a presence in the UK, including:

- Its sophisticated infrastructure and telecommunications;
- Its position as a leading financial centre;
- Its recognized and respected legal system;
- Its financial incentives and tax environment;
- Its stable political environment; and
- Its skilled workforce.

---

[1] Ernst & Young's UK Attractiveness Survey 2015

[2] United Nations Conference on Trade and Development - World Investment Report 2015 - Country Fact Sheet - UK

[3] FDI European Cities & Regions of the Future 2014/2015

[4] Ernst & Young's UK Attractiveness Survey 2015

Once a business has chosen to establish a presence in the UK, there are a number of factors, in addition to other, broader commercial issues, that need to be considered, including the following:

1. What type of entity should I choose?
2. What will the tax treatment be on my investment?
3. How do I go about employing people in the UK?
4. Which type of premises do I need for my investment?
5. Is the UK a good place to raise finance?
6. What if my business becomes involved in a dispute?

TYPE OF ENTITY TO BE CHOSEN

There are a number of entities or arrangements that may be chosen when establishing a business presence in the UK, including trading partnerships, limited liability partnerships, agency arrangements and European Economic Interest Groupings. However, the most common arrangements chosen by those investing or establishing a presence in the UK are the incorporation of a UK company (which may be a subsidiary of the overseas parent company) or the opening of a UK establishment (a branch or place of business in the UK).

UK companies and establishments are all regulated by UK companies' legislation. Companies House, operated by the Registrar of Companies, is the key government organisation that coordinates the registration and administration of businesses in the UK.

Where a business establishes a presence in the UK through a company or UK establishment, a number of consequences will follow, which will to some extent vary with the form or presence chosen, but will include obligations to file certain documents at Companies House and to submit tax returns to HM Revenue & Customs.

Establishing a UK Company

The most common method of establishing a business presence in the UK is through the incorporation of a limited liability company. The company may be incorporated as a wholly owned-subsidiary of a non-UK parent entity, or by one or more individuals. The company will have its own legal personality as an entity separate from its parent undertaking or individual shareholders, and will be able, therefore, to enter into contracts and operate in its own name.

In certain cases, the best way to develop a presence in the UK may be to partner experienced and established local representatives or undertakings through cooperation or joint venture arrangements, which will often be structured through a UK company as the joint venture vehicle. For further discussion on joint ventures, reference should be made to the chapter of this book entitled "Mergers and Acquisitions and Joint Ventures".

In order to establish a UK company, certain documents must be filed with Companies House, including the company's constitutional documents (namely, the Memorandum and Articles of Association). Depending on the nature of the company's business going forward, standard documents may be adopted, or these can be tailored to specific requirements (for which a solicitor's advice should be sought). Once the constitutional documents have been finalised, these and the other incorporation documents are filed at Companies House, and a certificate of incorporation and company number are issued. It can take as little as a day to register a company at Companies House.

Opening a UK Establishment

As an alternative to incorporating a UK company, a non-UK business may simply register a UK establishment in the UK. An overseas company will be required to register its UK establishment at Companies House and will also be subject to certain on-going accounting requirements and requirements to deliver returns. In simple terms, if an overseas company has a presence in the UK from which it regularly conducts business or premises in the UK where it may be contacted, this will constitute a UK establishment requiring registration. A single registration regime applies for all overseas companies that carry on business in the UK through a UK establishment, irrespective of whether it is a place of business or a branch.

THE TAX TREATMENT ON INVESTMENT

The format chosen for establishing a business presence in the UK will vary as a result of the taxation implications as well as the commercial considerations and objectives of the investors involved. The basic principles of UK corporation tax and the taxation consequences of each format are briefly set out below.

When deciding which entity would be most suitable for an inward investor, it should be noted that the tax implications of establishing a company, branch or a place of business/representative office in the UK may vary significantly from entity to entity depending on, for example, the size of the business or the nature of the trade that is being undertaken.

Since the taxation implications of any investment will vary from case to case and may be complex, it is advisable to seek more detailed tax advice from a solicitor specialising in UK tax before establishing any sort of UK presence.

Companies Resident in the UK

Generally, a company incorporated in the UK will be regarded as resident in the UK for tax purposes and will consequently be liable to pay UK corporation tax on its worldwide profits (subject to double taxation relief for foreign taxes).

In the UK, local and foreign-owned UK resident companies are taxed alike. Inward investors may have access to certain regional grants and incentives that are designed to attract industry to particular areas of the UK, but no tax concessions are granted.

The main corporation tax rate is currently 20%, down from 28% in 2010. The UK government aims to increase the UK's competitiveness from a tax perspective.

The UK has a fairly simple system of personal income tax, with a basic rate of 20% for income up to £42,385 (excluding personal allowances), a higher rate of 40% for income between £42,386 and £150,000 and a rate of 45% for income over £150,000. There is also a National Insurance system into which taxpayers and their employers make mandatory payments.

Companies that are not Resident in the UK

Companies that are not resident in the UK are subject to corporation tax only if the company trades through a permanent establishment in the UK. Profits that are attributable to the activities of a UK permanent establishment are subject to UK corporation tax as if the permanent establishment were a separate entity.

A non-UK resident company that does not have a permanent establishment in the UK, although not liable to corporation tax, may be liable to income tax on its UK source profits (e.g. rents from a UK property) at the basic rate of 20%, subject to certain limitations.

Where a company is resident in a country with which the UK has a double taxation treaty, the impact of that treaty must be considered.

The UK has recently introduced a new "Diverted Profits Tax" which can apply to certain artificial structures designed to avoid UK tax.

EMPLOYING PEOPLE IN THE UK

Businesses wishing to establish a presence in the UK have various options in relation to their staff. These, along with connected immigration issues, are discussed in more detail in the chapters 2.5 and 3.6 of this book.

Since the economic downturn, we have seen a steady improvement in the UK's employment data over the last few years; between February and April 2015, the number of people in work in the UK was 31.05 million and the unemployment rate was at 5.5% (down from 6.6% in the same period last year).[1]

Much of the employment legislation currently affecting the UK workforce originates from the European Commission in Brussels. EU regulations affect working patterns, wage structures and employee protection rights in the UK; for example, the European Working Time Directive creates an entitlement to minimum daily and weekly rest periods, an average working week limit of 48 hours, and restrictions on night work. As

---

[1] Office for National Statistics - Labour Market Statistics (June [2015]).

it has implemented the EU directives, the UK government has been proactive in trying to maintain its flexibility and competitiveness; for example, it has currently negotiated a special provision under the Working Time Directive that allows employees to opt out of the 48-hour working week limitations.

Whilst citizens of EEA Member States can usually enter the UK to live and work without restriction, migrants from other countries will usually require a visa. Individuals from certain countries can enter as business visitors for up to six months without applying for a visa in advance but their activities whilst in the UK are restricted. The UK immigration regime is dealt with in more detail in chapter 2.5 of this book.

RAISING FINANCE

The City of London is widely regarded as one of the leading financial centres in the world. London offers a huge variety of financial services, including:

- commercial and investment banking;
- insurance;
- venture capital;
- stock and currency brokering;
- fund management;
- commodity dealing;
- accounting and legal services;
- electronic clearing and settlement systems; and
- bank payments systems.

Notwithstanding continuing global economic uncertainty, London remains attractive to inward investors because of its solid regulatory, legal and tax environment, a supportive market infrastructure and a dynamic and highly skilled workforce.

UK government policies are intended to facilitate the free flow of capital and to support the flow of resources in the product and services markets. The principles involved in legal, regulatory and accounting systems in the UK are transparent, and they are consistent with international standards.

The London Stock Exchange (LSE) is one of the most active equity markets in the world, combining its robust and liquid nature with a high degree of integrity. An increasingly popular forum for inward investment into the UK, particularly for smaller companies, is the LSE's AIM market, which is examined in chapter 6.4 of this book "The AIM Market of the London Stock Exchange".

REAL ESTATE

The UK has one of the most dynamic and transparent property markets in the world, with a wide range of property options and flexible short term lease arrangements. For inward investors in the UK, one of the first decisions to make regarding real estate is whether to take a lease (or rent) premises (known as acquiring a "leasehold" interest) or to buy premises (known as acquiring a "freehold" interest). There are no restrictions on overseas companies either buying or leasing property in the UK.

Buying

Buying property in the UK is usually a relatively straightforward process and, importantly, there are no restrictions on overseas companies buying real estate. In addition to the price of the property, purchasers must pay stamp duty land tax ("SDLT") which is currently chargeable at a rate of up to up to 4% for commercial property and up to 15% of the purchase price or lease premium of residential property (depending on the statutory value bands). A similar tax called "Land and Buildings Transaction Tax" is payable in Scotland. Land Registry fees are payable on registration of purchases at the Land Registry and, in some circumstances, on a letting.

Leasing

Companies can either take a lease of premises that are already available or enter into what is known as a "pre-let". A "pre-let" is an agreement with a developer to lease premises before construction is completed, enabling prospective tenants to specify the design, layout and fittings of the building. Commercial leases in the UK typically run for a term of 5-10 years with the tenant paying a full-market rent, normally quarterly, and, usually, no premium is payable. It may be possible to negotiate "break rights", enabling the tenant to "break" the lease before the end of the term.

The majority of leases of commercial premises in the UK are let on "full repairing and insuring terms", which place the responsibility for all upkeep and decoration of the property on the tenant and require the tenant to reimburse the landlord's costs of insuring the building . In addition, most leases over 5 years in length will have a provision to increase the rent in line with market conditions at pre-determined points throughout the lease. The standard clause normally allows for "upwards-only" rent reviews at 3-5 yearly intervals. This means that if the market rent rises, so too will the rent payable under the lease, but the rent payable will not come down if the market falls.

Businesses choosing to take a lease of property must pay SDLT, which is calculated using the lease premium (if any) and the "net present value" of the rent payable, which is based on the value of the total rent over the life of the lease.

Companies purchasing or taking a lease of property should appoint an agent to represent them and are expected to pay legal fees, which incorporate conveyancing fees, as well as bank transfer fees and the costs for local authority and other conveyancing searches. An experienced property solicitor is necessary to assist in the preparation of all the required legal documentation.

Location

London may be the obvious choice for most investors establishing their business in the UK, due to its position as an internationally accessible city, its international time zone, its proximity to the EU and its excellent telecommunications infrastructure. However, running an office in London can be expensive, and some businesses may prefer to locate elsewhere in the UK.

DISPUTE RESOLUTION

Disputes in the UK are generally resolved through litigation in UK courts or by arbitration/mediation. Numerous disputes a year take place in London, many with an international dimension, reflecting London's strong position as an international centre for legal services[1].

The London Court of International Arbitration and the International Chamber of Commerce's International Court of Arbitration are leading international arbitration institutions. As a signatory to the 1958 Convention on the Recognition and Enforcement of Foreign Arbitral Awards (the New York Convention), the UK permits local enforcement on arbitration judgements decided in other signatory countries. The UK is also a member of the International Centre for Settlement of Investment Disputes and as such accepts binding international arbitration between foreign investors and the state.

Bilateral investment treaties (BITs) have been used as a means of protecting international investment and ensuring a more predictable and fair treatment of investors. The UK is party to 95 BITs that are currently in force[2]. A key feature of most of these BITs is investor-state dispute settlement arrangements that provide rights to those investing in the UK to seek redress for damages arising out of alleged breaches by the UK government of investment-related obligations. Key elements include provisions for equal and non-discriminatory treatment of investors and their investments, compensation for expropriation, transfer of capital and returns and access to independent settlement of disputes.

---

[1] Doing Business in the United Kingdom, 2013 Country Commercial Guide for US Companies - US Commercial Service

[2] Ibid.

CONCLUSION

For the reasons discussed throughout this chapter, the UK continues to be attractive to overseas businesses and inward investors.

1.4 GRANTS AND INCENTIVES WITHIN THE UK

Olaf Swanzy, PNO Consultants Ltd

INTRODUCTION

Thousands of different grant schemes, worth well in excess of £5 billion each year, are available for UK companies in an attempt to encourage, amongst others, innovation and economic development.

In general there are four types of public funding incentives available in the UK:

- **Grants** – where funding is secured ahead of the launch of a project.
- **Soft loans** – where loans are secured for projects that fall outside the parameter of normal business banking.
- **Tax incentives** – recognising advanced financial incentives for those with leading edge Research and Development (R&D) or capital programmes that are aligned with government strategy.
- **Awards** – that retrospectively recognise industry excellence in many functional areas of business – usually a financial prize, which has the advantage of significant PR.

Outside of the obvious fiscal benefits, for successful applicants the receipt of public funding can be also be used to achieve the following:

- Increased project leverage and project development.
- Improved company image (being awarded a grant is the equivalent of being awarded a quality stamp from a grantor body).
- A competitive advantage over others in your sector.
- Help raising additional 'harder finance' – comparable investment criteria.
- Establishment of collaborative relationships. Not all grants require a

collaboration, but those that do provide an ideal opportunity to work with academia or indeed other industrial organisations including potential customers.

In all cases, funding is used by a Governmental Body or Policy Maker to address key policy issues and to stimulate first movers by reducing financial risk in that area. Such incentives are therefore always in line with Government policies and key drivers. It is important that this is kept clearly in mind for any potential applicant when positioning their applications.

Although other forms of public funding are available, this article will focus predominantly on grants which represent the larger sums of money available for UK business.

MAIN GRANTS AND INCENTIVES IN THE UK

One of the key funding bodies to support UK businesses is Innovate UK (formerly the Technology Strategy Board), a fully public funded executive body established in July 2007. Innovate UK is our national innovation agency, dedicated to driving innovation for wealth creation in the UK, so that technology-enabled businesses sustain or attain global significance. It provides particular support for R&D to build partnerships between business, research and Government to address major societal challenges; and to run a wide range of knowledge exchange programmes to help innovation flourish. Funding is available for business and in some cases the academic base. The vision for Innovate UK is to make the UK a global leader in innovation and a magnet for innovative businesses, where technology is applied rapidly, effectively and sustainably to create wealth and enhance quality of life. Further information can be found at https://www.gov.uk/government/organisations/innovate-uk.

Other sources of guidance and support for UK investment include: www.ukti.gov. uk , www.scottish-enterprise.com, www.wales.gov.uk www.investni.com.

In general, the range of funding programmes available for UK businesses can be broken down into the following three principle areas:

1. Research and Development
2. Training and Education
3. Capital Investment

1. RESEARCH & DEVELOPMENT

Innovation remains the key focus area for the majority of UK funding bodies. A range of schemes are available for businesses irrespective of sector, company size and Technology Readiness Level (TRL). The key national funding programmes, designed to support businesses in their R&D activities, have been summarised below.

The Smart Programme (Innovate UK)

Smart is a UK small and medium-sized enterprise (SME) single company scheme, managed by Innovate UK. It is available on a rolling basis and is open to all sectors. Three types of grant are available:

- *Proof-of-market grant:* assesess the commercial viability of a project. Projects will last up to 9 months, have a maximum grant of £25k, and up to 60% of total project costs may be funded.
- *Proof-of-concept grant:* explores the technical feasibility and commercial potential of a new technology, product or process. Projects will last up to 18 months, have a maximum grant of £100k, and up to 60% of total project costs may be funded.
- *Development of prototype grant:* develops a technologically innovative product, service or industrial process. Projects will last up to 2 years and have a maximum grant of £250k; up to 35% of total project costs for medium enterprises, or up to 45% for small and micro enterprises, may be funded.

Applications are assessed every two months with an approximate 4-week assessment period.

Collaborative Research & Development (CR&D) Programme (Innovate UK)

CR&D is designed to assist the industrial and research communities to work together on R&D projects in strategically important areas of science, engineering and technology - from which successful new products, processes and services can emerge. Regular calls are announced throughout the year and topics vary with each call. Example calls have featured in ICT/Digital, Low Carbon Vehicles, Biotechnology, and Healthcare sectors. Projects must comprise industry led activity which is collaborative, either science-to-business or business-to-business interactions involving a minimum of two partners. Grant levels can be between 25% (for experimental development) and 50% (for applied research executed by Universities). Funding is typically £100K - £800K.

The Catalyst Programmes (Innovate UK)

Catalysts are run jointly by Innovate UK and the Research Councils. A Catalyst is a form of research and development funding which focuses on a specific priority area and aims to help take projects from research to as close to commercial viability as possible.

The Catalyst model supports projects in priority areas where the UK research base has a leading position and where there is clear commercial potential. Three levels of funding are usually available, varying according to how close a project is to commercialisation, with applicants able to join at any phase. Current Catalyst programmes include:

1. Biomedical Catalyst: :Open to both SME's and academics looking to develop innovative solutions to healthcare challenges either individually or in collaboration. Support will be available for projects arising from any sector or discipline that is aimed at addressing healthcare challenges. Two categories of grant available, depending on the maturity of the research, including Early Stage and Late Stage Awards (both Max grant £2.4 M, up to 50% support). Applications are accepted on a rolling basis with batch assessment dates typically every 4 months.
2. The Agri-Tech Catalyst to support businesses and academia in developing innovative solutions to challenges in the agri-tech sector. The Agri-Tech Catalyst will fund proposals relating to: primary crop and livestock production, including aquaculture, non-food uses of arable crops (for example, for biomass), food security and nutrition challenges in international development or challenges in downstream food processing, provided the solution lies in primary production.
3. The IB Catalyst to support the development and commercialisation of innovative Industrial Biotechnology (IB) processes.
4. The Energy Catalyst supports businesses and research organisations, including academia, to respond to challenges across the energy sector. It will fund projects delivering innovative solutions that address all elements of the energy trilemma. The Energy Catalyst can fund projects from early concept stage through to pre-commercial technology validation.

Small Business Research Initiative (SBRI) (Innovate UK)
The SBRI supports the engagement of the public sector with industry during the early stages of development, supporting projects across a range of industry sectors through the stages of feasibility and prototyping. The initiative is particularly suitable for SMEs and early stage businesses, as it provides them with vital funding for the critical stages of product development, and gives them a fast track and simplified process for working with the public sector. Typically, funding available is £100k for a feasibility stage project and £1 million for a development stage project.

Full information regarding all Innovate UK managed funding programmes can be found at https://interact.innovateuk.org/

EUREKA Eurostars (joint programme between more than 30 EUREKA member countries and the European Union)
This programme supports research-performing SMEs, to develop market orientated innovative products, processes and services in a transnational context i.e. involving at least one other partner from another Eurostars country. Any topic will be considered (with the exception of military applications).

The main programme criteria are:

- Consortium leader is an R&D performing SME from a Eurostars country which includes the UK.
- Eurostars R&D performing SMEs contribution is 50% or more of the total project cost.
- The consortium is well balanced (no single participant or country is responsible for more than 75%).
- The project duration is up to 3 years.
- Market introduction is within 2 years of the project's completion.
- Any topic can be considered (with the exception of military projects).

In the UK, only research-performing SME's are eligible for funding under Eurostars. UK Academics/universities and large companies are welcome to participate in a Eurostars project, but must fund their own participation or use funds from other sources. The same rules do not apply for other members states so for any potential collaboration please check the terms specific to that country. Up to 60% of eligible costs will be supported to a maximum grant level of €360,000 per UK partner in a Eurostars project. Further information can be found at https://www.eurostars-eureka.eu/.

Horizon 2020 (H2020) – European Funding
At a European Level, H2020 is the largest European funding programme for research and innovation, With nearly €80 billion of funding available over 7 years (2014 to 2020). Horizon 2020 is the financial instrument implementing the Innovation Union and a Europe 2020 flagship initiative aimed at securing Europe's global competitiveness. With the emphasis on excellent science, industrial leadership and tackling societal challenges, Horizon 2020's goal is to ensure Europe produces world-class science, removes barriers to innovation and makes it easier for the public and private sectors to work together in delivering innovation. Horizon 2020 is open to everyone, with a simpler structure than previous programmes – reducing red tape and time so that participants can focus on what is really important. This approach helps new projects to get off the ground quickly – and achieve results faster. Full details can be found at http://ec.europa.eu/programmes/horizon2020/.

2. TRAINING

Training or re-training of employees is of eminent importance to keep the workforce up to speed in rapidly changing environments. In some areas within the UK, these types of training courses may be eligible for public funding. The focus is on training for personnel below NVQ level 2 or minority groups such as asylum seekers.

3. CAPITAL INVESTMENT

Few CAPEX support programmes remain in the UK, with a greater number of smaller schemes available at a Regional/local level, depending on location. For larger scale investments, the main National funding programme is the Regional Growth Fund (RGF). RGF is a £3.2 billion fund, helping companies throughout England to create jobs between now and the mid-2020s. The payment of RGF money is spread between 2011 and 2017. RGF supports projects and programmes that are using private sector investment to create economic growth and sustainable employment. The bid threshold (a minimum amount of funding that can be applied for) is £1million. Any support will phased in line with expenditure and/or job creation/safeguarding. If you are considering an investment that will lead to job creation, it is worth speaking initially to your Local Enterprise Partnership about of the availability of funding https://www.gov.uk/government/publications/2010-to-2015-government-policy-local-enterprise-partnerships-leps-and-enterprise-zones/2010-to-2015-government-policy-local-enterprise-partnerships-leps-and-enterprise-zones.

THE GRANT APPLICATION PROCESS

Thorough preparation is the key to success in applying for grants. Having a credible business plan, a clear commercial or marketing strategy as well as a quality management team, before an application is submitted is a very important part of the application process. Application processing times differ significantly from scheme to scheme, with timescales ranging from four weeks to nine months. For any potential applicants it is important that project costs are not incurred before the grant application process is completed and grant agreements signed with the appropriate funding body.

Careful preparation of applications will naturally increase the chances of success, however there are no guarantees that an application will succeed, regardless of its merits, as the majority of UK grants are discretionary, meaning that they are awarded on a case-by-case basis and, more commonly, on a competitive basis. It is therefore of vital importance to ensure that the application is of the highest quality so that it stands out against the competition. It is also prudent to maximise the chances of success by developing a total grants strategy, rather than pinning everything on just one application.

Support in the Grant Acquisition Process

Finding the most appropriate grant and applying for funds can often be prohibitive. Successful grant procurement requires dedicated time and resources which companies often do not possess internally. As a result some businesses choose to maximise the funding opportunities available, appointing external expertise. Support advice and providers can be found through bodies such the UK Government Business Link network and the Enterprise Europe Network as well as specialist funding consultants.

One such public funding advisory is the PNO Group - Europe's leading innovation funding advisors. Employing just under 240 staff across the EU, PNO's core business is advising organisations, across all industrial sectors, in the context of the UK and EU grant funding landscape, helping them to identify and secure funds through available schemes.

Their client base include an extensive range of SME's, Universities and Multinationals which include companies such as HP, Microsoft, Philips, P&G and Solvay.(www.pnoconsultants.com). You can contact PNO's UK office to discuss the eligibility of any project ideas for funding potential on 0161 488 3488.

CONCLUSION

Public funding can provide a valuable means of supporting companies to achieve their strategic goals. For R&D activities in particular there are a range of schemes available to support projects across all stages of development from initial conception through to large scale demonstration.

With many businesses struggling to raise private and bank finance to advance their activities , it has never been more important to review all forms of funding available including public funds. If you are serious about being a market leader in your field, grant funding is the ideal mechanism to help you to achieve this.

NOTE:

Further information on_grants and incentives currently available in the UK may be found in UKTI factsheets on wwww.ukti.gov.uk.

1.5 A GUIDE TO THE UK'S LOCAL ENTERPRISE PARTNERSHIPS

Charles MacClelland, PA Consulting Group

WHAT ARE LOCAL ENTERPRISE PARTNERSHIPS?

In October 2010, the British Coalition Government published its proposals to replace the old Regional Development Agencies (RDAs) with Local Enterprise Partnerships (LEP) as the drivers of economic growth at the local level. The Government defined these new LEPs as "joint local authority-business bodies brought forward by local authorities themselves to promote local economic development". It was the Government's belief that local areas were better placed to determine their own priorities and shape more dynamic and entrepreneurial local economies then had previously been delivered by the RDAs, which were seen as depending too much on public spending to boost economic growth.

The new LEPs were intended to fit more appropriate economic geographies than the RDAs and allow greater input from local private sector interests who had direct experience of encouraging entrepreneurship. Therefore, when the nine RDAs were abolished they were replaced with thirty nine LEPs whose area had been defined through agreement between businesses and local authorities. On the board of each LEP is a mixture of private and public sector representatives, and more recently there has been an increase in the representation of local academic and research institutes. The only restrictions on membership of the LEP boards are that it must be chaired by a business person and half the members must be from the private sector.

These new LEPs took on a mandate to:

- Work with Government to set out key investment priorities, including transport infrastructure and supporting or coordinating project delivery;

- Coordinate proposals or bid directly for Regional Growth Fund monies;
- Support high growth businesses, for example through involvement in bringing together and supporting consortia to run new growth hubs;
- Make representation on the development of national planning policy and ensuring business is involved in the development and consideration of strategic planning applications;
- Play host to Enterprise Zones (see below for more information).

Since their creation in 2011, LEPs have been eligible to bid for a number of funding streams, some of which were substantial, so that by 2015 £18.5bn of public money has been allocated to them. Due to the increased level of funding and pro-devolution stance taken by the British Government LEPs have become significant economic agencies which can provide effective support for new investors looking to set up in UK, or existing investors who want to expand their operations.

Enterprise Zones are geographically defined areas, hosted by LEPs in which commercial and industrial businesses can receive incentives to set up or expand including tax incentives, simplified building regulations and millions of pounds in government funding for infrastructure. For example, businesses locating to an Enterprise Zone before 31st March 2018 are entitled to a business rate discount of up to 100% over a five year period (worth up to £275,000 per business) as well as Enhanced Capital Allowances for the purchase of machinery and equipment. Twenty four of them were established in April 2012 and since then they have attracted over 430 businesses, secured over £2bn in private sector investment and created over 12,500 jobs. They also allow businesses to cluster around centres of excellence in key sectors, and their clear focus on research and development is helping the UK up-skill its workforce to meet the demands of the future job market.

The disposition of LEPs geographically is illustrated in Figure 1.5.1.

Figure 1.5.2 LEP IMAGE 1

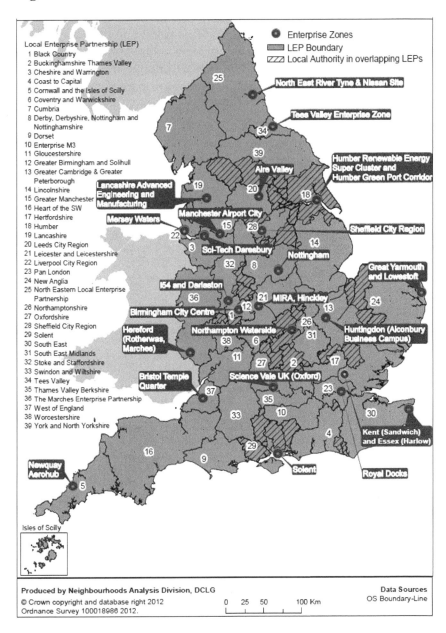

Local Enterprise Partnership (LEP)
1 Black Country
2 Buckinghamshire Thames Valley
3 Cheshire and Warrington
4 Coast to Capital
5 Cornwall and the Isles of Scilly
6 Coventry and Warwickshire
7 Cumbria
8 Derby, Derbyshire, Nottingham and Nottinghamshire
9 Dorset
10 Enterprise M3
11 Gloucestershire
12 Greater Birmingham and Solihull
13 Greater Cambridge & Greater Peterborough
14 Lincolnshire
15 Greater Manchester
16 Heart of the SW
17 Hertfordshire
18 Humber
19 Lancashire
20 Leeds City Region
21 Leicester and Leicestershire
22 Liverpool City Region
23 Pan London
24 New Anglia
25 North Eastern Local Enterprise Partnership
26 Northamptonshire
27 Oxfordshire
28 Sheffield City Region
29 Solent
30 South East
31 South East Midlands
32 Stoke and Staffordshire
33 Swindon and Wiltshire
34 Tees Valley
35 Thames Valley Berkshire
36 The Marches Enterprise Partnership
37 West of England
38 Worcestershire
39 York and North Yorkshire

Enterprise Zones
LEP Boundary
Local Authority in overlapping LEPs

Isles of Scilly

Produced by Neighbourhoods Analysis Division, DCLG
© Crown copyright and database right 2012
Ordnance Survey 100018986 2012.

0 25 50   100 Km

Data Sources
OS Boundary-Line

SETTING UP LOCALLY IN THE UK

LEPs are an essential part of the investment landscape and will be involved in assisting with most foreign direct investment into the UK. They either have their own inward investment arm, or a chosen delivery partner, who will work with foreign investors to ensure that they have as soft a landing in the UK as possible.

When an investor decides to invest in the UK they will usually contact UK Trade and Investment to ask for assistance and advice on how to accomplish their goal. If the investor is only interested in a single location then they will be put in touch with the relevant LEP, who will assist with the investment process. However, if the investor is unsure of the best possible location to establish their business then UKTI will select a shortlist of the most suitable, or make suggestions on how to narrow down the investor's existing choices. The LEPs whose area of responsibility covers the selected locations will then be asked to explain to the investor the attributes of their local area, so that the investor can make an informed choice regarding which location would best suit their business model.

Once a single geographical location has been selected the relevant LEP can begin to work with the investor and assist with process of establishing themselves in the UK.

This can manifest itself in a number of ways:

- *Funding signposts:* LEPs can point you in the right direction for relevant sources of business and property finance (grants, loans or equity) from both the public and private sectors.
- *Legislation and tax advice:* LEPs can offer tailored advice that suits a company's situation and requirements.
- *Premises:* LEPs can help investors search through the available commercial property in the area in order to find the most suitable property at the best price. If investors would like to design and build new premises then the LEP can assist with finding the necessary land and provide advice regarding the planning process.
- *Recruitment:* LEPs through their intimate knowledge of the local labour market can help companies recruit the right people with the right skills.
- *Research:* LEPs are more than happy to provide companies with bespoke research regarding the local labour market, the specific sector In which the company is active, the national and local economic landscape, and local supply chains.

Investing in a foreign country can be a difficult endeavour when one does not know the local economic, legal and political landscape. To offset this LEPs will help investors every step of the way to ensure a soft landing into the UK.

Case Study on LEP Collaboration:
The High Performance Technology Network
The High Performance Technology (HPT) Network is a collaboration of LEPs, Northamptonshire, Oxfordshire, South East Midlands, Buckinghamshire Thames Valley, Coventry & Warwickshire, and Leicester and Leicestershire LEPs, which aims to work with industry to develop a HPT cluster in Midlands. HPT covers Motorsport, Automotive, Defence, Aerospace and Marine. The Network contains thousands of members from SMEs to multi-national corporations, including Cosworth, Mercedes AMG, and Silverstone.

What the Network offers is access to:

- An established supply chain of motorsport, automotive & engineering businesses
- Industry-specialist technology parks and innovation centres
- Highly specialist test bed facilities
- University led applied research and collaborative R&D
- University Technical Colleges specialising in design and high performance and motorsports engineering
- Established pool of skilled engineers
- Funding

By working together with local industry, the HPT LEPs have developed a distinctive offer built on a world leading cluster of innovative HPT companies that provides a dynamic and innovative environment for HPT investors to establish themselves and take advantage of the high quality labour pool and supply chains.

OPERATING LOCALLY IN THE UK

Helping a company achieve a soft landing in the UK is not the end of the line; there are still many opportunities for LEPs to assist companies with their operational capabilities. LEPs are not just there for the special events such as the establishment and expansion of the company, but provide continual support to companies in their local area.

Several examples of the general business support are:

- *Connections:* LEPs are able to connect companies with industry networks, sector support agencies, media contacts and recommend professional services firms. They can also offer advice on collaboration possibilities with companies, universities and government.
- *Marketing:* LEPs have their own communications and marketing teams who work with both new investors and indigenous companies to promote their products and services in local, regional and specialist trade media.
- *Skills:* LEPs have created their own skills strategies and funds have been devolved from central government to see them realised. LEPs can therefore not only offer advice on skills training and help with access to training, but can also actively address any skills gaps in a local area.

Each company will be assigned an account manager by the LEP or UKTI who will be the main contact for companies to seek assistance from their LEP or UKTI. Companies are able to contact these individuals for advice and support where necessary, and they will be able to assist with the request.

LOCAL EXPANSION

LEPs are committed to supporting inward investors to grow, and they will each have their own individual initiatives, support services and funding programmes that are dedicated to realising this commitment. These can be accessed by contacting your local LEP and discussing your growth plans with them. They are able to help with all stages of development including planning a growth strategy, developing and commercialising new products, and advising on funding sources.

When a company wants to expand LEPs can help with:
- *Developing a growth plan:* Similar to the support offered by LEPs to inward investors looking to set up in the UK, they can assist established investors develop a growth strategy and offer advice that is tailored to the local area
- *Funding and finance:* LEPs have access to a number of funds, e.g. Regional Growth Fund, European Regional Development Fund, and use them to create their own funding and grant programmes aimed at helping businesses expand. Each fund or grant will have their own objectives and conditions. However they can be used to provide financial support for R&D, capital expenditure, taking on new staff and other activities associated with expanding a company, or offering new products and services.
- *Commercialisation:* If a firm has developed a new product/service which it would like to use as a platform to expand then LEPs can provide advice

regarding intellectual property rights and licencing, marketing strategy, and commercialisation of the product/service.

- *Relocation:* If an investor wants to move premises in order to expand then the LEP can help find new premises and support staff through the transition.
- *Recruitment:* Similar to the assistance LEPs can provide when establishing a business they can also use their intimate knowledge of the local labour market to find the right people when a company chooses to expand and take on more staff.

LEPs are well position to help non-indigenous firms expand due to their intimate knowledge of local markets and networks. Their business support programmes are well developed and they have a great deal of experience in helping businesses grow. It is well worth making use of what LEPs have to offer in this area and their help could be instrumental in ensuring the success of any expansion plan.

A LOCAL FUTURE

Over the past four years, LEPs have contributed a great deal to economic growth in the UK and will undoubtedly drive forward a great deal more over the coming years. The election of a Conservative Government and their commitment to the devolution of powers from central government to local areas has ensured that LEPs will continue to act as the main engine for local growth and their influence will only grow over the next five years.

With increased funding, resources and powers over local economic strategy, LEPs will provide essential support to foreign investors and along with UKTI should be the first port of call for anyone wanting to set up a business in the UK.

1.6 SCIENCE PARKS AND BUSINESS INCUBATORS

Nick Hood, Carter Jonas

THE INVESTMENT RATIONALE FOR SCIENCE PARKS

In our opinion Science Parks should be considered as a separate sector within the property investment market. Factors for investors to consider include:

- consistently high occupancy rates leading to reduced void costs for investors;
- new opportunities for investors to enter the market with the pressure on public sector investment into the sector;
- tenants often willing to take long leases leading to security of income;
- a key source of growth is derived from existing tenants who prefer to remain on the Science Park, moving to larger premises as they grow
- technology companies perform well at different times within the wider economic cycle diversifying the risk;
- preliminary evidence that investment returns have been better than office parks over one, three and five years.

These issues and the importance of Incubators are discussed in greater detail in this chapter.

SCIENCE PARKS

The Science Park movement in the United Kingdom is now over 40 years old; Cambridge Science Park has celebrated its 40th birthday and Herriot Watt Science

Park was established when the University relocated from central Edinburgh to a green field site to the west of Edinburgh in 1971. The movement started slowly but gathered momentum in the 1980s and the United Kingdom Science Park Association has celebrated its 30th birthday.

The Association continues to grow there are now over 88 full members and 22 Associates plus overseas members Affiliate members and business affiliates. The Parks vary in size and composition but all contribute to the promotion of the 'knowledge based economy' in the United Kingdom. UKSPA provides a useful definition of a Science Park as:

"A Science Park is essentially a cluster of knowledge-based businesses, where support and advice are supplied to assist in the growth of the companies. In most instances Science Parks are associated with a centre of technology such as a university or research institute."

All Science Parks will comply with some aspects of the definition but it is perhaps the human activities in the promotion of business support and interaction, coupled with the proximity and links to a centre of technology, which is the principal differentiator between a Science Park and a more conventional business park. The cluster effect is important and extends beyond the boundaries of an individual park. It is not therefore surprising that the more successful and prosperous Science Parks are located in cities with strong universities and research organisations. Edinburgh, Birmingham,Cambridge, Manchester and Oxford all have strong Science Parks.

Some of the important characteristics of these clusters are:

* Strong academic base in science
* Skilled workforce
* Effective research and development networks in the region
* Entrepreneurial culture
* Attractive environment so people wish to live in the area
* Good local schools
* Good local support infrastructure; access to finance, legal teams, accountants etc.

BUSINESS INCUBATORS AND INNOVATION CENTRES

Most Science Parks, but not all, will have a Business Incubator or Innovation Centre as part of their model. A Business Incubator or Innovation Centre does not necessarily need to be on a Science Park but where it is, it will often be considered a generator of tenants for the wider Science Park. The term Business Incubator, Innovation Centre or Enterprise Centre is widely used but they vary considerably in terms of what they seek to provide and some are actually no more than managed work space.

On a Science Park, a Business Incubator or Innovation Centre will provide small business suites with units of normally less than 100m² (1,000 sq ft) on short term 'easy in easy out' agreements with common services and meeting rooms as with most business centres. Space will normally be let at market rates but there will be additional business support services provided either directly or through third party partners at often minimal or low cost to the recipient. Indeed, a good Innovation Centre will be delivering these services to a wider area so that tenants do not need to be in the Centre or even on the Park which contributes to the marketing of the Park. The Centre will interact with the local business community and regional higher education institutes and research organisations to provide a catalyst for the growth of new and early stage business opportunities in their region. This activity will often be supported by the local authority but some parks will see this activity as the pipeline for future tenants not only for the Incubator/Innovation Centre but also for the park. A good Innovation Centre or Incubator will act as a Flagship in terms of generating activity and publicity for the benefit of the wider Science Park and will usually be focused on a particular sector or sectors of the technology market place.

The majority of Incubators and Innovation Centres will provide basic workshop or office specification space, usually with good high speed internet connectivity. A few will offer more specialised space for biotechnology or other laboratory users. Some have been established in response to the closure of a research organisation, such as Boots in Nottingham or Roche in Welwyn Garden City. The availability of specialised laboratory space at low or reduced cost, coupled with a skilled workforce, can provide a unique opportunity to create a new broader business base at a time when the potential job losses in the local market place is seen as a major problem.

In contrast, managed workspace will provide simple offices or workshops for small businesses without any additional management support or advice and while they may well serve a useful local need they are not Incubators or Innovation Centres. Business centres provide an additional level of service and provide active support to their tenants and seek to create a business community within the centre but will not be actively looking to promote economic activity. They are often supported by local authorities and well run centres can thrive in private ownership within a vibrant local economy but are unlikely to be actively supporting business incubation.

Incubators are often considered high risk investments given the short term nature of their agreements and the comparatively poor covenant strength of their tenants. However, they generally charge inclusive rental packages and in well managed centres can, once established, achieve consistently high occupancy rates with the opportunity to generate additional revenue from other activities such that the net rent to the investor can often match or better the income from conventionally let buildings. In over twenty five years the occupancy of the St John's Innovation Centre in Cambridge has very rarely fallen below 90% and then usually only when a larger tenant matured and moved onto new premises. If this can generate leads to the wider park, both from indirect marketing and tenants expanding, the centres can provide a positive contribution to a park.

A new business Incubator, The Exchange, was opened at Colworth Science Park near Bedford in 2012, through a partnership between Goodman and Unilever, to provide conference and catering facilities in addition to fully serviced laboratories and offices on flexible terms on this 500,000 sq ft park which specialises in food health and wellness. The partnership was sold to Palmer Capital and Wrenbridge in June 2014 which will be Palmer Capital's second venture into Science parks having bought Discovery Park in Kent in 2012. As a new source of funding into Science Parks this is a positive sign for the sector.

There are companies running Incubators who will take a direct investment stake into the businesses in their Incubators and will be actively involved in the business. This requires a different business model and is more closely akin to investment into a business rather than a property investment and has been successful in the USA.

OWNERSHIP

The Science Park movement is now reaching maturity and should be considered an investment sector in its own right. The original Science Parks were often funded by academic institutions seeking to promote the growth of businesses utilising the technologies within academia and to foster links between academia and the wider business communities. In general, while they were not considered on strict investment criteria, they were expected to deliver a return to their promoters in the longer term. These parks are generally found close to the major universities; The Surrey Research Park or Herriot Watt would be typical examples.

The success of these first parks encouraged others into the field and the public sector saw the potential benefits in the growth in knowledge based businesses. Local authorities started to encourage Incubators and Science Parks in association with their local higher education institutes and a number of publically funded research organisations also saw the benefit of promoting businesses alongside their own research. This support was further enhanced following the creation of the regional development agencies under the Labour Government. A number of leading Science Parks are joint developments between various stakeholders including local authorities and academic institutions such as Manchester Science Parks whereas Birmingham Science Park at Aston is a local authority initiative.

Today over 50% of Science Parks have a direct investment from an academic institution and a further 20% from publically funded research organisations and over 50% also have some aspect of funding from local authorities and development agencies. It is difficult to see significant further public sector initiatives, though the Local Enterprise Partnerships(LEPs) are beginning to become engaged, so it is a concern that there are few investment and development companies who have taken an interest in the Science Park movement. At present only about 20% of parks are controlled by the private sector and while some of these will also have public sector funding, they are expected to provide an economic return to their investors. These investment or development companies, such as Aviva, MEPC or the Best Network (LaSalle Investment Management), have appreciated the potential from Science Parks and can see that proactive management of their parks, coupled with knowledge of the sector(s) in which they are investing, can improve investment performance. Unfortunately there are too few private sector companies who understand the sector or are perhaps even aware of the opportunities it presents.

Innovate UK, formerly the Technology Strategy Board, is the UK's national innovation agency and has established nine Catapult Centres in response to a report by Herman Hauser in 2010. Their performance was reviewed by him in a report published in November 2014 in which he concludes that they have made a positive contribution and recommends further centres should be opened. The Centres themselves will have a physical presence but are primarily a catalyst for Innovation and Development in their specific sector. Through them Innovate UK will deliver other services to support business using their Knowledge Transfer Network and other initiatives. Science Parks should be working with the Centres operating in their region for the benefit of their tenants.

Sectors

Science Parks encompass a wide variety of uses and the building specifications will reflect this. Many technology companies are engaged in computing and software for which a standard office specification is appropriate, though possibly with enhanced cooling systems for server rooms and most investment companies or developers would be entirely comfortable with the specification. At the other extreme, a fully fitted biotechnology building will have an extensive fit out, probably costing rather more than the basic shell and core building. This requires a different approach by the developer/investor who may choose to simply provide a shell and core building, leaving the occupier to fund the fit out, usually on the basis of a 20 or 25 year lease with a rent geared to a proportion of an office rent. The basic shell and core will itself potentially be more expensive than a similar shell specification for a straightforward office use due to the requirement for the capacity for additional plant and equipment which might include an extra floor just for plant.

A more creative approach by a limited number of developers has been to split the package with a basic rent related to the shell and core building and a further 'rent' related to the fit out of the laboratory where the deal will be more related to a financial package than a traditional property one. Again the package may have different elements relating to the different elements of the fit out and the potential life expectancy of the components. This may give the occupier greater flexibility to modify the fit out as requirements change over time. Churchmanor Estates Company and Aviva Investors at Chesterford Research Park near Cambridge have successfully developed laboratory buildings and recently completed a 60,000 sq ft building pre-let to Biofocus where they assisted with the fit out.

The strength of the tenant covenant will play an important part in the negotiations as a specialised fit out may have limited value should a tenant vacate necessitating an expensive refit before the building is capable of occupation by another company.

Technology companies operate in growth markets often with higher margins than companies in more traditional markets. They are prepared to pay a premium for the right premises in the right location with the appropriate facilities to attract and retain their employees. Company failure rates on Science Parks are reputedly lower than average but this needs substantiation.

Science users are historically considered to come from the pharmaceutical sector but increasingly there is a confluence of life sciences and technology to the extent that physical and materials engineering are becoming inextricably linked to health care solutions. MEPC has recently acquired land adjacent to Silverstone race track and are developing buildings for technology rich enterprises who's work in motorsport leads to innovations that are applicable to med tech and all research and development activities.

There are a few parks where laboratories are provided for early stage businesses but these will generally be to a fairly basic specification, in terms of the fit out, with further adaptation required to meet individual needs of tenants. Babraham Research Campus in Cambridge has successfully developed Bioincubator buildings for early stage biomedical enterprises and has received Government funding to build more. MEPC is planning to develop an innovation centre at Milton Park in response to very strong demand from small and medium sized science companies often spinning out of academic institutions which will provide up to 30 much needed small laboratories with write up space.

FUNDING

The majority of existing Science Parks have been established through public sector funding in various forms, often working together and including universities, local authorities, the former regional development agencies and research organisations. While in some instances the initiative may have been in response to economic deprivation, in others it has been to exploit the economic potential of research within the local institutes. In the latter case the private sector can be involved in supporting the initiative as development can be economically viable.

Larger property investment funds will have an exposure to 'out of town business parks' and through these probably already have an exposure to science based tenants. These tenants will possibly have located to an area based on the potential 'cluster effect' and parts of the London market, the M4 corridor and Cambridge are typical.

The companies are looking for the right environment for their employees and their business and the criteria that make a good business park are equally valid for a science based company, including crèche facilities and good transport links. Larger companies will generate their own links with academia and research organisations and will therefore look for the best premises and terms to meet their requirements within a general geographical location. Science Parks should be seeking to provide a better environment to attract these businesses through the provision of services tailored to the specific needs of technology companies.

Technology companies will tend to be in growth sectors and, in our opinion, can often operate to slightly different economic cycles to the reminder of business in a region. If so they should also be considered as a separate asset class offering an opportunity to spread risk within the property sector. However, data is required to support this contention and at present, partly due to the nature of the ownership of a significant number of the parks, this is not available. With Parks which are in private ownership, or even where funds own an individual building on a Science Park, they will be assessing the performance of their assets by reference to the performance of other assets and, in particular, other property funds and as such are likely to provide information to the most widely used benchmark, the Investment Property Databank (IPD) Index. At present there is no IPD Index covering the Science Park sector.

CONCLUSION

As part of their 30th birthday celebrations in 2014 UKSPA carried out a Study to support their assertion of their catalytic role in supporting growth in the UK economy. The study provides an overview on the impact of science parks on the commercialisation of research, start ups and the growth of technology based firms, their contribution in creating high quality employment in a local area, the growth of exports and the attraction of foreign investment. The Science Park movement intends to use the findings to support them in attracting more funding from both the public and private sectors as only a small number of the property investment companies and government bodies are sufficiently aware of the sector and the potential it offers. It is essential that Science Parks promote themselves as a complimentary sector capable of offering competitive returns to investors and further spreading their risk from regional offices and business parks whilst offering job creation for local and national government.

Part Two:

The Regulatory Environment

2.1 COMPETETION LAW AND POLICY IN THE UK

Emanuela Lecchi, Watson Farley & Williams LLP

INTRODUCTION – SUBSTANCE & ENFORCEMENT

Competition law has two levels of complexity. First, it is *substantively* complex. Second, it is complex when it comes to *enforcement* due to the interplay between the workings of various regulators and courts both at the national level (in each member State of the European Union) and at the European level.

In this chapter[1] we aim to bring some clarity to the main concepts of competition law as it applies in the UK, and give a brief overview of recent reforms to the existing regime. Readers with an interest in competition law should consider a specialised text for an in-depth analysis.

COMPETITION LAW – THE SUBSTANTIVE RULES

Competition law at the European level and in most member States of the European Union (including the UK) is designed to deal with three main substantive situations, namely:

a. Anticompetitive agreements (Art. 101, Treaty on the functioning of the European Union ("TfEU"); Chapter I Prohibition, UK Competition Act 1998 ("UKCA 1998"));
b. Merger control (EU Merger Regulation; UK Enterprise Act 2002 (EA 2002); and
c. Abuse of a dominant position (Art. 102, TfEU; Chapter II Prohibition, UKCA1998).

---

[1] This chapter is condensed from a longer chapter on competition law published in [2009] in the Law Society Commercial Law Handbook, edited and co-authored by David Berry.

In addition, both at the European level and in some member States (including in the UK) the competition authorities (and, in the UK, the sector regulators) can investigate sectors which may show features (often structural features) which impede competition in some way (so-called "market investigations").

There are then two sets of rules often dealt with by lawyers specialising in competition law. These are, on the one hand, rules designed to deal with **State Aids** and rules designed to ensure a level playing field amongst companies **bidding for public works and services**; and, on the other hand, rules to ensure that **parallel imports** (usually of pharmaceuticals, or cars) are not impaired throughout Europe. State Aids, public procurement and parallel import have a "common market" *raison d'être* and are assessed, amongst others, with reference to underlying concepts of distortion of competition. Space dictates that they cannot be considered further here.

RECENT COMPETITION LAW REFORM IN THE UK – THE COMPETITION AND MARKETS AUTHORITY

In recent years there have been several important changes to competition law in an attempt by the UK Government to make the existing regime more effective in terms of enforcement and quality of decision making. The Enterprise and Regulatory Reform Act 2013 (ERRA), which received Royal Assent on 25 April 2013, contained a number of important reforms in relation to competition law.

The most notable change was made to the institutional architecture. In 2014 the Office of Fair Trading (OFT) and the Competition Commission (CC) were abolished and replaced by a new body, the Competition and Markets Authority (CMA). The rationale behind creating a single authority is that it will be able to deploy resources more effectively than the two separate bodies, the OFT and CC, were able to do. The CMA's single objective is to ensure the smooth running of the markets and protect the best interests of the consumers, businesses and ultimately, the economy. In practical terms, this reform has given the Government limited but increased powers to intervene in the assessment of mergers or the investigation of markets.

In addition, the CMA has gained additional powers, including in relation to information gathering and the use of interim measures in merger situations. The CMA is still in its first few months of operation A more detailed overview of the role of the newly created CMA is discussed where relevant below.

Following the Financial Services (Banking Reform) Act 2013, the Financial Conduct Authority (the "FCA") will have concurrent competition powers from April 2015 for the provision of financial services. As a consequence, the FCA will be able to enforce competition law in the financial sector in the same way as the CMA is able to. The financial services sector has been identified by the Government as a key sector of focus in the coming years. This is also highlighted by the formation of the new payment systems regulator, who will also have concurrent competition powers from 2015.

THE THREE MAIN SUBSTANTIVE SITUATIONS

In the experience of the authors, the following Figure 2.1.1 helps to understand the three main situations with which competition law is mostly concerned, by visualising each situation by reference to a bar designed to represent market concentration.

Figure 2.1.1 The three main situations addressed by competition law

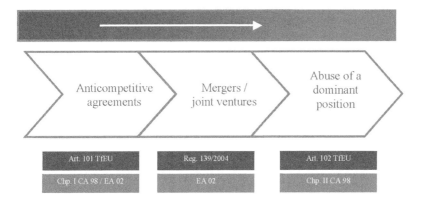

The left-hand side reflects a situation where the marketplace is close to a situation of perfect competition, progressively moving towards a situation of "dominance" and, on the extreme right, monopoly.

Anticompetitive Agreements
The first situation, *"anticompetitive agreements"*, occurs in a relatively unconcentrated marketplace, where there would remain a sufficient number of "undertakings" to compete, provided that the market remained competitive. If these undertakings enter into anti-competitive agreements, and, for example, agree to fix prices, or partition marketplaces, then the fact that there may continue to exist a number of undertakings is irrelevant as those undertakings will effectively agree to act as one single independent undertaking (a monopolist), rather than as an individual profit maximising firm might.

The most pernicious form of anticompetitive agreements is, of course, the "cartel". In Europe, the focus is on tackling cartels: leniency and immunity applications are accepted by "whistleblowers" and the amount of fines has increased considerably. A number of jurisdictions in the European Union have introduced criminal sanctions for executives involved in cartels (cfr. Ireland, the UK, Hungary and Romania amongst others). One of the more controversial reforms resulting from the ERRA is the removal of the requirement of "dishonesty" as an element to the offence. Some have argued that this effectively removes the *"mens rea"* of the offence. There is an exclusion where customers were given the "relevant information" which includes the names of undertakings involved and nature of the agreement. One issue with this is that it may not be commercial, or practical in some cases to publish information of a commercial nature and whether this will have a chilling effect on deals remains to be seen.

Defences to the cartel offence exist where the individual did not intend to conceal the nature of the arrangements from customers (or the CMA) and where reasonable steps were taken to ensure the nature of the arrangements would be disclosed to professional legal advisers for the purposes of obtaining legal advice.

Under the new CMA, Cartel enforcement remains a significant priority. The CMA aims to conduct a greater number of investigations and to resolve them more quickly. The programme of leniency for "whistleblowers" will continue, as will working closely with sector regulators to enhance competition in the energy, financial services, water and telecoms sectors.

When practitioners talk about "block exemptions", they refer to a set of guidelines and rules that can offer a "safe harbour" for agreements which may otherwise, on first consideration, be caught by the prohibition against anticompetitive agreements (the first situation, (a) above). Under no circumstances (at least under the law as it currently stands) can the block exemptions offer a "safe harbour" for conduct amounting to an abuse of a dominant position. The role of the block exemptions is often misunderstood: it is not the case that undertakings must ensure that their agreements fall within a block exemption to be permitted; agreement outside of the block exemption are not automatically void, but they do not benefit from a presumption of compliance with the competition rules. More information on the block exemptions is provided in Appendix 1.

There are limited exclusions from the prohibition on anticompetitive agreements in the UK. These are typically for public policy and national security reasons. Until 6 April 2011, there was a more general exclusion for land agreements. This exclusion has now been revoked and as of 6 April 2011, land agreements (whether entered into before or after that date) are subject to the Competition Act 1998.

Abuse of a Dominant Position

The third situation, *"abuse of a dominant position"* occurs in a relatively concentrated marketplace, where one undertaking (or a small number of undertakings together) can act in a manner that impedes competition, usually because of their market shares and the existence of reasons why these market shares cannot be eroded over time (for example, barriers to entry). The assessment of market dominance and of abuse is complex. There is no exhaustive list of conduct that constitutes abuse of a dominant position but competition lawyers distinguish between *Exploitative Abuses*, **those which** affect companies and entities dependent on the dominant undertaking (customers and suppliers) and *Exclusionary Abuses*, which relate to actions which have as their object the elimination of competitors and/or competition. There are two principal types of exploitative abuse: excessive pricing and price discrimination. Exclusionary conduct can be categorised as either price related or non-price related. Exclusionary price abuses include predatory pricing, margin squeezes and discounts. Exclusionary non-price abuses include refusal to supply and tying and bundling.

Under the ERRA, the CMA has power to compel individuals to provide information for the purposes of an investigation, and increased powers of intervention to impose interim measures where it considers that "significant damage" is likely. Previously this was set at the higher threshold of "serious irreparable harm", so interventions by the CMA pending investigative outcomes are likely to become more frequent.

Merger control

In the middle between anticompetitive agreements and abuses of a dominant position is *"merger control"*: markets become more concentrated as undertakings merge. Pre-screening of mergers is considered to be essential for the proper workings of the system. The European Commission has exclusive jurisdiction under the *EU Merger Regulation* ("EUMR") (Council Regulation (EC) No. 139/2004) to investigate mergers with a community dimension. Mergers must be notified to the European Commission if they meet each element of either of the tests set out in Appendix 2.

If a merger falls outside the scope of the EUMR, it is still necessary to determine whether clearance is required from any national merger authorities. (If the merger is notified to three or more countries within the EEA, the notifying party may request that the merger is referred to the European Commission (Art. 4(5) EUMR)).

When a merger taking place in the UK does not have a community dimension, the UK system of merger control needs to be considered. The UK currently has a voluntary merger notification regime. Parties are not required to notify mergers to the regulatory body, which is now, as of April this year, the CMA (as seen above). Although the system is voluntary, parties should be mindful of the CMA's ability to open own-initiative investigations into mergers after they have been completed. The CMA has jurisdiction to investigate mergers where either:

- The target has an annual UK turnover that exceeds £70 million; or
- The merging parties will together supply or acquire at least 25% of a particular description of goods or services in the UK, or in a substantial part of the UK, and the merger leads to an increment in share.

The thresholds will remain the same under the ERRA and the regime will remain voluntary; however a number of changes have been implemented, designed to strengthen the existing rules. These include penalties for parties for failing to respond to information requests from the CMA; suspension powers for proposed and completed mergers (previously these only existed for completed mergers); financial penalties of up to 5% of worldwide group turnover for breach of CMA orders and increased fees for filing merger notification forms.

The recent case of Ryanair/Aer Lingus has given rise to a pertinent debate about the interplay of merger control at EU and national level, particularly over the issue of minority shareholdings. In this context it is important to consider the likely implications in the UK of merger control reform in the EU. The EUMR applies a concept of change of control only where there is a lasting change of control, whereby only minority shareholdings that confer control or 'decisive influence' are caught by the rules.

In some national jurisdictions, notably in the UK, there are lower thresholds for change of control. In the UK, any mergers leading to the acquisition of "material influence" in the target are reviewable. Material influence is typically found in cases of shareholdings above 25% but could also be found in board representation or financial arrangements such as debt financing.

This disparity led to the European Commission launching a public consultation in June 2013 in which it proposed to broaden its powers to review non-controlling minority shareholdings. These proposals will centre around the idea that the European Commission could review mergers meeting a lower control threshold, similar to material influence in the UK in potentially problematic deals with an EU dimension.

MARKET INVESTIGATIONS

Where the CMA considers that particular features of a market may give rise to anti-competitive effects which may not be caught by the Art. 101 and 102 TfEU or UKCA 1998 provisions, it may investigate these markets where it considers that consumer harm may result. Generally speaking, these market investigations focus on industry practices rather than the actions of specific firms. Under the ERRA, the CMA has a shorter statutory timetable to conduct the market investigation than the Competition Commission had previously.

Following a market study, the CMA may make a market investigation reference to what is now known as the CMA Panel (which is the panel within the unified CMA which deals with issues previously dealt with by the Competition Commission). The reference can be made where the CMA has reasonable grounds for suspecting that any feature, or combination of features, of a market in the UK for goods or services prevents, restricts, or distorts competition in connection with the supply or acquisition of any goods or services in the UK, or a part of the UK. Under the ERRA, there has also been a reduction in the timetable for the reference period to 18 months. This can be extended up to 24 months where there are "special reasons" for doing so, with a six month time limit (extendable to ten months) for the implementation of remedies. In addition the ERRA has introduced formal information-gathering powers for the CMA in the market study phase. The CMA can impose interim measures to reverse pre-emptive action by parties. The Competition Commission did not have these powers under the prior regime. As was the case for the old regime, a reference may also be made by some sector regulators. If a market is found not to be working properly, the CMA could impose wide-ranging regulatory or structural reforms.

Whilst still in its relative infancy, the CMA has set out six areas of strategic significance for review where it considers there to be the greatest potential for consumer harm. They are: the online and digital economy; technology and emerging sectors; regulated sectors and infrastructure markets; the provision of public services; sectors that are important to economic growth and recovery; and conduct that leads to consumer exploitation. The approach of the CMA reflects the current European Commission's plans to harmonise EU regulation and competition law in the "digital age", and we should consequently expect a similarly focus on the digital economy here in the UK.

Alongside the digital economy, the CMA has also pledged to focus on the energy, financial services, public services and retail sectors in the coming years. The ongoing investigations into the Energy and Retail Banking markets are due to end in December 2015 and May 2016 respectively, both being conducted under the compressed timetable of 18 months discussed above.

CORE CONCEPTS IN COMPETITION LAW

In each of the three situations identified in Figure 2.1.1 above, there are two main concepts to be considered at the outset. First, that the rules apply to "undertakings". Second, that "market definition" is the foundation of competition analysis.

The Concept of an "Undertaking"

"Undertaking" is not defined in either the TfEU or the Competition Act 1998, which applies in the UK. The ECJ (now the Court of Justice of the European Union) has stated that the term "undertaking" "*encompasses every entity engaged in an economic activity, regardless of the legal status of the entity and the way in which it is financed*" (see *Höfner & Elser* v. *Macrotron* [1991] ECR I-1979).

Generally speaking, all companies, individuals and other entities (including charities) that engage in a commercial or economic activity will be undertakings for the purpose of competition law. There are two key difficulties with the definition of an "undertaking":

a. What activities are "economic activities"; and
b. Whether two legally separate bodies (such as two companies) can be considered a single undertaking.

A group of companies can be a 'single economic entity' if they have unity of conduct on the market. For example, a subsidiary company and a parent company may be one undertaking if they act as a single unit on the market, e.g. if the parent company is the directing mind of the subsidiary. Therefore, coordinated conduct between a parent and subsidiary company that distorts competition is unlikely to be prohibited as there is only one undertaking (the test under Art. 101 TfEU is that there are "two or more undertakings"). Similarly, commercial agents, such as those falling under the Commercial Agents Directive, and their principals will usually be considered to be the same undertaking for the purposes of competition law as the agent typically provides goods or services on behalf of the principal.

The Concept of a "Market"

An agreement can only be anticompetitive when it has as its "object or effect" the "prevention, restriction or distortion of competition" in a "market". Every one of the block exemptions will only confer a "safe harbour" provided that the parties to an agreement have a market share in a "relevant market" below prescribed thresholds (parties whose market shares are above the thresholds do not necessarily fall foul of the competition rules). Merger control is designed to prevent those (and only those) mergers that lead to a significant impediment to effective competition in a market. Equally, an abuse can only occur when an undertaking is "dominant" (can exercise market power) in a market.

An undertaking is said to have market power if it can raise prices without suffering a significant decline in demand.

The definition of a product market involves consideration of demand-side substitutability and supply-side substitutability. Demand and supply-side substitutability are used to delineate the products concerned by and the geographic scope of relevant markets, which in some (limited) scenarios will also have a temporal dimension; for example, in the case of markets where it is not possible for customers to substitute between time periods, as in the case of, e.g. the supply of train tickets at certain times of day (see OFT Notice on Market Definition, Guidance Notice OFT 403, section 5).

The exercise of market definition consists in identifying the effective alternative sources of supply for customers of the merging undertakings, both in terms of products or services and the geographic location of suppliers. Detailed rules on market definition apply.

ENFORCEMENT ISSUES

The CMA is the body responsible for enforcement. Where an undertaking is found to be in breach of the UK or EU competition rules, that undertaking can be fined up to 10% of its annual turnover. An "undertaking" means a single economic entity: a parent company can be fined up to 10% of the group's turnover if its subsidiary is in breach of competition law. Therefore, parent companies should take an active role in ensuring that all of their group companies are compliant with the competition rules.

Additionally, individuals that breach competition rules could be imprisoned, face personal fines and could be disqualified from being a director for fifteen years. In the UK, individuals may be extradited under the EA 2002 s.191, if they breach competition rules in the USA or in any other country that has a criminal offence that corresponds to the cartel offence in the EA 2002.

SECTOR REGULATORS

Utilities and communications services were historically provided by State-owned companies. With liberalisation, the sectors were opened up to competition. The UK regulators in the key sectors are listed below in Table 2.1.2.

Table 2.1.2 UK key regualators

Regulator	Responsibilities
Ofcom	Communications and post
Ofgem	Gas and electricity
ORR	Rail regulation
OFWAT	Water services
Utility Regulator NI	Northern Ireland energy, water and sewerage regulation
CAA	Aviation

COMPETITION ENFORCEMENT INSTITUTIONS

The key European and UK competition enforcement institutions, together with some of their responsibilities are set out in Table 2.1.2 below.

Table 2.1.2 Competition enforcement institutions

UK Institutions	
Competition Markets Authority (CMA)	• The Competition and Markets Authority (CMA) has replaced the Competition Commission and the competition functions of the Office of Fair Trading. • The CMA is responsible for enforcing the Competition Act 1998, carrying out merger control functions and conducting in-depth market investigations with a primary duty to promote effective competition. • The key sectoral regulators in Tab 2.2.1 above also have concurrent powers with the CMA in Competition Act cases and in-depth market investigations in their sectors. The sectoral regulators do not have the leading role in merger control cases in their sector.
Financial Conduct Authority (FCA)	• Regulates financial firms providing services to consumers and maintains the integrity of the UK's financial markets. • It focuses on the regulation of conduct by both retail and wholesale financial services firms.Powers include regulating conduct related to the marketing of financial products. • Responsible for regulating the consumer credit industry from 1 April 2014, taking over the role from the Office of Fair Trading.
Payment Systems Regulator (PSR)	• From April 1st 2015 the PSR will promote competition, to promote innovation, ensure that payment systems are developed and operated in the interests of service-users, working alongside the Financial Conduct Authority and Competition and Markets Authority, thus creating a more competitive banking industry.
Competition Appeal Tribunal (CAT)	• hears appeals on the merits of decisions made under Competition Act 1998 – appeals against decisions of the CMA or other sector regulators; • hears actions for damages under Competition Act 1998; • reviews mergers and market references; appeals against regulatory decisions of Ofcom.
High court	• Claimants can bring private actions for damages to the High Court. Claims can follow on from an adverse finding by the CMA or CAT or can be brought directly to the High Court.

EU Institutions	
European Commission (DG Competition)	• enforces competition rules of the TfEU; • reviews mergers with a European dimension (phase I and phase II); • publishes guidelines on the application of competition rules for consumers, industry and national competition authorities.
General Court (was Court of First Instance (CFI))	• Hears appeals against decisions of Community institutions, including DG Competition.
Court of Justice of the EU (was European Court of Justice (ECJ))	• hears references for preliminary rulings – the Court of Justice provides decisions or reasoned orders on specific points of law referred from national courts; • hears appeals against decisions of the General Court.

SUMMARY CHECKLIST

Activities in the contexts of:

a. Negotiating with customers
b. Cooperation with competitors
c. Mergers/joint ventures
d. Information gathering
e. Unilateral action by "dominant" companies

Activities which are likely to be permitted and those which are likely to be prohibited under EU Law are listed in Table 2.1.3 below.

The main block exemptions at the time of writing are identified in Appendix I and threshold for European notification under merger control are listed in Appendix II.

Table 2.1.3 Activities likely to be permitted and prohibited

LIKELY TO BE PERMITTED	LIKELY TO BE PROHIBITED
A. NEGOTIATING WITH CUSTOMERS OR SUPPLIERS	
<ul><li>Checking aggregated industry-wide statistical data.</li><li>Offering discounts to customers based on the suppliers' costs.</li><li>Setting recommended retail prices ("RRPs") for distributors, provided that there is no explicit or implicit pressure on the distributor to follow the RRPs and that you are not dominant.</li></ul>	<ul><li>Agreeing minimum or fixed resale prices with a distributor or a supplier.</li><li>Preventing a distributor from exporting a product to another EU member State.</li><li>Charging a distributor prices that vary according to whether the goods are to be resold in a specific country or exported to another EU member State.</li><li>Preventing a distributor from selling a product to a customer because they intend to export the product to another EU member State.</li><li>Preventing manufacturers of components from selling these components as spare parts.</li></ul>

LIKELY TO BE PERMITTED	LIKELY TO BE PROHIBITED
B. CO-OPERATION WITH COMPETITORS	
• Attending meetings of trade association. • Discussing health and safety. • Discussing proposed regulatory changes.	• Bid-rigging, i.e. allocating tenders between competitors. • Agreeing production quotas with competitors. • Agreements or arrangements with the effect of dividing product or geographic markets with competitors. • Warning a competitor to stay away from "our territory" or specialist field. • Discussing prices, profit margins, rebates or discounts with competitors. • Discussing the cost of key raw materials with competitors that also source similar materials. • Agreeing to boycott particular suppliers or distributors. • Discussing prices or profit margins with competitors. • Agreeing current or future prices with competitors. • Discussing terms of sale or supplier/customer business relationships. • Discussing strategic plans, such as pricing strategy or product/territorial expansion. • Agreeing with a competitor to fix the timing for the introduction of a new technology that has been developed independently. • Delaying quoting a price until you know a competitor's price.

LIKELY TO BE PERMITTED	LIKELY TO BE PROHIBITED
C. MERGERS / JOINT VENTURES	
• Entering into a research & development co-operation agreement with a competitor, where both parties are free to exploit the results independently.	• Agreeing with a competitor to fix the timing for the introduction of a new technology that has been developed independently.
D. INFORMATION GATHERING	
• Obtaining information on competitors' sales and prices from publicly available sources or from customers in the ordinary course of business. • Giving historical sales data to a third party which distributes aggregated, industry-wide sales figures to participants.	• Contacting customers specifically to gather competitors' pricing information ("fishing trip").

LIKELY TO BE PERMITTED	LIKELY TO BE PROHIBITED
E. UNILATERAL ACTION BY "DOMINANT" COMPANIES	
	• Excessively high pricing, i.e. where the price has no reasonable relation to the economic value of the product. • Selling goods below cost in order to foreclose competitors from the market. • Offering discounts to customers in a discriminatory manner, e.g. offering discounts to customers if they source all or most of their supplies from you. • Suggesting recommended retail prices to a distributor. • Refusing to sell a product to a purchaser with an existing business relationship. This will be permitted only if there are sound commercial reasons for refusing to sell, such as poor credit history. • Refusing to sell a particular product unless it is purchased with another non-essential product from your dominant market. • Insisting that a distributor must stock the whole range of your products.

APPENDIX 1

Block Exemptions

The main EU block exemptions in force at the time of writing are listed below:

Block exemption	Council Regulation
Vertical agreements – agreements between non-competitors – new block exemption	Regulation 330/2010 Expires 31 May 2022
Specialisation/production agreements – unilateral specialisation; outsourcing; reciprocal specialisation; joint production agreements	Regulation 1218/2010 Expires 31 December 2022
Research and development – joint R&D and joint exploitation of findings	Regulation 1217/2010 Expires 31 December 2022
Motor vehicle distribution – purchase, sale and resale of motor vehicles or spare parts; repair and maintenance services	Regulation 461/2010 Expires 31 May 2023
Technology Transfer Block Exemption Regulation – certain patents, knowhow and software copyright licensing agreements	Regulation 216/2014 Expires 1 May 2026
Insurance – joint establishment of calculations and tables; establishment of non-binding standard policy conditions for direct insurance	Regulation 267/2010 Expires 31 March 2017
Road and inland waterways groupings	Regulation 169/2009 Indefinite duration
Liner consortia – joint operation of liner shipping transport services	Regulation 906/2009 25 April 2020

The *Commissions Notice on Agreements of minor importance (de minimis notice) 2001/C368/07* applies to agreements where the combined market share of competing/ potentially competing undertakings ("horizontal agreements") is less that 10% and less than 15% for non-competitors ("vertical agreements"), provided they do not contain any hardcore restrictions.

APPENDIX 2

Merger Control:
Thresholds for European Notification

Issue	Primary test	Alternative test
Combined worldwide turnover	> €5,000 million	> €2,500 million
Individual EU-wide turnover	At least two parties > €250 million	At least two parties > €100 million
Presence in three member States		Combined turnover of all parties in at least three member States > €100 million AND Individual turnover of two or more of the parties in three of the member States referred to above > €25 million
Exception	A merger will not have a Community dimension if each of the parties achieves more than two-thirds of its EU-wide turnover in one and the same member State.	

The European Commission can refer the merger analysis to a national authority where the concentration would affect competition in a distinct market of a specific member State (Art. 4(4) or Art. 9 EUMR).

2.2 REGULATION OF FINANCIAL SERVICES

Ravinder Sandhu, Watson Farley & Williams LLP

INTRODUCTION

The existence of a legal and regulatory framework that provides investors and others with confidence in the market as a place to do business has never been more important than now.

The financial crisis that started in 2007 led to significant reforms to the system of financial services regulation in the UK, resulting in a new regulatory regime provided for in the Financial Services Act 2012 (FS Act) which came into force on 1 April 2013.

Until 1 April 2013, the structure of the regulatory system in the UK comprised a single central regulator, the Financial Services Authority (FSA), responsible for both the prudential and conduct regulation of all types of financial firms, and an overriding framework statute, the Financial Services and Markets Act 2000 (FSMA), governing businesses in the UK undertaking financial services – a term that encompasses a broad and diverse range of activities from banking and insurance to fund management, securities trading and even funeral contracts.

On 1 April 2013, the FSA was abolished and replaced with a "twin peaks" structure where the prudential and conduct of business regulation is to be carried out by two separate entities, the Prudential Regulation Authority (PRA), which is aimed at ensuring the stability of financial services firms, and the Financial Conduct Authority (FCA), referred to as the City's behavioural watchdog.

The Bank of England is responsible for the direct supervision of the stability of the whole of the UK banking system through its Financial Policy Committee (FPC), which can instruct the two new regulators.

The FS Act implemented significant changes to the UK financial regulatory framework. Its main role was to make extensive changes to the FSMA to establish the new regulators and to set out their additional powers.

THE FCA

The FCA is the financial services regulator responsible for both the conduct of all firms authorised under the FSMA (including those regulated for prudential matters by the PRA) and for the prudential regulation of firms not regulated by the PRA.

The FCA has taken on a majority of the FSA's roles and functions, including its function as the United Kingdom's Listing Authority (UKLA). In addition the market abuse regime is within the FCA's remit.

In carrying out its role, the FCA needs to comply with both its strategic objective of "ensuring that the relevant markets function well" and advance the following three operational objectives:

- The consumer protection objective – securing an appropriate degree of protection for consumers (which covers a broad spectrum of persons);
- The integrity objective - protecting and enhancing the integrity of the UK financial system; and
- The competition objective - promoting effective competition in the interests of consumers.

So far as is compatible with advancing the consumer protection objective or the integrity objective, the FCA is to discharge its general functions in a way which promotes effective competition in the interests of consumers.

THE PRA

The PRA is a subsidiary of the BoE and is responsible for the prudential regulation and supervision of banks, building societies, credit unions, insurers and major investment firms.

The PRA has a general objective to promote the safety and soundness of PRA-authorised persons. In promoting safety and soundness, the PRA focuses primarily on the harm that firms can cause to the stability of the UK financial system.

When dealing with insurers, the PRA must have regard to the insurance objective of contributing to the securing of an appropriate degree of protection for those who are or may become policyholders.

The Board of the PRA includes the Governor of the BoE (as Chairman) and the Chief Executive of the FCA.

THE FPC

The FPC is a committee of the Court of Directors of the BoE. It is chaired by the Governor of the BoE and other members include the PRA chief executive (who is also the BoE Deputy for prudential regulation) and the FCA chief executive.

Unlike the FCA and PRA, it does not have direct regulatory responsibility for firms. Instead, it is responsible for macro-prudential regulation – regulation aimed to mitigate systemic risks within the financial system as a whole.

The FPC has a primary objective of identifying, monitoring and taking action to remove or reduce systemic risks with a view to protecting and enhancing the resilience of the UK financial system. The secondary objective of the FPC is to support the economic policy of the government which includes growth and employment objectives. It is required to produce financial stability reports detailing how each action it takes is consistent with its objectives.

The FPC also has the power to give directions and make recommendations. In particular, it may give directions to the FCA or the PRA requiring it to exercise its functions so as to ensure the implementation, by or in relation to a specified class of regulated persons, of a macro-prudential measure described in the direction. The FPC's "macro-prudential toolkit" currently consists of the following tools:

a. The sectoral capital requirements (SCR) tool: this allows the FPC to adjust financial institutions' capital requirements against exposures to specific sectors over time;
b. The countercyclical capital buffer (CCB) tool: this allows the FPC to direct that firms' capital requirements should be increased in response to threats to financial stability. At the FPC meeting on 24 March 2015, the FPC decided to maintain the CCB rate for UK exposures at 0%;
c. The leverage ratio tool: this allows the FPC to set maximum ratios of total unweighted liabilities to capital and to change those ratios over time; and
d. The housing market tool: this permits the FPC to make directions on the owner - occupied mortgage markets relating to loan-to-value (LTV) ratios and debt-to-income ratios (DTI).

The FPC may also make recommendations to the FCA and the PRA about the exercise of their respective functions. The recommendations may relate to all regulated persons or to regulated persons of a specified description, but may not relate to the exercise of the functions of the FCA or the PRA in relation to a specified regulated person. Should the FCA and PRA decide not to implement recommendations made on a "comply or explain" basis, they are required by the FS Act to explain publicly their reasons for not doing so.

THE FSMA

The FSMA is a framework statute. Its principal provisions form the basis of the UK's regulatory system, with secondary legislation, rules and regulations being made under and pursuant to those primary provisions. The two main provisions setting the overall parameters within which financial services businesses are required to operate are the general prohibition on the carrying on of regulated activities (section 19, FSMA) and the restriction on the making of financial promotions (section 21, FSMA). These two sections provide that persons are prohibited from carrying on or promoting regulated business activities unless licensed, authorised or exempt by the FCA or PRA. These provisions are at the centre of the structure of the FSMA and form the basis for the regulatory system established beneath it.

General Prohibition

As noted above, the FCA's and PRA's regulation of financial services within the UK is based on a system of approval and licensing of market participants, whether they are commercial or investment banks, insurance companies, securities dealers, financial advisers or others. The system provides for minimum standards and criteria for persons to qualify for approval and licensing where the legislators consider that the end-consumers may require regulatory protection.

The activities requiring licensing are termed "regulated activities". The FSMA prohibits the carrying on of a regulated activity in the UK other than by authorised or exempted persons. This prohibition is referred to as the "general prohibition" and is the central building block around which the FSMA and secondary legislation is structured. A person who undertakes a regulated activity without authorisation will be subject to criminal and civil sanctions. Furthermore, an agreement that results from a breach of the general prohibition will be unenforceable against the other contracting party.

Although the FSMA provides examples of regulated activities, this term is not exhaustively defined in the FSMA itself. Instead, it is defined in secondary legislation - the Financial Services and Markets Act 2000 (Regulated Activities) Order 2001 (RAO) - and includes the following activities:

a. Accepting deposits (i.e. banking business);
b. Dealing in investments as principal or agent;
c. Arranging deals in investments;
d. Managing investments;
e. Safeguarding and administering investments;
f. Establishing or operating collective investment schemes;
g. Advising on investments; and
h. Insurance related activities, including (i) effecting and carrying out contracts of insurance and (ii) assisting in the administration and performance of contracts of insurance.

Investments are defined by the RAO and include deposits, contracts of insurance, shares, debt instruments, units in collective investment schemes and various derivative instruments.

As stated above, only authorised or exempt persons may carry out regulated activities. Such persons may include securities traders and advisers, firms of accountants or UK corporate finance firms that act as sponsors or brokers on a market listing. Exempt persons include recognised investment exchanges, such as the London Stock Exchange.

The regulated activities a person carries on determines whether it will be regulated by the FCA for conduct and prudential purposes (a FCA-Authorised Firm) or whether it will be regulated by the FCA for conduct purposes and by the PRA for prudential purposes (a PRA-Authorised / Dual-Regulated Firm). The FSMA (PRA-regulated Activities) Order 2013 (SI 2013/556), which came into force on 1 April 2013, identifies which of the RAO activities are PRA-regulated activities. Activities which are designated as PRA-regulated activities include accepting deposits and effecting and carrying out contracts of insurance.

Financial Promotion

In addition to regulating the activities described above, the FSMA also regulates communications made to third parties in relation to those activities. In particular, the FSMA prohibits a person from communicating, in the course of business, an invitation or inducement to engage in investment activity. This is more commonly known as the "financial promotion" restriction. The FCA is responsible for the regulation and supervision of financial promotions.

The financial promotion regime is based on similar foundations to the general prohibition and does not apply if the person making the communication is an authorised person under the FSMA, or if an authorised person approves the contents of the communication, or if the communication is covered by an exemption.

Breach of the financial promotion restriction may give rise to civil liability or constitute a criminal offence. Resulting agreements may also be unenforceable and recipients of the unlawful communication may be entitled to recover their investment and to claim compensation for any loss suffered.

Details of the financial promotion regime are set out in secondary legislation: the Financial Services and Markets Act 2000 (Financial Promotion) Order 2005 (FPO). The term "financial promotion" is itself cast in extremely broad terms to encompass any communication on whatever medium. It includes face-to-face oral representations and representations made during telephone conversations (referred to as "real time communications") as well as communications made in letters, emails or on a website (referred to as "non-real time communications"). Hence, communications with potential investors, inviting them to purchase shares or other investment products, will be caught, as will communications concerning insurance and banking products and the provision of investment management and investment advisory services.

Although the financial promotion restriction is wide, the FPO contains a large number of exemptions from the restriction. Examples of exemptions include intra-group communications and communications made by a company to its members, creditors or employees. The application of certain exemptions depends on the type of communication being made and whether or not it is solicited by the recipient. Exemptions may also apply by virtue of the nature of the recipients, for example, communications made to investment professionals, certified high net worth individuals or companies will (if they meet the specific requirements of the exemption) be exempt from the financial promotion prohibition, as such investors are not regarded as requiring higher levels of investor protection.

The financial promotion regime will generally apply to all communications with a UK link, irrespective of whether the recipients are located inside or outside the UK and whether the communication is an incoming or outgoing communication. Communications originating outside the UK will, however, only be caught if they are capable of having an effect in the UK, otherwise they are exempt. It is important to note that, if relevant, the general position may be altered by European Union (EU) legislation.

The intention is to regulate the provision of business advice or the making of statements upon which a customer or client (other than sophisticated investors) may seek to rely in making a financial or investment decision. The aim is to ensure that individuals and businesses establish the necessary credentials, legitimacy and expertise through a system of approvals and licensing before they engage with third parties and take a pecuniary reward as a result. This is supported by the FCA requirement to treat customers fairly by recommending that, when preparing and approving financial promotions, authorised persons consider whether the material:

- Is clear, fair and not misleading;
- Provides a balanced picture of the product or service;
- Matches what the product or service delivers; and
- Will be easily understood by their customers.

SECONDARY LEGISLATION AND THE FCA HANDBOOK

Secondary legislation is issued, modified, replaced and supplemented as the marketplace develops, and is tailored to particular kinds of businesses, such as the carrying on of deposit-taking businesses by banks, dealing in securities and derivatives and the operation and promotion of investment funds and other collective investment schemes.

Secondary legislation is further supplemented with rules and guidance issued by the FCA and the PRA and contained in the FCA Handbook (which applies to both FCA-Authorised Firms and PRA-Authorised Firms, containing conduct of business requirements that apply to all regulated firms and prudential requirements relevant to FCA authorised firms) and the PRA Handbook (which applies to PRA-Authorised Firms only, and contains the relevant PRA prudential requirements).

Both the FCA and the PRA Handbooks include overriding standards for all market participants, as well as detailed conduct of business rules and a code of market conduct. The FCA Handbook is also responsible for implementing the requirements of the Markets in Financial Instruments Directive (MiFID), which aims to harmonise financial services regulation within the European Economic Area and increasing competition and consumer protection in investment services. MiFID will be replaced by the MiFID II Directive and the Markets in Financial Instruments Regulation, under which Member States must publish and adopt measures transposing the MiFID II Directive into national law by 3 July 2016, and must apply those provisions from 3 January 2017, subject to certain exceptions.

Conduct of Business Rules
The FCA's Conduct of Business rules apply to all firms with investment business customers in the UK. The extent to which the rules apply depends upon the nature of the products and services provided, and the type of client to which they are offered. The rules are set out in the Conduct of Business Sourcebook (COBS).

The COBS is designed to provide guidance on the regulatory requirements across the range of activities that may be carried on by regulated persons and covers, amongst other things:

- Financial promotions;
- The provision of information and advice to clients;
- Dealings in investments; and
- The management of investments.

The most recent COBS came into force in 2007 and is intended to enable companies to design their business processes and promotional material to suit their particular circumstances to design their business processes and promotional material to suit their particular circumstances and those of their customers. To this end, the COBS is based on general principles rather than detailed rules and processes. The COBS also implements the conduct of business requirements of the MiFID.

Market Abuse
Although the FSMA primarily regulates financial services through a system of authorisation and licensing, it also sets out a framework for tackling wrongful

behaviour in the financial markets (better known as market abuse), which complements the criminal offence of insider dealing. These rules are designed to enhance market integrity and confidence for the benefit of market participants.

The FCA has taken over the FSA's responsibilities for regulating the market abuse regime and targeting market abuse is a regulatory priority, particularly in an uncertain economic climate where market instability can increase the scope for market abuse.

The current market abuse provisions implement the Market Abuse Directive (MAD), and harmonise the requirements relating to insider dealing and market manipulation across the EU.

Market abuse arises in circumstances where market participants have been unreasonably disadvantaged (whether directly or indirectly) by others in the market who, amongst other things, have:

- Used to their own advantage information that is not generally available;
- Created a false or misleading impression; or
- Distorted the market.

Under the FSMA, the FCA has the power to impose financial penalties for market abuse. The FCA has published a Code of Market Conduct, which forms the first chapter of the FSA's Market Conduct sourcebook to supplement the provisions that deal with market abuse and provide guidance as to whether or not behaviour constitutes market abuse.

MAD is to be repealed in accordance with legislation implementing the Market Abuse Regulation (MAR) and the Directive on Criminal Sanctions for the Market Abuse (CSMAD) with effect from 3 July 2016. Together, MAR and CSMAD will introduce an updated EU market abuse regime, incorporating a wider range of sanctions.

Other Provisions

In addition to the above, the FSMA also establishes the FSA's powers of intervention, which include broad powers of investigation and powers to penalise persons contravening the FSA's rules or the provisions of the FSMA, including the ability to fine contraveners or withdraw a person's authorisation.

The FSMA is a comprehensive statute. This chapter provides a summary of the principal provisions upon which financial services regulation in the UK is based, but the FSMA also makes provisions in relation to other relevant matters, including provisions for:

- The official listing of securities, derived from EU legislation;
- An investors' compensation scheme;
- The establishment and operation of an independent financial ombudsman to

whom investors and market participants can complain;

- The establishment and operation of regulated and unregulated collective investment schemes; and
- Changes of control over authorised persons.

In addition, under the FS Act, there is a prohibition on certain kinds of market behaviour, including making false or misleading statements or creating false or misleading impressions, which are in addition to the provisions relating to "market abuse" referred to above.

2.3 INTELLECTUAL PROPERTY

Mark Tooke, Watson Farley & Williams LLP

INTRODUCTION

Intellectual property rights ("IPRs") play an important and often essential role across business activities. There are many different types of IPRs that include the protection of intangible business assets, such as know-how, reputation and goodwill, and the products of creative effort. Most IPRs have a commercial value and can be bought, sold and licensed.

It makes good business sense to identify the IPRs you have (particularly where your business is investing in innovation and research, or sells goods or services on the basis of its reputation) and to ensure that they are properly protected. It is also important, where you can, to identify as early as possible areas of potential conflict with IPRs owned by third parties, so that infringements of their IPRs can be avoided.

Some IPRs attract protection automatically on their creation or commercialization; others require registration with an official body (usually the UK Intellectual Property Office; IPO) before they are recognized and afforded protection by the courts. This chapter gives a description of the main commercially significant IPRs that may be protected and exploited in the UK.

COPYRIGHT AND RELATED RIGHTS

Copyright is the collective name for the body of law that grants to makers of written, dramatic, musical and artistic works the ability to control how their creations are used. Both economic and moral rights are provided under the copyright law of the UK:

- Economic rights allow the creator to control the commercial exploitation of their work and to prevent it from being copied without permission.
- Moral rights protect works from being manipulated or distorted in a way that is detrimental to the interests or reputation of the creator.

In the most basic terms, copyright is a right to prevent unauthorized copying. Rights related to copyright include the ability for the owner of a work to prevent others from doing things that, although not strictly copying, are essential to the commercial exploitation of a work; for example, the public performance of music, the adaptation of a play or the broadcasting or public showing of a film or television programme.

Automatic Protection

Copyright protection covers original literary, dramatic, musical and artistic works, published editions, sound recordings, films and broadcasts, where the creator has expended a sufficient level of "skill, judgement and labour" in creating the work.

Protection is automatic as soon as the work is recorded, in any form or medium. There is no official registration system in the UK and, therefore, there are no fees to pay or formal action required in order to obtain copyright protection. However, it is good practice to keep a detailed record of how and when the work was produced in case a creator is ever obliged to prove (e.g. in court) that they created the work and that it was not copied. Although not a legal requirement in the UK, owners can mark their work with the international copyright symbol ©, together with their name and the year of publication.

As well as receiving and affording reciprocal protection to nationals and residents of other EEA states, the UK is a member of several international copyright conventions, and works created by UK nationals or residents are automatically protected by the copyright law of other signatory countries; nationals or residents of these countries are automatically afforded reciprocal protection in the UK.

Ownership and Duration

Copyright can be bought, sold, inherited, transferred or licensed (wholly or in part). As a result, the economic rights to a copyright work can belong to someone other than the creator. Moral rights can be waived, but cannot be transferred. The length of protection offered by copyright depends on the type of work and there are specific rules for each work, but in general, the length of protection is as follows:

- Literary, dramatic, musical or artistic works and film: the life of the author, plus 70 years;
- Sound recordings and broadcasts: 50 years or 70 years (depending on whether a sound recording has been published or played in public); and
- Published editions: 25 years.

Infringement

Copyright infringement occurs when a work is copied or used without permission. Matters of infringement are ultimately decided in court. Infringement will not occur if the work is used with the permission of the owner or in relation to certain very limited purposes, which include non-commercial research, private study, criticism, review and teaching in schools.

DATABASE RIGHT

A database, for the purposes of protection, can be defined as a collection of independent works, dates or other materials that are, firstly, arranged in a systematic and methodical way and, secondly, are individually accessible by electronic or other means. Copyright protection will apply to a database if there is originality in the selection or arrangement of the contents. If there has been substantial investment in the creation of a database then, in addition to copyright protection, a separate, stand-alone database right may also apply. Copyright and the database right can both apply to the same database.

Database right gives automatic protection as soon as a database exists in recorded form and applies to both electronic and paper databases. It provides protection against the unauthorized appropriation and distribution to the public of the whole or a part of the contents of a database, and lasts for 15 years.

TRADEMARKS AND PASSING OFF

A trademark is a distinctive sign that identifies certain goods and/or services as those produced or provided by a particular person or enterprise. The owner of a registered trademark has the exclusive right to use or identify goods and/or services using that trademark. If a sign is being used by a business as a trademark but is not registered, it may be capable of protection using the law of passing off.

Trademarks can greatly assist the customers of a business by serving as a badge of origin for the business's goods and services. Registered trademarks also offer businesses the ability to protect the investment it makes in its brand identity and in the reputation of its goods and services. Additionally, without trademark protection the competitors of a business may try to take unfair advantage by using confusingly similar, distinctive signs to market their products and services.

Types of Trademark

Trademarks may be words, letters, numerals, symbols, drawings, fragrances, colours used as a distinguishing feature and/or three-dimensional signs (eg. the shape and packaging of goods and sounds, as long as the trademark is capable of being represented graphically). Although the possibilities are many, and may seem almost limitless, a trademark must be distinctive and capable of distinguishing the goods or services of one undertaking from that of another.

Registration Process

To be registered, a trademark must be distinctive, not similar to any earlier marks and not be deceptive, or contrary to law or morality. Both British trademarks and European Community (EC) trademarks have effect in the UK. There are two main ways to acquire such a trademark:

1. Apply to the IPO for a British trademark; or
2. Apply to the Office for Harmonization in the Internal Market for an EC trademark.

Official fees must be paid to obtain both types of registered trademarks. A British trademark offers protection in the UK only. An EC trademark has effect in every member State of the EC, as well as the UK, but the application process is generally more expensive and slower than for a British trademark.

A trademark application must specify the types of goods and services in respect of which protection is sought (the more types, the more expensive the application). Prior to registration, the application can be rejected by the relevant office on a number of grounds, or challenged and blocked by third parties. Once granted, registration lasts for 10 years but can be renewed indefinitely on payment of a renewal fee for successive ten year periods as long as the trademark is being used.

Benefits of registration

Registering R trademark confers on the owner the exclusive right to use the mark for the goods and services it covers in the UK. Once a trademark has been registered, the symbol ® can be put next to the trademark to warn others from using it. Care must be taken, however, as use of the symbol ® for unregistered trademarks is a criminal offence.

Other benefits conferred to the owners by registered trademarks include the following:

- The ability to sell or license the trademark;
- The ability to commence legal action against anyone who uses it without permission;
- The generation of value in an asset that may be used as collateral for financing; and
- The ability to involve the UK Trading Standards, the police and the other law enforcement agencies, who can bring criminal charges against counterfeiters and pirates.

Passing Off

If an unregistered mark is used without the owner's permission, it may be possible to claim protection from the courts under the law of passing off. To be successful in a claim for passing off, a claimant must prove that:

- He/she is the owner of the unregistered trademark and has built goodwill or reputation attached to the goods and services he/she supplies to the public;
- The defendant has made a misrepresentation to the public (intention is irrelevant), leading or likely to lead the public to believe that goods or services offered by the defendant are the goods and services of the claimant; and
- He/she has suffered or is likely to suffer damage from the illegitimate use of the mark.

A legal action claiming passing off can be expensive, as proving the sufficient reputation or goodwill in an unregistered trademark is often difficult for the claimant, and usually involves showing an extensive and lengthy prior use of the trademark in the UK (five years or more).

PATENTS

If you have invented a product that is new or a new way of doing something, a patent may be granted. A patent having effect in the UK can be acquired in two ways:

1. By application to the IPO for a British patent; or
2. By application to the European Patent Office for a European patent (which is in fact a single-application process, leading to the grant of a "bundle" of separate national patents, including a UK patent).

(NB At the time of writing, August 2015, not all of the steps necessary for establishment of an EU unitary patent have been taken). Irrespective of which application process is used, a UK patent (once granted) has effect only in the UK, and lasts for 20 years from the date of filing of the application provided the prescribed annual renewal fees are paid following the expiry of the fifth year. A patent may not be the best or only way to protect an invention. It may be possible to protect aspects of the invention as registered or unregistered designs, registered trademarks or using the law of copyright.

Scope

In basic terms, a patent is designed to protect how things work, what they are made of or how they are made. To be granted a patent, the invention in question must be new, must involve an inventive step, must not be obvious to someone with knowledge and experience in the subject and must be capable of being applied on an industrial scale.

A patent will not be granted for certain types of innovations, including:

- Scientific or mathematical discoveries;
- Literary, dramatic, musical or artistic works;
- Most computer programs;
- Animal or plant varieties;
- Methods of medical treatment or diagnosis; and
- Inventions that are deemed against public policy or morality.

Application Process

The process of applying for a patent can be complicated, and the assistance of a qualified patent attorney is recommended. It is also recommended that a search of published patents and existing public know-how (so-called "prior art") be conducted before an application is made to confirm that the invention is new and has not already been patented.

The registration process requires full disclosure to the IPO of information explaining how the invention works, and this information is made available to the public whether the application is successful or not. Once a patent is granted, yearly renewal fees must be paid for the rights to continue.

Protection

The owner of a patent can prevent anyone from using, distributing, selling or commercially making the invention without permission. If a patent is infringed, it is up to the owner to take appropriate action.

DESIGNS

In the UK, a design may be legally protected in one of the three ways.

- Registered designs: the look of a product (including its surface decoration, colour and ornamentation) may be protected by seeking registered design protection, provided certain requirements are met, the main ones being that the design is new and has individual character (i.e. it is distinctively different from existing designs). To obtain a registered design, an application must be made to the IPO, with the required fee. Registration lasts for a maximum of 25 years.
- Design right: the shape or configuration of a product may be protected from illegal copying by use of the law of unregistered design right. Design right is free and, subject to certain qualifications, arises automatically where the shape of a new product is original. Design right lasts for the shorter of the 10-year period after the first marketing of products that use the design or the 15-year period after the creation of the design. Licences of right (meaning that anyone

is entitled to a licence to make and sell products copying the design) may be available toward the end of the protection period. Design right does not protect two-dimensional designs (in respect of which registered designs or copyright may be relevant).

- Copyright: if an original design is artistic and is not intended to be mass-produced, it will be protected against illegal copying by the law of copyright.

PLANT VARIETY RIGHTS AND GEOGRAPHICAL INDICATIONS

There are a number of IPRs that, although less well known than those mentioned previously, can be valuable to those engaged in certain specialist areas of business. These include the following:

- Plant variety rights (which offer protection to plant breeders); and
- Geographical indications (which offer protection to producers of foodstuffs with a strong connection to a particular area, eg. Stilton cheese).

CONFIDENTIAL INFORMATION AND TRADE SECRETS

Information that is not covered by one of the IPRs may nonetheless be protected by its owner if it is not public knowledge and the owner keeps it a secret. The law imposes or implies certain duties of confidentiality in particular situations, but these can be strengthened or widened by contract; for example, a new and distinctive business proposition may not meet the requirements for patent protection, but before disclosing it to potential new business partners the owner may require them to sign a confidentiality agreement that will prevent them from using the idea themselves or disclosing it to third parties.

REMEDIES FOR INFRINGEMENT

A range of remedies is available to the owner of an IPR depending on the IPR in question. These include the following:

- Account of profits: if the defendant has made profit out of infringing another's IPRs, the IPR holder can elect to have this awarded instead of damages.
- Damages: damages are usually calculated on a loss of profits or on a royalty basis. Generally, they are compensatory in nature and are to put the holder back in the position that they would have been in if the infringement had not occurred.
- Criminal penalties: serious infringement of certain IPRs, such as copyright, trademarks and patents, may amount to a criminal offence (eg. piracy on a commercial scale), leading to criminal sanctions including imprisonment and fines.

Other remedies include delivery up and destruction of articles infringing IPRs. Injunctions ordering a defendant not to carry on certain activities may be granted by the court; however, injunctions are discretionary remedies and may not always be awarded, and interim injunctions (awarded before the final decision of the court in an action for infringement) are granted only if it is a matter of urgency or in the interests of justice.

EMPLOYEES AND IPRS

In many cases, the IPRs created by an employee in the course of their employment will, according to UK law, belong automatically to their employer. However, the type and nature of the IPRs created and the scope of the employee's duties can sometimes result in the employee being considered the first owner of the IPRs; for example, a junior employee who invents something that is not directly connected with the main business of the employer may claim that they are the first owner of the invention, on the basis that it was not created in the course of their employment or as part of their normal duties.

To avoid such problems, it is strongly recommended that every UK employment contract contains clauses that expressly set out who will be the first owner of the IPR created while the employee is employed by the employer.

Where the creator of an IPR is not an employee of the business but is a contractor engaged by the business, the usual rule (that the business is the first owner of any IPRs created at its request) does not apply in the absence of an express agreement between the parties to the contrary. In this situation, the IPRs will usually belong to the consultant who created it, with an express or implied licence being granted to the business to use the IPRs. Although in some circumstances it may be inferred that a contractor is under an obligation to assign the IPRs to the business, a clear written agreement between all parties engaged in the work is highly recommended.

THE PATENT BOX

There are a range of incentives for R&D administered by HM Revenue & Customs, particularly for small and medium enterprises (SMEs). A new addition to these incentives is the Patent Box, which came into effect in April 2013 and seeks to reward those innovations that result in a qualifying patent. In simple terms, profits that arise from certain patents will be taxed at 10%. The regime will also apply to other qualifying intellectual property rights such as regulatory data, supplementary protection certificates and plant variety rights.

2.4 COMPANY FORMATION – METHODS AND LEGAL IMPLICATIONS

Mark Jackson, Mazars

INTRODUCTION

The UK has an open and transparent system for setting up companies. No permission is required to set up a business, although some industries, such as financial services, may require specific authorisation before they can commence trading. This chapter looks at the options available to investors wishing to set up a new enterprise in the UK or expand an existing one.

COMPANY TYPES

In the UK, there are four main types of company that can be separated into two categories:

Unlimited Liability
The owners of organisations having unlimited liability are personally liable for all the debts that the business may incur. Should the enterprise fail, the owners may have to liquidate some (or all) of their personal assets in order to pay the enterprise's outstanding debts. Examples of such businesses are sole traders, unlimited companies and partnerships.

Limited Liability
The owners of these types of business are only liable for the amount that they originally invested in the company. Should the business fail, investors in the failed company will only lose the original value of their investment or the amount they agreed to contribute, as set out below.

In the UK there are three main types of Limited Liability Company:

1. A private company limited by shares – the liability of members is limited to the amount unpaid on shares they hold.
2. A private company limited by guarantee – members are only liable for the amount they agreed to contribute to the company's assets should the company be wound up.
3. A public limited company – these companies are permitted to sell shares to the general public, and their liability is limited to the amount unpaid on shares they hold.

FORMING A COMPANY

The majority of businesses setting up in the UK register as limited companies and are therefore subject to the Companies Act 2006. This Act sets out the rules governing the setting up and day-to-day running of companies.

To set up a company in the UK, you can use a company formation agent, arrange for your professional adviser (solicitor or accountant) to form the company, or you can incorporate a company yourself by using the web incorporation services operated by Companies House.

Companies House is the government agency responsible for incorporating, dissolving and registering companies, and making company information available to the public.

Eligibility for Company Directorship

Any company setting up in the UK must have formally appointed officers. The number of officers depends on the type of company that is being set up:

- A private company must have at least one director and may have a company secretary. The company's sole director cannot also be the company secretary.
- A public company must have at least two directors and the company secretary must hold a formal qualification.

Procedure to Incorporate a Company

To register a private or public limited company, the following documents must be sent to Companies House:

- A Memorandum of Association
- Articles of Association
- Form IN01

The Memorandum of Association is a document that sets out the company's name and the address of its registered office (which must be a valid UK address).

The Articles of Association set out the standard rules and procedures that state how the company runs its internal affairs. A company can adopt the model articles in their entirety as prescribed by the Companies Act 2006.

Form IN01 provides details of the first director(s) and company secretary (if appointed), the address of the company's registered office, a statement of the issued share capital on incorporation and the names and addresses of the subscribers (first shareholders). The directors must also include personal details such as their address, date of birth, occupation, nationality and country of residence.

CAPITAL FOR PRIVATE AND PUBLIC LIMITED COMPANIES

When first registering, the first members of the company must each agree to take at least one share and their names must also be included on the memorandum. Shares have a par value, which can be of any amount. The value of the shares held by the shareholders (number of shares multiplied by their par value) is the company's 'Issued Share Capital'.

The amount of share capital required differs depending on the type of company you are setting up and the requirements of the business. A private limited company has no maximum or minimum authorised or issued share capital required in order to commence trading, save that it must have at least one share in issue unless the regularity requirements of its particular industry require a specific minimum. The rules for public limited companies are more complex.

Capital for Public Limited Companies

For a public limited company to trade, the requirement is that it must have at least £50,000 or Euro equivalent of issued share capital, of which 25% must have been paid up and the whole of any premiums (that is the amount investors are asked to pay for the shares less the par value) on these shares. As with private companies a company operating in a particular industry may be required to have a significantly higher issued share capital.

Once the share capital has been paid the company will need to send the relevant information to the Registrar of Companies, who will then issue a 'Certificate to commence business and borrow'. Without this certificate the company cannot trade or carry on business.

MANAGEMENT OF COMPANY

A private limited company must have at least one director, and a public limited company must have at least two directors. In both types of company, the directors are responsible for the day-to-day running of the business, and are personally responsible for any decisions made. The main responsibilities include:

- Producing the annual accounts and making sure that a copy of these is sent to Companies House (a legal requirement for both public and private limited companies);
- Making sure any other information required by Companies House is sent there (for instance, notification of a change in address of the company's registered office or a change in the identity of the directors of the company).

Some of these responsibilities are required by law and, as such, any breach by the directors is a criminal offence for which the penalties can be severe (prosecution, fines, and/or imprisonment).

OTHER FORMS OF COMPANY

Sole Traders
Sole traders are businesses set up by individuals. They are typically small and usually financed by the individual. They are unlimited liability businesses, so the owner is responsible for meeting all the debts of the business. Sole traders are not required to publish annual accounts, although they must keep financial records for tax purposes.

Partnership
Regarded as a step up from a sole trader, this is where a group of two or more individuals set up a business together. Partnerships are regulated by the Partnership Act 1890 (as amended). Normally, a partnership agreement is drawn up before trading commences and this agreement usually contains information on the names of the partners of the business, how profits and/or liabilities will be shared, how the partnership will be run, and the procedures for dissolving the partnership.

As with a sole trader, partnerships have unlimited liability, with the partners jointly and severally liable for all debts, that is, if one or more of the partners is unable to meet these debts, then the remaining partners will become liable for them. A partnership in England and Wales does not have a separate identity from its partners, as a company has from its members. Partnerships are not required to publish their annual accounts, although they must keep financial records for tax purposes.

Limited Partnership

It is still possible to register a limited partnership under the Limited Partnership Act 1907, although they have been superseded in the main by the Limited Liability Partnership (see below). Limited partnerships are very similar to partnerships with these exceptions:

- There are two types of partner: general partners, who are liable for all the businesses debts, and limited partners, who have limited liability up to the amount of money they have invested as capital in the business. Limited partners cannot take back any money invested in the business during the partnership's lifetime, nor can they have a management role in the business.
- By law, limited partnerships must be registered at Companies House by sending a form signed by all partners giving the name of the business, what the business does, and details of all the money invested by the limited partners.

Limited Liability Partnership (LLP)

The Limited Liability Partnerships Act 2000 created a new business vehicle, the Limited Liability Partnership (LLP) which combines the organisational flexibility and tax status of a partnership with limited liability for its members.

Members of limited liability partnerships benefit from limited liability because the partnership, rather than its members, is liable to third parties. However where the members of an LLP are professional people, a negligent member's own personal assets may still be at risk because under general law, a professional person owes a duty of care to his or her client. While the government originally intended to restrict the use of LLPs to members of regulated professions, the LLP Act makes LLPs available to two or more persons carrying on any trade or profession. In view of this, as the LLP combines the tax/NIC (National Insurance Contributions) advantages of partnerships with incorporation and limited liability, it may well become a popular vehicle for small businesses.

LLP profits are taxed as if the business were carried on by partners in partnership, rather than by a body corporate. There are no special tax treatments, or reliefs, available to LLPs or members of LLPs beyond the treatments or reliefs available to partners and partnerships.

The European Public Limited-Liability Company

The European Public Limited-Liability Company or 'Societas Europaea' (SE) is available to businesses operating in more than one member state. It has been possible to set up this type of legal entity in the UK since October 2004.

The purpose of the SE is to make it easier for businesses to structure and carry out cross-border activities within the EU. In practice, however, they are probably of more value for presentational purposes, although the ability to change the domicile of an SE by an administrative procedure can prove to be useful in certain circumstances.

The SE European Public Limited – Liability Company

An SE may be created on registration in any one of the Member States of the European Economic Area (EEA). Member States are required to treat an SE as if it is a public limited company formed in accordance with the law of the Member State in which it has its registered office. UK national laws that apply to public limited companies also apply, in many respects, to SEs registered in the UK.

Overseas Companies Carrying on Business in the UK

Some companies might still want to do business in the UK without registering a company in the United Kingdom. This can be done by setting up a branch.

A branch is part of an overseas limited company that employs local representatives in the UK to carry out its trading activities. To register a branch with Companies House, the company must complete a OSIN01 Form (this lists details such as the company's name and directors, and details of the branch being set up), the most recent set of audited company accounts, and a certified copy of their constitutional documents (both these must be in the home language of the company). If these are not in English, then a certified translation made in the country where the company was incorporated must also be submitted. A non-UK company can establish one or more branches and must register each one separately, but it is only necessary to file the constitutional documents once.

Overseas companies may also wish to set up a joint venture with a UK firm, usually through a partnership or a limited company.

2.5 UK IMMIGRATION

Angharad Harris and Devan Khagram,
Watson Farley & Williams LLP

INTRODUCTION

The UK government is keen to promote economic opportunities by encouraging overseas investment and the immigration of skilled individuals. The government implemented a points-based system (PBS) in 2008 to replace the various immigration options that were previously available to individuals wishing to enter the UK to seek employment or to explore business and investment opportunities. The aim of the PBS is to enable the UK to:

- Control migration more effectively;
- Tackle abuse; and
- Attract the most talented workers into the economy.

This article sets out an outline of the main business immigration options and key requirements under each category.

CAN I VISIT THE UK ON BUSINESS?

It is possible to enter the UK as a visitor to carry out limited business activities, although there are restrictions on the type of activities that can be undertaken. Permitted activities include:

- Board-level directors attending board meetings in the UK, provided they are not employed by a UK company (however, they may be paid a director's fee for attending the meeting);

- Attending meetings, including interviews that have been arranged before coming to the UK, or conferences;
- Negotiating or signing deals or contracts;
- Speaking at a conference where this is not run as a commercial concern and the conference is a "one off";
- Internal audits (including financial, regulatory, manufacturing and health and safety audits) carried out by auditors from within global corporations based overseas;
- Undertaking fact-finding missions; and
- Undertaking permitted specific, one-off training in techniques and work practices used in the UK, provided this is not on-the-job training.

Advisers, consultants, trainers or troubleshooters entering the UK as visitors must be employed abroad, either directly or under contract, by the same company (or group of companies) to which the UK company belongs. In addition, they must not get involved in actual project management or provide direct consultancy services to clients of the UK company.

A visitor must:

- Only intend to transact business directly linked to his/her employment abroad;
- Normally live and work abroad and have no intention of transferring his/her base to the UK (even on a temporary basis); and
- Receive a salary from abroad (although reasonable expenses may be paid for travel and subsistence during the visit).

In restricted circumstances, secondees from overseas companies that are not linked to the UK company may also qualify as business visitors.

HOW DO I KNOW IF I NEED TO OBTAIN A VISA BEFORE TRAVELLING TO THE UK?

Not all individuals travelling to the UK require a visa if they are visiting the UK. The Home Office website has a list of all countries from which nationals will require a visa before travelling to the UK to visit.

Entry Clearance
For longer term categories, if an individual is already legally in the UK but is changing their immigration status from one category to another, they can sometimes "switch" their immigration status without leaving the UK. This requires the applicant

to make an application to the Home Office before their current leave to remain ends, although they will need to check whether they are eligible to "switch" in-country.

Most visa applications under the PBS will require an application for prior entry clearance before the individual can travel to the UK. If an application for entry clearance is required, the applicant must make their application to a British Embassy/Visa Application Centre in their country of nationality or legal residence before travelling to the UK.

IF I HAVE A SCHENGEN VISA, DOES THIS ALLOW ME TO TRAVEL TO THE UK?

A Schengen visa allows an individual to travel freely among certain European member countries. The UK is not part of the Schengen Treaty and therefore having a Schengen visa will not permit someone who would otherwise need a visa and/or other immigration permission to enter the UK (although, for those applying at certain UK Visa Application Centres in China, the UK authorities, together with their Belgian counterparts, have recently introduced a combined application process so that a Schengen visa and UK visitor visa can be obtained at the same time). As of July 2015, the Schengen Treaty countries are:

Austria	Greece	The Netherlands
Belgium	Hungary	Norway
Czech Republic	Iceland	Poland
Denmark	Italy	Portugal
Estonia	Latvia	Slovakia
Finland	Liechtenstein	Slovenia
France	Lithuania	Spain
Germany	Luxembourg	Sweden
Switzerland	Malta	

Schengen visas are issued for varying amounts of time, but an individual will be allowed a maximum stay of 90 days within any six-month period. The scheme is intended for individuals who wish to move around Schengen member states for the purposes of business and tourism. A Schengen visa does not provide a right to work in a Schengen participating country, and in order to do so, an individual will generally need to obtain permission to work from the relevant country.

WHAT RIGHTS DO I HAVE AS A EUROPEAN UNION NATIONAL?

Nationals of certain countries have the right to live and work in the UK. This is known as a right of residence. Nationals with a right of residence include:

- nationals of the European Union (EU);
- nationals of Iceland, Liechtenstein and Norway; and
- Swiss nationals.

Iceland, Liechtenstein and Norway are not EU countries but are part of the European Economic Area (EEA) Agreement, which provides nationals of these countries with the same rights to enter, live and work in the UK as EU citizens. Swiss nationals are also included in the definition of "EEA nationals". Although not essential, people from the EEA can apply for a UK residence permit.

Croatia has now joined the EU. However, Croatian nationals will still need to obtain authorization to work before starting any employment. Once they have been working legally in the UK for 12 months without a break, they will acquire full rights of free movement; they can then apply for a residence permit confirming their right to live and work in the UK.

Where an individual has a right of residence, their spouse/partner, dependent children under 21 and other dependant relatives may generally join them in the UK. However, if their family members are non-EEA nationals, they should get an EEA family permit, which is a form of entry clearance (like a visa) prior to travelling to the UK, followed by a Residence Card once here. The spouse/partner of an EEA national is permitted to work in the UK.

If an individual is not an EEA national or the family member of an EEA national, they will generally require permission to undertake employment in the UK. Permission will be required even if they are going to undertake work-based training for a professional or specialist qualification, or a period of work experience.

TIER 1 OF THE PBS

The Tier 1 (General) visa which was designed to allow highly skilled workers to come to the UK has now closed to all applicants, and those who currently hold a valid visa in this category will need to switch into another route or leave the UK before their visa expires.

CAN I ESTABLISH A BUSINESS IN THE UK?

Under Tier 1 (Entrepreneur) of the PBS, an individual may apply for entry into the UK in order to set up, take over and be actively involved in the running of one or more businesses. To apply under the PBS and be accepted into the Tier 1 (Entrepreneur) category, an applicant must pass a points-based assessment, and must score a minimum of 75 points for attributes, 10 points for English language and 10 points for available maintenance (funds). They will need to have access to £200,000 (see exceptions below) for 90 days prior to submitting the application, which must be in a regulated financial institution and disposable in the UK. They must also provide the Home Office with a letter from each financial institution holding the money, confirming the amount of money available, as well as additional evidence if they are receiving third-party funding.

This £200,000 fund should be invested into a new or existing UK business. The amount of money invested must not include the value of any residential accommodation, property development or management.

Recent changes to this category have made it more attractive for those setting up business in the UK. It is possible for an entrepreneur to team up with another entrepreneur as part of an entrepreneurial team to rely on the same £200,000 to qualify under this visa category whereas previously they would have needed to show £200,000 each. Furthermore, those applicants who have access to £50,000 from a venture capitalist firm regulated and listed with the Financial Conduct Authority ("FCA"), from a UK entrepreneurial seed funding competition endorsed by UK Trade and Investment or from a UK government department can now also apply for a visa under this category. Applicants switching into this Tier 1 (Entrepreneur) category from the (Tier 1 Graduate Entrepreneur) visa (this is separate from the Tier 1 (Entrepreneur) category), may also benefit from these and other similar provisions.

The Home Office has also introduced a "genuine entrepreneur" test to allow them to assess whether the applicant genuinely intends to set up a business in the UK. Entrepreneurs must now submit evidence that they are genuine businessmen, including CVs and business plans, when applying for their visas.

One of the requirements for an extension under this visa is to create the equivalent of 2 full time jobs for persons settled in the UK, for a period of 12 months. Where an Entrepreneurial team has been granted a visa, both team members can rely on the jobs created by the team at the point their visas are extended. In addition, the applicant must also have registered as the director of a new or existing business, or registered as being in self-employment with HMRC, no more than 6 months after the grant of their visa.

Those who are very successful in their business in the UK and create the equivalent of 10 full time jobs for a period of 12 months have an accelerated route to settlement and can obtain Indefinite Leave to Remain ("ILR") in 3 years (usually it takes 5 years). Entrepreneurs who have generated business income of at least £5 million during a 3 year period also have an accelerated route to settlement.

Tier 1 (Entrepreneurs) can now spend as much as 180 days per year outside the UK and still qualify for ILR. However, please note that the permitted absences for nationality are more restricted (see below). Therefore, if the applicant's aim is to obtain British citizenship they will have to spend a greater amount of time in the UK.

There is also a Tier 1 (Graduate Entrepreneur) category that provides for UK graduate migrants with an endorsement from an authorised UK higher education institution or overseas graduates with a UK Trade & Investment endorsement to establish a business in the UK. The migrant must have formed a genuine and credible business plan and be seeking to set up their business in the UK. This visa can be used as a stepping stone to the Tier 1 (Entrepreneur) visa.

ARE THERE SPECIAL RULES FOR INVESTORS IN THE UK?

An application under the Tier 1 (Investor) category is suitable for individuals who have substantial capital assets available to invest in the UK. In order to be granted leave to enter the UK under this category, an applicant needs to show that they have at least £2 million to bring to the UK, which is held under the applicant's control in a regulated financial institution, and which is disposable in the UK.

These funds need to be held by the applicant for the three months prior to the application or they need to show the source of the funds in a manner specified by the Home Office. The applicant must also open a UK bank account with an FCA-regulated bank before they apply. Within three months of the visa being granted or the date they first enter the UK under this visa, the applicant must bring £2 million into the UK (if it is not here already) and invest their capital in UK government bonds, or in share capital or loan capital in active and trading UK registered companies (other than property related companies), subject to certain restrictions, for the duration of their stay in the UK under this visa.

Applicants are permitted to seek employment or can be self-employed or non-executive directors/consultants, but there is no obligation on them to take up employment in the UK.

In addition, it is possible for a potential investor currently in the UK under certain other immigration categories to "switch" into the Tier 1 (Investor) category. Furthermore, once established in the UK, the investor can extend their stay in the UK, provided that they can show sufficient evidence that they have invested at least £2 million within three months of arriving in the UK and still have permitted investments to this level.

To provide an incentive for applicants as Investors in the UK, the government have provided for an accelerated route to settlement for those who invest £5 million or £10 million in the UK. Whilst a Tier 1 (Investor) is usually eligible for ILR after 5 years in the UK, if the applicant invests £5 million in the UK they can obtain ILR after 3 years and if they invest £10 million in the UK they can obtain ILR after 2 years. It should be noted that the fast track is for ILR only. Those who invest £5 million or £10 million still have to be in the UK for 5 years before they are eligible to apply for British citizenship. Whereas investors who invest £2 million will have to be in the UK for 6 years.

Like Tier 1 (Entrepreneurs), Tier 1 (Investors) can now spend as much as 180 days per year outside the UK and still qualify for ILR. However, the permitted absences for nationality are more restricted (see below). Therefore, if the applicant's aim is to obtain British citizenship they will have to spend a greater amount of time in the UK.

Unlike most of the other categories, there is no English language or maintenance requirement to qualify for this visa.

TIER 2 OF THE PBS

Tier 2 of the PBS incorporates and adapts the old work permit regime. The main change to the system is that employers require a sponsorship licence and are required to issue certificates of sponsorship to employees they wish to employ. To obtain a sponsorship licence, a company will have to apply to the Home Office and provide various prescribed documents to show that they are a genuine and actively trading company. A sponsor will also have to implement various compliance obligations which will be assessed by the Home Office on a compliance visit either before or after the licence is granted.

The employee will then apply to their local British Embassy/Visa Application Centre for entry into the UK to work, at which stage the Home Office will assess the application to ensure the applicant scores sufficient points to qualify. Points will be awarded based on prospective salaries and the circumstances around their recruitment as well as the level of need in any given sector. Tier 2 (Skilled Migrant) is available in two categories:

1. Tier 2 (Intra-Company Transfer); and
2. Tier 2 (General).

Tier 2 (Intra-Company Transfer) applications involve a simplified procedure where the employee of a global company is transferring to a skilled post in a UK-based branch of the same company. The category is split into 4 subcategories:

1. Long-term Staff - for those who have worked for the company outside the UK for 12 months or more and who's annual salary will be £41,500 or more. They are permitted to come to the UK for up to 5 years;
2. Short-term Staff - for those who have worked for the company outside the UK for 12 months or more and whose annual salary will be more than £24,800. They are permitted to come to the UK for up to 12 months;
3. Graduate Trainees - to allow multi-national organisations to transfer recent graduate recruits to the UK business for up to 12 months of training; or
4. Skills Transfer - for migrants to transfer to an organisation or UK business to learn or transfer skills and knowledge to/from the UK offices for a period of 6 months.

Before an application is made under this category, the applicant must have:

- a valid sponsor; and
- certificate of sponsorship.

When an application is made, the applicant is awarded points based on their:

- future expected earnings;
- sponsorship; and
- available maintenance (funds).

When applying for permission to come to the UK under this category, or extending their permission to stay, the applicant does not have to meet the English language requirement.

Other applications, usually where the individual does not already work for the organisation abroad, may fall within the Tier 2 (General) category and this usually requires the employer to show that it cannot fill the post with a "resident worker" (including EEA nationals). This involves advertising the post in accordance with the Home Office specifications. Those earning more than £155,300, those in shortage occupations or exempt categories or certain students are exempt from the advertising requirements. By contrast to Tier 2 (Intra Company Transfer) all applicants under Tier 2 (General) need to meet the full English language requirement.

Those migrants applying under Tier 2 (General) from outside the UK and whose prospective earnings are less than £155,300 will be subject to the monthly limit on migrants. Their employer will have to apply for a restricted certificate of sponsorship and this will be granted if the applicant scores sufficient points to come within that particular month's limit.

Those already in the UK in certain other specified categories, those extending their stay or those whose prospective earnings will be more than £155,300 are not subject to the annual limit on economic migrants.

CAN I COME TO THE UK AS A SOLE REPRESENTATIVE OF AN OVERSEAS FIRM?

A sole representative application is only suitable where an overseas company that does not have a presence in the UK wishes to send one of its existing employees to set up a wholly owned subsidiary or register a branch. The overseas parent company must be in genuine operation; where it has been established for less than one year, it is unlikely to be deemed an eligible sponsor for these purposes.

In order for an application to be considered, the individual must:

- be authorised to take operational decisions on behalf of the overseas parent company without reference to the overseas parent company;
- have been recruited to the overseas parent company from outside of the UK;
- be directly employed by the overseas parent company; and
- have been employed by the overseas parent company for some time and hold a senior post.

The employee must not, however, be a majority shareholder in the overseas parent company and should not intend to carry out any other work while in the UK. In addition, the individual must be able to support themselves (and any dependants) in the UK, without recourse to public funds.

A sole representative application is normally made by the individual employee at a British Embassy/Visa Application Centre in their country of nationality or legal residence. Applicants are expected to spend a minimum of nine months a year in the UK; those who spend less time than this are not considered to be making genuine efforts to establish a commercial presence.

Once an application has been successful, the sponsor company must continue to conduct the majority of its business overseas. It will not be permitted to gradually move its operation to the UK by exploitation of this category.

INDEFINITE LEAVE TO REMAIN (SETTLEMENT)

Generally speaking, an individual will become eligible to apply for ILR after they have spent a requisite period of time in the UK; for most people, this is five years of continuous lawful residence in a qualifying category (although note the accelerated route for Tier 1 (Entrepreneurs) and Tier 1 (Investors)). Qualification for ILR has been restricted and those entering under the Tier 2 (Intra-Company Transfer) category can no longer apply for settlement (unless they were in the UK before 6 April 2010). Those in the UK under Tier 2 (General) can currently apply for ILR. From 6 April 2016, Tier 2 (General) migrants applying for ILR must be paid at least £35,000 per annum in order to qualify for settlement.

Adult applicants (aged 18-65) are required to demonstrate knowledge of language and life in the UK, in addition to meeting the usual requirements for settlement. Most applicants now will need to pass a "Life in the UK" test and applicants will also need to demonstrate that they have sufficient English language skills, either by way of a degree taught in English, or having passed an approved English language test. Nationals on the Home Office's list of majority English-speaking countries, such as Australia and New Zealand, automatically meet the latter requirement.

Once settlement is granted, there will no longer be any immigration related restrictions on the work or business the individual may do in the UK, and no time limits on their stay here, provided that in general they do not spend longer than two years outside of the UK, maintain ties here and consider the UK to be their home.

BRITISH NATIONALITY

An individual can normally apply for naturalization as a British citizen one year after being granted ILR and as long as they meet the residence requirements and they have been in the UK for 5 years in total.

There are various requirements that will need to be satisfied, such as age, capacity, residence requirements, good character, language skills and intention. The applicant will also need to pass an approved English language course and the "Life in the UK" test (if they did not do so at the ILR stage). If the application is approved, the applicant will be required to attend a citizenship ceremony after which a certificate of naturalization is issued. Once naturalized, they are eligible to apply for a British passport.

When applying for British citizenship an applicant is only permitted absences from the UK of up to 450 days over 5 years with no more than 90 days in the final year.

CONCLUSION

The UK immigration system consists of many complex categories and rules and can be difficult to navigate. However, for employers who plan in advance and have a genuine need to employ a skilled migrant worker, there are routes to bring those migrants to the UK. It is always important to bear in mind the long term intentions in respect of that migrant, for example will they want to settle in the UK, how many migrants do you wish to bring etc. It is also important to allow sufficient time to go through the whole visa process.

The information contained in this chapter is correct at the time of writing, but the authors would recommend that readers check the current position. All salary levels mentioned are periodically updated by the Home Office.

2.6 COMPLYING WITH THE UK'S MONEY LAUNDERING REGULATIONS

Kim Hurst, Mazars

The UK's Money Laundering Regulations came into force in December 2007, replacing and updating the existing regulations; their purpose is to protect the UK financial system. Any business covered by the regulations must implement controls to prevent it being used by criminals or terrorists for money laundering activities. Failure to comply with the law could have serious consequences.

WHICH BUSINESSES ARE COVERED BY MONEY LAUNDERING REGULATIONS?

Regulations apply to a number of business sectors, including:

- Most UK financial and credit businesses such as banks, currency exchange offices, cheque cashers or money transmitters;
- Independent legal professionals;
- Accountants, tax advisers, auditors and insolvency practitioners;
- Estate agents;
- Casinos;
- 'High Value Dealers' - businesses that accept cash payments for goods worth 15,000 Euros or more either in a single transaction or in installments;
- Trust or Company Service Providers.

If your business falls into one of these business sectors there is a requirement for it to be monitored by a supervisory authority. It may be the case that your business is already monitored, for example by a professional body, such as the Law Society, or by the Financial Conduct Authority, but if it is not you will probably need to register with the UK Revenue & Customs (HMRC).

To register with HMRC under Money Laundering Regulations you must complete an application form (MLR100) to register each place where you carry on business activities that require supervision. There is a fee for registering each business premises and a subsequent annual renewal fee.

If your business is a Money Service Business or a Trust or Company Service Provider, you are also required to apply for the 'fit and proper' test (form MLR101) in addition to registering with HMRC. The 'fit and proper' test must be taken by all those people who are involved in the running of the business.

CRIMINAL OFFENCES UNDER THE ANTI-MONEY LAUNDERING LEGISLATION

Money Laundering is the term used for a number of offences involving the proceeds of crime or terrorist funds. It includes possessing, or in any way dealing with, or concealing, the proceeds of any crime. It also involves similar activities in relation to terrorist funds, which include funds that are likely to be used for terrorism, as well as the proceeds of terrorism.

Someone is engaged in Money Laundering if they:

- Conceal, disguise, convert, transfer or remove (from the United Kingdom) criminal property;
- Enter into or become concerned in an arrangement which they know or suspect facilitates (by whatever means) the acquisition, retention, use or control of criminal property by or on behalf of another person;
- Acquire, use or have possession of criminal property.

Criminal Property is very widely defined, but, in summary, property is Criminal Property if it:

- Constitutes a person's benefit in whole or in part (including pecuniary and proprietary benefit) from criminal conduct; or
- Represents such a benefit directly or indirectly, in whole or in part; and
- The alleged offender knows or suspects that it constitutes or represents such a benefit.

Criminal Conduct is conduct that constitutes an offence in any part of the United Kingdom or would constitute an offence in any part of the United Kingdom, if it occurred there (subject to the exemptions listed below). This includes tax offences committed abroad if the action would have been an offence were it to have taken place in the United Kingdom. There is no need for there to be any consequential effect on the United Kingdom's tax system.

However, no offence is committed in any of the following circumstances:

- Where the persons involved did not know or suspect that they were dealing with the proceeds of crime;
- Where the act is committed by someone carrying out a law enforcement or judicial function;
- Where the conduct giving rise to the criminal property was reasonably believed to have taken place outside the UK, and the conduct was in fact lawful under the criminal law of the place where it occurred, and the maximum sentence if the conduct had occurred in the UK would have been less than 12 months (except in the case of an act which would be an offence under the Gaming Act 1968, the Lotteries and Amusements Act 1976 or under sections 23 or 25 of the Financial Services and Markets Act 2000, which will fall within the exemption even if the relevant sentence would be in excess of 12 months).

It is a general rule that an element of intent is required before many criminal offences can be committed. For example, theft can only be committed where the offender is dishonest and has intent to deprive permanently. In some cases, where the monetary proceeds of a suspected theft or tax fraud are small, it may be that the perpetrators were acting in error or in the mistaken impression that they had permission to act as they did.

It is also important to note that for indirect tax, section 167(3) Customs & Excise Management Act 1979 provides that a wide range of innocent/accidental errors are criminal offences (although they are in practice generally dealt with under the civil penalty regime).

For the avoidance of doubt, Criminal Property includes (but is by no means limited to):

- The proceeds of tax (direct or indirect) evasion including the under declaring of income and the over claiming of expenses.
- A benefit obtained through bribery and corruption (including both the receipt of a bribe and the profits earned from a contract obtained through bribery or the promise of a bribe).
- Benefits obtained through the operation of a cartel.
- Benefits (in the form of saved costs) arising from a failure to comply with a regulatory requirement, where that failure is a criminal offence, e.g. a breach of health and safety regulations.

- Property, even of minimal value, acquired by theft (including, for example, not telling a customer that they have erroneously paid twice or an overdrawn director's current account in a relevant company).

The following can constitute a criminal offence:

- Providing assistance to a money launderer to obtain, conceal, retain or invest funds if you knew, or in some cases, if you should have known that the funds were the proceeds of serious criminal conduct. Making a report precludes a charge of assisting a money launderer.
- Tipping off a person, or any third party, in connection with an investigation into money laundering. This could include, for example, informing someone of your money laundering suspicions.
- Failing to report a suspicion of money laundering if the suspicion was acquired in the course of your employment (or, as the case may be, your profession). It is a criminal offence not to comply with the Regulations and a criminal offence may also be committed by anyone who has consented to or connived at non-compliance with the Regulations, including where such non-compliance is attributable to their neglect.

There are thousands of criminal offences in the United Kingdom that, if committed, are likely to result in a person benefiting from an offence and thereby having Criminal Property. The key point to note is that Proceeds of Crime Act (POCA) introduced an 'all crime' reporting regime. That is, Money Laundering offences can relate to the proceeds of any criminal activity not just, for example, drug trafficking.

In addition to the offences under the POCA, there is also an obligation for businesses to report belief or suspicion of the proceeds from, or finance likely to be used for, terrorism, or its laundering, based on information which came to them in the course of its business or employment.

MONEY LAUNDERING CONTROLS AND PROCEDURES

Businesses covered by the Money Laundering Regulations must put controls in place to prevent them being used by criminals or terrorists for money laundering purposes. The controls include:

- Assessing the risk of the business being used by criminals to launder money
- Appointing a 'nominated officer'
- Implementing a procedure to check the identity of customers and 'beneficial owners' of corporate bodies and partnerships and keeping all relevant documents

- Ensuring employees are aware of money laundering regulations.

The 'nominated officer' must be a person in the business; they cannot be an external consultant. As it is an important role, it must be undertaken by a person who:

- Has access to all customer records and documentation;
- Can make the decision, without reference to others, whether or not to report suspicious activities;
- Can be trusted with the responsibility.

If you are a sole trader in a regulated business with no employees, you must act as the 'nominated officer' yourself.

The duties of the 'nominated officer' include:

- being the first point of contact for reports of suspicious activity from any employee in the business;
- considering all information and assessing whether evidence of money laundering or terrorist financing exists;
- reporting any suspicious activities or transactions to the National Crime Agency (NCA);
- requesting permission from NCA to continue with any transactions that they have reported, and ensure that no transactions are continued illegally.

All employees, particularly those in customer-facing positions, must receive regular training to ensure that they are aware of the money laundering laws, understand how the business' procedures affect them and appreciate the penalties of non-compliance. They should also be able to recognise suspicious activity and know what to do about it.

WHAT ARE THE PENALTIES FOR NOT COMPLYING WITH THE MONEY LAUNDERING REGULATIONS?

If you do not comply with Money Laundering Regulations there are various measures that can be taken, from warning letters to criminal prosecution. Although criminal prosecution is a last resort, the penalty may be harsh; depending on the severity of the offence, the courts can impose penalties ranging from unlimited fines to lengthy imprisonment, or both.

Part Three

Operating a Business and Employment in the United Kingdom

3.1 FINANCIAL REPORTING AND ACCOUNTING: AN OVERVIEW

Stephen Brown, Mazars

INTRODUCTION

All limited and unlimited companies in the UK, regardless of whether they are trading or not, are required to keep accounting records throughout the period. This chapter sets out the key financial reporting and accounting requirements for companies trading or investing in the UK.

GENERAL PRINCIPLES

Where formal accounts are required, in particular for limited companies, these must include for accounting periods commencing after 1 January 2015:

- An Income Statement;
- A Statement of Financial Position signed by the director;
- A Directors' Report signed by a director or the company secretary;
- A Strategic Report signed by a director (if applicable);
- Notes to the accounts; and
- Statement of Cashflows (if applicable);
- Consolidated Financial Statements (if applicable);
- An Auditor's Report signed by the auditor (if required).

In general, all private and public limited companies are required to send a full copy of their accounts to Companies House every year.

Once received, all accounts filed and held at Companies House are available to the general public on request. For this reason the option to file abbreviated accounts is attractive to some small companies.

Small companies are entitled to certain disclosure exemptions in relation to the accounts they must send their shareholders, and can, in addition, file abbreviated accounts with the Registrar of Companies. Medium-sized companies can also send abbreviated accounts to the Registrar but the reduction in disclosure in these accounts is negligible. In both instances they must, however, provide a full set of accounts for their shareholders. For both small and medium-sized companies, the production of abbreviated accounts is entirely voluntary.

A company/group filing small company abbreviated financial statements does not need to file a Directors' Report, Income Statement and can include fewer notes to the financial statements.

For a company to qualify as small, at least two of the following conditions must be met:

- Turnover must be less than £6.5 million;
- Gross assets must be less than £3.26 million; and
- Average number of employees must be less than 50.

A company filing medium abbreviated financial statements has a limited option to reduce disclosure but does need to include a Directors' Report, an Income Statement and notes to the financial statements.

For a company/group to qualify as medium-sized, again, at least two of the conditions below must be met:

- Turnover must be less than £25.9 million;
- Gross assets less than £12.9 million; and
- Average number of employees less than 250.

The time normally allowed for companies to deliver their accounts to Companies House is:

- 9 months from the ARD (Accounting Reference Date) for a private limited company.
- 6 months from the ARD for a public limited company.

The ARD is the period-end date to which all accounts are prepared and normally covers a period of 12 months, although this can be extended to a maximum of 18 months. Filing of financial statements for a first year entity must be within 21 months of incorporation. Late delivery of accounts to Companies House will result in a late filing penalty, which is, technically, a criminal offence for which Directors can be prosecuted.

ACCOUNTING

Regulations regarding the presentation of the primary financial statements in the UK are found in several sources such as UK company law and UK and international accounting standards. Note that subsidiaries of overseas firms incorporated outside the UK are subject to the normal UK accounting practices. Branches or places of business of overseas firms have special registration procedures.

Accounting Principles

All accounts in the UK are prepared in accordance with two fundamental accounting concepts:

- Going concern – the accounts are prepared as if the company will be trading in the foreseeable future (at least 12 months from the date of signing the financial statements).
- Accruals basis – income and expenditure should relate to the period in which it occurred, not the period in which it was received/paid.

Whichever accounting policy is selected, they must be transparent and reflect industry and sector norms.

Financial Reporting

Until recently, Financial Reporting Standards were developed solely by the Accounting Standards Board ("ASB"). These standards, in conjunction with the requirements of UK companies legislation (principally the UK Companies Acts), helped make up what is known as UK GAAP, which gives guidance to companies and auditors on how UK accounts should be prepared to give a 'true and fair' view of the company's financial position.

However, due to increasing globalisation in the world economy, it became necessary to produce a set of International Financial Reporting Standards ("IFRS") so that potential investors can compare firms on a global scale.

EU firms with securities that are publicly traded on a regulated stock exchange are required to apply EU-adopted IFRS when producing consolidated accounts. In the UK, this means any company listed on any of the markets of the London Stock Exchange. Individual subsidiary companies are not yet required to prepare financial statements under IFRS.

At present, only the types of company detailed above are required to adopt IFRS. However, even companies not required to do so can choose to adopt these new standards. A company that chooses to use IFRS to produce its accounts for one financial period cannot change back to UK standards in the following years. There are limited exceptions to this, such as if the company becomes a subsidiary of a group that uses UK standards as opposed to IFRS, in which case the company can revert back to using UK standards.

UK companies were required to adopt a new financial reporting framework for accounting periods beginning on or after 1 January 2015 when the extant FRSs, SSAPs and UTIFs were withdrawn from UK GAAP.

The new framework has been updated to achieve greater convergence with international standards and is split into three tiers (based on public accountability and size) for financial reporting purposes.

Listed and AIM companies must use IFRS in their group accounts - AIM companies because the listing rules require it and full listed companies because regulations require that all companies listed on an EU regulated market use IFRS, as adopted in the EU, in their group accounts.

Other entities that are not required to use IFRS had the following choices:

- IFRS – any entity, except a charitable one, can adopt IFRS if they wish.
- FRS 101 – ('IFRS' with reduced disclosures) - this is only available to subsidiaries of parent companies who have adopted IFRS, and it allows the subsidiaries to adopt IFRS but with reduced disclosures;
- FRS 102 – the standard that has replaced UK GAAP;
- FRS103 – Insurance contracts is a fourth standard added to the framework which is relevant to entities that are applying FRS102 that have insurance contracts; and
- FRS105 – the financial reporting standard applicable to micro entities.

FRS103 should be applied by an entity that applies FRS102 and issues insurance contracts and/or holds reinsurance contracts. This FRS should also be applied to financial instruments (other than insurance contracts) that it issues with a discretionary participation feature.

"Small" companies/groups as defined by the Companies Act have previously had the option to use the FRSSE, for accounting periods beginning on or after 1 January 2015 FRSSE (effective 2015) has replaced FRSSE (effective April 2008).

The amendments to FRSSE primarily reflect that FRS 102 is replacing existing SSAPs and FRSs from January 2015. The key differences between FRSSE (effective April 2008) and FRSSE (effective 2015) are as follows:

- An annual assessment is required of whether there are any indications of impairment of any assets.
- If unable to make a reliable estimate of the life of goodwill or intangible assets the maximum life shall not exceed five years (changed from 20 years).
- The definitions regarding related party transactions and key management personnel have been aligned with FRS 102.

- The exemption for disclosure of intra-group related party transactions where any subsidiary party to the transaction is 100% owned by the group has been included.

FRSSE (effective 2015) will be withdrawn from 1 January 2016 at which point companies/groups that are "small" but not "micro" (meaning they cannot apply FRS 105) may use FRS102 for smaller companies.

FRS102 for smaller companies (which is an amendment to FRS102 by way of a new section 1A for small entities) requires entities to apply the full recognition and measurement principles contained in FRS102, but retain presentation and disclosure requirements that are appropriate to a small company.

Companies that meet the "micro" criteria have the choice of applying FRS105 for micro entities. For a company to qualify as micro-sized, at least two of the conditions below must be met:

- Turnover must be less than £632,000;
- Net assets less than £316,000;
- Average number of employees less than 10.

For a company to be eligible to apply FRS105 it can not meet any of the following criteria:

- Companies excluded from the small companies regime;
- Financial institutions including credit, insurance and banking institutions;
- Charities;
- Small parent companies who choose to prepare consolidated financial statements;
- Companies that are included in consolidated financial statements; and
- Public companies.

FRS105 is effective for accounting periods commencing on or after 1 January 2016 which means that there will a one year period where "micro" companies that have previously applied FRSSE (UK GAAP applicable to smaller entities) will have to adopt FRSSE (effective 2015) or FRS102 for smaller companies before FRS105 becomes effective.

FRS105 requires only two primary statements and the information contained on these primary statements will be condensed. Amongst other simplifications assets can not be measured at fair value or at revaluation under FRS105.

As before FRS105 and FRS102 for smaller companies are not mandatory and a company could instead use full FRS 102 or indeed IFRS if it so desired.

Other entities that are not "small" or "micro" and are not required to use IFRS end up with various choices, depending on their situation.Charitable companies are expected to use FRS 102 and a new Charities SORP (SORP 2015) was issued to update the changes to UK GAAP in line with the adoption of FRS 102 for accounting periods commencing on or after 1 January 2015.

AUDIT

Audits must be carried out by someone authorised to provide an audit, by:

- Being a member of a Recognised Supervisory Body ("RSB"); and
- Having the necessary qualifications/eligibility of that RSB to be an auditor.

An RSB can be a professional body such as the Institute of Chartered Accountants for England and Wales. UK companies are required to be audited unless they are designated as 'small' in size (and can satisfy 2 out of the three criteria), or are dormant. This 'small' exemption is subject to a number of detailed conditions which must be met in order for it to apply.

If a UK small company is part of a group of companies (UK or worldwide), the group in its entirety must meet the definition of 'small', otherwise the small UK company will be subject to an audit regardless of its individual size.

There are circumstances where a parent company can guarantee the liabilities of a UK trading subsidiary and this can allow it to take advantage of an exemption from audit regardless of its size.

If a group of companies (UK or worldwide) contains a listed entity with its shares traded on a recognised stock exchange anywhere in the world, then any UK company which is part of that group will require an audit regardless of its own individual size.

Note here that exemption from the audit requirement does not exclude the company from having an audit if it so wishes.

Auditors are normally appointed in the following ways:

- They are appointed by a newly formed company, or by an existing company that requires a new auditor.
- They are reappointed by a company for which they are already existing auditors.
- They are ordered to be auditors of a firm by the Secretary of State.

This last case occurs when a company requiring an audit fails to agree to appoint an auditor.

The company's auditors are appointed/reappointed each year by either majority vote of the shareholders, or for a private company the provisions of deemed re-appointment of an existing auditor may apply. Directors have the authority to fill a vacancy that arose during the year but this will need to be later confirmed by the shareholders before the new auditor may continue in office for subsequent financial years.

Upon appointment, the auditor should send the company an engagement letter confirming their appointment as auditors, and setting out other items relating to the audit, such as the work they will carry out, confirmation of their independence and payment of audit fees. The auditor should also seek professional clearance from the previous auditors before accepting any audit appointment.

An auditor ceases to audit a company in the following ways:

* They resign from the post of auditor of the company.
* They are removed by the company.

If an auditor resigns they must provide a written notice to the company and a statement of circumstances to the Registrar of Companies and anyone else entitled to copies of the company accounts.

If the members of a company wish to remove the existing auditor, the auditor has the right to have written circularisation to all members and the right to be seen and heard at the company's general meeting at which their removal is proposed.

3.2 BUSINESS TAXATION

Andrew Ross, Mazars LLP

INTRODUCTION

This chapter is divided into the following parts:

- The key forms in which an overseas company could set up in the UK with a view to carrying on business.
- The basis of taxation in the UK, summarising the key taxes an investor needs to be aware of.
- Setting out the basis of calculation of taxable profits, noting the key rules on tax deductibility of expenditure and certain important tax reliefs and anti-avoidance provisions.

VEHICLES FOR DOING BUSINESS IN THE UK

There are several different vehicles that could be used when doing business in the UK, each with their own legal and commercial peculiarities. When considering the most suitable form of vehicle to use, investors would be recommended to consider such factors in addition to taking account of the differing tax treatment of each.

Representative Office

It is important to distinguish between "trading in" and "trading with" the UK. An overseas person will not be subject to UK tax on profits simply because they are transacting with UK entities, even if the goods are delivered to UK locations or services are carried out within the UK.

This can be the case even if the overseas investor has set up an office within the UK, although this will depend on the nature of the activities carried out by that office.

If, however, those activities cross a certain line, this could result in the creation of a taxable branch or permanent establishment.

In this context, it should be noted that in 2013 the OECD commenced a project referred to as "BEPS" – Base Erosion and Profit Shifting. The objective of this project is to review the current rules on allocation of taxable profits between territories, including the extent to which profits are allocated to locations which differ from where the actual business activity takes place. The UK Government supports the introduction of BEPS and it is likely that UK tax law will be amended once agreed proposals have been issued by the OECD. This will be particularly relevant to overseas companies intending to set up operations in the UK via a representative office or branch/"permanent establishment".

In addition, for profits arising on or after 1 April 2015, the diverted profit tax ("DPT") applies, under which a 25% tax is charged on profits relating to UK activities of multinational enterprises which are diverted (avoiding the UK tax net) using "contrived" arrangements. One example of this might be where a non-UK resident company operates in the UK in such a way that whilst it earns (significant) profits from the UK, its operations are structured in such a way as to avoid the creation of a taxable permanent establishment (on which, see below).

Branch / "Permanent Establishment"

The UK branch (referred to for tax purposes as a "permanent establishment" or "PE") of a foreign company will be subject to tax in the UK on profits that are attributable to the branch. UK domestic legislation gives a definition of a PE which is broadly similar to that contained in many double tax treaties. Typically, a foreign company will have a UK PE if:

- it has a fixed place of business in the UK through which the business of the company is wholly or partly carried on; and/or
- an agent acting on behalf of the company has and habitually exercises in the UK authority to do business on behalf of the company (except where that agent is of independent status acting in the ordinary course of his business).

There are exceptions to this where, for example, the fixed place of business is for the storage of goods or purely for purchasing or information-gathering functions. In such a situation, the foreign company may not have a UK taxable presence.

Subsidiary

A UK incorporated subsidiary will be subject to UK tax on all of its trading profits, wherever those profits are earned (subject to the possibility of claiming an exemption from UK tax for profits within overseas branches).

A non-UK incorporated company can also be treated as UK tax resident (and so taxable in the UK on its worldwide profits) if its "central management and control" is located in the UK. Therefore care needs to be taken where a non-UK company is operating in the UK to ensure that the company as a whole does not become UK tax resident.

Branch v Subsidiary

From a UK tax point of view, there is generally little difference in the basis of taxation between a branch and a subsidiary. UK corporation tax is charged at the same rates on branch or subsidiary profits and no withholding tax is charged on the remittance of funds by a branch to its head office or on dividends paid by a subsidiary to its parent company.

Therefore, a decision on the most appropriate form will generally need to be based on commercial & legal factors and the non-UK tax implications.

One potential tax advantage of using a UK branch (particularly in start-up ventures) is that tax losses of the branch may (depending on the law of the relevant overseas country) be available to offset non-UK profits arising in the same foreign company. At the same time, those tax losses can also be carried forward to shelter future profits of the branch from UK tax (although the flip-side of this is that there may be less double tax relief to shelter those same future profits from tax in the overseas country).

Joint Ventures

Where an investor wishes to enter into a UK joint venture-type arrangement with a 3rd party, the parties will likewise need to agree on the form of the joint venture, for example:

- Contractual joint venture: Each party (through its own legal entity) enters into a contract with a view to carrying out a business transaction or a project.
- Partnership: This is a more formal legal structure involving the carrying on of a business in common with a view to profit. Each party (again through its own legal entity) will enter into a formal partnership agreement. The basis for sharing profits will be set out in this partnership agreement.
- Company: A company is set up to carry out the joint venture business, with the joint venture parties owning shares in that company. The relationship between the joint venture parties may also be governed by a shareholders' agreement.

Again, commercial and legal considerations must be taken into account in determining the most appropriate vehicle. The tax treatment of each will also vary.

BASIS OF TAXATION

The main taxes payable in the UK may be summarised as follows.

Tax on Company Profits

Corporation tax is payable on the taxable profits (both income and capital) of a UK subsidiary or the UK branch of an overseas company. The rate of corporation tax is the same for both a branch and subsidiary.

Tax is calculated based on the profits of an "accounting period", which will normally coincide with the period for which the company prepares its financial statements.

Historically, there were two rates of corporation tax - the main rate and the "small profits rate", although these rates have now converged, resulting in a single rate of 20%.

The current and proposed future rates of corporation tax are:

Profits arising in year from 1 April to 31 March:	2015/16	2016/17
Main rate of corporation tax	20%	20%
Small profits rate of corporation tax	n/a*	n/a

Effective 1 April 2015 the small profits rate (20%) was unified with the main rate (previously 21%), such that there is now only one rate of corporation tax.

In the 2015 Summer Budget, it was announced that the main corporation tax rate would reduce to 19% for the years starting 1 April 2017, 2018 and 2019 and to 18% for the year starting 1 April 2020.

In charging corporation tax on companies with year ends other than 31 March, a proportionate part of profits for an accounting period is taxed at each of the applicable rates. For example, the main rate of tax on taxable profits of a company with a 31 December 2015 year end is 20.25%.

In the past, rates of corporation tax were impacted by the number of associated companies. Post 1 April 2015, the number of associated companies only really impacts on whether a company is required to pay its corporation tax liability by quarterly instalment payments ("QIPs"). A company must make QIPs during the accounting period where it is 'large,' i.e. its profits exceed £1.5m (divided by the number of associated companies) and it was either large in the previous accounting period or its current period profits exceed £10m (again, divided by the number of associated companies). From 1 April 2015, an associated company arises where one company is a 51% subsidiary of another, or both companies are 51% subsidiaries of a third.

Pursuant changes announced in the 2015 Summer Budget, the precise timing of payments under QIPs will depend on the profitability of the company.

From 1 April 2013 a new "Patent Box" regime was introduced, giving reduced corporation tax rates which ultimately result (from 1 April 2017) in a 10% corporation tax rate for "patent derived profits" (including royalties) for both new and existing patents.

The current patent box regime will be closed to new entrants from June 2016 following which companies with IP which already qualified (patents which are already registered) may continue to apply the reduced 10% tax rate until June 2021. At present there is no indication as to whether a replacement regime will be introduced.

For "large" companies (as defined above) the corporation tax liability for an accounting period is due and payable quarterly, the first instalment being six months and 14 days after the beginning of the period (and hence estimates of the forecast tax for a particular year will need to be made for at least the first two quarterly payments). For companies not within the quarterly payment obligation, tax is due in a single payment, nine months after the end of the company's accounting period. Interest is payable to/receivable from HMRC on any under/over and late/early payment of tax.

Tax on individuals

Individuals are liable to income tax on trading profits, employment income, interest, dividends and other income and are subject to capital gains tax on chargeable gains. The rates for the tax year commencing 6 April 2015 are:

Taxable income (£)	Tax rate on income	Effective tax rate on UK/overseas dividends	Tax rate on capital gains*
up to 31,785	20%	Nil	18%
31,786 - 150,000	40%	25%	28%
over 150,000	45%	30.6%	28%

A reduced rate of 10% is payable on the first £10m of gains made in a taxpayer's lifetime, on the disposal of qualifying business assets ("Entrepreneurs' relief").

Based on announcements in the 2015 Summer Budget, from April 2016, only the first £5,000 of dividend income will be tax-free for basic rate tax payers. Above this level, a basic rate tax payer will pay tax at 7.5% and a higher rate tax payer will be subject to tax at 32.5%. Over £150,000 of income, dividends will be subject to 38.1% income tax.

An individual who is trading in partnership is assessed to income tax on their share of the tax-adjusted trading profits for the accounting period of the partnership ending in the tax year. The basis of calculation of taxable trading profits is broadly the same as for a company.

The rules for the calculation of individuals' capital gains differ from the rules for companies in that "indexation allowance" (an allowance for inflation) is not available to individuals, whilst there are other reliefs available to individuals that are not available to companies (e.g. Entrepreneurs' relief).

Interest income is taxable when received. In most cases, UK interest is paid to individuals net of basic rate income tax. The gross income is taxable, with credit given against the tax liability in the tax year for the tax deducted. Where the tax liability is less than the tax deducted, the excess withholding tax is repayable.

Income tax on trading and other income that is not subject to PAYE (see below) is due in two instalments – on 31 January within the relevant tax year and 31 July following the end of the tax year.

Payroll Taxes/National Insurance Contributions

An employer is obliged to make deductions from pay for employee income tax and employee national insurance contributions (NIC), using the "pay as you earn" (PAYE) system.

Employer NIC is an additional cost payable by the employer based on each employee's wages plus benefits in kind. The rates of employer NIC vary depending on whether the employer offers a final salary pension scheme and has contracted out of the state earnings related pension scheme. The rates for the year commencing 6 April 2015 are:

Weekly earnings	Monthly earnings	Contracted in	Contracted out
Up to £156	Up to £676	Nil	Nil
£157 to £815	£677 to £3,532	13.8%	10.4%
Excess over £815	Excess over £3,532	13.8%	13.8%

The employer has to make monthly remittances to HMRC (by mandatory electronic funds transfer) of the amounts they deduct for employee income tax and NIC, along with the employer NIC. All employers are required by law to report to HMRC on a real-time information basis ("RTI"). This means that the employer files a RTI notification to HMRC via the Government Gateway every time an employee is paid. The RTI return is filed either in advance of or along with the remittance to HMRC. This is viewed as the most significant change to PAYE since its introduction in 1944.

VAT

All businesses investing or trading in the UK must register for UK VAT if they have a "business establishment" or usual place of residence in the UK. This test differs from the corporation tax tests of residence and it is therefore possible for an overseas investor to be required to register for UK VAT even though it may not have a branch that is liable to corporation tax.

VAT registered businesses are generally required to file VAT returns quarterly by way of electronic returns and therefore any VAT payable will usually be payable by not later than one month and seven days after the end of the relevant quarter. However, VAT-registered businesses with an annual VAT liability in excess of £2.3 million must make interim payments at the end of the second and third months of each VAT quarter as payments on account of the quarterly VAT liability. A balancing payment for the quarter is then made with the VAT return.

Stamp Duty Land Tax ("SDLT")

SDLT is payable on the acquisition of any interest in land situated in the UK regardless of whether the acquirer is an individual, a partnership or a company or whether the acquirer is UK or non-UK resident.

The most common rate of SDLT when a capital sum is paid to acquire non-residential land or an interest in such land (whether the acquisition is ownership of the land or on the grant or assignment of a lease) is 4%. Lower rates of SDLT apply if the purchase consideration is less than £500,000. Different rates of SDLT may apply to the acquisition of residential land. There are exceptions for intra-group transfers. Care must be taken, in particular, where residential land which was valued at more than £2 million on 1 April 2012 is to be acquired by a company (or other collective investment vehicle) since an Annual Tax on Enveloped Dwellings may also be payable. This £2m threshold is reduced to £1m for returns relating to 2015/16 and £0.5m post 1 April 2016.

On grant of a non-residential lease, in addition to the SDLT on any premium, the tenant is liable to pay SDLT at 1% of the net present value of the total rent payable under the lease, less a deduction of £150,000.

Stamp Duty

Stamp duty, at 0.5%, is payable by the person acquiring shares or convertible loan notes of a UK registered company. There are exceptions for intra-group transfers. No duty is payable on the transfer of ownership of other assets, for example loan notes, goodwill or trade debtors. There is no duty on the issue of shares or convertible loan notes.

Withholding Taxes

The UK does not impose withholding tax on dividends.

A 20% withholding tax is generally imposed on interest payments made by

1. A company,
2. By or on behalf of a partnership of which a company is a member,
3. By a person to another person whose usual place of abode is outside the UK.

However, the rate may be reduced under an applicable double tax treaty or the EU Interest and Royalty Directive, provided that certain conditions & formalities are complied with prior to the payment of the interest.

There is no withholding from payments of interest by a UK company to UK companies or to UK branches of overseas companies (which will include, in particular, UK branches of overseas banks), or on payments of interest on certain quoted loan stock. Where securities are issued at a discount, no withholding is applied on the discount element.

For royalties, a 20% income tax withholding applies, subject to lower rates in the relevant applicable double tax treaty or under the EU Interest and Royalty Directive.

Rent paid to a non-UK resident person is subject to a 20% withholding deduction, unless the landlord has met the requirements of HMRC's "non-resident landlords' scheme".

Under the construction industry scheme, there may be a withholding requirement on payments made by contractors to sub-contractors in relation to building projects.

No withholding tax is applied on service fees, technical fees or management charges.

DETERMINATION OF TAXABLE PROFITS OF A BRANCH/SUBSIDIARY

The rules for the calculation of the taxable profits of both a branch and subsidiary are essentially the same. The key issue for a branch is the extent to which profits of the relevant overseas legal entity should be allocated to the head office or the UK branch.

Taxable Trading Profits

The taxable result from trading is based on the profits for the year, as shown in the company's financial statements (provided the financial statements are prepared in accordance with IFRS or UK GAAP).

Costs that are not deductible for tax purposes include entertainment expenditure, fines and penalties, expenditure of a capital nature and non-specific provisions. Depreciation, amortisation and gains/losses from the disposal of fixed tangible assets are not allowed or taxed. For tax depreciation, there is a statutory relief for certain classes of assets (see capital allowances, below).

Until the 2015 Summer Budget, tax relief was available on the cost of the acquisition of intangible fixed assets (for example goodwill) if acquired after 31 March 2002 from a non-connected person. The amount that was tax deductible was the charge in the profit and loss account or, if an irrevocable election was made, a 4% p.a. straight line writing down allowance. Based on the proposals announced in the 2015 Summer Budget, from 8 July 2015 onwards tax relief will no longer be given for purchased goodwill and certain customer related intangibles acquired as part of the acquisition of a business.

Remuneration paid to employees is deductible on an accruals basis providing payment to the employee is no later than nine months after the year end. Remuneration paid more than nine months after the year end is tax deductible in the period when payment is made. Tax relief for payments made by the employer into a pension scheme is generally given when the payment is made (rather than on an accruals basis), although relief may be spread where there is a large increase (> £500,000) in the level of contributions from one period to the next.

Capital Allowances

Capital Allowances is the UK term for the statutory code for deducting the cost of capital expenditure from trading profits. The main class of asset that is eligible for capital allowances is plant and machinery. This includes plant within a building or structure (e.g. electrical, heating, water and air conditioning systems, lifts, escalators, sanitary ware). No allowances are given for the cost of buildings.

Eligible expenditure on plant and machinery qualifies for tax relief at one of two rates. Certain specified expenditure can obtain allowances at a rate of 8% per annum and all others at 18% per annum. For both, allowances are calculated on a reducing balance basis.

Assets in the 8% expenditure category include:

- Those with an expected life when new of more than 25 years
- Some plant within buildings
- Cars with emissions of more than 130 g/km (from 1 April 2013) of CO_2.

For expenditure incurred in the period 1 April 2014 to 31 December 2015, up to £500,000 of a company's annual expenditure on eligible assets, other than cars or assets for leasing out, is subject to 100% tax relief in the year of purchase. This is known as the "annual investment allowance". From 1 January 2016, the amount of the annual investment allowances will reduce to £200,000 per year. When the company is a member of a group only one annual investment allowance is given to the whole group.

Full relief is also available in the year in which it is incurred (100% tax allowances) for:
- Environmentally beneficial or energy saving plant (which includes cars with CO_2 emissions of no more than 75 g/km (from 1 April 2015);
- Plant for research & development activities;
- Expenditure of up to €20 million (Euro) on renovating empty commercial buildings until 11 April 2017.

On disposal of plant, the net sale proceeds, up to a maximum of cost, are deducted from the accumulated net pool of qualifying expenditure.

Interest and Finance Income and expense

In general, interest is taxed or relieved in accordance with the treatment in the company's financial statements.

Tax relief for finance expenses in "large" (as defined) corporate groups may be restricted due to the "worldwide debt cap". This restriction is considered after making any transfer pricing (thin capitalisation) adjustments (on which, see below). Broadly speaking, the intention of the worldwide debt cap is that the tax deductible finance expense relieved against a group's UK profits should be no greater than the external finance expense in the consolidated results of the group. However this regime will not apply if the UK net debt is less than 75% of the group's consolidated gross debt. This is a complex area on which further advice should be sought.

Dividends Received

The UK has a comprehensive dividends received exemption which applies to dividends a UK-resident company receives from UK or non-UK companies. Various conditions must be met, although there is no minimum holding period or minimum ownership percentage.

Sale of Capital Assets

The taxable gain on the disposal of a capital asset is calculated as net proceeds received less the acquisition cost and costs incurred on improvements. "Indexation allowance" (an allowance for inflation) may also be given to disposals by companies. Gains on certain assets can also be deferred by reinvesting the proceeds in certain replacement assets ("rollover relief").

The UK has a form of participation exemption, which can exempt from tax the gain or loss on the disposal by a company of shares in a trading company or trading sub-group - the exemption is called the Substantial Shareholdings Exemption (SSE). SSE, along with the dividends received exemption, are core features that make the UK an attractive location for holding companies.

The SSE rules contain several detailed requirements and therefore professional guidance should be sought as to whether it applies, not least because a group's non-trading activities do not necessarily need to be substantial for the group not to be regarded as a "trading group" and hence not qualify for the relief. An advance clearance application can be made to HMRC where there is uncertainty as to whether SSE applies to a particular disposal.

Transfers of capital assets (including intangibles) between UK members of a group takes place on a tax neutral basis regardless of the value of the asset or the price paid (see chapter 3.3). However, if the transferee subsequently leaves the group still holding the asset within six years of the transfer, this can create a "de-grouping" tax charge based on a deemed disposal (and re-acquisition) of the asset at its market value at the date of the intra-group transfer. Depending on the circumstances, this de-grouping charge may be taxable either in the transferee company that leaves the group or in the company selling the shares in the transferee.

Reliefs may apply to the transfer of a trading business to a company (a business incorporation) and to corporate acquisitions effected by a share-for-share exchange.

Losses

A company may claim to set a trading loss against all of its taxable profits within the same accounting period, and against the profits of the immediate preceding period, providing the company was carrying on the same trade in the previous period. Alternatively, or in addition, it may transfer some or all of a trading tax loss to other UK members of a 75% group, for use against the other companies' profits within the same accounting period only. This is known as "group relief".

A trading loss not applied to the current or previous accounting period and which has not been surrendered via group relief is carried forward and used against profits of the same trade arising in later periods, without time limit.

Tax relief for a non-trading company's finance expense in excess of the company's profits for an accounting period may be claimed against financial profits of the previous year. Alternatively, this expense can pass to another UK group member for use against that member's profits, in the same accounting period under the "group relief" provisions. Any unrelieved finance expense is carried forward, without time limit, to be used against future non-trading profits of the company.

Capital losses are set against chargeable (capital) gains of the company for the same period, with any excess being carried forward, without time limit, for use against net chargeable gains of subsequent periods.

There are several anti-avoidance provisions which may deny the carry forward of all types of tax losses when a group purchases a company with existing tax losses, and the main reason for the acquisition is to access these tax losses.

Research and Development Tax reliefs

Enhanced tax relief is available to companies which conduct R&D for the purposes of resolving scientific or technological uncertainty with a view to achieving an advancement in science or technology, or an appreciable improvement in existing technology.

There are two schemes of relief. One for small and medium sized companies (SME's), including so-called "larger SME's", and one for large companies.

For these purposes, an SME is broadly a company with less than 500 employees and not more than either €100m turnover or balance sheet total of €86m, taking into account certain linked and partner enterprises (e.g. group companies). An SME may claim an enhanced tax deduction of 230% of its qualifying R&D spend. If the SME is loss making, it may instead trade in losses for a cash rebate of 14.5% of the enhanced tax deduction (i.e. just over 33p in the £ of the actual qualifying spend), based on the rate applicable from 1 April 2015, thereby creating an additional source of cash-flow for the company.

Large companies may claim a tax deduction of 130% of their qualifying spend and do not currently have the cash-back option. However, for accounting periods commencing on or after 1 April 2013 a "Research and Development Expenditure Credit" (RDEC) credit scheme has been introduced. Under this scheme, in a large company's financial statements, the RDEC credit will be recognised as a reduction in R&D expenditure in the Profit and Loss Account. For tax purposes, the RDEC credit will be treated as a taxable receipt of the trade. For large companies with no corporation tax liability, or with a CT liability less than their RDEC credit, the key advantage of this new scheme is that such companies can claim an immediate benefit from their R&D claim through a payable credit of 11% of qualifying R&D expenditure. RDEC will operate as an alternative to the super-deduction scheme until April 2016 when only the RDEC scheme will be available.

A UK R&D tax relief claim must be made via the company's tax return and must be made within 24 months of the accounting year end of a company.

Transfer Pricing on Debt

The UK has transfer pricing rules, which substitute arm's length amounts to transactions with connected persons. These are broadly aligned to the OECD transfer pricing guidelines. The transfer pricing rules apply to both the interest rate (such that interest at a rate in excess of market value would not be deductible) and the amount of the borrowing (i.e. thin capitalisation, whereby a tax deduction will not be given for the whole of the interest on the element of debt in excess of that which would have been loaned by a 3rd party acting at arm's length).

Exemptions from transfer pricing rules or reduced documentation requirements apply to small and medium sized enterprises although in some circumstances, HMRC can issue a direction for medium sized companies to comply with transfer pricing legislation.

There are no safehavens with regard to debt:equity ratios or interest cover ratios (e.g. EBIT:interest or EBITDA:interest). Each has to be negotiated separately with HMRC. In order to be non-discriminatory with regard to the EU, the transfer pricing rules apply to all connected party transactions, including those between UK enterprises.

The transfer pricing rules can also apply to the provision of finance by lenders who do not control (or even have no shareholding in) the borrower where those lenders are "acting together" with other persons who between them have control over the borrowing company.

INVESTING IN THE UK – MAZARS, YOUR INTERNATIONAL PARTNER

Mazars provides specialist expertise to businesses like yours everyday. From company formation, choosing the most effective tax structure, getting your people paid and setting up the back-office, we help you to keep everything in order so you can stay focused on growing your business.

For further information please contact: **Toby Stanbrook, Outsourcing Partner**
T: +44 (0)20 8661 4120 • **E:** toby.stanbrook@mazars.co.uk

www.mazars.co.uk

SCIENCE PARKS
ARE IN OUR MAKE UP.

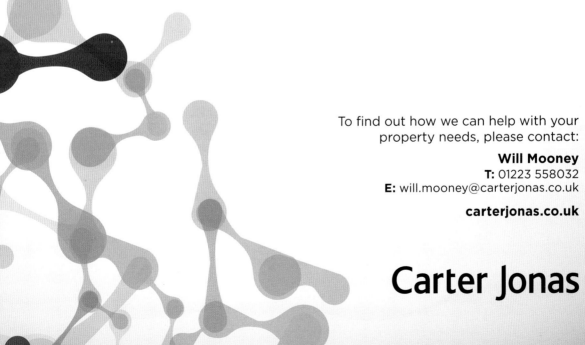

To find out how we can help with your
property needs, please contact:

Will Mooney
T: 01223 558032
E: will.mooney@carterjonas.co.uk

carterjonas.co.uk

Carter Jonas

Inspire Improve Impact

Are you looking for R&D grant funding opportunities?

PNO Consultants

PNO Group is Europe's largest independent public funding advisory, employing more than 230 staff across 12 European countries. Supporting small businesses, large enterprise and universities across all research disciplines and sectors, PNO has extensive experience of all principal national and European funding programmes with a service model that covers the entire grant acquisition process. This includes the identification of grant funding opportunities to support project ideas and company activities, a comprehensive but flexible writing service that includes full writing support through to peer review guidance and support in the post award reporting process to ensure that the full draw down of a grant is achieved once an individual project is underway. PNO also offers an extensive range of project services including project management, technology intelligence, development of exploitation strategies and dissemination. With a client base of more than 15,000 organisations throughout Europe, PNO can also help with finding suitable project partners as well as identifying potential projects for our clients to join.

Our Services:

1. Initiate
   - Assessment of projects for grant potential
   - Linking with potential partners/ projects
   - Grant education and training
2. Apply
   - Bid writing support: Full support, co-writing and peer review
   - Development of project budget
   - Contract negotiation with Grantor Body
3. Comply
   - Advice on administrative requirements
   - Project management assistance
   - Support to ensure full draw down of grant
   - Managing project spend against project deliverables

Grant Schemes

There are a range of funding programmes available for UK businesses that aim to help take projects from research to as close to commercial viability as possible to support the development of new products, processes or services. Key national funding programmes include:

- **SMART -** a single applicant scheme open to all R&D performing UK SME's from any sector
- **Collaborative R&D** – supports industrial and research collaborations in strategically important areas of science, engineering and technology
- **Catalyst Programmes -** a form of research and development funding which focuses on a specific priority area. Current areas include Industrial Biotechnology, Energy, Agri-Tech and Biomedical
- **Small Business Research Initiative (SBRI) -** supports the engagement of the public sector with industry during the early stages of development across a range of industry sectors.

Key European R&D funding programmes include **H2020** and **Eureka Eurostars.**

Contact Us:
Olaf Swanzy, Director
Telephone: 07810 837479 **/** 0161 488 3488
Email: olaf.swanzy@pnoconsultants.com
Web: www.pnoconsultants.com

INNOVATION PLACE
Projects, networks and funding
Sign up to our free online innovation portal
www.innovationplace.eu

IPR LICENSE

THE FUTURE OF RIGHTS LICENSING

WWW.IPRLICENSE.COM

Legend Press

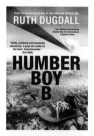

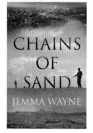

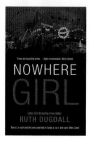

@legend_press

www.legendpress.co.uk

10 Years of Award-Winning Publishing

Dorset...
the natural place to do business

invest in
DORSET

Contact: Jo Rufus, Dorset Local Enterprise Partnership
Inward Investment Team
01305 224797
j.c.m.rufus@dorsetcc.gov.uk
Website www.investindorset.co.uk

The UK – number one for European headquarters

With easy access to Europe, a single market of over 500 million consumers, and consistently attracting more headquarter operations than any other European location, choose the UK.

Flight paths
Europe

BUSINESS IS GREAT
BRITAIN & NORTHERN IRELAND

gov.uk/ukti

Visualisation: UCL World

3.3 BUSINESS TAXATION AND PLANNING

Andrew Ross, Mazars LLP

INTRODUCTION

This chapter follows on from the overview of the UK business tax system set out in chapter 3.2 and covers various areas of UK tax planning that an investor should consider, both with a view to realising tax savings and also avoiding unnecessary tax costs.

ACQUISITION OF A BUSINESS: ASSETS V SHARES

Asset Acquisitions

An asset (business) purchase could be effected using a UK company or a UK branch of the overseas company. As discussed in Chapter 3.2, a UK branch of an overseas company and a UK company are subject to UK tax on profits in broadly the same way. Therefore, an overseas investor wishing to purchase a business in the form of an asset purchase will need to take into account commercial, legal and non-UK tax factors in deciding a preferred route.

One of the key non-tax advantages of an asset purchase is that any liabilities or exposures within the selling company do not automatically transfer across to the purchaser.

Share Acquisitions

A company is a separate legal entity and, as such, when an investor acquires a company it is acquiring all of that company's history and liabilities. Therefore, any unknown or contingent liabilities (as well as those which the purchaser is aware of) will effectively be inherited by the purchaser. For this reason, a purchaser will normally seek to obtain from the vendor an indemnity against such liabilities, whether or not they had crystallised as at the date of the sale (together with warranties over the company's tax position).

One of the first questions an investor will need to address is the vehicle to be used to make the acquisition, i.e. should the acquisition be made:

- directly by the overseas investor;
- by an intermediate holding company set up in the UK; or
- by an intermediate holding company set up in a 3rd territory.

Each investor will have its own particular fact pattern that may influence the choice and, as such, specific advice should be taken. But examples of factors that could, from a tax point of view, influence a purchaser towards one or other of these acquisition vehicles include:

- Where overseas tax rates are higher than UK rates, there could be an advantage to making the acquisition using the overseas investing company in order to benefit from any financing tax deductions in that territory.
- But where the overseas investor does not have sufficient profits to offset financing costs, a UK debt-financed acquisition vehicle may be preferable.
- If the investor wishes to create a sub-group to facilitate the cross-border expansion of the target business, it may be appropriate to set up an intermediate holding company (either in the UK or elsewhere).
- Whether the overseas territory has a favourable tax regime for the holding of shareholdings and how any local "controlled foreign company" rules may affect this.

Asset v Share Purchase

When acquiring shares in a company, the existing tax profile of the target company will remain and so the purchaser effectively inherits this.

From a buyer's point of view, the potential tax advantages of buying assets or shares include:

Assets

- Ability to obtain tax relief for the goodwill element of the deal price. (However, pursuant to announcements made in the 2015 Summer Budget, such tax relief will no longer be available for acquisitions on or after 8 July 2015.)
- Can claim capital allowances for plant & machinery and other qualifying fixed assets based on the consideration allocated under the Business Purchase Agreement rather than on the existing tax value of those assets within the target company (assuming the former is higher).
- Avoids 0.5% stamp duty (although stamp duty land tax would be payable if land is being acquired).

Shares

- Existing tax losses transfer across (but subject to anti-avoidance legislation aimed at preventing the acquisition of companies solely or mainly to enable the purchaser to benefit from these tax losses).
- If the current tax value of fixed assets is greater than the purchase price allocated to those assets, a share acquisition avoids a reduction in the amount on which capital allowances can be claimed.
- Avoids stamp duty land tax, which could be significant if there is valuable non-residential land within the target business (although there will be a 0.5% stamp duty charge on the consideration paid for the shares).
- Greater flexibility to enable the vendors to reduce or defer tax where the vendors are to retain a direct or indirect stake in the target business (e.g. by exchanging shares in the target company for new shares in the purchaser).

There will often be a conflict between the interests of the sellers and the buyers and it is important that a buyer appreciates this when negotiating a transaction. Buyers typically prefer to purchase assets in order to benefit from the advantages listed above. By contrast, sellers will often prefer to sell shares because:

- Individual sellers may be able to benefit from Entrepreneurs' relief, such that they only pay tax on the resulting capital gain at 10%.
- A corporate seller may be able to claim an exemption from tax on any gain (taking advantage of the "substantial shareholdings" exemption).
- An assets sale could give rise to a double tax charge on the seller – a first tax charge crystallising within the company making the disposal and a second tax charge on the shareholder when extracting the net proceeds from the company.

See below for exit considerations that a buyer will also need to take into account when investing.

ACQUISITION OF A BUSINESS: FINANCING

The funding for an acquisition could be sourced in a number of different ways – e.g. existing cash resources within the investor, 3rd party borrowings, equity injection by the ultimate shareholder(s) – and this will need to be taken into account when determining the optimal financing structure from a tax point of view.

Likewise, a review will need to be carried out of the tax regimes of both the overseas territory and the UK in determining the optimal place for locating interest deductions if the funding is to be effected through loan finance.

Questions that may need to be considered include:

- *Is the acquisition to be made by the overseas investor directly or by a UK acquisition vehicle?* Clearly, if the investor is to make the acquisition directly, any external funding will need to be taken out by the investor (even if the assets of the target business are used as security, which has been possible over recent years following the relaxation of the "financial assistance" rules).

-

- *What capacity do the investor and the target company each have to utilise interest deductions against forecast taxable profits?* No benefit will accrue from deducting interest in a territory in which there are insufficient taxable profits against which those deductions can be offset.

-

- *Is the corporate tax rate in the investor's home territory higher or lower than the UK rate?* The preference may be to locate borrowings (and hence interest deductions) in the territory with the higher tax rate.

-

- *What restrictions apply to the deductibility of interest in the UK and the overseas territory?* In relation to the UK, for example, transfer pricing/thin capitalisation considerations and the "worldwide debt cap" will need to be taken into account even if all or some of the finance is being provided by a 3rd party (see Chapter 3.2 for more detail).

-

- *Will the borrower be required to withhold tax on payment of interest?* 3rd party lenders will often include a gross-up clause such that any withholding tax will effectively be a cost to the borrower rather than a lender. Therefore the borrowing may need to be structured in such a form or location that avoids or minimises any withholding taxes.

Consideration will also need to be given to how interest payments are to be financed. Where the acquisition is funded out of existing cash resources provided by the investor, this may be less of an issue. But where 3rd party lenders are involved, the investor will need to have a clear plan on how payments of interest are to be funded. A UK company can remit cash to an overseas parent free of UK tax, whether by way of dividend or an upstream loan (although such a loan should itself be interest-bearing in order to meet transfer pricing rules), but the parent will need to consider the taxation of such receipts under its local tax regime. In this regard, it should not be assumed that an upstream loan would be tax-free to the investor, as some tax regimes can treat such loans as deemed dividends.

REPATRIATION OF PROFITS

No withholding taxes are charged on a repatriation of profits. This applies to dividends paid by a UK company, irrespective of the identity of the shareholders, as well as to repatriation of branch profits to head office.

As well as the use of dividends, groups should also consider the extent to which other charges should be levied on the UK business – for example, royalties, service fees and management charges. Provided that such charges relate to the UK business and are calculated on an arm's length basis (in compliance with transfer pricing legislation), those charges can be deducted against UK taxable profits. The withholding tax position on such payments is covered in Chapter 3.2.

TAX GROUPS

Where an investor has an existing UK business, there will be advantages to structuring the acquisition so as to create a UK tax group. The main advantages are:

- Current period UK trading profits of one company can be sheltered from tax by using trading losses of another UK group company arising in the same accounting period. This is known as "group relief".
- Capital assets can be transferred between UK members of the tax group without crystallising a tax charge. This would enable the tax-neutral combination of two UK businesses, if commercially desirable.
- Capital gains arising in one company can effectively be offset against brought forward non-trading losses (including capital losses, expenses of management and non-trading loan relationship debits) of another company in the UK group.

Where investors are part of a consortium, it is also possible in certain scenarios to use some of the current period tax losses arising in the consortium-owned company to shelter taxable profits arising in one of the consortium members (or vice versa).

The definitions of "group relief" groups and capital gains groups differ and so care must be taken where companies are not 100% owned, since in some situations not all of the above benefits of tax grouping will be available.

"Group relief" group : Comprises companies in which a shareholding of at least 75% is held directly or indirectly by the parent company (provided that the shareholder is also entitled to at least 75% of profits available for distribution and assets on a winding up). Non UK resident companies can be taken into account when tracing 75% ownership. In Figure 3.3.1, tax losses can be surrendered between UK 1 (owned 80% directly) and UK 3 (owned 81% indirectly). However, UK 2 is owned only 72% by Overseas Co. and therefore UK 2 cannot surrender losses to UK 3 (or vice versa).

Figure 3.3.1 – Example of how "group relief" may be applied according to levels of ownership

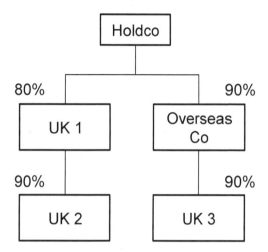

Capital gains group : This comprises companies which are held at least 75% by their immediate parent and which are indirectly held more than 50% by the top company in the group (provided also that the top group company is also entitled to more than 50% of profits available for distribution and assets on a winding up). Thus, in the above diagram UK 1, UK 2 and UK 3 are all part of the same capital gains group.

A tax group cannot be formed unless there is a common corporate parent company. Therefore, if an individual investor directly owns a number of UK companies, that investor will need to interpose a common holding company (which need not be a UK company) in order to create a tax group as in Figure 3.3.2:

Figure 3.3.2 – Creating a tax group

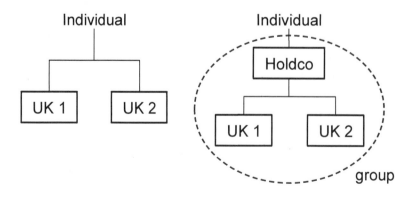

Even where there is no tax group in place, i.e. the individual holds both companies directly, the relationship between the two UK companies is such that they may still be regarded as associated or connected with each other for certain UK tax purposes. Hence:

- Transfer pricing rules can still apply to transactions or dealings between the two companies, to ensure that they are taxed on an arm's length basis.
- Transfers of assets must be for an arm's length consideration, failing which HMRC can substitute an arm's length value for the actual consideration.
- In determining the corporation tax rate payable by each company and, particularly, whether the small profits rate or marginal relief is available, both companies must be taken into account in calculating the number of "associated companies" – see Chapter 3.2 for the impact of this on the corporation tax rate payable.

EXIT CONSIDERATIONS

When structuring an acquisition, an investor should also be mindful of the likelihood of a future exit, what form that exit might take and the tax implications of such an exit event.

Business Held via a UK Branch of an Overseas Company

- The disposal would need to be effected via an asset sale (assuming that a sale of the overseas company would not be feasible).
- This will trigger a UK tax liability, with any gains on the sale of chargeable assets being taxed at the prevailing corporation tax rate. Overseas tax may also be payable (subject to double tax relief for UK tax paid, depending on the tax regime in the overseas territory).
- The branch could be packaged up into a new UK company, with the overseas investor selling that new company. This is a more complex area and could give rise to both UK tax charges in the new company and overseas tax charges in the overseas company.

Business Held within a UK Company

- Gives the flexibility to sell via a sale of assets or sale of shares.
- A sale of shares would generally not give rise to a UK tax liability within the target company (although a "de-grouping charge" could arise if the UK company holds assets that were transferred into it from another UK group company within the preceding six years). If the overseas parent company benefits from a

"participation exemption" regime, this could enable a sale of the business, by way of a sale of shares, free of both UK and overseas tax.

- A sale of assets would generally be less tax effective, since a UK tax charge would arise in the UK company on any gains and an overseas tax charge could arise on a subsequent remittance of the disposal proceeds by the UK company.

EMPLOYEE INCENTIVISATION

Where an investor wishes to incentivise or recruit/retain key employees by means of the issuing of shares in the target business, there are a number of different share plans that can assist in achieving this objective in a tax efficient way. Ultimately, the most appropriate plan will be dependent on commercial requirements and the characteristics of the investors (e.g. UK v overseas; company v individual).

The area of share options and employee incentivisation is a complex one on which specialist advice should be sought.

INVESTOR TAX RELIEFS

There are also incentives aimed at encouraging UK resident individuals to invest in smaller, higher-risk trading companies, by offering tax reliefs for the purchase of new shares in such companies. So far as direct investment in companies is concerned, the main schemes are as follows.

Enterprise Investment Scheme (EIS) – Under EIS, an investor can claim income tax relief (i.e. a reduction in their income tax liability) of up to 30% of the amount invested (up to a maximum investment of £1,000,000 in a single tax year). The investor can also use the amount invested to defer other capital gains (whether or not on shares), with the deferred gain crystallising when the EIS shares are disposed of. In addition, disposals of EIS shares after three years may be free from capital gains tax. EIS is aimed at smaller, unquoted companies and enables such companies to raise up to £5m in any 12 month period.

Seed EIS (SEIS) – An individual subscribing for shares that qualify for SEIS can claim income tax relief of up to 50% of the amount invested (up to a maximum annual investment of £100,000). In addition, disposals of SEIS shares after three years may be free from capital gains tax. There is also a relief equal to 50% of capital gains tax payable on gains realised from the disposal of other assets, where the gains are reinvested in SEIS shares within the same tax year. This relief is also subject to the same £100,000 annual investment limit. SEIS is targeted at companies whose trade is less than two years old and whose assets (pre-subscription) do not exceed £200,000.

3.4 UK TAXATION FOR FOREIGN NATIONALS

Paul Barham, Mazars

This chapter gives a brief overview of the UK tax considerations for a foreign national coming to the UK to work. By necessity, it only highlights the areas to consider and gives some indication of the current law. Advice should be sought in all respects, preferably before coming to the UK.

BASIS OF TAXATION

There are two concepts which need to be understood with regard to taxation in the UK. These are:

1. Residence
2. Domicile

Residence

Up until 5 April 2013, the question of residence in the UK was always a matter of case law and interpretation by the UK tax authorities, being broadly the number of days a person spends in the UK and their connections to the UK.

A new statutory residence test has been introduced from 6 April 2013. The legislation contains three parts detailing rules which will result in conclusive non residence, conclusive residence and a list of 'connecting factors' which will determine residence for the individuals who do not fall within the conclusive tests.

The tests are looked at in a certain order and only if a test is not satisfied do you move on to the next test.

The new rules are extensive and exhaustive but generally if a person comes here to work full time they will be resident in the UK for tax purposes. Although the tests are meant to give certainty, HMRC have issued substantial interpretation and guidance which indicates they are not necessarily as straightforward as they first look. There are also anti avoidance rules to ensure that the rules are not used in a way that the UK Government did not intend.

"Overseas workday relief" is available if certain conditions are satisfied. It only applies to non UK domiciled individuals (see below) and will, in limited circumstances give the "remittance basis" to foreign employment duties.

Domicile

Domicile is a concept of general law; not a tax law and it is determined in a different way to residence. It is only relevant to taxation in the UK if a person is not domiciled in the UK.

There are three types of domicile relevant to Income Tax ("IT") and Capital Gains Tax ("CGT"). These are:

- *Domicile of origin:* An individual will normally acquire a domicile of origin from their father at birth. An individual's domicile of origin need not be the country in which the individual was born. This is determined by the relevant parent's domicile at the child's birth.
- *Domicile of choice*: An individual has the legal capacity to acquire a new domicile at the age of 16. Whilst it is possible to acquire a domicile of choice, this means much more than simple residence and a person must settle in another country permanently and sever ties with the country of origin. It is extremely difficult to acquire a domicile of choice.
- *Domicile of dependence:* A child under 16 cannot have a domicile of choice. Whilst under 16 their domicile will follow that of the person on whom the individual is legally dependent.

In the 2015 Summer Budget, it was announced that changes would be made to the taxation of non-UK domiciled individuals who have been UK tax resident for more than 15 years and for non-UK domiciled individuals who own UK residential property.

Under these measures due to apply from April 2017:

- Non-UK domiciled individuals who have been tax resident in the UK for 15 out of the last 20 tax years will be treated as UK domiciled for all UK tax purposes.
- An individual with a UK domicile of origin who has established a domicile of choice elsewhere will be treated as UK domiciled for all tax purposes as soon as he becomes tax resident.
- All UK residential property held by a non-UK domiciled individual, whether directly or indirectly, including UK residential property held by offshore

companies, offshore trusts and non-UK partnerships will be subject to UK inheritance tax.

UK Taxation

In general, individuals resident in the UK will be liable on all their worldwide income and gains, known as the "arising basis" of taxation. This means that they will pay UK tax on all of their income as it arises and on their gains as they are realised, wherever that income and those gains arise in the world.

Whilst an individual is non-domiciled he can choose whether to use the "remittance basis" of taxation which is discussed later in this chapter.

Personal Allowances

In general, individuals resident in the UK are entitled to an income tax personal allowance. This is set at £10,600 for the 2015/16 tax year and is the amount of income each individual can receive before they are liable to tax. For individuals with income over this amount, tax is only charged on income in excess of £10,600.

However, a personal allowance will not be available in certain circumstances, and so the individual will be chargeable to tax on all of their income. The allowances are withdrawn either where the income is in excess of £100,000 (and it is withdrawn gradually), or where the remittance basis is being claimed under certain circumstances.

There is also a CGT annual allowance available to reduce chargeable gains, which is currently set at £11,100 for the 2015/16 tax year.

UK Tax Rates

Most forms of income are chargeable to tax at the following rates for the 2015/16 tax year:

£0 - £10,600	0%*
£10,601 - £42,385	20%*
£42,386 - £150,000	40%*
£150,000 +	45%

* If the personal allowances are still available.

CGT for individuals is currently 18% if their marginal rate of income tax is 20% or below and 28% if their marginal rate of income tax is 40% or above.

Access to the Remittance Basis

Where an individual is resident in the UK, but not domiciled in the UK, they will have a choice whether to use the arising basis of taxation and therefore be taxed on their worldwide income or gains as they arise or to use the remittance basis of taxation.

If a claim for the remittance basis is made then the individual will only be liable to tax on income and gains arising in the UK and any overseas income and gains "remitted" (i.e. brought to or used to benefit the individual) in the UK.

Where an individual has been in the UK for less than 7 years, he can claim the remittance basis without paying for the privilege, however this will result in the loss of his personal allowance and CGT allowance.

Long term residents in the UK (broadly resident seven out of nine years) must pay a £30,000 remittance basis charge (RBC). Furthermore, where an individual has been in the UK for 12 out of the last 14 years, this RBC is increased to £60,000 per annum. From 6 April 2015, a higher charge of £90,000 per annum applies to individuals who have been UK resident for 17 out of the last 20 years. From April 2017, the remittance basis of taxation will no longer be available to individuals who have been resident in the UK for 15 out of the last 20 tax years.

This is a particular area which needs specialist advice and would require a whole book to cover the rules, planning and anti avoidance in sufficient detail.

ON ARRIVAL

There are no specific tax forms which need to be completed on arrival in the UK, other than to register with HMRC as necessary. There are likely to be two registrations, one to obtain a National Insurance number and one to register with HMRC for tax purposes. Both of these are discussed briefly below.

National Insurance Contributions

Both employers and employees, including self-employed people, make compulsory National Insurance Contributions (NIC) to HMRC in order to pay for a number of social benefits including the state pension and jobseeker's allowance. Men over the age of 65 and women over the age of 60 are exempt from making these contributions, although the age limit for women is in the process of rising from 60 to 65 to equalise with men. For employees, their employers will calculate their NIC and deduct this from their gross pay using PAYE; self-employed persons must work out their contributions themselves.

All UK residents over the age of 16 must have a National Insurance number if they wish to work in the UK and have their contributions credited to their "account".

So, before working in the UK, an individual will need to obtain a National Insurance number. This can be obtained by contacting HMRC and arranging for either an 'Evidence of Identity' interview or agreeing to submit a postal application in limited circumstances.

If an employee is being sent to the UK by his employer, the position in respect of social security will vary depending on the country from which the employee is being sent. It may be possible for the employee to continue paying social security in their home country or it may even be compulsory. Either way, agreement will need to be obtained from the tax authorities to ensure the appropriate compliance requirements are met.

In some circumstances, a 52 week NIC holiday may be appropriate, where the employee continues to pay social security in their home country for the first 52 weeks and then commences paying NIC in the UK.

National Insurance rates for 2015/16 are 12% for employees up to the higher rate of income tax and 2% thereafter, and for employers they are 13.8%. There is a small exemption broadly equivalent to the personal allowance.

UK Tax Return Requirements

The UK tax year runs from the 6 April one year to 5 April of the next. The UK operates a "self assessment" system meaning that the responsibility to ensure the correct amount of tax is paid rests with the individual taxpayer. A UK tax return is likely to be required where the following circumstances apply:

- the individual is the director of a company in the UK; or
- he chooses to make a claim for the remittance basis; or
- he has income which is subject to tax (or a further tax liability) in the UK.

If an individual needs to be within the self assessment system he needs to complete form SA1 (obtainable from HMRC) to be registered.

HMRC does not generally assist an individual in the preparation of his tax return but they can ask questions and challenge certain items on the return. In general they are able to do this for up to a year after the return has been filed, though in certain cases this can be extended for up to 6 years.

HMRC may request that a return is prepared, but if they do not request a return, the individual is responsible for notifying HMRC that he is required to prepare a return for a particular tax year.

Completed tax returns need to be filed with HMRC by 31 October following the tax year end where the individual files a paper tax return. In most cases tax returns should be filed online as this provides a much more efficient service from HMRC and in addition, this extends the filing deadline to 31 January following the end of the tax year.

If the tax return is filed late, an automatic penalty of £100 will be charged which may be increased if the delay in filing is extended beyond 3 months.

Any additional tax liability will need to be paid to HMRC by 31 January following the end of the tax year. Provided the return has been processed by this time the taxpayer should receive a reminder from HMRC, providing details of how to pay and a payslip to use when making the payment.

If the individual's return has not been processed by this time, he is still liable to pay his tax by 31 January.

If the tax is paid late, interest will be charged from the day after the due date. In addition, if the tax has not been paid within a month of the due date, a surcharge of 5% of the outstanding balance will be levied. Further charges may be raised if the tax liability remains unpaid after this date.

For an individual coming to the UK, the date of arrival and some brief details on the individual intentions should be disclosed in the annual income tax return for the tax year of arrival.

OTHER TAXES

Capital Gains Tax

Mention has been made earlier of CGT with regard to the annual allowance and the tax rates at which it is charged. CGT is broadly charged on any gain made on holding an investment, such as shares or property.

There are several valuable exemptions, the most important one being an exemption for an individual's main residence. In addition, there are certain tax breaks which are available to encourage investment. One of those is Entrepreneurs' Relief, described below.

Entrepreneurs' Relief

Entrepreneurs' Relief (ER) is available for "qualifying business disposals". The effect is to reduce the rate of Capital Gains Tax from 18% or 28% to 10%, for total lifetime gains of £10 million.

A claim for ER can be made more than once, but the total cumulative gains cannot exceed £10 million. If this is the case, any gains over this limit will be subject to the higher rates of CGT.

A "qualifying business disposal" includes a disposal of shares in a trading company, or the holding company of a trading group.

ER is normally available provided that, for a period of 12 months ending with the date of the sale, the individual holds at least 5% of the ordinary share capital; can exercise at least 5% of the voting rights and is an officer or employee of the company or of one or more of the companies which are members of the trading group.

Compliance with the rules should be checked carefully.

Business Investment Relief

This relief is aimed at UK resident non domiciled individuals and has been introduced to encourage inward investment. Subject to certain conditions, overseas income and gains can be remitted into the UK for investment into eligible trading companies, without triggering a tax charge on those funds being remitted to the UK. There is no limit to the investment and although there are some anti avoidance provisions, the rules appear to be relatively generous.

This relief is relatively new and advice should be taken to ensure any remitted funds qualify before investment.

Inheritance Tax

The charge to Inheritance Tax ("IHT") is based on where the asset is situated and the domicile of the person concerned; the place of residence is irrelevant.

Deemed Domicile

Currently, the concept of deemed domicile only applies for IHT purposes, and is essentially an anti-avoidance provision. In the 2015 Summer Budget it was announced that the concept of deemed domicile will be extended to all taxes from April 2017 where an individual is resident in the UK for 15 of the last 20 tax years

At present, if an individual comes to the UK he will be deemed domiciled in the UK once he has been resident in the UK for 17 out of 20 years. Certain Double Taxation Treaties may override these rules and should be checked carefully.

Basis of Taxation

IHT is an integrated lifetime transfer and estates tax, and is a tax on capital transfers of value by an individual on certain lifetime gifts which are taxed immediately, lifetime gifts where the donor dies within seven years from the date of the gift and the chargeable estate upon the individual's death.

Each individual is entitled to a nil rate band ("NRB") (currently £325,000 for 2015/16). Only transfers of value exceeding this band are liable to IHT. Any unused NRB can now be shared by spouses/civil partners on second death. The NRB is not an annual exemption. It is a seven year cumulative band which takes into account the previous seven years' chargeable transfers when determining whether a transfer has exceeded the NRB.

IHT is currently charged at rates of: 20% for lifetime transfers and 40% on death.

There are three types of lifetime gift: exempt transfers, potentially exempt transfers and chargeable lifetime transfers.

Upon death an individual is deemed to have made a transfer of value equal to the whole of their chargeable estate, which is the total value of all their capital assets less any amounts owing at the date of death.

Examples of the most common exempt transfers are transfers between spouses and civil partners, gifts to UK registered charities, the annual exemption – (the first £3,000 of gifts made each tax year) – and small gifts up to £250 de minimis. There are other valuable exemptions available.

The most common chargeable lifetime transfers (CLTs) are gifts to trusts. Most gifts to trusts (except charitable trusts or trusts for the disabled) are CLTs.

Potentially exempt transfers are all lifetime gifts between individuals. During the donor's lifetime the transfers are treated as exempt from IHT and if the donor survives seven years from the date of the gift the transfer is completely exempt.

If the donor dies within seven years of the date of the gift the transfer becomes chargeable, although the amount chargeable depends on how many years have passed between the date of the gift and the date of death.

It was announced in the 2015 Summer Budget that a main residence NRB will be phased in from 2017/18. By 2020/21 this should be worth £175,000. The main residence NRB will effectively be transferable between spouses so on the death of the second spouse a family home worth £1million could be passed on to their descendants without incurring an IHT charge. This relief will be withdrawn gradually where the net value of the estate exceeds £2million. Advice will need to be taken to ensure that the appropriate amount of relief is claimed.

OTHER CONSIDERATIONS

Remuneration Packages

Any benefits provided to an employee, either in the UK or in their home country, will need to be considered when calculating the UK tax position and some of the more popular benefits are mentioned briefly below.

It is also possible to use share schemes and incentives to remunerate in a tax efficient manner and these are discussed elsewhere in the book.

Common Benefits

If accommodation is provided rent free or at a subsidised rate, the relevant benefit of that will be chargeable to both tax and NI. If the value of the property provided is in excess of £75,000, the tax benefit is particularly high and there are ways of minimising the tax liabilities.

If the employer helps with the move to the UK, there are some valuable reliefs worth up to £8,000 but it is important that advice and planning is undertaken before the move takes place.

If an employee is sent to the UK on a temporary secondment for less than 24 months it may be possible to claim tax relief in respect of the expenses in attending the "temporary workplace" in the UK. These expenses would include, but not restricted to accommodation costs, utilities, ordinary commuting to the temporary workplace and subsistence. This relief may extend to cover travel between the UK and their home country.

The taxable benefit of a car is generally calculated on its CO_2 emissions and the list price before discounts. This has led to a move towards more fuel efficient cars and can make a difference to the overall taxable benefit.

Double Taxation

It is always worthwhile to remember that there is a guiding principle that no one should suffer double taxation on the same income, gains or assets in more than one country. However, how this relief is given depends on the country of origin and any double taxation treaty which may be in force with the UK.

Taxation could be due in both countries, the country of origin only, or the country where the source is "arising". This changes depending on the type of income or gains and whether there is an old treaty, a new treaty or even no treaty at all.

Once again, if at all possible, the interaction between the countries should be checked before the foreign national arrives in the UK.

3.5 FINANCIAL COMPLIANCE AND AN OUTSOURCED SOLUTION

James Smalley, Mazars

INTRODUCTION

After setting up a company in the UK there are various statutory and fiscal returns that need to be completed as the company develops. Typically, an overseas company will engage an accounting and outsourcing firm to provide these services, By engaging an external provider to provide this compliance it can release a company's senior management team from often time consuming and burdensome fiscal compliance, allowing them to focus on the activities that really matter to the growth and success of the business and giving them peace of mind that the company is being looked after and penalties are not being incurred.

TYPICAL FINANCIAL COMPLIANCE REQUIREMENTS

After a company has been formed, typically it will have the following compliance requirements:

Initial set up
- Company formation
- Registration of taxes (Corporation tax, VAT)
- Set up of PAYE payroll
- Set up of pension scheme under Auto-enrolment

Common on-going requirements may include
- VAT returns to prepare and submit (typically quarterly)
- Corporation tax returns

- Statutory accounts
- RTI monthly reporting of payroll
- Auto-enrolment pension administration
- P11D and P11D(b) benefit returns
- National statistics return
- ECSL or Intrastat returns for European trade
- Maintaining suitable accounting and statutory records

WHY OUTSOURCE FINANCIAL FUNCTIONS?

The above compliance requirements can be delivered by the company but there is often not the breadth of technical knowledge to deliver them within an organisation. These compliance areas are often looked after by a third party provider from whom the following benefits can be derived.

Compliance

When someone creates a company in the UK and becomes a director there are a number of responsibilities that the individual takes on. There are both civil and criminal penalties if these rules are not complied with. One responsibility is to maintain proper accounting records and outsourcing the financial function can help in ensuring local legislation is met. This is a key benefit to outsourcing the finance function and can give the security and peace of mind that the business is compliant.

Risk Management

Every business investment carries a certain amount of risk. Markets, competition, government regulations, financial conditions and technologies can all change quickly. An external outsourcing provider is responsible for keeping abreast of regulatory changes and ensuring that the business is up-to-date and fully compliant. This is particularly relevant for inward investment organisations where the parent company and the management of the organization operate outside of the UK and are therefore less exposed to or aware of regulatory changes. The result of non-compliance can be hefty penalties and fines.

Local Knowledge

Using an external provider with local knowledge and experience ensures the investor is aware of the country-specific taxes and concessions that may be available to them. This is an area where a proactive provider may be able to save the business both time and money.

Staffing and Recruitment

It can be expensive to recruit a new resource and getting the right resource to cover all requirements can be difficult when a business is in its early stages. There tends not be enough work for a full-time financial controller and issues can arise which need a greater level of skill than a regular book-keeper can provide. Recruiting and training staff can also take time which can be avoided with the use of a suitably experienced outsourcing provider.

Additional Resource

If staff are recruited there may be busy times of the month or year when extra support may be needed. This could be to meet deadlines, provide cover for a member of accounting staff on long term leave, assist with accounting reconciliations or incomplete records, or to enable post acquisition accounting alignment. In these situations an external outsourcing provider can be flexible in the level of resourcing provided, both in terms of skills and manpower, enabling the business to cope with the peaks and troughs in its workflow. This can provide greater continuity in the staff engaged and ensure that knowledge is not lost.

Variable Costs

Outsourcing converts fixed costs into variable costs. In the early stages of a new business venture when the pace of growth is uncertain, outsourcing can help management control costs by managing them flexibly.

Legal Redress

An external supplier will provide services in line with a legally binding contract which has financial penalties and legal redress. This gives the business a level of accountability and assurance which does not exist when services are provided by an internal team. However consideration should be given to the size and reputation of the firm delivering the service and its ability to resolve any issues that might arise.

Focus on the Core Business

Productivity can be increased as an external provider can take on volume transactions or labour-intensive procedures and carry them out quickly and efficiently using tried and tested processes. This allows the company's management team and staff to focus on the core functions of the business where they add most value. An increase in productivity can directly influence the bottom line.

Technical Expertise and Core Skills

Using an external provider can give you access to a larger pool of talent and technical knowledge. This may manifest itself in the production of consolidated reporting or the consistent reliability of monthly reporting deadlines being met. It also means that you have a quick route to deal with business critical matters such as resolution of tax queries or the settlement of payments on a local basis.

Payroll

The key area to any business is the people who drive it forward. With international business and personnel being transferred across borders there can be both visa issues and tax issues for the individual and the company. Outsourcing the payroll, expatriate tax advice and immigration support to one provider means that employees are looked after when overseas and local legislation is complied with. This means that they are paid on time and local tax issues are dealt with.

WHICH FUNCTIONS CAN BE OUTSOURCED?

When a company outsources the financial and accounting compliance additional non-core areas of the business are often considered as well. This is often to take advantage of the third party providers' intellectual capital and the technical knowledge they have of system implementation and to deal with other non-core administrative areas:

Management Accounting & Reporting

- Management accounts production
- KPI reporting
- Consolidation packs

Legal & administration
- Company secretarial services
- Fiduciary services

Interim accounting solutions
- Provision of manpower
- Accounting support
- Emergency accounting

High volume business processes
- General ledger
- Accounts receivable
- Accounts payable
- Payroll
- Fixed assets

Non-financial solutions

- *HR*
- Procurement
- Insurance claims
- IT Support

3.6 EMPLOYMENT LAW

Asha Kumar, Watson Farley & Williams LLP

INTRODUCTION

Employment law in the UK has changed over the decades to reflect social and political changes, and has also been affected by the UK's membership of the European Union (EU). The UK Government has made various amendments to the law in this area, with the aim of deregulating it and making the UK more competitive and a more attractive place to do business. Any business considering the UK as a place of business needs to be aware of the employment and immigration laws that operate in the UK. Those investing in the UK will have to deal with different aspects of employment protection according to the mechanism used to invest in the UK, and it should also be noted that special protection is afforded to employees where there is a merger or acquisition of a business.

This chapter seeks to assist those unfamiliar with UK employment law by providing an overview of the rights and obligations afforded to individuals through the employment relationship.

EMPLOYMENT STATUS

In common with other European countries, UK employment law distinguishes between "employees", "workers" and the "self-employed". This status is important because it determines the statutory employment rights to which a person is entitled.

Significant rights are conferred upon employees who, traditionally, have been seen as individuals with full-time jobs working under indefinite employment contracts. However, as new working arrangements emerge, the UK has seen an increase in the number of individuals whose working arrangements fall outside the traditional pattern.

There is no statutory definition of "employee", and while case law has developed in this area, the actual finding of employment status depends upon the circumstances of each particular case. As a consequence, the growth of legislation that applies to "workers", a term wider than "employees", embraces certain types of self-employment. It should also be noted that there is now limited employment law protection for qualifying temporary agency workers.

In addition, a new status of "employee shareholder" has been recently created. This is a new type of employment status, whereby employees give up certain employment rights, such as unfair dismissal (apart from dismissal on the grounds of discrimination and in relation to health and safety) and statutory redundancy payments, in return for an award of shares worth at least £2,000.

CONTRACTS OF EMPLOYMENT

A contract of employment comes into existence as soon as someone accepts an offer of employment in return for pay. It is legally binding between the employer and employee, and can be written or oral, express or implied, or a combination of these. In addition, some employment terms are imposed into contracts by statute.

While employers are obliged only to provide a written statement of the main employment particulars (see below), it is recommended that employees are given a full written contract, as it provides certainty and may help to avoid later disputes. However, even a written contract may not necessarily reflect all of the terms that apply in an employment relationship, and terms are often implied into a contract. These may be necessary to make the contract workable or may reflect custom and practice.

A contract can be for an indefinite duration, terminable on an agreed period of notice, or for a fixed term. Protection is afforded to a fixed-term worker so that he/she cannot be treated less favourably than an equivalent permanent worker, unless the treatment is objectively justified. In certain circumstances, fixed-term contracts automatically become permanent contracts.

Written Particulars of Employment

The Employment Rights Act 1996 obliges employers to provide employees with a written statement of employment particulars. The written statement is not necessarily a contract, but can provide evidence of the terms and conditions of employment. It must be provided to the employee within two months of the employment commencing and must contain certain basic information, including:

- the names of the employer and employee;
- the rate of remuneration and the intervals at which it is to be paid;
- the hours of work; and
- holiday entitlement.

An employee who has not been provided with the required particulars may make a complaint to the Employment Tribunal, which may award him/her between two and four weeks' pay. For these purposes, a week's pay is currently capped at £475, and this generally increases annually on 6 April each year.

Policies and Procedures

Often written contracts are supplemented by the use of policies and procedures that describe the employer's more general employment practices, such as email and internet use.

MINIMUM STATUTORY PROVISIONS

In the UK, employees (and sometimes workers) are provided with minimum terms, which are aimed at providing decent minimum standards and promoting fairness at work. Many of the minimum standards were introduced in order to implement European directives, and consequently similar provisions apply throughout Europe. Minimum terms related to the following cannot be overridden:

- the national minimum wage;
- statutory sick pay;
- working hours;
- notice periods;
- employers' liability insurance; and
- health and safety.

National Minimum Wage

The National Minimum Wage Act applies to almost all workers and sets minimum hourly rates of pay. The national minimum wage is reviewed annually. The rates vary for different groups of workers and as of 1 October 2015, were set as follows:

- £6.70 an hour for workers aged 21 and over;
- £5.30 an hour for 18-20 year olds;
- £3.87 an hour for all workers aged 16-17; and
- £3.30 for apprentices.

Statutory Sick Pay

Eligible employees are entitled to receive statutory sick pay (SSP) for up to 28 weeks in one period, or more than one linked period, of sickness (periods with eight weeks or less between them are linked). A helpful SSP calculator can be found on the HM Revenue and Customs website.[1]

[1] http://www.hmrc.gov.uk/calcs/ssp.htm

The rate of SSP is reviewed annually and is currently £88.45 per week. In certain circumstances, an employer may be able to recover some or all of any SSP they have paid to their employees.

As a matter of policy, employers may choose to pay employees full pay (inclusive of SSP) for a limited period; this is referred to as "contractual sick pay".

Working Hours

The Working Time Regulations implement a European directive aimed at protecting the health and safety of workers by ensuring that working time does not adversely affect a worker's health. In summary, the regulations provide details of:

- the 48 hour week;
- rest breaks; and
- annual leave.

The 48-hour Week

An employer cannot require an employee to work more than an average of 48 hours a week, although there are a number of exceptions to this rule for senior employees and certain other categories of employment. Unlike many other European countries, Britain has negotiated an opt-out whereby this limit does not apply if an employee agrees in writing with his/her employer that it is not to be applied. It should be noted that the employer cannot compel the employee to opt-out and that the employee can reverse this opt-out by giving appropriate notice.

Rest Breaks

Workers have the right to an uninterrupted rest period of at least 11 hours between working days, and to a 24-hour period clear of work each week. Additional rest breaks must be provided to workers whose pattern of work puts their health and safety at risk. The regulations also provide the right to a rest break of at least 20 minutes after six hours of consecutive work. Special provisions apply to night workers.

Annual Leave

Workers currently have the right to a minimum of 5.6 weeks' paid annual leave. This right applies from the first day of employment and accrues at the rate of one-twelfth of the annual entitlement per month worked. A "week" reflects the employee's working week. So, where an employee works a five-day week, he/she will be entitled to 28 days' annual leave, and if an employee works three days a week, he/she will be entitled to 16.8 days' annual leave. In practice, many employers offer employees the statutory minimum inclusive of bank holidays and will provide employees in senior roles with additional annual leave.

Grievance and Disciplinary Procedures

When resolving workplace disputes there is a requirement for both parties to comply with a code of practice developed by the Advisory, Conciliation and Arbitration Service (ACAS). The ACAS Code provides basic practical guidance to employers, employees and their representatives and sets out principles for handling disciplinary and grievance situations in the workplace. If an employee or employer is unreasonable in its failure to follow the new code of practice, employment tribunals will be able to order an increase or decrease in awards of up to 25 per cent.

Notice Periods

The minimum legal notice periods to be given by an employer are:

- one week's notice if the employee has been continuously employed by the employer for at least one month but for less than two years; or
- two weeks' notice if the employee has been continuously employed by the employer for two years, plus an additional week's notice for each further complete year of continuous employment, up to a maximum of 12 weeks.

An employee's contract of employment may, however, provide for a longer notice period. An employment contract may be terminated without advance notice where the employee has committed an act of gross misconduct.

In the absence of any contrary contractual provisions, an employee who has been employed for one month or more must give their employer at least one week's notice to terminate their employment.

Employers' Liability Insurance

Every employer in the UK must have employers' liability insurance, which covers employers against damages and legal costs following injury or disease to its employees during their employment.

Health and Safety

In the UK, employers have legal obligations to ensure a safe workplace. The health and safety obligations are extensive and if breached may give rise to criminal liabilities. Further details can be obtained from the Health and Safety Executive's website.[1]

Work/life Balance

Over the years, legislation has been brought in to enable employees to achieve a better work/life balance. It has been particularly targeted at parents to enable them to spend adequate time bringing up their children by allowing them to work around their commitments.

---

[1] http://www.hse.gov.uk

Maternity Leave

All pregnant employees are entitled to 52 weeks' maternity leave. All employment benefits including non-contractual benefits connected with an employee's employment that are not "remuneration", continue to be provided for the full period of maternity leave.

Employees on maternity leave who are eligible are also entitled to receive up to 39 weeks' statutory maternity pay (SMP) at the rate set by statute. The first six weeks of SMP are earnings-related, and an employee is entitled to 90 per cent of her average weekly earnings with no upper limit. The remaining 33 weeks are paid at a lower rate, which is currently £139.58 (or 90 per cent of earnings if this is less).

Employees who are not eligible for SMP may be entitled to a Maternity Allowance for up to 39 weeks. This is currently £139.58 per week (or 90 per cent of earnings if this is less) and is claimed from the Department for Work and Pensions. Similar provisions to those set out above apply on the adoption of a child.

Shared Parental Leave

On 5 April 2015, the Children and Families Act 2014 introduced a new system of "shared parental leave" (SPL) for eligible employees and agency workers. The new statutory shared parental leave scheme allows parents to share the statutory maternity leave and pay that is currently available only to mothers (and adoptive parents to share the adoption leave and pay currently only available to the primary adopter). Parents can share up to 50 weeks of SPL and 37 weeks of Shared Parental Pay. Leave does not have to be taken consecutively so both parents may be absent from work at the same time if they elect to do so.

Paternity Leave

Eligible employees whose partners are expected to give birth will be entitled to time off at or around the time of the birth. They are entitled to take either one or two consecutive weeks' leave as paid paternity leave. Statutory paternity pay is either 90 per cent of an employee's weekly earnings or the prescribed amount (currently £139.58), whichever is the lesser.

Parental Leave

Parents who have at least one year's continuous employment may take up to 18 weeks' unpaid parental leave for each child up to that child's 18th birthday.

Time Off to Care for Dependants

In the UK, all employees have the right to take a reasonable amount of time off, without pay, to care for dependants. The right to time off is intended to enable employees to deal with an emergency in the short-term and/or, where necessary, to make longer-term care arrangements.

Right to Request Flexible Working

Changes to the flexible working regime in the UK have finally been put in place, so now any employee with 26 weeks' continuous service has a right to request flexible working.

Part-time Working

Protection is also afforded to those who work on a part-time basis. Regulations have introduced provisions that prevent part-time workers from being treated less favourably than equivalent full-time employees, unless this is justifiable. Part-time employees should also have access to the same rights and benefits as full-time employees, albeit on a *pro-rata* basis.

EQUALITY PROVISIONS

In the UK the Equality Act 2010 outlaws discrimination on the grounds of gender reassignment, marriage and civil partnership, pregnancy and maternity, sex, race, disability, sexual orientation, religion or belief and age. Generally, the law recognizes the following types of discrimination:

- Direct discrimination: this is where someone is treated differently because of their sex, race, etc. It is not necessary to show an unlawful motive; it is the reason for the treatment that matters.
- Indirect discrimination: this is a less obvious form of discrimination. It occurs where certain requirements, conditions or practices imposed by an employer, although applied equally to all employees, have a disproportionately adverse impact on one group or other.
- Harassment: this is where one person subjects another to unwanted conduct related to their sex, race, etc., which has the purpose or effect of violating the other's dignity, or creating an intimidating, hostile, degrading, humiliating or offensive environment for them.
- Victimisation: this is where a person is treated less favourably because they have started proceedings, given evidence or complained about the behaviour of someone who has been harassing them or discriminating against them.

Special provisions apply to disability discrimination and age discrimination. Under the disability discrimination provisions, an employee with a particular condition may receive additional protection where this amounts to a "disability" as defined under the legislation.

MISCELLANEOUS MATTERS

Whistleblowing

Protection is given to employees who disclose or "blow the whistle on" wrongdoings at work. Employees are protected if they blow the whistle and, if they are dismissed or receive detrimental treatment as a result of their action, they can present a claim in an Employment Tribunal. Compensation for whistleblowing is uncapped. Whistleblowers are protected where they disclose in good faith something that relates to:

- the commission of a criminal activity;
- failure to comply with a legal obligation;
- a miscarriage of justice;
- a health and safety issue;
- damage to the environment; and/or
- the deliberate concealing of information about any of the above.

Any disclosure must be made in the public interest.

Data Protection

The UK has data protection or "privacy" laws. Data transfer to companies outside the European Economic Area (EEA) is permitted only when the receiving country has data protection laws that are considered "adequate" by the European Commission. UK data protection laws may give individual employees access to information held on them by their employer, provided that certain conditions are satisfied.

Reporting and Consultation Requirements

The Information and Consultation of Employees Regulations 2004 (ICE) give employees the right to be informed and consulted about the business they work for, including information on the employer's activities and any possible threats to their employment. ICE applies to all undertakings with at least 50 employees. The aim of ICE is to encourage people to develop their own voluntary arrangements tailored to their particular circumstances.

TERMINATION OF EMPLOYMENT

In the UK, employees have the statutory right not to be unfairly dismissed. Generally, this right accrues after an employee has accrued two years' service. A dismissal in the UK will only be "fair" if it falls under one of the following prescribed reasons, namely:

1. capability;
2. conduct;
3. Employment breaching a statutory restriction
4. redundancy; or
5. some other substantial reason that justifies dismissal.

Even though a fair reason may be established, the employer should follow a fair procedure when dismissing an employee, and the parties are required to comply with the ACAS Code.

Where a dismissal is found to be unfair, an employee can recover compensation which is capped at the lower of £78,335 (reviewed annually) or one year's salary of the employee. There are, however, a number of circumstances, including in the event of whistleblowing or discrimination, where 2 years' service is not required and in which an employment tribunal can ignore the cap on compensation and award unlimited compensation. If the reason for dismissal is redundancy, an employee is generally entitled to a statutory redundancy payment, up to a current maximum of £14,250.

Employers should note that there are special rules concerning redundancy. An employer who proposes to make 20 or more employees redundant must consult with the relevant trade union or employee representatives beforehand. Failure to do so may result in compensation of up to 90 days' pay for each affected employee.

Breach of Contract

In addition to statutory rights that apply on dismissal, if an employer does not comply with a term of the employment contract, this may be a breach of contract. An employee can bring a claim for damages for "wrongful dismissal" if they do not receive their notice entitlement under their contract of employment. A fundamental breach of contract will also usually entitle an employee to resign and claim unfair "constructive dismissal". Similar principles apply where an employee breaches their employment contract.

When awarding compensation for breach of contract, UK courts will seek to place the innocent party in the position they would have been in had the contract been properly performed.

MERGERS AND ACQUISITIONS

Where a business or part of an entity is transferred to another by way of a business transfer, the employees in the transferring part are given significant legal safeguards under the Transfer of Undertakings (Protection of Employment) Regulations 2006. These safeguards apply only when there is a transfer of assets and not where the employing entity is the same, as might be the case where the transfer is of shares in the company. These special provisions also apply in certain outsourcing situations.

The special protections include:

- appointment of employee representatives who must be informed (and possibly also consulted) in advance of the transfer;
- inheritance of past (undischarged) liabilities of the employer by the buyer;
- changes to an employee's terms and conditions of employment being rendered potentially unlawful; and
- dismissals in connection with the transfer being rendered unlawful, unless they are for certain specified reasons.

CONCLUSION

It might seem at first sight that employers in the UK are subject to a considerable amount of legislative requirements. It should, however, be borne in mind that many of the provisions, particularly in the area of equal opportunities, were introduced as a result of European directives and thus apply to all EU member states. Further, in many areas the UK has managed to water down the impact of the legislation by opting out of certain provisions.

3.7 PENSIONS IN THE UK

Matthew Beaman, Mazars

This chapter gives a brief overview of the UK pension's regime for both corporations and individuals. Pensions law is subject to regular change, especially over recent years, and this section is merely a high level guide to the current position. Independent advice should be sought in all respects especially in relation to employer responsibilities or the recently introduced individual "pension freedoms."

SOCIAL SECURITY

Like many countries the UK pensions system is based on three tiers:

1. Compulsory membership (UK resident) of a low level state provision, maintained on an unfunded pay as you go basis (Basic State Pension);
2. A small top-up based loosely on earnings during the working life, excluding the self-employed (GRB, SERPS and S2P); and
3. Private provision (both employer sponsored and individual).

The UK social security system as it stands today is based on the Social Security Contributions and Benefits Act 1992 and Social Security Administration Act 1992, as amended by the Social Security Act 1998, the National Insurance Contributions Act 2002 and the National Insurance Contributions and Statutory Payments Act 2004. A dual social insurance and social assistance scheme, as far as pensions are concerned, only provides a very basic level of income at retirement based on the individuals contribution record through their working life as paid by both the employer and employee (both compulsory for UK residents.) It is underpinned by a means tested 'pension credit' system to guarantee a minimum level of income.

Assuming full entitlement the current flat rate basic state pension (BSP) is £115.95 per week for a single person or £185.45 per couple per week. There is also possibly

179

a smaller additional element from two earnings related pensions SERPS (as was) and now S2P again dependent upon national insurance record.

The Pensions Act 2014 made provisions for a new single flat rate state pension to replace (but still recognise) previous elements. This is expected to be implemented from 2016.

State retirement age is currently in transition and will be equalised at 65 for both men and women by November 2018. The retirement age is then set to continue to rise to 67 between 2026 and 2028. Continued rises are expected and a mechanism has been established to review the state pension age every five years.

PRIVATE PROVISION

Until recently there was no requirement for an employer to offer any kind of employer sponsored workplace scheme. Previous attempts to encourage saving included the Stakeholder legislation, but as no employer contribution was required, these were met with little enthusiasm from workers.

The key benefits of UK private provision are the tax relief on contributions (within limits), the fact that the fund(s) can be drawn upon from age 55 even whilst still working if required and that up to 25% of the fund can be taken free of tax as a cash sum.

Since 1ˢᵗ October 2012 that has all changed with 'Auto-Enrolment' as legislated for in the 2008 Pensions Act.

AUTO-ENROLMENT

Transitioning through to 2018, auto-enrolment began with the largest companies and works down in size (based on employee numbers). From a given date "staging date" set by the Department of Work and Pensions (DWP), ALL employers will be required to auto-enrol any qualifying employees into a nominated pension scheme, at least every 3 years. There are a broad ranging and significant set of statutory fines for non-compliance and breaches, and The Pensions Regulator has already demonstrated its ability to enforce these on employers where they deem necessary.

This date is determined by the number of employees on the employer's largest PAYE schedule as was at 1ˢᵗ April 2012. This date could be amended however following any company acquisitions or mergers that have occurred since April 2012. Staging dates cannot be put back, although employers can postpone auto-enrolling employees by up to 3 months. Employees can opt-out but must be re-enrolled every 3 years.

Employers must nominate an appropriate scheme or category to be used for auto-enrolment as a "QWPS" - a qualifying workplace pension scheme. This may be an existing company arrangement, providing it meets certain qualifying criteria or another scheme such as "NEST2 (National Employment Savings Trust) which is available to employers to auto-enrol their employees. Any Scheme used for auto-enrolment however must meet certain standards as confirmed by the Pensions Regulator including the following:

- All member charges are transparent and represent value for money (there are charge caps.);
- Contributions must meet the required minimums (explained in the next section);
- Employees must be auto-enrolled without having to give their consent (no application form);
- There must be an appropriate Scheme default investment fund (employers responsibility to select);
- All employees must receive relevant Scheme information before being auto-enrolled.

Employee Categories

Employers are required to regularly assess their workers (usually via payroll records) to determine how they must be treated under the regulations. The automatic enrolment regulations define 3 different types of worker based on their *total qualifying earnings* as follows:

Earnings/Age	16 - 21	22 - (SPA)	SPA - 75
Under threshold (£5,824 in 2015/16)	Entitled Worker		
Between threshold and trigger (£5,824 - £10,000 in 2015/16)	Non – Eligible Jobholder		
Over trigger (£10,000 in 2015/16)	Non - Eligible	Eligible Jobholder	Non - Eligible

This categorisation then in turn determines the employer duties as follows:

Type of worker	Employer Duty
Eligible Jobholder	Must be automatically enrolled in a qualifying scheme and employer must make minimum contributions for these workers as long as they remain in the scheme.
Non-eligible jobholder	Must be offered the opportunity to opt into an automatic enrolment scheme and employer must make minimum contributions as long as they remain active.
Entitled worker	Must be offered a pension scheme for them to make contributions if they wish. There is no obligation on the Company to contribute.

Contributions

From October 2018, employers will be required to contribute at least 3% of defined employee earnings for all those to be enrolled in the pension scheme.

Employees must be assessed on their total qualifying earnings but contributions can be paid on a chosen definition of earnings, e.g. total pay, qualifying band earnings (£5,824-£42,385) or basic / pensionable pay. Contributions can also be phased from staging date to October 2018, to help employers meet the additional costs they will face on auto-enrolment.

Communications, Records and Registration

Employers have a responsibility to provide employees with communications surrounding their entitlements and options at various stages. There is also the requirement to register the workplace scheme and complete and declaration of compliance within 5 months of staging. As with real-time PAYE there is the requirement to keep records such as any opt-out requests and the data sent to the pension provider.

TYPES OF OCCUPATIONAL SUPPLEMENTARY PLANS

Since the 6th April 2006 when the Finance Act 2004 came into force a single set of conditions now applies to all types of pension plan whether occupational or personal, contract or trust based. Legacy benefit limits based on length of service and/or earnings have been replaced by a lifetime allowance (LTA) which is effectively a total benefit cap and an annual allowance which is a contribution limit. Breaching these limits triggers punitive tax liabilities.

Types of scheme effectively fall under two categories trust based and contract based.

Trust Based Plans

1. Defined Benefit – Promises to provide a retirement income as a percentage of final salary (or averaged salary over the last few years prior to retirement). Entitlement is earned by years of service providing a fraction of final salary per year of service. So, for example, 40 years salary might equate to 40 x 1/60th i.e. 2/3rds final salary. Outside of the public sector (civil service, teachers etc.) these schemes are increasingly rare, however many companies and scheme trustees still have liabilities and scheme management responsibilities to bear which can be increasingly costly with low interest rates and increasing life expectancy.

2. Career Average – career average, is a lower cost scheme to the employer as it looks at earnings over the employee's entire service rather than just earnings prior to retirement.

3. Defined Contribution – Historically trust based, this plan largely moves risk from the employer to the employee as the employer contribution is fixed and the outcome is largely fund dependent. Again with the introduction of auto-enrolment, and due to the responsibilities on trustees, many of these schemes have now closed and converted to non trust based defined contribution.

Contract Based Plans

1. Stakeholder – The Welfare and Pensions Reform Act 1999 required most employers (unless they already had an occupational scheme or less than 5 employees) to offer access to a Stakeholder scheme. No contributions were required from the employer however. In reality therefore these schemes did not really take off, but they did help drive pension charges down in the market in general. Now, with the introduction of auto-enrolment, Stakeholder schemes are generally either being amended to comply with the updated regulations or replaced with a new scheme.

2. Group Personal Pensions – Each member has a personal contract under a group 'umbrella' usually to improve charges and for ease of employer administration. The pot is accrued from the combination of employee and employer contributions and the fund can be used at retirement in various ways to provide income (which may include capital sums).

There are also potentially "SSAS's" (small self-administered scheme) and "SIPP's" (self-invested personal pension) being contributed to through company payrolls, particularly in relation to senior management or directors, as they often allow more individual investment control and asset types. Other than to be aware of their existence, their detail is outside the scope of this chapter.

PENSIONS FREEDOMS

The recent changes (effective on pensions to which individuals become entitled on or from 6 April 2015) have been the subject of much press coverage. Initially announced in the 2014 Budget, the Taxation of Pensions Bill was introduced to Parliament in October 2014. Ultimately the aim was to allow individuals to access their money purchase pension savings as they wish during retirement, subject to their marginal rate of tax.

Income options therefore now include one or a combination of the following;

1. An Annuity – several types but generally they an insurance contract which provides a guaranteed income in exchange for an agreed capital sum. With low interest rates and increasing longevity income levels have dropped significantly in recent years. Along with the loss of capital on death annuities are seeing a decline in popularity. Types of annuity include lifetime, with profits and flexi/ fixed term.
2. Flexi Access Drawdown ("FAD") – allows the choice of income from the fund without reference to any rates or limits other than the size of the fund. Up to 25% of the fund can usually be taken as a tax free lump sum, and the remainder is subject to income tax at the individual's marginal rate.
3. Uncrystallised Funds Pension Lump Sum ("UFLPS") – an alternative option to FAD allows withdrawals directly from the pension funds flexibly. 25% of any amount taken is tax free cash and the rest is taxed income. It is important to note that once any funds are taken using the UFPLS option, a reduced money purchase annual allowance applies. This restricts any further tax relievable money purchase contributions to £10,000 per annum with no carry forward available.
4. Phased retirement – either using annuities or drawdown.

3.8 EMPLOYEE BENEFITS AND INCENTIVE PLANS

Liz Buchan and Rhodri Thomas, Watson Farley & Williams LLP

INTRODUCTION

In the UK it is usual for an employer to provide its employees with a mix of benefits including one or more of: pension arrangements, insured benefits, childcare vouchers and/or stock/share options, in addition to basic salary. Pension arrangements are dealt with in chapter 3.7, but this chapter summarises the other types of benefits which are most common in the UK.

INSURANCES

Introduction
It is very common for employers to provide employees with insured benefits, such as life insurance, private medical insurance and permanent health insurance. These benefits are summarised below.

Life Insurance
This benefit pays out a lump sum in the event of the death of the insured employee. Typical arrangements will provide for a lump sum payment based upon a multiple of the insured employee's annual salary, sometimes up to a maximum salary level. Where an employer provides this benefit through a group life insurance plan (see below), the level of cover that can be provided is capped at four times an employee's annual salary.

Where life insurance is provided as an employee benefit, this will usually be done by the employer establishing a group life assurance plan for which the employer pays the plan premium. Individual employees can then be entered into the plan. The provision of life insurance by an employer (where the group policy meets certain HMRC requirements) does not constitute a taxable benefit in the hands of an employee who is entered into the policy.

Private Medical Insurance

This benefit provides cover to meet the costs of treatment of short-term curable illness or injury of an employee, and consequently ensures that the employee has access to such treatment with as little delay as possible. Certain conditions may, depending on the scope of the policy, be excluded from the cover provided (for example, any conditions pre-existing on commencement of the policy will often be excluded).

Similarly to life insurance plans, group private medical insurance may be arranged by an employer, and individual employees may then be entered into the plan. This will usually decrease the 'per capita' cost of cover, as the employer is able to obtain lower premiums for the group policy than would be available to an individual. However, the value of the premiums paid by the employer in respect of an employee is a taxable benefit for the employee, and the employee will therefore be required to pay income tax on this amount (at the employee's prevailing marginal rate) to HMRC.

Permanent Health Insurance (PHI)

Where an employer provides this benefit to an employee, in the event that the employee becomes unable to work due to illness or accident, the insurer will pay a percentage (usually between 50 and 75%) of the employee's salary for the duration of the employee's incapacity. Sometimes the policy will provide benefits for a maximum fixed period of time, for example, two or five years; in other cases they may pay until the employee's retirement date (provided the employee continues to be incapacitated). PHI policies will usually provide either that an employee must be unable to perform his or her own occupation, or that the employee must be unable to perform work of any kind, in order to receive benefits, although other forms of policy are available.

Payments will begin after a deferment period during which time the employee must be incapacitated (within the meaning prescribed in the policy). Deferment periods of six months are common, although the period may be longer or shorter. Shorter deferment periods will increase the premium payable on the policy. Often the employee will be eligible to receive company sick pay from the employer for some or all of the deferment period, following which the employee may become eligible to receive benefits under the policy.

Where an employer provides PHI as a benefit to employees, it will normally do this by establishing a group plan, into which individual employees may be entered. Where an employer sets up a plan in this way, the provision of PHI cover to an employee is not a taxable benefit in the hands of the employee. However, should an employee become eligible to receive benefits under the PHI policy, those benefits will be taxable as income (this is in contrast to where an individual arranges PHI independently, where any benefits received will not be subject to tax).

CHILDCARE

Many larger employers operate a childcare voucher scheme. Often this runs with a "salary sacrifice" which involves National Insurance advantages for participating employers. A new government sponsored tax-free childcare voucher scheme will be introduced in early 2017. Under the scheme working families will be able to claim 20% of qualifying childcare costs for children under 5 (and children with disabilities under 17). There are plans to make it available for all children under 12. To qualify, all parents in the household must be "in work" earning on average at least £50 a week, although there will be dispensations for certain workers. The new scheme will not be available to families where either parent earns over £150,000. Claims will be capped at £2,000 per child per year. The new scheme will not depend on participation by employers and will not involve a salary sacrifice arrangement. It will be operated via a Government website. Parents who are signed up to the current childcare voucher scheme will be able to remain in the scheme, so they will not be disadvantaged by the proposed 2015 changes. However, if they move to a new employer after the introduction of the new scheme, they will be considered to have left the current scheme and be forced to switch to the new arrangements.

EMPLOYEE INCENTIVE PLANS

Introduction
There are various types of share and share option plans that an employer can establish as a potentially tax efficient way of rewarding and incentivising its employees. The choice of plan or plans will depend on the needs and objectives of the employer. An employer will need to decide whether it wishes to put in place:

An option plan, (in which case Company Share Option Plans (CSOP), Save As You Earn Plans (SAYE), and Enterprise Management Incentive Plans (EMI) may be of interest);

A share plan, (in which case Share Incentive Plans (SIP) or Long-Term Incentive Plans (LTIP) may be of interest); or

A cash based plan which replicates an option or share plan (in which case a "Phantom" Plan may be of interest).

Further details in relation to share and share option plans can be found on HM Revenue & Customs' website. www.hmrc.gov.uk/shareschemes.

Employee Shareholders

Additionally, while not strictly 'employee incentive plans', the concept of 'employee shareholder' employment status was introduced in the UK in 2013, where an employee gives up certain employment rights and protections (including the right not to be unfairly dismissed in certain circumstances) in exchange for shares in their employer. The shares granted to an employee shareholder must have a minimum value (at the time of grant) of £2,000. Tax-favourable treatment applies to all grants of shares to employee shareholders up to a value of £2,000, and on disposal of up to £50,000 of employee shareholder shares.

"Tax Advantaged" and "Non-Tax Advantaged" Plans

Share and option plans are often categorised as "tax advantaged" or "non-tax advantaged" depending on whether or not they attract tax-favourable treatment. Again, employers will need to decide whether a tax advantaged or non-tax advantaged scheme, or even using a tax advantaged scheme together with a non-tax advantaged one, will best suit their objectives. It is also open to employers simply to grant standalone share options (including tax advantaged EMI options), outside of any formal scheme.

Broadly, an employee who is granted a non-tax advantaged option will not normally be charged income tax on the grant of the option itself, nor when the option becomes exercisable. Income tax and National Insurance contributions will, however, be charged following exercise of a non-tax advantaged option on the excess (if any) of the market value of the shares acquired, at the time of acquisition, over the amount paid by the employee to acquire the shares. Capital Gains Tax ("CGT") may also be payable on any increase in value between the date of exercise and the date of disposal, although reliefs may be available to minimise any charge. There may also be PAYE and National Insurance implications for the employer on grant or, more likely, exercise of the option.

By contrast, options granted under the terms of a tax advantaged option plan may, subject to conditions, be exercised without giving rise to a charge to income tax or National Insurance. The employee may still be liable to CGT when he ultimately sells the shares acquired on exercise, but certain tax advantaged plans do offer CGT benefits. CSOPs, SAYEs, SIPs, and EMIs as described below are all tax advantaged plans.

Company Share Option Plans (CSOP)

Summary

A CSOP is a tax advantaged plan under which employees are granted an option allowing them, during a set period of time, to buy up to a specified number of shares at a price fixed at the date of grant. The employer (or company in which the shares are to be acquired) must either be listed on a recognised stock exchange, or free from the control of another company. The price of the shares must not be less than the market value of the shares at the time of grant. To qualify for favourable tax treatment, CSOP options must generally be exercised not less than three years and not more than 10 years after the time of grant.

Under a CSOP the employer is, broadly, free to set its own rules as to the circumstances in which the options may be granted or exercised, provided that any performance-related conditions are objective and not subject to the exercise of discretion by any one person, and that the plan's rules do not contain elements which are neither essential nor reasonably necessary to its operation.

Participation and Limits

The employer can decide on a discretionary basis which of its employees or full time directors can take part in its CSOP. There is, however, a limit of £30,000 on the maximum value of shares over which tax advantaged options granted under a CSOP may be held by an individual at any one time.

Further information on CSOPs can be found on the HMRC website, see p.190.

Save As You Earn Option Plans (SAYE Plans)

Summary

SAYE plans are tax advantaged plans, and as with CSOPs there are eligibility requirements that an employer must satisfy to be able to use a SAYE plan. Employees are given a share option to buy a certain number of shares at a fixed price at a particular time. The shares can only be purchased using amounts saved under special HMRC approved savings arrangements. Employees are required to make savings contributions out of net income over a number of years.

At the end of the fixed period the savings arrangement pays back the contributions, interest thereon, and a bonus, out of which the shares can be purchased, by exercise of the share option. If employees do not exercise their options, they will still receive the proceeds of their savings arrangement, including the bonus.

Participation and Limits

SAYE plans are all-employee plans under which all qualifying employees and directors must be eligible to participate on similar terms. The employer may specify a qualification period of up to five years' employment. Participants may choose to exercise their options at the end of fixed three or five year terms and monthly savings must be between £5 and £500.

Further information on SAYE Plans can be found on the HMRC website, see p.190.

Enterprise Management Incentive Plans (EMI plan)

Summary

EMI plans can be established by qualifying independent trading companies that have gross assets not exceeding £30 million. Certain trades (such as property development) are excluded. Unlike other forms of tax advantaged plans, an employer can seek advance HMRC confirmation that it is eligible to grant EMI options.

Participation and Limits

There are no restrictions on the number of employees who may participate in an EMI plan. Options over shares worth up to £250,000 at the time of grant can be issued to each employee. However, there is an overall limit on the value of unexercised options at any time of £3 million.

There are no rules about when the options may be exercised (although options must be exercised within 10 years of grant to obtain tax and National Insurance relief) or about the price at which options may be granted. Tax relief is limited if the options are granted with an exercise price of less than market value at the time of grant.

A qualifying employer under an EMI plan must have fewer than 250 employees, must not be under the control of any other company and must be carrying on a qualifying trade. It must also have a permanent establishment within the UK.

Individuals, whether they are new recruits or existing employees, must work for the employer for at least 25 hours a week, or if less than 25 hours, for at least 75% of their working time, to qualify for EMI. The purpose of the grant of the option must also be to recruit or retain an employee, and not for the purpose of tax avoidance.

Further guidance on EMI plans can be found on the HMRC website, see p.190.

Share Incentive Plans (SIP)

A SIP is a tax advantaged plan, which operates by providing employees of a company with shares in the company, through a trust. All shares acquired under a SIP must initially be held in a UK resident trust, whose trustees hold shares in the employer on behalf of the employees who join the plan.

In order to obtain the full tax benefits, employees must normally leave their shares in the plan's trust for at least five years. Cash payments are made to the plan's trustees, who buy shares in the employer which are then appropriated to each employee in the plan.

There are four ways by which an employee can obtain shares:

- Free Shares: An employer can award an employee up to £3,600 worth of free shares per annum (with a choice of performance related awards).
- Partnership Shares: An employee can buy shares out of pre-tax remuneration. The maximum percentage of salary which can be used to buy the shares is 10%, with an overall limit of £1,800 per annum.

- Matching Shares: An employer can match the partnership shares bought by an employee by awarding up to two free shares for every partnership share issued.
- Dividend Shares: An employee can use any dividends from their plan shares each year to reinvest in further plan shares.

Further details in relation to SIPs can be found on the HMRC website, see p.190.

Long-Term Incentive Plan (LTIP)
Summary
This is a flexible, non-tax advantaged plan whereby employees receive a deferred right to shares, or to exercise an option to acquire shares at nil (or close to nil) cost. Rights are generally made conditional upon the attainment of pre-set performance targets. The plan is intended to afford incentives for future performance over a period of (usually) three years. Many plans also provide that at the end of the period over which performance is measured, the employees' rights to sell the shares are deferred for a further period of another one, two or three years (i.e. up to six years in total). The plans are often aimed at company executives, to encourage them to become long-term shareholders in the employer.

When shares are ultimately transferred to (or sold on behalf of) the employee under an LTIP, they receive the full value of those shares, not merely, as in the case of a traditional share option, the growth in the value over the option period. This is because, should the targets be met, shares are usually transferred to the recipient at no (or very low) cost.

Participation and Limits
Any employee may participate in the plan at the discretion of the directors/shareholders. Since LTIPs are not tax advantaged plans, there are no limits on the amounts up to which individuals may participate in the plan.

Tax Treatment for the Employee
The tax treatment for the employee will be as described above in relation to non-tax advantaged plans, the employee generally being liable to income tax and National Insurance contributions when shares are received. There may be PAYE and National Insurance considerations for the employer, which generally do not apply to tax advantaged plans.

"Phantom" Share Options ("Phantoms")
Summary
Phantoms are a type of deferred cash bonus arrangement, mirroring the cash benefits that would result from the grant and exercise of a share option, and the immediate sale of the shares acquired. As Phantoms are merely a method of calculating a cash bonus, they are not capable of being tax advantaged plans.

The amount paid as a bonus is calculated by reference to the increase in the market value of a fixed number of shares over the "option period". The employee is granted a right to call upon the employer to pay him a cash sum calculated as the amount of the difference between the "exercise price" (usually the market value at the time of grant) and the market value of those shares at the time of exercise.

Participation and Limits

Any employee or director, at the discretion of the directors/shareholders, is able to participate in the plan. As Phantoms are not capable of being tax advantaged plans, there are no restrictions on the number of shares referable to, or on individual participation.

Tax Treatment for the Employee

The cash bonus paid forms part of the employee's emoluments and is subject to income tax and National Insurance contributions.

Regulatory and HMRC Matters

It is important to note that the UK's Financial Services and Markets Act 2000 (and the underlying Prospectus Rules) may impose requirements on an employer when seeking to establish an employee share or share option plan. There are various exemptions in the legislation which will often mean that no steps need to be taken, or that compliance will be straightforward, but it will always be important to check that the relevant regulatory requirements are being satisfied.

Additionally, all employee share and share option arrangements will need to be registered with HMRC, and declarations as to compliance with statutory requirements will be necessary in respect of tax advantaged plans.

Listed Companies

Listed companies are subject to various additional rules, guidelines and codes of best practice relating to the adoption and amendment of employee share and share option plans. In particular, certain provisions of the UK's Listing Rules and Corporate Governance Code will apply, and listed companies are expected to conform to the ABI Principles of Remuneration, issued by the Association of British Insurers and the Institutional Voting Information Service. The principles are designed to provide a framework to enable companies to operate the full range of employee share plans within prudent limits, which avoid undue dilution of the interests of existing shareholders.

Part Four

Investment in Energy and Regeneration

4.1 INVESTING IN UK REGENERATION PROJECTS

*Jon Pickstone, UKTI's Regeneration
Investment Organisation (RIO)*

Why the UK is so attractive for property investment is a question that UKTI's Regeneration Investment Organisation (RIO) never tires of. The answer includes a combination of attractive financial returns, a secure and low-risk business environment, strong government support, and a wide range of opportunities that meet a diverse range of investor interests.

THE RIO MODEL

RIO was launched by the Prime Minister in November 2013 with a remit to complement the work of commercial agents in helping international finance find and flow into the most suitable UK property development projects. These projects are located across the country and in a wide range of sectors, including commercial, industrial, residential, and leisure.

Such developments contribute to the regeneration and renewal of UK towns and cities, but are not necessarily on previously developed land. The continued prosperity of places also relies on growth and expansion, an ambition that is being met by increasing flows of international capital into UK property investment.

Sir Michael Bear - RIO Chairman and UK Special Envoy for Sustainable Urbanisation, China - explains RIO's role: *"the criteria for projects are straightforward - they must have planning consent and existing partners, and have a value of more than £100m, though sometimes a couple of smaller projects can be bundled together to meet this threshold."* From seasoned experience Sir Michael notes that *"there may be one piece of the jigsaw to come, such as an anchor tenant, a construction partner or a crucial element of infrastructure. RIO helps overseas investors understand risks and returns and how long projects could take to come to fruition. We know the system and how it works. We have the ear of government."*

To help grow investor certainty, RIO can also introduce interested international parties to UK companies with a wealth of development expertise, or to one of several blue-chip domestic investors interested in co-funding models. Seeking to facilitate business-to-business partnerships is a key part of RIO being a one-stop-shop for regeneration investment. A recent example of this was when RIO helped bring together EcoWorld, a Malaysian investor, with Ballymore, a UK developer. The resulting joint venture is expected to bring forward a £2.2bn, primarily residential, London development portfolio.

Case Study: Peak Resort
Announced during the Prime Minister's visit to the USA in January, RIO helped facilitate an investment commitment to create Peak Resort, a new £400m integrated year round leisure, health, sport and education destination. A partnership between UK development company Birchall Properties and US firm Grand Heritage Hotel Group, the US investor was identified by UKTI Denver who – along with other colleagues across North America – sourced potential investors for the scheme. The project will be developed near Chesterfield in Derbyshire, bringing to life a former open-cast mining site, and creating over 1,000 full time equivalent jobs and many more in the construction phase.

RIO has a pipeline of £115bn (Gross Development Value) of projects with over 50 of these currently in commercial dialogue (total value £32bn). Further details of these projects are available from RIO's pages on the UK government's website: www.gov.uk/government/organisations/regeneration-investment-organisation

RIO is supported by being part of UKTI, the UK government's dedicated Department for Trade and Investment. UKTI encourage and support overseas companies to look at the UK as the best place to set-up or expand their business. RIO's work is reinforced by UKTI's professional advisers around the UK and staff across more than 100 countries. This global network provides broad and deep reach into international investment markets and also the ability to respond to multi-sectoral project ambitions, including where property forms a component.

A GREAT TIME TO INVEST

Although live data on the current value of property developments across the UK is limited, both temporal and geographical comparisons evidence this being a favourable time for investing in UK property markets. Figures reported by PwC and the Urban Land Institute show the UK to be the number one destination for property investment in Europe. In Q1-Q3 of 2014, 47bn Euro was invested in UK property, more than 50% more than the next European country, Germany. Deloitte note that US-based companies and funds have been highly active, aided in part by a favourable exchange rate, targeting portfolios and a wide range of property types at a time when UK institutional funds have also been increasing their exposure to real estate.

Deloitte report that "UK commercial property achieved a total return of 17.1% over 2014, according to IPD, which placed it ahead of the majority of countries covered by their data. Among the major investment locations, only Ireland outperformed the UK."

Figures from CBRE show that flows of international capital into this sector have increased every year since the nadir of the 2008 global economic downturn. Inflows from Asia, Europe, and the Americas have all risen substantially.

So, why is the UK evidentially particularly attractive for property investors? Jon Neale, Head of Research at Jones Lang LaSalle, explains:

"The UK's relatively positive economic prospects and high demographic growth, alongside a strong planning system, are probably the most obvious reasons why. However, there are other factors at work. Firstly, there is a long history of protecting the rights of property owners, alongside a well-developed legal, advisory and professional framework. Secondly, a city such as London offers a scale of proposition and a level of liquidity that only a handful of cities (Paris, New York) can match; there is sufficient depth and breadth of interest for a buyer to reassured that they will find a seller. Thirdly, the market is transparent and there is plentiful information on pricing and property ownership. Finally, soft factors are undoubtedly important – familiarity and the English language, to name just two."

RIO is working across government to ensure that these advantages are harnessed effectively and that regeneration is well integrated with wider local economic growth programmes. An example of this was the successful Investment into Cities event that RIO helped organise at Number 10 Downing Street where representations from Birmingham, Bristol and Leeds impressed a range of key investors with development plans and the support of strong local government. Such events and the sectoral and geographical diversity of RIO's pipeline evidence the range of competitive opportunities available across the UK.

OPPORTUNITIES ACROSS THE UK

RIO has seen growing interest in development sites outside London, and Deloitte point to pricing and availability being the key factors drawing property investors to locations outside the capital. Two-thirds of those canvassed for the PwC/Urban Land Institute 2015 Emerging Trends Europe report say "there's a need to consider secondary markets or assets. Their willingness to take on more risk is reflected in this year's ranking of city investment prospects: Birmingham in the UK has moved up to 6th place [in Europe], from 17th last year."

CBRE data on flows of international capital into UK commercial property show that since 2011 higher growth rates have been experienced outside of London. Mat Oakley, Director of Commercial Research at Savills PLC tells a similar story: *"Commercial property investors have clearly rediscovered the joys of the UK regions, with 58% of the total investment in the UK going to markets outside London in 2014. Furthermore, non-domestic investor demand is spilling out into the regions, with 2014 seeing the highest ever level of investment activity by non-domestic investors outside London."*

Momentum and direction of travel is similar in the residential sector where Jim Ward, also a Director at Savills, comments that:

> *"With regard to residential led regeneration, it's all about the strength of our undersupplied residential market, with demand spilling out of the higher value markets of London and other centres of employment, into other well connected markets where this creates the market conditions for value uplift. Investment in new rail links is increasing the reach of this regeneration potential, as is the cyclical pattern of house price inflation which we now expect to shift from London to other parts of the UK."*

THE NORTHERN POWERHOUSE

The Chancellor of the Exchequer's sound economic rationale for the Northern Powerhouse initiative is that increasing the interconnectivity between northern English cities and helping them pool their strengths will increase economic growth in the manner that agglomeration has supported major global cities such as London or Paris.

The scale of these urban areas is similar. The North of England's largest conurbation is Manchester with a population of 2.7 million people, but within 40 miles of Manchester, is a belt of cities and towns that contains 10 million people, including Liverpool, Leeds and Sheffield.

The high-speed rail links between these cities and down to London are increasing investor appetite as are growing airports and ports, cost-competitive workforces, and increasing government support that will drive higher productivity in a region already benefitting from 4 of the world's top 100 universities e.g. through science, technology, advanced manufacturing, and the digital and creative sectors *(Source: QS World University Ranking 2014/15)*.

These investments continue a long history of innovation in an area once the crucible of the industrial revolution, which has regularly advanced the world since, be that Liverpool and Manchester being linked by the world's first inter-city railway, Rutherford splitting the atom, the world's first stored-program computer, or the first isolation of graphene.

A high quality of life here also attracts people to live, work, study and invest. The Northern Powerhouse initiative recognises the importance of continued government investment in quality cultural institutions that enhance a region blessed with several beautiful national parks and a world-renowned heritage of football and popular music.

Regeneration is at the heart of many of these ambitions. Whether it is building incubators for exciting hi-tech firms, or providing Grade A office space to service increasing demand in key locations, RIO introduces international investors to local governments and developers with proud records of getting things done.

Key Northern Powerhouse Projects

Liverpool Waters - www.liverpoolwaters.co.uk

Liverpool Waters is a £5.5bn, 60 hectare, mixed-use development of historic docklands sites. Combining residential and leisure uses with an extension of the city's central business district, it forms an integral part of Liverpool's iconic waterfront. The development sits within the Mersey Waters Enterprise Zone, where additional government tax incentives are available to many investors. The scale of development and World Heritage Site designation make this one of the most significant waterfront regeneration and investment opportunities in Europe. Liverpool Waters is part of the wider c.£75bn Atlantic Gateway plans to reinforce a strategic corridor stretching 40 miles from the Port of Liverpool to the City of Manchester.

Newcastle Science Central - www.newcastlesciencecentral.com
Newcastle is the largest city in North East England - compact and energetic with stunning National Parks and beautiful sandy beaches on its doorstep.

Science Central is its new landmark location for science, business, living and leisure. Spanning 10 hectares of prime development land in Newcastle's city centre, it has excellent transport links, not only locally, but also via the main Edinburgh to London railway line. Science Central is designed to support a thriving community, rewarding jobs and groundbreaking scientific advances. Further bespoke development plots are available with outline planning permission, state-of-the-art telecommunications, infrastructure and utilities plugged-in.

OTHER HIGH VALUE REGENERATION PROJECTS IN THE UK

In a time of favourable market conditions for UK property development, underpinned by robust government support, RIO provides a one-stop-shop for interested international investors. RIO not only promotes a diverse range of high-value regeneration projects in England, Scotland, Wales and Northern Ireland, it also helps guide investors through UK development processes.

This is through the provision of RIO's own advice, connections with professional service providers, and RIO's ability to bring international investors together with UK companies whose standing and expertise helps de-risks projects, especially for newer entrants to UK regeneration markets.

More of RIO's projects are shown below, and many others are showcased at: www.gov.uk/government/organisations/regeneration-investment-organisation RIO will be delighted to explore opportunities with inward investors, contact via: rioenquiries@ukti.gsi.gov.uk

Scotland: Clyde Gateway, Glasgow - www.clydegateway.com
Glasgow, with a population of 1.2 million people, is the commercial capital of Scotland and the UK's largest retail centre after London. It is also one of Europe's top 20 financial centres, and home to many of Scotland's leading businesses.

The Clyde Gateway is the continuing regeneration of 840 hectares of land to the east and south east of Glasgow City Centre, spurred by sites that played host to the 2014 Commonwealth Games. Development is supported by a government-backed urban regeneration company offering regeneration investment opportunities in hotel, commercial, retail and residential. Over £1.5bn of infrastructure development is already complete and new investors and occupiers are moving-in across industrial, office, residential and leisure markets.

Northern Ireland: Titanic Quarter, Belfast - www.titanic-quarter.com

Belfast is the world's top destination city for financial services technology investment, which has led to over 800 international companies establishing themselves there. Recent investors include Allen and Overy, Seagate Technology, Fujitsu, Bombardier Aerospace, Microsoft, Citi, Liberty Mutual, the Allstate Corporation and Baker and McKenzie LLP.

Titanic Quarter - a major new 75 hectare waterfront urban regeneration project – is a leading example of the accommodation high-end occupiers seek. The scheme is market ready; planning has been secured for 370,000 sqm of space of which 140,000 square metres has been completed. Around 5,000 people already live and work there and 100 companies are on site. The scheme will provide homes and employment for a further 50,000 people within a high quality public realm.

Wales: Cardiff Pointe - www.cardiffpointe.co.uk

Cardiff is a high-growth city benefitting from qualities that define competitive locations – from commerciality, connectivity and environment, to culture, character and quality of life and opportunity.

Cardiff Pointe and Cardiff International Sports Village are high-profile seafront regeneration projects in the Welsh capital. A 3,000-seat ice arena is due to open in the sports village at Christmas 2015, with a "real snow" indoor ski slope planned to sit alongside other retail, leisure and hotel facilities. Meanwhile, £700m of neighbouring residential development overlooking Cardiff Bay continues to be released to market, providing 800 new houses and apartments to service the increasing attraction of Cardiff as the principal centre for government, media and finance in Wales.

England's Midlands: Boots Enterprise Zone, Nottingham
- www.investinnottingham.com/enterprisezone

In March 2011 the Alliance Boots UK HQ site was designated as an Enterprise Zone by the UK Government with tax incentives available for some forms of investment. The Group's vision is to create a UK centre for innovation in health, beauty and wellness in Nottingham. Alliance Boots, now part of Walgreens Boots Alliance, already employ over 8,000 people on the site as part of their HQ operation.

As the freeholder, Walgreens Boots Alliance is spearheading development. The site has outline planning permission for around 90,000 square metres of new commercial opportunities and 675 new homes as well as opportunities to reuse existing buildings. Up to 40 hectares of brownfield land is available for development, proximate to Nottingham Science Park and the world class University of Nottingham.

England's South: Royal Pier Waterfront, Southampton
- www.royalpierwaterfront.com/

Southampton, only 80 miles from London, is one of the largest cities in Southern England. Famous for its docks, they remain one of Europe's busiest ports.

Southampton's Royal Pier Waterfront is being redeveloped as part of a wider Southampton City Centre masterplan. Leisure focused development plans include 40-50 new premium shops, waterside restaurants, cafés and bars, an epicurean market, 730 contemporary apartments, a 250 bed 4 or 5* signature hotel, office space and a casino. A cultural, arts and technology hub celebrating Southampton's links with land, sea and air is central to the development as well as improvement of Mayflower Park, site of the world-renowned PSP Southampton Boat Show.

4.2 RENEWABLE ENERGY: A UK PERSPECTIVE

Conall Mullen, Investment Advisor, UKTI Services Team

The UK is currently undergoing an energy revolution with huge investment being undertaken in renewable technologies. Between 2009 and 2013 the UK installed 10GW of renewable electricity generating capacity. The latest figures show that at the end of 2014 17.8% of the UK's electricity demand was being sourced from renewables. Under the EU Renewable Energy Directive the UK must source 15% of its energy from renewables by 2020 (which equates to 30% of electricity, 12% heat and 10% transport) so investment will continue.

The chart below from the Department of Energy and Climate Change illustrates the increase in renewable electricity capacity over the past 5 years. The largest gains in renewable capacity have been made through investment in onshore wind, offshore wind and solar photovoltaic.

FIGURE 4.2.1 – Renewable energy capacity

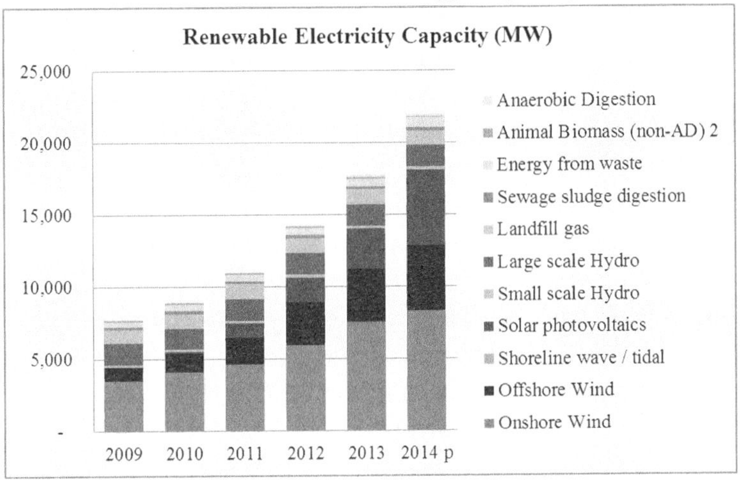

Renewable Electricity Capacity (MW)

Investment has been backed by government through financial schemes for renewable generators. Small scale generation has been incentivised by Feed-in-Tariffs and the Renewable Heat Incentive, whilst large scale technologies have been supported by the Renewables Obligation and Contracts for Difference (CfDs). For more information on these please refer to the Department of Energy and Climate Change website.

Project finance is being provided through the government's Green Investment Bank (GIB). GIB's investments help fund the creation of new energy and waste infrastructure across the UK and with that, new jobs in construction and operations. The bank primarily invests in three sectors: Offshore wind, energy efficiency, waste and bioenergy. GIB works with private sector finance in order to leverage the maximum impact from its own investments.

Although the UK has made large steps towards its 2020 targets there is still a long way to go. The next 5 years will see sustained investment in renewables and opportunities exist for overseas companies to get involved. The UK requires companies at all levels of the supply chain and UKTI is well placed to demonstrate all that the UK has to offer. This article summarises the main drivers for investment in the UK's largest renewable energy sectors.

OFFSHORE WIND (SEE ALSO CHAPTERS 4.3 AND 7.2)

The UK is the largest global player in offshore wind with 5GW of capacity either operational or under construction/approval. In fact, the UK currently has the same offshore wind capacity as the rest of the world combined. The UK also boasts the largest pipeline of upcoming instalments with 64GW promised in the 3rd round of the Crown Estates Leasing Rounds. The government has made repeated commitments to development and it is therefore unsurprising that the UK is considered the most attractive destination for offshore wind investment (EY, Renewable Energy Country Attractiveness, March 2015).

The UK offshore wind sector has attracted £3bn worth of capital investment from across the globe in the past financial year. However, currently a large proportion of the physical content of the UK's offshore wind farms are being imported from Europe (mostly Denmark and Germany). The Offshore Wind Developers Forum (a forum of developers and government) pledged to push towards a target of 50% UK content in new offshore wind farms. Through concerted efforts by the government and developers (as laid out in the UK Offshore Wind Industrial Strategy) the UK has now attracted investment from two OEMs that will supply future wind farms: Siemens will manufacture blades in Hull and Mitsubishi Vestas Offshore Wind will manufacture blades on the Isle of Wight. There has also been significant investment in other components of wind farms, including transition pieces and cables. The government and industry are encouraging manufacturers to invest in the UK to manufacture other components, including towers, jackets, substations, transmission cables and monopole foundations.

The government is supporting the growth of the Tier 1 and 2 supply chains through GROW:OffshoreWind. Shaped by industry leaders, the service offers English based business direct access to market experts, technological know-how and funding support. The aim of the scheme is to grow the UK content percentage of manufactured products used in future UK wind farms. For businesses supplying the offshore wind industry or keen to break into it, GROW:OffshoreWind has up to £500k of funding available - per company - to invest directly.

The GIB has been supporting projects in the offshore wind sector and has so far invested over £1bn in 7 wind farms with a total capacity of 2.7GW. The bank invests directly in to projects in the construction phase and in operational offshore wind farms, allowing developers to recycle their capital.

The attractiveness of the UK does not end at manufacturing opportunities as the UK has some of the best offshore wind R&D resources in the world. Driving down the cost of offshore wind is a key focus in the sector with industry aiming to reach £100/MWh by 2020. As a prime example, the Offshore Renewable Energy Catapult (OREC) boasts, amongst other facilities, a tried and tested 50m test facility, and a new forward facing 100m facility, designed and built to accommodate the next generation of longer blades being developed for the offshore wind market. OREC offers its services to both industry and SMEs and supports the development of innovative offshore wind technology across the UK.

The UK's success in attracting offshore wind investment is the result of the collaborative effort of UKTI, BIS, DECC, the global embassy network and industry. Opportunities for foreign companies are abundant and there is still time to get involved. UKTI can provide bespoke advice and assistance to an offshore wind company seeking to enter the UK market.

Case Study: Siemens Blade Facility
In March 2014, Siemens Wind Power selected Green Port Hull and Paull as the locations for nacelle assembly and blade manufacturing for their next generation offshore wind turbines. This £310m investment (£160m from Siemens and a further £150m from their port partner Associated British Ports) will bring 1,000 jobs to the Humber. Since March, Siemens has received continued on-going support from the UK to encourage regional investment from companies that can both supply their new plant and increase its competitiveness. The project was granted consent by Hull City Council in May 2015 and construction will soon begin.

SOLAR

It may be surprising for some to consider that the UK currently has 8GW of installed solar capacity and is ranked as the 3rd fastest growing country in terms of ground mounted solar globally. The government is supporting the growth of solar in the UK through its Solar PV Strategy which clearly outlines the direction of travel for the industry in the UK and underpins policy decisions.

The growth of solar in the UK is being driven by the availability of government subsidies at both a domestic and industrial level and by the rapidly falling costs of solar cells. The Green Deal provides incentives for homeowners to install renewable technologies for generation and has been used to install photovoltaic (PV) systems on more than 3,700 occasions. In addition, in May 2014 the UK announced that it will end RO support for large solar farms (>5MW) in 2015/16 and transition to CfDs. This has sparked a rush of installation across the country to get online before the closure of RO. These incentives are complimented by the fact that solar is now one of the cheapest forms of renewable technology available. Advances in technology and the ease of import of solar cells are the key reasons for the price drop.

FIGURE 4.2.2 – Solar cells price

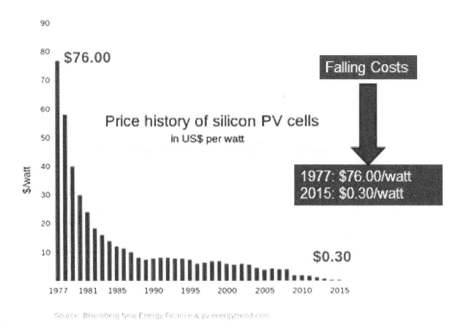

The move from the Renewables Obligation to Contracts for Difference will cause a change of pace for the industry but the fact that 5 solar farms were supported in the first allocation round gives support to the industry. The UK solar sector is expected to continue to grow in coming years with 15GW predicted to be installed by the end of 2016.

The general opportunity that the UK offers is complimented by specific opportunities arising from commercial organisations and government: the largest of which is the drive for roof top mounted systems. The UK has seen a recent surge in the desire for roof top solar systems: as an example in March 2015 Marks and Spencer's installed a 6.1MW system on its warehouse in Castle Donington (the largest rooftop system in the UK). A recent government decree that systems can be moved if the owner relocates has put further incentive behind installation and activity has been increasing. In addition, the government has pledge to install 1GW of solar systems across its estate. DECC has stated that is will "make sure that not one inch of suitable government roof space is wasted" as it rolls out solar PV across public buildings – including MoD property and hospitals. The first tranche of investment will include 500MW so contract opportunities will be abundant for investors.

The UK is also leading the world in R&D with some of the most innovative solar developments coming out of UK universities. For example, Sheffield University have recently developed spray-on solar cells which will follow a process similar to putting paint on cars and graphic printing and could be used for high volume manufacturing.

Other opportunities that will arise from the growth of solar include energy storage and grid capacity updating. Energy storage allows for electricity generated through solar to be stored and used by consumers when required. In terms of grid capacity, the distribution network requires updating to deal with the inflows of electricity from domestic solar and network operators must respond to demand.

Opportunities are present to provide solar systems at both a domestic and industrial scale and the government is keen to attract investment across the supply chain spectrum. The government is especially looking to attract investment in the areas of manufacturing, innovative technologies and R&D.

BIOENERGY

As set out in the UK Renewable Energy Roadmap, bioenergy is an important part of the Government's plans to meet the Renewable Energy Directive objectives in 2020.

The Bioenergy Strategy set out the Government's approach to securing the benefits of bioenergy and outlines how bioenergy could deliver up to 11 per cent of the UK's primary energy demand by 2020. As of the end of 2014 the UK had 6.5GW of installed bioenergy capacity which is mostly comprised of plant biomass, energy from waste and landfill gas.

As with solar, the bioenergy sector has been able to capitalise on incentives for domestic and industrial level energy production. The Renewable Heat Incentive provides incentive for small-scale domestic and non-domestic energy users to install a green heat source. Likewise, industrial companies have been able to avail of the Renewables Obligation through installing biomass electricity generation systems – for example Iggesund in Workington, Cumbria have an adjoining bioenergy facility to their 200,000 tonnes per annum paperboard mill. In addition, local governments have been supporting the installation of bioenergy facilities on waste treatment sites.

Currently there are strong opportunities for investors in the energy from waste division of bioenergy. According to the GIB, to date the main focus of investors has been with local authority PPP / PFI waste projects. The majority of the required investment in this area is now largely behind us, although there are some important projects still outstanding. The bank now believes that the energy from waste market must move towards "merchant projects" that utilise private, specialist fuel supplies such as refuse derived fuel, commercial and industrial waste and waste wood. It is estimated that this commercial and industrial waste presents a £5bn investment opportunity that could create 6,000 jobs and provide electricity for 1 million homes.

Case Study: Ireland's Electricity Supply Board, Port of Tilbury
In March 2015, Irish electricity utility Electricity Supply Board (ESB) and the Green Investment Bank made a combined commitment to invest £70 million in a new £190m renewable power facility at the Port of Tilbury, Essex. The facility will require 270,000 tonnes of waste wood per year and marks ESB's first investment in the UK's waste and biomass sector. The Tilbury Green Power facility is expected to generate 300 GWh of green electricity per year, enough to power more than 70,000 homes, when it is commissioned in early 2017.

CONCLUSION

This chapter has given an overview of the main opportunities in the renewable energy sector today. However, other opportunities exist in the onshore wind, marine and tidal and hydroelectric sectors – for example the UK has recently approved a contractor for the 320MW Swansea Bay Tidal Lagoon, the first of 4 planned tidal lagoons. China Harbour Engineering Company Ltd has pledged to use 50% UK content in the delivery of the lagoon.

UKTI is working closely with other government departments to provide the best possible environment for overseas companies interested in the UK renewables sector. Please get in touch for more information.

4.3 THE UK OFFSHORE WIND INDUSTRY
Danny Dunne, Head of UKTI's Offshore Wind Team

INTRODUCTION

The United Kingdom is...

*   The global market leader in offshore wind:
    The UK has 5.7GW installed or under construction, and is on track to deliver 10GW by 2020, representing the largest expansion in any class of renewable energy technology.
*   The most attractive location for offshore wind investment in the world:
    The UK consistently tops international rankings as the best place to invest in offshore wind, and has been successful in attracting investment from across the globe. The offshore wind pipeline presents an investment opportunity of between £16 to £21bn from 2014 to 2020. Innovative funding models are being created to attract new sources of capital into the sector.
*   A stable and predictable policy regime:
    The UK enjoys a reputation for operating stable and predictable policy regimes to support investment in renewable electricity infrastructure. The UK's Electricity Market Reforms provide long term stable revenues for low carbon energy projects and reduce investor risk.
*   Home to a growing supply chain capability:
    Industry and Government are working together to build a competitive and innovative UK supply chain that delivers and sustains jobs, exports and economic benefits for the UK. UK companies lead the world in services for the design, development, financing, construction and operation of offshore wind plant. Suppliers like Siemens have already chosen the UK as the site for future world class manufacturing facilities, and there are great opportunities for further investment in the supply chain.

The Existing Landscape

Stable and supportive conditions have seen offshore wind expand dramatically in the UK, attracting a growing pool of international investors and delivering the largest installed capacity anywhere in the world.

Why Offshore Wind?

- The United Kingdom is home to the world's largest offshore wind portfolio in a stable regulatory environment.
    - * The UK has committed to the renewal of its electricity system, aiming to maintain secure and affordable supplies whilst delivering on our ambitious 2050 carbon reduction commitments.
    - * The UK Government has established a robust new market framework designed to deliver investment in new low carbon power capacity.

- Offshore wind will be at the forefront of this expansion
    - * The UK is already the world leader in offshore wind, and the sector is on track to deliver 10GW by 2020, representing the largest expansion in any class of renewable energy technology.
    - * Offshore wind is a proven technology which has developed in the UK through 16 years of government support. Active programmes of technological development are driving improvements in yields, reduction in costs and acceleration in deployment.
    - * The local supply chain is already expanding to meet demand, with leading equipment manufacturers choosing UK sites as the centre for growing operations.

- Investment is needed today, across the value chain
  A growing, dynamic sector presents a diverse range of opportunities for investment in:
    - * Technology and IP
    - * Manufacturing facilities and supply chain
    - * Wind farm projects in development and construction
    - * Construction management and contracting
    - * Installation plant and vessels
    - * Operating wind farms
    - * Plant operation and maintenance

- United Kingdom offshore wind offers favourable returns in a stable, regulated environment
  Offshore wind farms present an attractive investment profile, summarised in

Table 4.3.1 :

* Long-dated assets with 25 year asset lives and up to 20 years of contracted revenues
* Inflation-linked revenue streams backed by UK Government legislation
* The Crown Estate offering 50 year lease terms

Table 4.3.1 Status of UK offshore wind progamme

UK Offshore Wind Programme	
Installed Capacity*	4 GW
Under construction	1.7 GW
2020 potential	10 GW
Potential investment 2014-20	£16tn to £21 tn
Further potential for investment beyond 2020	

*Capacity of wind farms that have been fully commissioned.
Source: data supplied by The Crown Estate.

PROJECT PIPELINE

A continuing programme of development and construction will present further investment opportunities as the UK's offshore wind capacity doubles to 2020.

UK projects have attracted a broad range of integrated suppliers, independent power producers, and sovereign wealth funds as Figure 4.4.2 indicates.

Figure 4.3.2 - Developer shares in each phase – May 2015

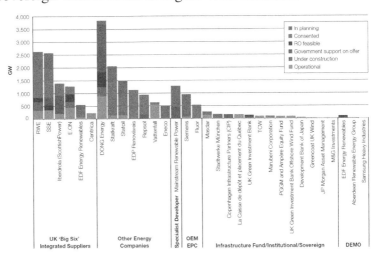

Opportunities exist to invest across operating assets, wind farms in construction and projects in development identified in Figure 4.4.3 .

Figure 4.3.3 – UK offshore wind project pipeline – May 2015

Operational: Total capacity of wind farms that have been fully commissioned.

No.	Project name	Capacity MW
01	Barrow	90
02	Blyth	4
03	Burbo Bank	90
04	Greater Gabbard	504
05	Gunfleet Sands Demonstration	12
06	Gunfleet Sands I	108
07	Gunfleet Sands II	65
08	Inner Dowsing	97
09	Kentish Flats	90
10	Lincs	270
11	London Array 1	630
12	Lynn	97
13	Methil Demonstration – Samsung	7
14	North Hoyle	60
15	Ormonde	150
16	Rhyl Flats	90
17	Robin Rigg East	90
18	Robin Rigg West	90
19	Scroby Sands	60
20	Sheringham Shoal	317
21	Teesside	62
22	Thanet	300
23	Walney (Phase 1)	184
24	Walney (Phase 2)	184
25	West of Duddon Sands	389
Total		4,039

Under construction: Total capacity of wind farms that are under construction or where the developer has confirmed a final investment decision, but are not yet fully operational.

No.	Project name	Capacity MW
26	Burbo Bank Extension	258
27	Dudgeon	402
28	Gwynt y Môr	576
29	Humber Gateway	219
30	Kentish Flats Extension	50
31	Westermost Rough	210
Total		1,715

Government support on offer: Total capacity of wind farms that have secured a Contract for Difference or whose publicly stated timescales are consistent with accessing the Renewables Obligation (RO).

No.	Project name	Up to capacity MW
32	Beatrice	664
33	Blyth Demonstration	99
34	East Anglia ONE	714
35	Galloper[1]	340
36	Heron Wind (Hornsea)	600
37	Neart na Gaoithe (NNG)	448
38	Njord (Hornsea)	600
39	Race Bank[1]	580
40	Rampion[1] (Southern Array)	400
41	Walney Extension	660
Total		5,105

Consented: Total capacity of wind farms that have planning consent and for which government support is not yet in place.

No.	Project name	Up to capacity MW
42	Aberdeen Demonstration	66
43	Creyke Beck A (Dogger Bank)	1,200
44	Creyke Beck B (Dogger Bank)	1,200
45	East Anglia ONE	486
46	Inch Cape	784
47	MacColl (Moray Firth)	372
48	Rampion (Southern Array)	300
49	Seagreen Alpha (Firth of Forth)	525
50	Seagreen Bravo (Firth of Forth)	525
51	Stevenson (Moray Firth)	372
52	Telford (Moray Firth)	372
53	Triton Knoll	1,200
Total		7,402

In planning: Total capacity of wind farms for which a consent application has been submitted.

No.	Project name	Up to capacity MW
54	Breesea (Hornsea)	900
55	Hywind 2 Demonstration (Buchan Deep)	30
56	Navitus Bay (West Isle of Wright)	970
57	Optimus (Hornsea)	900
58	Teesside A (Dogger Bank)	1,200
59	Teesside B (Dogger Bank)	1,200
Total		5,200

Grand total	23.46GW

1 RO feasible based on published grid connection dates as per TEC register – May 2015

NOTE: Quoted capacity refers to the property rights held with The Crown Estate and does not necessarily reflect the build out capacity permissible under current or future statutory planning permissions.

SUPPLY CHAIN: OPPORTUNITIES FOR INVESTMENT

The UK is committed to delivering a capable, competitive, and innovative local supply chain. Investors like Siemens have already committed to new manufacturing facilities in the UK, and many more opportunities exist for investment to boost existing manufacturing capability. The UK is a strong platform for exports to Europe and beyond and companies are already seizing this opportunity.

Vision for the industry

Industry and Government are working together to build a competitive and innovative UK supply chain that delivers and sustains jobs, exports and economic benefits for the UK.

Government's work to support this vision:

• Providing market confidence and demand visibility – critical for investment by

developers and the supply chain
- Building a competitive supply chain – to support UK based companies to develop the capability and capacity to bid for, and win, contracts in open and fair competition
- Supporting innovation – vital to achieve cost reduction and enable new players to enter the market with new product designs
- Finance – support to access finance for developers and the supply chain
- Building a highly skilled workforce – to deliver the right skills at the right time

Offshore wind cost reduction
The supply chain is innovating to reduce costs and deliver a competitive product for UK and international markets.
Aim for cost reduction
The UK set up the Offshore Wind Cost Reduction Task Force as a joint collaboration between Government and industry to delivery on the point of cost reduction. The Crown Estate in support of the Offshore Wind Reduction Task Force concluded a detailed review of offshore wind costs in 2012. This concluded that costs can be reduced to around £100/MWh for a project financed in 2020.

Progress
The Cost Reduction Monitoring Framework* was established in order to provide a consistent way to measure the cost of offshore wind projects in the UK. The report shows that levelised costs have fallen faster than anticipated, from £136/MWh for built projects in 2010/11 to £121/MWh for projects taking FID in 2012-2014 with the main driver being the move to larger, more efficient turbines.

Future
The results of the first CfD auction on 26 February 2015 also confirm that costs are falling, with the clearing prices over 14% lower than the administrative strike price of £140/MWh. Contracts have been offered to Neart na Gaoithe, a 448 MW site in the outer Forth estuary which cleared at £114.39/MWh and the 714 MW East Anglia One project which cleared at £119.89/MWh.

*https://ore.catapult.org.uk/our-projects/-/asset_publisher/fXyYgbhgACxk/content/cost-reduction-monitoring-framework

UK SUPPLY CHAIN: INVESTMENT OPPORTUNITIES

UK based manufacturers are in a strong position to access the largest global market for offshore wind, detailed in the range of opportunities summarised below.

Component	Investment opportunity
Offshore turbine manufacturing	Siemens have committed to manufacture blades and assemble nacelles on the Humber. Market demand is sufficient to support further UK based turbine manufacturing facilities. The UK pipeline to 2020 alone will demand an estimated 800 wind turbines – around 50% of the European market.
Offshore turbine towers	Existing European facilities do not have the capacity to deliver the volume of offshore towers required by the market – new investment is required. The UK offers significant logistical advantages due to challenges and costs of tower transportation.
Foundations	The market continues to generate high demand for extra large monopiles and transition pieces. Offshore Structures (Britain), a JV between EEW and Bladt, have now committed to delivering transition pieces from their recently acquired Teesside factory. The UK has the capability to deliver jackets and secondary steel, with opportunities for partnership and investment to deliver serial jackets production.
Cables	The UK market presents a strong investment opportunity for cable manufacturing with high volume contract opportunities for export cables and interconnectors. The UK already has a strong track record in inter-array cables, supplying the UK and EU markets.
Substations	The UK project pipeline requires an estimated 8 substations by 2020. UK fabricators bring experience from the offshore oil and gas sector, and have a track record in supplying projects in the UK and wider EU market. Partnership opportunities exist to build on this existing capability for future orders.

ACCELERATING TRADE AND INVESTMENT

UKTI's Offshore Wind Team is here to support your business to succeed in this sector, and can point you towards the wider government support available to investors and exporters. Innovative funding models are being created through government and the Green Investment Bank to attract new sources of capital into offshore wind.

UKTI's Offshore Wind Team
The Offshore Wind Team offers dedicated support to potential UK investors, and can support your company to export from a UK base to markets in Northern Europe and globally.

UKTI's Offshore Wind Team is working with industry to support delivery of a strengthened UK offshore wind supply chain.

UKTI's aim is to deliver:

- Growth of existing UK players in the supply chain
- New investment in UK facilities by foreign owned companies
- Export opportunities for new or existing UK operations

UKTI's support for companies includes:

- Work with developers to support delivery of UK supply chain strategies
- Support investors by sharing market insight, linking companies to Government financial support and local partners
- Facilitate partnerships between new investors and existing UK companies where appropriate
- Support UK businesses in developing and implementing strategies to win contracts in the largest trade markets
- Build relationships with opportunity providers, collect information on forthcoming and current export opportunities
- Build strong relationships with key UK businesses able to deliver against these opportunities

UKTI helps companies to navigate government and access the best possible support.
UKTI works together with the Department of Energy and Climate Change, the Department for Business Innovation and Skills, UK Export Finance, and local partners in the Devolved Administrations and English Regions.

Notes for the reader:
Figures and policy information used in this publication date to June 2015 and readers should account for industry developments since then.
Figures on UK offshore wind capacity are sourced from The Crown Estate, May 2015.

4.4 ISSUES FOR INVESTORS IN THE UK UPSTEAM OIL AND GAS SECTOR

Heike Trischmann of Watson Farley & Williams LLP

SUMMMARY

Although considered a mature basin and despite the current low oil price (forecast by some to remain below US$100 per barrel until well into the next decade[1]), the UK oil and gas sector still offers a wide range of opportunities for, and continues to attract, a large amount of investment.[2] The experience gained over the past decades of oil and gas exploration and production in the UK has given the country a dependable regulatory regime and a set of responsive and efficient regulatory authorities. The UK Government's stated aim[3] of ensuring security of supply through economic extraction of remaining oil and gas reserves will continue to give confidence to new and existing participants that the environment for further investment will remain favourable for the remaining life of the UK oil and gas resources.

INTRODUCTION

Oil production offshore the United Kingdom, i.e. on the United Kingdom Continental Shelf ("UKCS"), commenced in the 1960s and today the area is regarded as a mature

---

[1] See: http://knoema.com/yxptpab/crude-oil-price-forecast-long-term-2015-to-2025-data-and-charts

[2] See: http://www.offshoreenergytoday.com/uk-awards-offshore-blocks-in-biggest-ever-licensing-round/

[3] See: https://www.gov.uk/government/uploads/system/uploads/attachment_data/file/65643/7101-energy-security-strategy.pdf

petroleum producing region. Production peaked in 1999 but is now in decline as easily accessible reserves are depleted. However, recent data shows that substantial recoverable reserves remain, amounting to approximately 5.3 billion barrels of oil and 2.5 billion barrels of oil equivalent ("boe") of gas.[1]

By comparison, the UK onshore oil and gas industry started back in the early 1900s but so far has yielded much more episodic success. However, the UK is said to have significant unconventional oil and gas reserves onshore and the extent of those currently stands at approximately 1,300 trillion cubic feet (approximately 2.4 trillion boe).[2],[3],[4]

Ongoing economic extraction will require both exploration of new areas and further development of existing fields by employing new and more efficient technologies. While the UK Government recognises that the scope of future UK oil and gas activities will be dictated by "geological inheritance" (that is, the amount and accessibility of oil and gas remaining in place) and global oil prices, it is conscious of the need to present flexible, attractive and predictable regulatory and fiscal regimes[5] to encourage new investment from existing and prospective participants (see the section on Taxation further below in this chapter). At the same time, the industry offers attractive opportunities to the services sector in the decommissioning of aging and disused installations and other facilities (see the section on Decommissioning at the end of this chapter).[6 and 7]

As the UK's domestic oil and gas resources are depleting, they must increasingly be supplemented by imports. In the interest of maintaining and increasing security

---

[1] See: https://www.gov.uk/oil-and-gas-uk-field-datea for estimates of UK additional potential resources for [2015].

[2] See: https://www.gov.uk/government/uploads/system/uploads/attachment_data/file/[66170]/uk-onshore-prospectivity.pdf

[3] See: http://www.bgs.ac.uk/research/energy/shaleGas/howMuch.html

[4] See: http://www.lse.co.uk/AllNews.asp?code=ftpo[58]g[5]&headline=UK_Government_To_Announce_Onshore_Oil__Gas_Licensing_Round_Results

[5] See: https://www.gov.uk/government/uploads/system/uploads/attachment_data/file/[420028]/OGA_Framework_Document_April_[2015].pdf

[6] See: http://www.theguardian.com/environment/[2015]/feb/[03]/uk-can-become-a-world-class-hub-for-decommissioning-oil-platforms

[7] See: http://www.bbc.co.uk/news/uk-scotland-north-east-orkney-shetland-[32832972]

of energy supply to the country, the UK Government had to focus on attracting the necessary investment in the infrastructure for gas importation, storage and associated facilities (see the section on Offshore LNG Unloading and Gas Storage further below in this chapter).

Initially and for ease of reference, however, this chapter presents an overview of the main regulatory requirements for investment in oil and gas, focusing on offshore conventional and onshore unconventional petroleum exploration and production in the UK, and the necessary infrastructure to import and/or store additional volumes particularly of natural gas.

OFFSHORE – SEAWARD LICENCES

UK legislation relating to offshore (and onshore) petroleum licences provides that all rights of "searching and boring for and getting" petroleum are vested in the Crown.[1] The Secretary of State for Energy and Climate Change ("Secretary of State") is empowered, on behalf of the Crown, to grant licences to such persons and on such terms and conditions as he thinks fit.[2] The legislative structure giving discretion to the Secretary of State in this manner has remained largely unchanged throughout the active life of the oil and gas industry in the UK, and certainly in relation to the UKCS. Although this has led to some historical complexity, it has also allowed the licensing regime to adapt quickly to commercial change.[3]

Types of Licences
There are currently four types of Seaward Licences allowing for intrusive exploration and production of licence areas (known as "blocks"). There is also one type of offshore licence allowing for non-intrusive exploration of areas not currently covered by any other production licence. However, for the purposes of this chapter we are

---

[1] Section 2(1) Petroleum Act 1998 (**Petroleum Act**). The "Crown" is an imprecise concept but in this context means the UK State.

[2] Sections 3(1) and (3) Petroleum Act.

[3] However, please note that following a review undertaken by Sir Ian Wood, the Oil and Gas Authority (**OGA**) will be fully established as a new oil and gas regulatory body by the Energy Bill 2015 which is currently passing through Parliament. OGA became an Executive Agency of the Department of Energy and Climate Change (**DECC**) on 1 April 2015 and will be transformed into a "government company" with fully independent powers and functions, although it will remain under the governance of the Secretary of State. Certain functions have already passed from DECC to OGA such as the UK's licensing regime for onshore and offshore exploitation of hydrocarbons; DECC continues to administer offshore environmental regulation and the decommissioning of offshore oil and gas installations and pipelines.

concentrating on Seaward Production Licences, just touching on Seaward Exploration Licences further below.

Seaward Production Licences are split into three successive periods, known as "terms", the duration of which depends on the type of licence. During each term the licensee is required to carry out its activities pursuant to "Minimum Work Programmes" that must be pre-agreed with OGA. The initial term usually involves exploration of the relevant licence area, including obtaining seismic data and drilling or another similarly substantive activity. Licensees may only progress to the next term, if and when the Minimum Work Programme for the previous term has been completed and the prescribed proportion of the licence area relinquished (i.e. handed back to the UK Government). If during the second term a commercial discovery has been made and a development plan approved for it, the licence will normally continue into its (extended) third term that is intended for the production phase.

The four types of Seaward Production Licences mainly differ in the length of the respective terms, minimum work requirements and the size of the licence area that has to be relinquished in each case, giving maximum flexibility to the relevant investor.[1]

Licensees are required to pay an annual rental rate (per square kilometre) in respect of all licence types which is based on the area covered by the licence. The rate increases over time as the field moves towards production, which provides an incentive for licensees to relinquish voluntarily additional unused or unexplored areas.

Seaward Exploration Licences

Seaward Exploration Licences are aimed primarily at companies that collect seismic data for sale. Seaward Exploration Licence holders are able to explore acreage covered by Seaward Production Licences only with the consent of the Seaward Production Licence holders.

Model Clauses

The standard terms and conditions applicable to petroleum licences, known as "Model Clauses", are set out in secondary legislation made under the Petroleum Act and incorporated (historically by reference but now set out in full) into each Seaward Production Licence or Exploration Licence. The Model Clauses which apply to a Licence are those that were in effect on the date of the grant of that Licence (so the terms and conditions of a Licence do not change during its term by amendments to the underlying legislation).

There is one set of Model Clauses for all four types of Seaward Production

---

[1] See: https://www.gov.uk/oil-and-gas-petroleum-licensing-guidance

Licences[1], and one set for Seaward Exploration Licences[2].

Licence Application Process

The majority of Seaward Production Licences are awarded through competitive licensing rounds. Applications are invited on an annual basis and the latest round (the 28th Seaward Licensing Round) closed on 25 April 2014. Despite the low oil price, this latest licensing round attracted huge interest and a total of 134 licences covering 252 blocks were awarded in November 2014 and a further 41 licences in July 2015.[3]

However, very few companies are willing or able to take on the entire risk and expense of being the sole licensee on a Seaward Production Licence, so companies often bid for licences together as a group (the bid is usually coordinated by the intended operator (see below)). Regardless of whether applications are made on an individual or group basis, all licensees share joint and several liability vis-à-vis the UK Government for all operations under a Licence; i.e. the Government may pursue each licensee for the total cost of any liability that may arise from such operations.

From time to time, OGA will also consider "Out of Round" applications for Seaward Production Licences.

Acquisition of Licence Interests

Parties can also acquire interests in Seaward Production Licences by buying all or part of the licence interest from an existing licensee.

Companies acting together on a Seaward Production Licence usually do so by way of an unincorporated joint venture pursuant to a joint operating agreement ("JOA"). The JOA will specify the undivided percentage interest that each party has in the licence and will regulate the relationship between the relevant parties. Subject to consent from OGA (and normally the other licensees), each licensee is entitled to assign part or all of its licence interest to a third party, which provides opportunities for new parties to enter the licence agreement at every stage of the life of a licence.[4]

---

[1] The Petroleum Licensing (Production) (Seaward Areas) Regulations 2008 (SI 2008/225)

[2] The Petroleum Licensing (Exploration and Production) (Seaward and Landward Areas) Regulations 2004 (SI 2004/352)

[3] See: http://www.offshoreenergytoday.com/uk-awards-offshore-blocks-in-biggest-ever-licensing-round/ and
http://www.offshoreenergytoday.com/uk-awards-new-offshore-licences-in-one-of-the-largest-rounds-in-five-decades/

[4] Applications for approval of licence assignment is now made to DECC through its new e-licence administration system (PEARS: the Petroleum E-Licensing Assignment and Relinquishments System).

The UK offshore oil and gas operators have, in conjunction with what was then a function of DECC, taken steps to facilitate licence transfers. Standard transfer documents such as the Master Deed[1] and the Approved Model Deed of Assignment[2] are aimed at cutting costs of external advisors and providing transferors and transferees with certainty.

Competencies

Given the different types of operations that are necessary to fully exploit the remaining UKCS hydrocarbon reserves, OGA is keen for a wide range of companies to participate in UKCS oil and gas activities, whether by open tender for new, or private purchase of existing, licence interests. There are, however, minimum criteria for participants (whether applying for a Licence or acquiring a licence interest by way of assignment) to ensure that they are financially and technically capable of operating in the UKCS, and to ensure that the UK can benefit from any resulting tax revenue.

a. Financial capacity

All companies seeking to be included on a Seaward Production Licence must demonstrate that they have sufficient financial capacity to meet the actual costs which may reasonably be expected to arise under a Licence. The level of financial capacity required is not prescribed and will depend on a number of factors.

b. Technical capacity

One of the parties to a JOA must be designated as the operator under the relevant Licence, whose role it will be to exercise day-to-day control of the exploration or production activities under the Licence. OGA requires that as well as demonstrating financial capacity, the party acting as operator must also demonstrate the necessary technical capacity to carry out the role on behalf of its co-licensees. OGA will review the track record of potential operators, including in other jurisdictions, in deciding whether a particular company is a suitable operator.[3] Each co-licensee must demonstrate the level of technical capacity that will enable it to exercise responsible oversight of operations (through decisions made under the JOA), although this standard is lower than that required of the operator.

---

[1] The Master Deed provides a voluntary mechanism for licensees to transfer licence interests on pro-forma terms and without the need to collect signatures from all licensees on all transfer documents. See: http://www.masterdeed.com/masterdeed.cfm for further details.

[2] See:
https://www.gov.uk/government/uploads/system/uploads/attachment_data/file/[15109]/licguideapp[4-1].doc

[3] This will be done through PEARS.

c. Environmental capacity

Licensees are also required to demonstrate environmental competence in relation to their proposed operations including, amongst other things, arrangements for pollution liability and environmental management. Oil and gas operators are subject to extensive environmental regulation.[1]

Following the major oil spill caused by the explosion of BP's Deepwater Horizon rig in the Gulf of Mexico, the European Commission reviewed member states' safety of offshore oil and gas operations and rapid accident response strategies.[2] As a result of its findings, the Commission adopted Directive 2013/30/EC on the safety in offshore oil and gas operations[3] in an effort to set an EU-wide minimum standard in health and safety and environmental protection in the European offshore oil and gas industry. The Directive addresses eight main issues, including obligatory *ex ante* emergency planning, which "operators" of offshore installations will have to comply with in order to commence and continue operations.

Although the UKCS has a good safety record and robust regulatory regime (largely introduced in response to the Piper Alpha disaster in 1988), in response to the Deepwater Horizon accident referred to above contingency plans were strengthened further and existing temporary forums made permanent to drive the industry on to further improvements. The UK Government also introduced amendments into existing UK oil and gas legislation to transpose the provisions of Directive 2013/30/EC. These amendments came into force on 19 July 2015.[4]

d. Corporate capacity

All companies with interests in the UKCS must have a place of business within the UK, which means (i) it is a UK registered company, or (ii) it is a UK registered branch of a foreign company, or (iii) it has a staffed presence in the UK.[5] Licensees in producing fields must have a staffed presence in the UK or be a UK registered company. Operators must also demonstrate that they have sufficient proximity to the licence area to adequately control operations.

---

[1] See: https://www.gov.uk/oil-and-gas-offshore-environmental-legislation

[2] See: http://ec.europa.eu/energy/oil/offshore/standards_en.htm

[3] See: http://eur-lex.europa.eu/legal-content/EN/ALL/?uri=CELEX:32013L0030

[4] See: http://www.hse.gov.uk/offshore/directive.htm and

[5] See: https://www.gov.uk/oil-and-gas-petroleum-licensing-guidance

Taxation

Taxation of offshore oil and gas activities is complex and specialist advice should be taken prior to any investment. This complexity is derived largely from successive governments seeking to find a balance between providing financial incentives for exploration and development while ensuring the UK economy as a whole derives significant benefit from the country's natural resources.

In its 2015 Summer Budget, the newly elected UK Government announced the introduction of various measures which will take effect from autumn 2015 and which are intended to encourage additional investment in the UK oil and gas industry (both conventional offshore and unconventional onshore) in the current low price – high cost environment. The measures include, amongst other incentives, a simplification of the existing system of offshore field allowances, a cut in the supplementary charge and in the petroleum revenue tax.[1] The package is expected to lead to at least 120million boe of additional reserves, increasing production by 15%, equivalent to 1% of the UK's gross domestic product, by 2019/20.

An explanation of applicable tax rates, allowances and reliefs applicable in the UK oil and gas industry can be found on HMRC's website.[2]

ONSHORE – LANDWARD LICENCES

Types of Licence

Petroleum Exploration and Development Licence ("PEDL") is the full name of the UK Landward Production Licence. A PEDL is similar to a Seaward Production Licence and, as with a Seaward Production Licence, applicants must prove technical, financial and corporate competences as well as awareness of environmental issues before an offer of a PEDL will be made. The rules concerning application for and assignment of a licence interest that are applicable to Seaward Production Licences also apply to PEDLs.

Once granted/acquired, PEDLs confer a similar right to search for, bore for and get hydrocarbons, but, contrary to Seaward Production Licences, PEDLs do not confer any exemption from other legal/regulatory requirements such as any need to gain access rights from a private landowner, health and safety regulations and planning

---

[1] See: https://www.gov.uk/government/uploads/system/uploads/attachment_data/file/[443232]/[50325]_Summer_Budget_[15]_Web_Accessible.pdf and

http://www.offshoreenergytoday.com/uk-oil-and-gas-authority-to-be-able-to-issue-fines-and-revoke-licences/

[2] See: https://www.gov.uk/oil-and-gas-taxation

and https://www.gov.uk/government/collections/petroleum-revenue-tax-prt-and-government-revenues-from-uk-oil-and-gas-production permission from relevant local authorities, which must be obtained independently.[1] Decommissioning will also be dealt with as part of the relevant planning regime rather than through DECC.

As mentioned above, the onshore oil and gas industry has been operating in the UK for well over 100 years. There are currently some 28 onshore oil fields and 10 onshore gas fields in production in the UK; all of them from conventional hydrocarbon sources. However, this type of onshore production currently only contributes approximately 1.5% of overall UK oil and gas production and increasing attention is focused on unconventional petroleum sources.

Onshore Shale Gas Exploration and Production

Shale gas production has been of increasing importance in the US for some years but exploration only just started in the UK. In 2008, the 13th Round of Oil and Gas Onshore Licensing resulted in the award of several blocks for shale gas exploration, though bids were often based on a quest for conventional and unconventional prospects as the regulatory regime was identical for both.

Cuadrilla Resources' Preese Hall No. 1 well drilled in 2010 was the first exploration well drilled to specifically test for UK shale gas. However, all operations under that licence had to be suspended in May 2011, pending the investigation of two seismic tremors experienced in the area during initial drilling operations.

In light of the results of that investigation and recommendations of a thorough review of the suitability of the current UK regulatory regime for unconventional oil and gas exploration, in 2012 the Secretary of State announced that, subject to new regulatory controls, the suspension of Cuadrilla's operations near Preese Hall would be lifted.[2] The new controls principally relate to the management by operators of potential seismic activity triggered by the specific methods employed in shale oil and gas exploration activities.

Accordingly, amongst other things, operators have to review more carefully available information on geological faults in the relevant area and monitor background seismicity before operations commence, as well as in real time during the life of such operations. These operations will be subject to a "traffic light" regime so that operations can be quickly paused and data reviewed if unusual levels of seismic activity are observed. Operators will also have to submit a "fracking plan" before consent can be

---

[1] Note, however, that this part on PEDLs does not cover the various environmental, health and safety and planning consents that must also be obtained. See instead: http://www.gov.uk/oil-and-gas-petroleum-licensing-guidance

[2] See: https://www.gov.uk/oil-and-gas-onshore-exploration-and-production#resumption-of-shale-gas-exploration

given by OGA to any such activities.[1]

DECC also established a new Office of Unconventional Gas and Oil to maintain and strengthen the coordination between the regulatory bodies currently involved in overseeing activities in this area, this mainly being OGA, the Environmental Agency and the Health and Safety Executive.[2]

The results of the 14th Round of Onshore Oil and Gas Licensing which opened in July 2014 are expected to be announced imminently and expected to increase the importance of unconventional oil and gas exploration in the UK.[3]

OFFSHORE LNG UNLOADING AND GAS STORAGE

As mentioned at the beginning of this chapter, while oil and gas production in the UK continues to decline, the UK gas demand continues to increase, forcing the UK to import more and more of the gas it uses. Some reports suggest that the UK will be importing 80% of its gas needs by 2020.[4]

Liquefied natural gas ("LNG") and piped gas imports became the major sources of natural gas to fill the growing gap between demand and the UK's domestic supply capabilities. Gas is imported into the UK through three existing onshore regasification terminals[5] and the offshore import terminal at Teesside[6] as well as through the Langeled

---

[1] See: https://www.gov.uk/government/news/new-controls-announced-for-shale-gas-exploration

[2] See: https://www.gov.uk/government/policy-teams/office-of-unconventional-gas-and-oil-ougo

[3] See: http://www.lse.co.uk/AllNews.asp?code=ftpo58g5&headline=UK_Government_To_Announce_Onshore_Oil__Gas_Licensing_Round_Results

[4] See: http://www.europeanoilandgas.co.uk/article-page.php?contentid=11530&issueid=352

[5] The 3 terminals are the LNG import terminal at the Isle of Grain in Kent (total annual import capacity of 118.8TWh), the South Hook LNG import terminal (total annual import capacity of 125.4TWh) and the Dragon LNG terminal (total annual import capacity 66TWh) both of which are located at Milford Haven, South Wales. The South Hook and Dragon LNG terminals together are capable of supplying up to 30% of the UK's current gas requirements.

[6] The Teesside Gasport has a peak unloading capacity of 0.187TWh/day using the Energy Bridge floating regasification technology.

pipeline from Norway[1], the Interconnector[2] from Belgium and the BBL[3] from The Netherlands.

However, ongoing concerns about security of energy supply mean that the UK Government has to continue to attract sufficient investment in gas importation and storage and associated infrastructure, both onshore and offshore. While the regulatory regime regarding such activities and infrastructure onshore the UK has been well developed for some time, a regime concerning offshore gas importation and storage activities and infrastructure was only introduced in the UK legislation in 2008.

The Energy Act 2008 (Energy Act)

The Energy Act covers three main activities: (a) offshore LNG regasification and unloading, (b) offshore gas storage, and (c) offshore carbon capture and storage ("CCS"), each of which the UK Government expects will increase in importance over time in ensuring security of energy supply and at the same time reducing carbon emissions.

a. Offshore gas storage

Gas storage provides obvious benefits: gas can be injected during periods of low demand, when the gas is cheap, and can be withdrawn during periods of high demand when the gas is more expensive. The UK currently has approximately 66TWh of onshore (including LNG peak shaving) and offshore gas storage capacity which, by 2021, is set to increase approximately 200TWh.[4] More than three-quarters of this increase will be achieved by storage in depleted/near depleted oil and gas fields that are located offshore on the UKCS.

b. Offshore LNG regasification and unloading

The advantages of Floating Storage and Regasification Units ("FSRU"s) over

---

[1] The Langeled pipeline is a forward flow gas pipeline only with an annual capacity of 280.5TWh which represents 20% of Britain's current peak gas demand.

[2] The Interconnector is a forward flow and reverse flow gas pipeline between Bacton in the UK and Zeebrugge in Belgium with an export capacity from the UK of 220TWh per annum and an import capacity into the UK of 280.5TWh per annum.

[3] The Balgzand Bacton Line (**BBL**) is a forward and non-physical interruptible reverse flow gas pipeline between Balgzand in The Netherlands and Bacton in the UK with an annual import capacity of 211.2TWh.

[4] See: http://infrastructure.planninginspectorate.gov.uk/wp-content/ipc/uploads/projects/EN030001/3.%20 Post%20Decision%20Information/Decision/130409_EN030001_Chris_Le_Fevre_Report.pdf

conventional onshore LNG regasification terminals include their short implementation time (18 to 24 months), cost-effectiveness and reduced upfront capital requirements, and enhanced delivery flexibility. Using FSRUs, LNG can be loaded conventionally at LNG liquefaction plants and then either (i) shipped to an offshore unloading facility (such as the Teesside Gasport) where it is regasified aboard the floating unit and the regasified LNG delivered through a high pressure gas connection to, for example, a subsea buoy moored in the hull of the unit or (ii) discharged as a liquid at any conventional onshore LNG receiving terminal.

Although the LNG industry is currently undergoing a profound change with more liquefaction projects coming on stream within the next 2 to 3 years thereby increasing supply well above demand at least in the short to medium term, Europe is expected to absorb a large part of any uncommitted quantities. This means that despite the relatively large number of LNG import terminals that already exist in the UK, new projects are expected to come on stream, such as the FSRU-based Port Meridian offshore North Wales.[1]

c. Carbon Capture and Storage ("CCS")
Coal and natural gas are the predominant fuels used for power generation in the UK. However, the UK has committed to at least an 80% cut in greenhouse gas emissions by 2050 against a 1990 baseline and CCS is seem both domestically in the UK and the internationally as a cornerstone method of reducing greenhouse gas emissions from the continued use of fossil fuels, particularly the use of coal in power generation.

Cost is a central issue when planning to develop viable CCS projects along with the large-scale demonstration of the integrated capture, transport and storage technologies of carbon dioxide (CO_2) and the UK Government has pledged its support for the construction of a CCS demonstration plant in the UK.[2]

Offshore licensing regime
The Energy Act provides for a licensing regime governing offshore gas storage, unloading of regasified LNG as well as the permanent subsurface storage of CO2

---

[1] See: http://portmeridian.com/

[2] See: https://www.gov.uk/uk-carbon-capture-and-storage-government-funding-and-support

that is administered by DECC.[1,2] The regime applies to storage and unloading within the offshore area comprising both the UK territorial waters[3], and the area extending beyond the territorial sea that has been designated under the Energy Act[4] as a Gas Importation and Storage Zone ("GISZ").[5]

The relevant licence will provide the framework for regulatory consent to the physical activities at the relevant offshore site. Similar to Seaward Production Licences covered earlier in this chapter, the Secretary of State will assess each applicant's operating competence (technical and environmental) and financial viability and has discretion to decide whether or not to issue such an Energy Act licence, and if so, to whom and on what conditions.

The licence conditions for an offshore gas storage licence are based on those of a Seaward Production Licence and are similar to those of a gas unloading licence.[6] Please note that there is no pro forma CO2 storage licence available yet.

If the licence is in respect of gas storage or CO2 storage activities and the gas/CO2 is stored in a depleted/near depleted offshore oil and gas reservoir, the developer will also have to apply to OGA for a Seaward Production Licence.[7] This is because native

[1] For CO^2 storage licensing these provisions form part of the transposition into UK law of EU Directive 2009/31/EC on the geological storage of CO^2. The Storage of Carbon Dioxide (Licensing etc.) Regulations 2010 (SI 2010/2221), which transpose many other requirements of the Directive, came into force on 1st October 2010 and were subsequently amended by the Storage of Carbon Dioxide (Inspections etc.) Regulations 2012 (SI 2012/461).

[2] The Storage of Carbon Dioxide (Licensing etc.) Regulations 2010 (SI 2010/2221)

[3] Territorial waters are defined as that part of the sea that is located within 12 nautical miles from the coast line.

[4] Section 1(5) Energy Act 2008. See also Exclusive Economic Zone Order 2013 (SI 2013/3161). This is in addition to the rights granted under the Energy Act 2004 concerning the Renewable Energy Zone (**REZ**) in this area.

[5] The GISZ includes the waters beyond the territorial sea to 200 nautical miles from the coast line.

[6] The Offshore Exploration (Petroleum, and Gas Storage and Unloading) (Model Clauses) Regulations 2009 (SI 2009/2814) set out the model clauses for exploration Licences for gas storage (and regasified LNG unloading activities), using non-intrusive methods such as seismic data gathering and shallow drilling. The Offshore Gas Storage and Unloading (Licensing) Regulations 2009 (SI 2009/2813) set out the model clauses for gas storage (and unloading) Licences and cover the relevant activities themselves.

[7] See: https://www.gov.uk/oil-and-gas-petroleum-licensing-guidance

gas from the relevant reservoir will co-mingle with any non-native gas injected into the reservoir for storage and will inevitably be produced from the reservoir when the gas is recovered from storage.

In addition, a lease from The Crown Estate[1] is required for activities involving the seabed of the UK territorial waters or the GISZ as the right to conduct certain activities in these areas is vested in the Crown by virtue of the Energy Act. The grant by The Crown Estate of a lease will be coordinated with the Secretary of State granting the relevant Energy Act licence(s) and having approved any development plan(s) that are necessary for the relevant activity.

Under certain circumstances, The Crown Estate's grant of rights will be subject to compliance with competition requirements, which are likely to require an open, transparent and potentially competitive process. However, in the case of a depleted/ near depleted oil and gas reservoir that is subject to a current Seaward Production Licence, DECC or OGA will most likely have run a competitive licensing round that is considered sufficient to avoid the need for further tender processes.

CABLES AND PIPELINES

If any of the developments referred to above require the laying of new cables or oil and gas pipelines that will cross the seabed within the UK territorial waters or transit the GISZ, additional consents will be required as mineral rights or offshore wind farm developments may be affected.

Under Part III of the Petroleum Act, a "Pipeline Works Authorisation" is required for the construction and/or use of a "pipeline" in the UK territorial waters or GISZ.

Permission in the form of a lease or a licence is also needed from The Crown Estate as the relevant landlord to obtain the rights to lay, maintain and operate cables and pipelines on the seabed. However, care needs to be taken as The Crown Estate owns some, but not all, of the UK offshore areas, and consents may therefore be required from other regional bodies.

THIRD PARTY ACCESS (TPA) TO OFFSHORE INFRASTRUCTURE

The evolution of offshore infrastructure on the UKCS has been characterised by field owners developing pipelines and processing plants for sole usage, but, as production levels started to decline, ullage (spare capacity) was progressively made available to third parties against payment of a tariff. Field-dedicated infrastructure is economically

---

[1] The Crown Estate is a statutory body which acts on behalf of the Crown in its role as landowner within the area of the territorial sea and as owner of the sovereign rights of the UK seabed beyond the territorial waters. The Crown Estate operates as a commercial landowner under the provisions of the Crown Estate Act [1961].

viable when fields are relatively large but become less so as fields get smaller. To ensure that new and smaller players in the UKCS can develop and bring on stream discoveries that would require the use of otherwise expensive infrastructure, in 2004 industry participants adopted a code of practice for TPA to offshore infrastructure ("Code")[1]. The Code is voluntary in nature and sets out principles and best practice procedures to guide all those involved in negotiating TPA to upstream oil and gas infrastructure on the UKCS.

Under the Code, companies seeking access for their hydrocarbons to such infrastructure must apply in the first instance to the owner of the infrastructure in question. However, if by following the Code a third party is unable to agree satisfactory terms of access with the owner of the relevant offshore infrastructure, legislation[2] gives that third party the right to make an application to the Secretary of State to require access, and to determine the terms on which such access is to be granted. The Energy Act 2011 strengthens the Secretary of State's powers in this regard by giving him the right to require, on her own initiative, from the infrastructure owner the necessary access to, and, under certain circumstances, the necessary expansion of, that infrastructure[3].

While the Code applies to offshore pipelines, processing facilities and other infrastructure, it does not apply to the actual offshore gas storage or LNG unloading facilities, or CO_2 storage facilities. Provisions concerning negotiated TPA to offshore gas storage facilities are contained within sections 17C and 17D of the Petroleum Act,

---

[1] The Code of Practice on Access to Upstream Oil and Gas Infrastructure on the UK Continental Shelf. See: http://www.oilandgasuk.co.uk/publications/viewpub.cfm?frmPubID=[243]

[2] The first and second Gas Directives ([98]/[30]/EC and [2003]/[55]/EC) introduced provisions for TPA to pipelines, LNG importation and other essential facilities by providing a choice between negotiated and regulated TPA. The UK adopted a regime of negotiated TPA to such infrastructure by amending the Petroleum Act in respect of offshore downstream gas pipelines (section [17]B). The TPA regime to submarine pipelines is administered by the Secretary of State. In accordance with Article [22] of the second Gas Directive [2003]/[55]/EC, section [17]A of the Petroleum Act now also provides that the Secretary of State may under certain circumstances grant an exemption from the requirement to offer negotiated TPA to offshore downstream gas pipelines. The right of negotiated TPA to downstream gas processing facilities is set out in section [12] of the Gas Act [1995], as amended by the Energy Act and further amended by the Energy Act [2011]. The provisions granting negotiated TPA to upstream gas processing and oil processing plants are contained in section [82] of the Energy Act [2011]. The right of negotiated TPA to (offshore) upstream petroleum pipelines is also set out in section [82] of the Energy Act [2011] but rights of negotiated TPA to other (offshore) pipelines continue to be covered by section [9] of the Pipe-lines Act [1962] and section [17] of the Petroleum Act, both as amended by the Energy Act [2011].

[3] Sections [83] and [84], Part [2], Chapter [3], Energy Act [2011]

which follows the TPA regime applicable to onshore gas storage facilities as set out in the Gas Act 1986.

The EU's Third Energy Package[1], among other measures, introduced a mandatory regulated regime of TPA to LNG import facilities. These provisions were introduced into UK law in November 2011[2] and apply to offshore (and onshore) LNG unloading facilities. It is worth pointing out that this remains the only access regime in the UK that works on a regulated rather than negotiated basis. For this reason, Ofgem[3], which administers this regime, has produced guidance notes on how it will apply this regime in practice.[4]

As far as CO2 storage facilities are concerned, the Storage of Carbon Dioxide (Access to Infrastructure) Regulations 2011[5] extend the regime of negotiated TPA that applies to pipelines and oil and gas processing facilities, to CCS infrastructure.

DECOMMISSIONING

Offshore

The UK Government is required, under international law[6], to remove (or have removed) all offshore installations or structures on the UKCS which are abandoned or disused in accordance with generally accepted international standards.[7] However, it

[1] For the purposes of this article, the relevant parts of the Third Energy Package are Gas Directive 2009/73/EC, and Gas Regulation 715/2009.

[2] See: http://www.legislation.gov.uk/ukdsi/2011/9780111513965/contents

[3] The Office of the Gas and Electricity Markets Authority (the regulator of the gas and electricity markets of Great Britain). See: https://www.ofgem.gov.uk/home

[4] See: http://www.ofgem.gov.uk/Markets/WhlMkts/CompandEff/Documents1/Guidance%20on%20the%20regulated%20Third%20Party%20Access%20regime%20for%20Liquefied%20Natural%20Gas%20Facilities%20in%20GB.pdf

[5] SI 2011/2305

[6] Arts. 60(3) and 80 of the UN Law of the Sea Convention 1982 21 I.L.M. 1261 (UNCLOS) www.un.org/depts/los/convention_agreements/texts/unclos/unclos_e.pdf and the Oslo and Paris Convention for the Protection of the Marine Environment of the North East Atlantic 1992 (OSPAR)

[7] The standards adopted are the draft Guidelines and Standards for the Removal of Offshore Installations and Structures on the Continental Shelf and in the Exclusive Economic Zone, as adopted by the Assembly of the International Maritime Organisation on 19 October 1989. See: http://www.imo.org/blast/mainframe.asp?topic_id=1026

is permitted some discretion as to whether installations are removed in their entirety.

Although, these obligations rest with the UK Government, it passes them on to the relevant licensees through Part IV of the Petroleum Act to protect the UK taxpayer from having to pay the relevant costs for decommissioning. The Petroleum Act empowers the Secretary of State, by written notice, to demand an "abandonment programme"[1] for each offshore installation[2] setting out the measures to be taken to decommission an installation, along with projected costs and timing and any continuing maintenance that may be necessary.[3] The notice can be served on a number of parties, including the owner and the operator of the installation, co-licensees, parties to the relevant JOA and associates of any of the above (that is, their parent company/ies or affiliates).[4]

In practice, DECC usually serves this notice on the licensees once commercially exploitable quantities of oil or gas have been discovered and a development plan in respect of them has been approved, putting the licensees on notice and requesting an abandonment programme at a date often to be determined in the future. Where licensees change through the life of a licence, the Secretary of State reserves the discretionary right to withdraw this notice in relation to the exiting companies.

Once the programme is approved, all parties who submitted the abandonment programme bear joint and several liability for carrying it out. If the parties fail to do so, the Secretary of State can herself arrange for abandonment work to be carried out and recover the cost (plus interest) from the defaulting parties. The Secretary of State also has the power, whether before or after approval of the abandonment programme, to take such security as is necessary to ensure that sufficient funds are available.[5]

Parties to a JOA are understandably concerned that all other parties have made financial provision for what can be fairly onerous obligations. It is therefore common practice for parties to enter into a decommissioning security agreement, under which parties make regular payments to a separate trust fund (protected from creditors as far

---

[1] The term "abandonment" is used interchangeably with "decommissioning" in this context, although the latter is the preferred term, as stipulated by the Guidance Notes to the Decommissioning of Offshore Oil and Gas Installations and Pipelines under the Petroleum Act [2008].

[2] The Energy Act extended the definition of "offshore installation" to include installations associated with the conversion, storage or unloading of gas (which would include gas storage, CCS and LNG importation). See section [44], Part IV, Petroleum Act [1998].

[3] Section [29] Petroleum Act [1998].

[4] Section [30]([1]) Petroleum Act [1998], as amended by the Energy Act [2008].

[5] See: https://www.gov.uk/government/uploads/system/uploads/attachment_data/file/[69754]/Guidance_ Notes_v6_[07].[01].[2013].pdf

as possible) as security for future decommissioning costs.[1]

However, what is the oil and gas companies' onerous obligation is the services companies' welcomed business opportunity, with required expenditures expected to be between £35bn and £50bn.[2]

Onshore

As stated before, decommissioning of onshore facilities will be dealt with as part of the relevant planning regime for those facilities rather than through DECC but this is beyond the scope of this chapter.

---

[1] See: https://www.gov.uk/oil-and-gas-decommissioning-of-offshore-installations-and-pipelines for examples of approved decommissioning programmes

[2] See: http://www.bbc.co.uk/news/uk-scotland-north-east-orkney-shetland-32832972 and http://www.theguardian.com/environment/2015/feb/03/uk-can-become-a-world-class-hub-for-decommissioning-oil-platforms

Part Five

Investing in UK Advanced Manufacturing

5.1 UK AUTOMOTIVE – UNRIVALLED OPPORTUNITIES FOR AUTOMOTIVE INVESTORS

Tom Fardon, UKTI's Automotive Investment Organisation

For automotive investors, the UK offers Europe's best business opportunity underpinned by growing demand for UK products at home and overseas. The UK provides an innovation landscape which brings together companies, universities and specialist automotive R&D centres to deliver transformational R&D, and the UK has the most supportive business environment in Europe for the automotive industry.

Between 2012 and 2015 the UK automotive sector attracted more than £15 billion of foreign investment. Already 11 of the world's largest vehicle manufacturers assemble vehicles and engines in the UK, and 770,000 people are employed in the automotive industry.

Figure 5.1.1 Vehicle plant locations & Output 2014

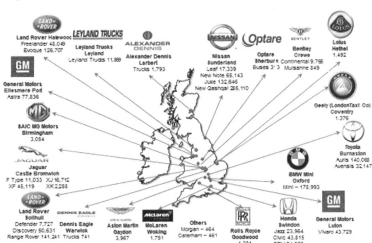

The Automotive Investment Organisation (AIO) is the part of UKTI whose task it is to promote UK automotive overseas and to bring investment into the country. For investors, the AIO is the gateway into a UK-wide network of advice, expertise, funding and support.

> *"We were delighted to receive such strong support from the UK Government for our investment into the UK. The Government's close cooperation has been fundamental to ensuring we can drive forwards our UK business successfully. We are aiming to open our new facility by early 2016, giving us the platform to win future business within the Brose Group."*
> **Juergen Zahl, Managing Director of Brose.**

WHY THE UK?

A Leading Business Environment for Automotive
The UK has the most competitive business environment for automotive of any major economy in Europe. Overseas automotive investors have benefitted from the lowest corporation taxes in the G8 and significant further tax support, particularly for R&D. This includes an effective corporate tax rate of 10% from patents registered in the UK or European patent offices. The UK's highly competitive business environment is a strong incentive for global automotive companies to base their Headquarters or R&D operations in the UK. This includes Fiat Chrysler Automobiles, who moved their Global HQ to London in 2014.

A Cohesive and Supportive Policy Environment
The UK has a coherent and established industry-led approach to automotive policy – setting the standard for a stable and forward-looking investment environment. Automotive policy is driven by the Automotive Council – the joint Government and private sector body which includes representation from all the major manufacturers and suppliers in the UK. One of the core commitments of the Automotive Council is to promote further overseas investment into the UK. The UK Government at both the local and national level also has a track-record of providing financial and in-kind assistance to the automotive sector to ensure that company business cases are, and remain, globally competitive.

A Low-cost and Highly-skilled Workforce.
The UK has a skilled, low-cost, flexible and highly productive labour force – bucking the stereotype for workforces in the major Western European economies. At €20.90 in 2014, average labour costs per hour are substantially lower than France, Germany and Italy, and lower than those in Spain. Nissan Sunderland is recognised as one of the most productive car assembly plants in the world. The UK automotive workforce is

the most productive in Western Europe. With the support of Government and industry, an additional 10,000 apprentices and 2,000 graduates will be recruited into the sector by 2018. Industry relationships have been revolutionised, and are characterised by a stability which underpins the sector's efficiency.

Figure 5.1.2 Production volume chart

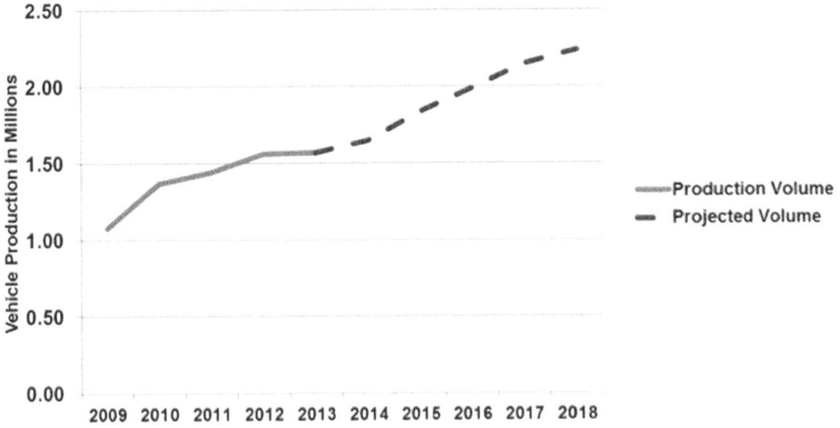

Source - SMMT

Rapid Growth in Production

Vehicle production in the UK has increased at an unprecedented rate. Between 2009 and 2014 production in cars grew by 50% to over 1.5 million units a year with a record turnover of £64 billion in 2013. A vehicle now rolls off a UK production line every 20 seconds and the country is the 3rd largest car manufacturer in Europe. This growth is predicted to continue, with production set to exceed 2 million vehicles a year.

This record growth is driven by a steady increase in demand. Sales of vehicles in the UK continue to grow, with year-to-date registrations for 2015 up 6.4%. However exports have been the main driver. For many manufacturers the UK is the gateway to Europe and the world. In 2014 over 78.2% of vehicles produced in the UK left to over 100 countries. Exports totalled in excess of £34 billion, up 9% on 2012 and an all-time record. Much of this growth has been in key emerging markets – including China, with UK exports to the country increasing seven fold since 2009, and India, where exports increasing nine fold in the same period. This diversity of global markets means that demand in the UK is more resilient than in countries which rely more heavily on domestic purchasing levels.

"We have an exemplary work force and labour relations, a ready market, an increasing appetite for capital investment and a supportive relationship with Government, allowing us to grow a sustainable business in the UK. Calsonic Kansei's ability to produce high quality and cutting edge products at a price which is competitive is opening up exciting opportunities to export our product to a global market."

James Davies, CEO and Chairman of Calsonic Kansei Europe

KEY INVESTMENT OPPORTUNITIES

The UK Automotive Supply Chain [key investment opportunity 1]

Continued rapid growth in demand for UK vehicles has driven the accelerated expansion of the UK supply chain. UK domestic automotive supply chain sales increased by over £1 billion over 2013-2014, with 19% growth in 2014 alone. The UK Automotive Council estimates that there is a further £4 billion worth of unfilled demand from domestic manufacturers for UK sourced Tier 1 components. A further £2 billion of unfilled demand exists for components from UK-based suppliers in Tier 2 and below.

This £6 billion in total of unfulfilled demand for UK manufactured supply chain components has been recognised by overseas investors as a unique opportunity. Since the AIO's establishment in 2013 we have attracted over £750 million of overseas investment in the UK supply chain which has secured or created over 10,000 jobs. The Japanese companies Calsonic Kansei and Nifco, the German company Brose and the US Fortune 500 company Lear are four examples of major overseas investors who the AIO has worked with to establish and grow their presence in the UK.

Innovation and Automotive R&D [key investment opportunity 2]

The UK has a burgeoning automotive R&D sector, with over £1.9 billion invested in 2013.

This is driven by an innovation ecosystem which brings together companies, universities and specialist automotive R&D centres to deliver transformational R&D. The growth in UK vehicle production also presents a ready market for the commercialisation of innovative R&D projects.

> *"We are proud of our close association to the UK – a country whose automotive industry we recognise is riding a tide of optimism and growth. The UK offers great labour flexibility, very competitive taxes, low staff and production costs compared to elsewhere in Europe, and a Government approach that actively encourages and supports automotive investment and expansion."*
>
> **Gideon Jewel, Lear Corporation's President for Europe and Africa**

Overseas investors have been harnessing the UK's innovation landscape to provide valuable support to their mainstream UK business or to base a stand-alone R&D centre in the UK. Investors have also recognised that the UK is a premier destination for globally mobile R&D projects.

The Innovation Landscape

The UK Government and industry has invested heavily in the UK innovation landscape to ensure that the UK is a leading centre for R&D. This includes a network of Catapults and centres which are the focus of public and private sector collaboration across a range of areas – including composite materials, transport systems, advanced propulsion, high-value manufacturing, and advanced forming technologies. All of these are accessible to overseas automotive investors, including the associated funding opportunities.

Fig: Automotive R&D Centres

Fig: UK catapult network

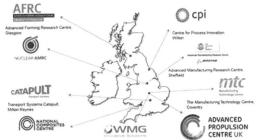

This is further supported by a network of world-class vehicle test facilities - such as MIRA, Silverstone and Millbrook - where automotive investors can also establish a low-cost presence for the design, production and testing of cutting-edge technologies.

The UK is the global leader in the most R&D intensive part of automotive - motorsport. The sector generates £9 billion a year for the UK economy. 7 out of 10 of the current F1 teams are based in the UK, and there are 4,500 other UK motorsports companies, many with unique offers. Investors therefore have unrivalled access to cutting-edge expertise, and a growing number of technologies have moved to the mainstream automotive sector. Buses in London which use F1 derived hybrid technology and the increasing use of composites in cars are examples of this.

UK Leading the Way on Low Emission Technologies

With 2.4 million engines produced annually, the UK has a long track record of success in engine design and development. Now Government and industry are ensuring that the UK remains in pole position for the next generation of low-emission engines and technologies. The joint Government and industry £1 billion investment in the Advanced Propulsion Centre to support the commercialisation of innovative propulsion solutions, and a £900 million Government investment in subsidies and infrastructure for ultra-low emission vehicles, has consolidated the UK's world-leading position. The UK is also leading the way on light-weighting and composite technologies for automotive – including through a £25 million investment by the Government and the European Union in the National Composites Centre.

5.2 LIFE SCIENCES – A GLOBAL HUB FOR SUCCESS

Mark Treherne, Chief Executive,
UKTI Life Sciences Organisation (LSO)

In December 2011, the Prime Minister made a firm commitment to build on our scientific and commercial heritage and exploit innovation in the life sciences sector, announcing the Government's ten-year Strategy for UK Life Sciences.

Since then, the changes and new investments we have made are already opening up our scientific, clinical and healthcare infrastructure to new partnerships, while at the same time establishing a more efficient and integrated life science ecosystem to attract and stimulate industrial growth. The UK life sciences sector is a combination of Government, the National Health Service (NHS), the UK research base, research charities and industry. It presents a new deal for businesses, the life sciences economy, and patients, whereby all stakeholders share the inherent risks in research and development but also together reap the rewards. The UK is now the international partner of choice to tackle the global healthcare challenges and realise value for businesses and for patients.

THE LSO COMMITMENT TO BUSINESS

To help achieve the commitments of the Strategy and to signal the importance of the life science sector to the UK economy, UK Trade & Investment (UKTI) established a dedicated unit – the Life Sciences Organisation (LSO) in 2012 - to support overseas investment into the UK from the earliest R&D collaborations through to clinical trials, commercial and manufacturing operations and partnerships. It offers inward investors a bespoke service, tailoring support to the requirements of the client.

The LSO recognises the need to support every component of the pathway. From bench to bedside, we are making it easier to discover, develop and deliver healthcare innovation in the UK. Businesses benefit from the support and investment we provide to protect the UK's vibrant research base and create the right environment for experimental medicine, clinical translation and commercialisation.

THE STRATEGY THREE YEARS ON

In November 2014, LSO working with the Office for Life Sciences (OLS) reported joint success three years on from the launch of the Strategy for UK Life Sciences - recording £3.5 billion of investment in the UK to create more than 11,000 jobs.

The life sciences sector is critical to the UK economy and now accounts for 183,000 UK jobs and with a total annual turnover of £56 billion. Already underpinned by a long-term industrial strategy since 2011, the UK life sciences sector was further enhanced by the appointment of a dedicated Minister for Life Sciences in 2014, unique in the world.

On announcing the success of the Strategy three years on, the Minister for Life Sciences, George Freeman said: "NHS leadership in health research is attracting new investment into our life sciences research sector, generating the health and wealth we need to be a modern economy. I want to ensure that patients up and down the country can get access to important innovations as soon as possible. By revolutionising the way in which we look at getting medicines and devices into the NHS we will make sure that this country is the best place in the world for 21st Century medical innovation."

LSO – RECORDING INCREASED RESULTS

Each year the LSO is tasked with delivering on key investment projects and focuses on bringing value adding investment to the UK. For 2014/15 the LSO recorded an increase of more than double the number of new jobs and financial investment compared to last year's results and saw a greater than 20% increase in the number of wins recorded.

LSO has placed a strong focus on supporting priority subsector and activity themes which deliver real value to businesses and the UK economy and align with the Strategy for Life Sciences – 69% of wins align with a subsector theme, and by activity.

Twenty per cent of the LSO's inward investment successes were for global, international, or European headquarters projects, while nearly 25% involved a manufacturing element, and around half were linked to R&D. Priority source markets such as the USA continued to perform strongly while there was a notable increase in new investors from India and China. £94 million was also recorded in Venture Capital related wins.

The 3-year View

Figure 5.2.1 – 3-year FDI wins

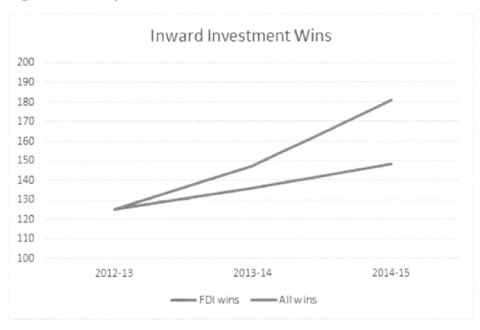

Figure 5.2.2 – 3 year FDI jobs and CAPEX

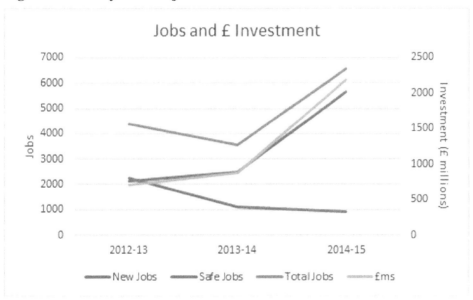

Case Studies

UKTI LSO worked with Tokyo Electron and the Local Enterprise Partnership to establish an open innovation centre for Smart Cell Processing Technologies, based at the Stevenage Bioscience Catalyst. The new centre will enable the company to work with ecosystem partners from academia and industry to develop standardised technologies for cell culture and inspection. Tokyo Electron has unique experience in automation and quality management frameworks from decades of innovation and development in the semiconductor industry, so is well placed to lead on the transfer of these techniques into life sciences. Leveraging their base in Stevenage, the LSO team now looks forward to supporting Tokyo Electron's international plans.

UKTI LSO was a key partner helping Pfizer to establish its London-based Genetic Medicine Institute and the Pfizer Rare Disease Consortium. The consortium is a novel and innovative framework agreement between Pfizer and over 18 UK universities, which enables collaboration in the area of rare diseases with the overarching intent to develop new therapies for these currently poorly served patient groups. UKTI LSO worked with ministers and Pfizer's senior leadership in the UK and USA to secure high-level support for the investment. It also provided practical help to identify suitable laboratory space for Pfizer's Genetic Medicine Institute at the London Bioscience Innovation Centre, and in the high profile launch of the Pfizer Rare Disease Consortium in September 2014, accessing a suitable venue and identifying high level delegates and speakers.

UK LIFE SCIENCES WEB PORTAL

A new UK Life Sciences web portal – www.lifesciences.ukti.gov.uk - has been launched to provide a single access point to the UK life sciences landscape. It provides an online platform to allow UK and international companies, academia and R&D organisation to connect.

The initiative is led by LSO and OLS and in collaboration with data partners, stakeholders and industry. One of the key features of the site is access to a database of around 4,500 UK life science companies that are developing, producing and marketing products and services in the pharmaceutical, medical technology and medical and industrial biotechnology markets.

For the first time the capabilities and strengths of the UK life science industry are showcased to facilitate the identification of potential collaborators, suppliers and customers. The database is accessed through the Company Mapping Tool feature on the site that allows you to search for companies based on location and also on sub-sector segmentation.

Another key feature is the Access to Funding Tool that highlights Government funding for science, engineering and manufacturing activities available to the health life sciences sector.

The highlighted funding opportunities cover UK-wide and national programmes in addition to funding initiatives that may also be available indirectly through collaboration with academic or other industry partners. Links to wider business support are also provided.

Phase three of the web portal will be developed during 2015 and this will represent the Access Route Map. The route map will support access to the UK Life Sciences ecosystem and including contact points for market intelligence, service and product information, partners and organisations.

INNOVATIVE MEDICINES AND MEDICAL TECHNOLOGY REVIEW

In March 2015 the Innovative Medicines and Medical Technology Review was announced with the objective to give NHS patients quicker access to innovative medicines and medical technology.

The review will improve the speed at which medical innovations such as precision medicines, digital devices, apps, diagnostics and new therapeutic technologies get to patients and their families.

The review is being led by Sir Hugh Taylor, Chair of Guy's and St. Thomas' NHS Foundation Trust. He is being supported by an expert advisory group headed by Professor Sir John Bell, Regius Professor of Medicine at Oxford University. The review is supported by the Wellcome Trust.

The aim of the review is to ensure that the UK is the fastest place in the world for the design, development and widespread adoption of medical innovations. This will help stimulate new investment, jobs and economic growth to support a stronger NHS.

The review's terms of reference show how it will explore opportunities to get innovative medicines, devices and diagnostics from the lab to NHS patients as quickly and safely as possible.

It currently takes on average over a decade and can cost £1 billion to develop a new drug – from the early pre-clinical research right through to being available for patients. The review will make recommendations to accelerate this and tackle regulatory obstacles.

The review will examine:

- How new approaches to the development of medicines, diagnostic and devices, based on precision medicine and emerging technologies, could speed up access to innovative products for NHS patients.
- How more collaborative work between companies and regulatory and evaluation bodies could ensure that innovative products can be assessed more quickly, using better data.

- How charities and patient groups can play a greater role so that NHS patients can get access to cutting-edge treatments.
- What more can be done to promote the rapid adoption of important medical innovations into clinical practice.

The review will:

- Make recommendations to Government on reforms to accelerate access for NHS patients to innovative medicines and medical technologies (including devices and diagnostics), making the UK the best place in the world to design, develop and deploy these products. These recommendations could include the role of statutory bodies including NICE and MHRA.
- Look specifically at three key areas of potential reform:
  - *Regulation* – how we could more quickly assess the safety and efficacy of innovations by adapting systems and better exploiting our unique advantages as an integrated healthcare system with world-renowned research medicine ethics and infrastructure;
  - *Reimbursement* – how we might adapt our systems of health economic assessment to: reflect technological advances in genomics, precision medicine and informatics; take time and risk out of the traditional Research and Development model; and better exploit the potential of our integrated healthcare system to pioneer new models of reimbursement for innovative products, including payment by results and Evaluation through Commissioning;
  - *Uptake* – how the NHS can better support and drive medical innovation (including through specialist commissioning).

The outcomes from the review will include:

- Consideration of how the UK system could generate long-term incentives for development in currently under-incentivised therapeutic areas;
- Short and medium/long-term recommendations for action, up to a 10 year horizon;
- Setting out of clear steps for implementation and accountable monitoring of measureable success metrics so that third parties can have confidence in implementation;
- Respect for the existing statutory responsibilities of NHS bodies and the European legislative frameworks for regulation and procurement of medicines and medical technologies.

MEDICINES MANUFACTURING INDUSTRY PARTNERSHIP

The Medicines Manufacturing Industry Partnership (MMIP) was established in 2013 to bring the UK's medicines manufacturing industry together to create an attractive and innovation-rich environment to drive UK competitiveness, and build international recognition, in medicines manufacturing.

The UK Medicines Manufacturing Industry Partnership provides a view of common issues in manufacturing and a common vision, from industry. MMIP is led by industry and works closely with government organisations, including the LSO. LSO is working with the MMIP to facilitate the growth of the existing footprint of medicines manufacturing and seek its expansion from investment by UK and international companies.

The UK's medicines industry is one of our leading manufacturing sectors, with exports worth £24bn and generating a trade surplus of £5bn in 2013. Medicines manufacturing is a key area of focus for the LSO and one that will continue to grow over the next few years. MMIP's view is that there is at least £1bn in manufacturing investment earmarked for the UK between 2013-2017, across small molecules, large molecules and cell and gene therapies.

MMIP sees opportunities to strengthen UK medicines manufacturing across small molecules, biologics, and cell and gene therapies. Each of these sub-sectors are at different stages of evolution and require different types of support. However, there are sufficient synergies to view the broad and collective strength of all three areas as a key element of a vibrant and dynamic ecosystem for medicines manufacturing that will drive growth. Specifically, there is an opportunity to build on industry product innovation, particularly in the area of personalisation of patient therapies, and to pioneer, in collaboration with the NHS, 'whole service' solutions for medicines supply to patients.

MMIP is supported by the ABPI and the BIA, and includes senior leadership from major companies based in the UK.

GLOBAL ACCESS

LSO catalyses and coordinates life sciences inward investment across the whole of the UK. We promote the UK as the leading European nation for biomedical innovation and the global location of choice for life sciences companies and investors. We work with UK-based businesses of all sizes to provide advice, expertise and support to successfully export products/services.

Our combined network of Government and private-sector specialists in the UK and in our British Embassies and Consulates overseas offer practical advice and free and confidential support in the following key areas:

- Access to government incentives, tax breaks, regulatory and business planning issues;

- Site and property search assistance and information on staff recruitment;
- Key contacts and links with centres of excellence and leading organisations;
- Relationship management and aftercare through on-going support.

LSO can assist companies to maximise their global potential. LSO can help companies once established in the UK to take advantage of new business opportunities and branch out to new locations, both in the UK and overseas through our export-oriented FDI programme.

www.gov.uk/ukti/lso
www.lifesciences.ukti.gov.uk
Twitter: @UKTI_LSO
Email: lifesciences@ukti.gsi.gov.uk

5.3 AGRICULTURAL SCIENCE AND TECHNOLOGIES

Prof Janet Bainbridge OBE,
Chief Executive, UKTI's Agritech Organisation

The UK has a very strong R&D base and its researchers are able to work in an interdisciplinary environment to bring academic research through many developmental stages to commercial realisation. The UKTI Agriculture technology organisation is now almost 2 years old and has established considerable success in attracting Foreign Direct Investment into the UK and helping indigenous companies trade their goods and services around the world. This success is leading towards an agricultural revolution, creating new approaches to food and farming systems and helping to support food security across the globe.

Significant breakthroughs in plant resilience, animal breeding, remote sensing, meteorological prediction and the exploitation of data are driving global investment in Agri-tech, encouraging a more competitive, productive and resilient market that simultaneously addresses the issues of environmental sustainability. UK farmers have been drawing on this world class innovation to grow their businesses, leading the way for an effective and efficient agricultural industry that competes globally and works seamlessly with consumer–driven retail sector.

Global issues of climate change, urbanisation, energy shortages, rapid population growth and demand for more meat-based food products are changing the landscape of the market rapidly. Awareness of food security and supply is universal, as is the drive to produce healthy food and educate the consumer. The irony is that amidst the concerns about food security, obesity is also an issue of concern- not just in the West but also in developing economies, as increased wealth fuels the desire for processed and refined foods.

With its world-leading supply chains and traceability, as well as some of the safest food in the world, the UK offers exciting R&D and manufacturing opportunity for both UK and foreign businesses. Each year the UK governments have been investing more than £400 million in Agri-food research to address these global challenges. The UK launched its cross Government strategy for agricultural technologies in July 2013, to build up on the existing strengths of the UK Science and Technology base by transforming research capabilities into commercial output. Additional funding of around £160 million over the coming years will continue to accelerate the commercialisation of research and encouraging UK food and farming businesses to innovate and drive UK growth.

Of these funds, more than £90 million is being used to establish world class centres for Agricultural Innovation which will help businesses develop, adopt, and exploit new agricultural technologies, as well as supporting the large scale adoption of innovative technology applied to the food chain. Each centre will be designed and operated in close partnership with the agri- industry. The first of these centres has recently been announced; the Agricultural Informatics and Metrics of sustainability centre (AIMS) consisting of a consortium led by the University of Reading, Rothamsted, The National Institute of Agricultural Botany (NIAB) and Scotland's Rural College (SRUC) but supported by eight other UK partners. The consortium received 52 letters of support from industry and academia. The UK has some of the world's best and most complete data-sets in healthcare, demographics, weather reports, agriculture and the environment, consumer behaviour. AIMS will develop ways to interrogate existing data sets and develop new ways of data handling to convert the information into useful forms for accurate decision-making by players across the food chain from farmers to retailers

A further £60 million fund is supporting projects an Agri-Tech Catalyst to support 'proof of concept' development of near-market agricultural innovations. To date, a wide range of innovative businesses have received a share of £4 million of funding from Government and industry to develop their innovative business ideas and launch them on the road to full scale commercialisation. The projects range from cultivation of algae in aquatic pens, Cultivation of the European lobster, Development of tractor –mounted wheat protein sensors, hydroponic systems for urban environments, identification of traits for optimum feed conversion by ruminants, natural sources of novel pesticide etc.

These initiatives are already making a difference, in ATO has been very busy identifying key markets and working with potential investors. Current outputs indicate that we have attracted over £120 million in new trade opportunities for UK companies and have attracted more than 20 investments. To date, the largest of these is £300 million with over 100 new jobs created

WHY INVEST IN UK AGRI-TECH?

The UK has a long history of global influence in the agri-tech industry that continues to push and focus on making extraordinary advancements that are leading the world in expanding this sector.

Currently the UK possesses:

- Fully integrated agricultural food supply chain worth £96 billion annually;
- World leading researchers across all disciplines relevant to Agri-Tech with a track record of delivering for business and working together across the sectors;
- Launch location for European and global markets;
- Fair and transparent regulatory environment;
- Internationally competitive tax regime;
- Business environment that encourages and rewards R&D through generous tax credits;
- Robust IP protection and tax relief for patents developed in the UK;
- Government financial support to de-risk projects;
- Highly skilled and flexible workforce;
- Dedicated team within UKTI of sector experts available to deal with queries and support overseas companies including brokering contacts with leading R&D.

Companies Collaborating with the UK's World Leading Centres have:

- Developed unique products that have given them competitive advantage and long term revenue streams.
- Added value to their reputation through new, high quality innovative products.
- Overcome technical barriers to improve products and processes.
- Discovered new talent and developed existing staff.

The UK has a unique R&D Ecosystem with a world-class academic and research environment:

- UK universities generate an astonishing 13.8 percent of the world's most highly-cited scientific papers (second only to the US).
- UK universities' ability to win funding from the European Union, with collaborative research grants and regeneration programmes, increased by 19 percent year on- year basis and the UK stakeholders are already becoming a significant players in Horizon 2020.

A competitive package for tax and incentives:

- The main rate of corporation tax fell to 20 percent by 2015 – one of the most competitive rates in the world;
- 'Patent Box' initiative (reduces corporation tax on profits from patents to 10 percent);
- Generous research and development tax credit scheme;
- Companies have the opportunity of locating in an Enterprise Zone providing even more enhanced tax incentives administered by Local Economic partnerships;
- A wide range of Government-funded assistance and grants supporting all stages of the innovation process, from initial concepts through to commercialisation.

A robust system of protecting intellectual property:

- World-class intellectual property system providing strong protection for new ideas, concepts and developments.
- UK complies with all main international agreements on intellectual property rights and works closely with the World Intellectual Property Organization, the European union and the World trade organisation.

Globally-recognised measurement and standards systems to underpin innovation:

- The National Physical Laboratory (NPL) develops and applies the most accurate measurement standards. They also produce the best science and technologies available to underpin the International System of Units 'SI' and support innovation in various disciplinary technologies. Working with over 2,400 companies each year, NOL generates more than £630 million of financial benefits through measurement innovation. This expertise underpins the 'SI' and supports innovation in various disciplinary technologies.
- UK-based BSI is one of the largest providers of standards in the world and is at the forefront of shaping new industry standards globally in areas such as management systems, governance, anti-bribery and financial services.
- The UK also has a well-established infrastructure for testing and certification, underpinned by the internationally-recognised United Kingdom Accreditation Service.

UK academic and corporate research institutes consistently produce world-leading research to address all fundamental challenges facing the agri-tech sector. UK is especially renowned for the ability of researches to work across traditional disciplinary boundaries.

In Plant Science:

- *The Rothamsted Research* established the Broadbalk Winter Wheat Experiment in 1843 and is the world's longest running agricultural experiment. This is a unique experiment that has charted the long-term effects of agricultural practices on crops, soils and farmland ecosystems. In 2012, Rothamsted's 20:20 wheat programme was launched to deliver wheat yields of 20:20 tonnes per hectare over 20 years, doubling yield and generating £1.5bn at the farm gate.
- *The National Plant Phenomics Centre* located in Aberystwyth University, uses automation and state-of-the art imaging technologies to electronically monitor (and non-destructively) the growth of tens of thousands of individual plants in containers. Results yield how much feed and moisture the plants use and how their physiology responds under different conditions.
- *The Stockbridge Technology Centre* in Yorkshire is growing tomatoes, raspberries, broccoli and many other products for our retail green groceries. These products are cultivated indoors in vertically banked rows under LED lighting to identify the right 'light regime'. This is done through researching the specific wavelengths from the photosynthetically active spectrum in collaboration with the University of Lancaster and retail partners.
- *East Malling* conducts strategic and applied research, development and innovation in horticulture, with a particular emphasis on perennial and clonally propagated crops. They hold international licences for many tree fruits, soft fruits and other plants and continue to produce and service public and private customers. One current project involves a Chinese company that is looking at new fruit varieties for processing into soft drinks.

In Animal Science:

- *Moredun Research Institute* addresses the needs of the livestock farming industry and has developed many vaccines, diagnostic tests and improved treatment strategies for farm animals across the globe.
- *The Pirbright Institute* in Surrey investigates solutions to combat animal diseases and the increasing threat of zoonotic pandemics spreading in humans e.g. avian and swine flu viruses. Additionally, Pirbright contributed to key technological advancements in thermo stable vaccines that are developed through a global collaboration over several decades to eradicate the Rinderpest virus (cattle plague).
- *The Roslin Institute* in Edinburgh was the home of Dolly the sheep, and is a world leader in animal and poultry genetics.
- *Farming Practice* is a pioneering research farm platform at North Wyke in Devon tests the practical implementation of farming technologies.

UK Case Studies in Agri-tech

- *It's Fresh!* developed by Food Freshness Technology, and already used in Tesco and Marks & Spencers, is a simple pad which absorbs and locks away ethylene gas, the natural plant ripening hormone, and so radically slows the ripening and decay of fresh fruit, vegetables and flowers in the supply chain, reducing waste and assuring consumer product quality.
- *Well Cow Smart Sensor*, the world's first automated, long term measurement device for monitoring pH and temperature in dairy herds has been developed by Well Cow Ltd. and Silsoe Research Institute, and will allow farmers to optimise diets for their cattle and prevent the occurrence of sub-acute rumen acidosis.
- *i-crop*™ is a web-based revolutionary crop management system, developed by PepsiCo UK in partnership with Cambridge University, bringing together data drawn from soil moisture probes in the fields and the local weather station to help farmers make informed decisions about when to irrigate and how much water to use, and produce more by using less water.

Part Six

Banking, Property and Financial Services

6.1 SETTING UP A FINANCIAL SERVICES INSTITUTION IN THE UNITED KINGDOM

Salim Kawadri, UKTI's Financial Services Organisation

The UK is the leading global financial services centre and the most internationally-focused marketplace in the world. As a global financial services hub, London is recognised as the gateway to the rest of the world: the destination of choice for any financial services business looking to internationalise.

THE UK HAS A RICH BUSINESS HERITAGE UNDERPINNED BY AN INHERENTLY INNOVATIVE ENVIRONMENT

London is Europe's largest international banking centre; and the fourth largest globally. All major global banks and financial institutions in the world have a presence in London.

London is, of course, central to the UK's international position but other cities, such as Edinburgh and Glasgow in Scotland; Birmingham, Bristol, Leeds, Liverpool and Manchester in England; Cardiff in Wales; and Belfast in Northern Ireland are also important financial centres.

The UK has more cross-border banking than any other financial centre worldwide. We have Europe's largest asset management industry and its biggest insurance market. The UK is the largest exporter of financial services in the world. The UK's trade surplus in financial services is double that of the next largest trade surpluses recorded by Luxembourg and Switzerland.

The UK is the leading European centre for investment and private banking, hedge funds, private equity, exchange traded derivatives, and sovereign wealth funds.

In support of the financial services sector are of course the UK's world class associated business and professional services sectors. Half of the world's top eight international law firms by revenue are based here, as are over half of the world's biggest accountancy networks.

The UK remains the most attractive destination for inward investment in Europe and is proud to be one of the most open economies in the world. It already benefits from a highly skilled workforce and continues to grow as the destination of choice for high-calibre internationally mobile professionals. This ensure that the UK remains a platform which brings together talented, creative and innovative world class individuals.

The UK beneficial geographic location allows firms to conduct business with Asia in the morning and the Americas in the afternoon. More overseas financial institutions choose to do business in the UK than in any other country. The UK is not only a world class location in its own right, providing investors with an encouraging and rewarding environment in which to do business; it is also a springboard from which to export to other markets across Europe and the globe.

Financial institutions operating in the UK have access to over 500 million potential investors and consumers across Europe and the largest stock market in Europe, and benefit from the lowest corporate taxation rate in the G7.

A WELCOMING ENVIRONMENT FOR INVESTORS

With a highly trained workforce, robust regulatory framework and legal system, ideal geographic location, competitive tax regime, global links, excellent ICT infrastructure, supportive stance for innovation, and a pool of business support services to draw upon, the UK provides an attractive environment in which to set up a financial services institution.

But the UK financial services sector is by no means saturated. New entrants are setting up in the UK every day and the opportunities are abundant. Furthermore, the UK Government welcomes new entrants to the market and is making great efforts to ensure that the UK has the most enabling business environment for investors to grow.

By working closely with industry partners, the UK Government is actively engaging with and pursuing new entrants to the market, championing the UK's status as the preeminent international financial centre. Indeed, ensuring the UK is remains competitive in the global market is one of the government's key priorities.

A FORWARD-THINKING GOVERNMENT

The UK Government recognises that it has job to do in creating the right conditions for businesses to thrive in the UK, to attract inward investors to our shores, and to help companies take full advantage of global opportunities.

Over the next 10 to 15 years an estimated 90% of global demand will be generated outside Europe. It is important that financial services companies based in the UK, whether indigenous or foreign-owned, are able to tap into this growth potential and take advantage of new international business opportunities. It is the government's job to create the right environment for UK-based firms to access these markets and to support them to gain market share, especially in emerging economies where new investors, savers and opportunities are appearing.

The Government strongly supports the financial services industry, and is committed to creating the right conditions in which British business can thrive in an increasingly competitive global marketplace.

To that end, the Government has identified key areas where it can work in partnership with the industry to pursue and secure new trade and investment opportunities. These efforts will make the UK a more attractive place to set up, and will help financial services organisations (both indigenous and foreign owned based in the UK) to increase their market shares overseas and cement the position of the UK as the pre-eminent global financial centre.

DEVELOPING LONDON AS THE GLOBAL HUB FOR OFFSHORE RENMINBI

In order to export to fast growing economies like China, and attract more investment to our shores, the UK recognises the importance of ensuring China's currency is used and traded here.

Through progressive thinking and a forward leaning Government, London has established itself as the Western hub for offshore Renminbi (RMB) trading, and agreements are in place that lay the groundwork for London to become the Western hub for investment into China too. Not only is the flow of RMB funds through London expected to increase, but doing business in China will become easier for UK-based companies. Almost two-thirds of all RMB payments outside China and Hong Kong now take place in London and almost a third of all international RMB payments are made in the UK, the most outside Hong Kong and mainland China.

Figures from the City of London Corporation show that London's RMB business volumes continued to grow during the first half of 2014 as the international use of the Chinese currency increased. There was substantial growth across all three principal RMB product categories: trade-related services, forex and deposits. RMB forex trading (both deliverable and non-deliverable) in the first half of 2014 increased by 116 percent compared with the second half of 2013 to reach US\$54,651 billion.

INVESTMENT MANAGEMENT

The UK is one of the largest markets in the world for investment management, and by far the leading European centre. TheCityUK's Fund Management report shows that the UK's fund management sector was responsible for a record £6.2 trillion of funds at the end of 2013. Over a third of these funds, some £2.2 trillion, came from overseas clients. The 2013 figures represent the sector's fifth consecutive year of growth, with a 14 percent increase due to both an inflow of new funds, and strong investment returns. Nearly two-thirds of funds under management in 2013 came from institutional clients. Retail clients generated a further 16 percent, with the remainder accounted for by private client funds and alternative funds.

The Government published its UK investment management strategy in March 2013, setting out action to grow the UK's share of this global business , and UKTI's comprehensive guide "Fund Management in the UK" is available online.

London is the largest centre for hedge fund managers after New York. London's 18 percent global share in 2012 was slightly down on the previous year, but more than double its market share ten years earlier. The UK remains by far the largest centre for hedge funds in Europe, and is also the leading centre for hedge fund services such as administration, prime brokerage, custody and auditing.

The UK private equity market is the most developed outside the USA. Private equity funds based in the UK accounted for 10 percent of global investments and 6 percent of funds raised in 2012. Over the past two decades, the UK private equity industry has invested over £200 billion in around 30,000 firms worldwide.

THE GLOBAL CENTRE FOR ISLAMIC FINANCE

The UK is the leading Western country and Europe's premier centre for Islamic finance, with US$19 billion of reported assets. An important feature of the development of London and the UK has been Government policies intended to broaden the market for Islamic products. Six banks offer fully Sharia-compliant services and at least 20 other financial firms offer Sharia-compliant windows – more than any other Western country.

In June 2014 the UK became the first country in the Western world to issue sovereign Sukuk, the Islamic equivalent of a bond. The issuance of the £200 million Sukuk successfully attracted orders from investors in the UK, Middle East and Asia which amounted to more than ten times its size.

The launch of Sharia-compliant Sukuk will act as a further means of attracting investment for infrastructure projects. Islam prohibits the earning of interest, but Sukuk bonds entitle investors to a share in the returns generated by an underlying asset, such as a property or construction development. Further developments announced in October 2014 will help to strengthen the UK's status as the Western hub for Islamic finance. UK Export Finance expects to be able to provide Sharia-compliant support for British exporters in the next few months. The Bank of England is looking at establishing Sharia-compliant liquidity facilities to help Britain's Islamic banking sector grow.

The UK is also an international leader in Islamic finance education and research. World-class universities and business schools across the UK offer a range of specialist courses and qualifications in this subject, ranging from foundation courses to postgraduate research.

EUROPE'S LARGEST INSURANCE SECTOR

The UK insurance industry is the largest in Europe and third largest in the world. Its strong international position is indicated by the fact that:

- The UK is the largest source of both insurance funds and pensions in Europe.
- UK companies feature prominently in rankings of the world's largest insurance companies.
- 22 percent of global marine insurance premiums were transacted on the London Market in 2012, more than in any other country.
- London accounts for around a 10 percent share of total world reinsurance.

A study by the London Market Group and Boston Consulting Group confirms the London Market's position as the largest global hub for commercial and specialty risk, reaching £60 billion of gross written premiums in 2013, with £45 billion of this written in London and backed by London capital. The study shows that, based on business written in London alone, the market is nearly double the size of Bermuda and Zurich and 11 times bigger than Singapore.

The Government published the UK Insurance Growth Action Plan in December 2013. The plan sets out a package of measures to strengthen the insurance sector's contribution to the UK economy and enhance the UK's position as a global leader in the industry.

LONDON: THE FINTECH CAPITAL OF EUROPE

Technology is transforming the financial services industry – and the UK is leading the way. Management consulting firm Accenture reports that investment in financial technology (Fintech) is growing faster in the UK and Ireland than anywhere else in the world. The volume of deals, mostly connected to London, has grown at an annualised rate of 74 percent since 2008, compared with 27 percent globally and 13 percent in Silicon Valley. London alone accounts for 53 percent of total European investment in the sector. Figures from CB Insights show that London-based Fintech firms attracted more than US$539 million in the 11 months up to November 2014 – triple the amount raised in 2013.

Many of the biggest players in Fintech have chosen to have a base in the UK. Particular investment opportunities exist in four subsectors: payments, platforms, software, and data analytics. For more information on the strengths and opportunities in the UK Fintech ecosystem see the UKTI publication "Fintech – the UK's unique environment for growth".

PRACTICAL SUPPORT SETTING UP A FINANCIAL SERVICES INSTITUTION

There are, of course, a number of considerations that any company has to take into account when setting up a financial services institution in the UK. Many of these are around compliance with regulation and regulatory processes. Financial institutions must satisfy the regulators that they are well prepared and are capable of operating a successful business in the UK.

Other considerations may be around deciding what might be the right corporate structure; the choice of location and obtaining suitable premises and workforce; obtaining visas for migrant workers and non-UK employees; tax arrangements and IT infrastructure.

The UK Government's aim is to make the UK as welcoming as possible to any inward investor wishing to set up a financial services institution. And to help investors set up in the UK, practical assistance is available.

The Government's message is clear: we want the UK to be the most attractive place to set up and establish a financial services institution. Practical assistance is on hand, and, should your business require it, UKTI, working with local partners and across government, is here to help. To summarise, Britain is open for business and UKTI will make your investing in the UK as easy as possible by providing practical help. Once here, UKTI will do all it can to help your business succeed internationally.

6.2 MERGERS AND ACQUISITIONS AND JOINT VENTURES

Richard O'Brien, Watson Farley & Williams LLP

INTRODUCTION

The phrase "mergers and acquisitions" (M&A) refers to the aspect of corporate strategy, finance and management dealing with the purchase, sale and merging of different companies and businesses. The term "acquisition", also known as a takeover, is used to describe a wide variety of transactions involving the sale and purchase of either a business or a company. Through the acquisition of a UK target, an inward investor is able to gain immediate local presence, expertise and name recognition. The same principal issues are common to most acquisitions, whatever the size or nature of the parties or the entity being acquired.

The basic forms of business combination are:

- the purchase of shares of a target company;
- the purchase of the target's underlying business; and
- joint venture arrangements.

This chapter is divided into four sections: the first considers the private acquisition of companies and businesses; the second deals with the acquisition of public companies; the third covers joint ventures; and the final section provides an overview of merger control.

PRIVATE COMPANY AND BUSINESS ACQUISITIONS

There are generally two methods of acquiring a business: one is to buy the shares of the company that owns the business; the other is to buy the assets that make up the business. In either case, the buyer will achieve its commercial objective of acquiring the business that is being run by the target company, although the legal effects of the two types of acquisition are fundamentally different.

If shares in a company are purchased, all its assets, liabilities and obligations are acquired (even those that the buyer does not know about). The contract is made between the buyer and the owner of the shares (the seller). There is no change in the ownership of the business; it remains in the ownership of the company. Alternatively, the business may be purchased in its entirety as a going concern, together with all its assets and liabilities or, if appropriate, only those identified assets and liabilities that the buyer agrees to acquire.

A share sale is generally the quickest way to effect an acquisition because legally this only requires a share transfer. On a business sale, by contrast, transfer arrangements will need to be put in place for each asset being purchased. Tax issues will also play a central role in determining the best route to be followed.

Exclusivity

As an acquisition will involve a prospective buyer investing a substantial amount of time, effort and money, the buyer will often require the seller to agree not to negotiate with other parties for a given period while it undertakes its due diligence (investigation of the target business). An exclusivity (or "lockout") period for the buyer will often be agreed in a separate exclusivity agreement entered into with the seller.

Confidentiality Agreement

As most acquisitions will involve the buyer having access to significant information about the target business (and, to a certain extent, the seller and its group), some of which will be confidential, it is standard practice for a seller to ask any prospective buyer to enter into a confidentiality agreement requiring the buyer and its professional advisers to treat all disclosed information as confidential, and to agree it may only use the disclosed information for the purposes of the acquisition or otherwise with the seller's consent.

Due Diligence

For acquisitions subject to English law, the principle of *caveat emptor*, or "buyer beware", will apply, which effectively means that there is only limited statutory and common law protection for a buyer under the law. It is, therefore, essential for a buyer to learn as much as possible about the target business and the issues that will be relevant to the acquisition as early as possible in the acquisition procedure through the process of due diligence.

Due diligence is intended to identify risks so that these can be allocated between the buyer and the seller. The review usually comprises legal, financial, tax and commercial due diligence, and will help to determine the contractual protections which the buyer will require from the seller, as well as the risks the buyer should avoid completely. The information-gathering process will aim to identify information that may impact upon the negotiation process and, in particular, on the price the buyer is prepared to pay. The buyer will seek to obtain contractual protection from the seller in relation to issues of concern to it and other risks in the form of warranties and indemnities in the acquisition agreement.

Warranties

In simple terms, warranties are contractual promises made by the seller to the buyer regarding the state of affairs of the target company/business.

Warranties serve two main purposes: one is to elicit information about the company and business from the seller by way of disclosure or qualification of the warranties—a process linked to the due diligence investigation discussed above; the second is to provide the buyer with a remedy (a claim for breach of warranty) if the statements made about the company/business later prove to be incorrect and the acquisition turns out to be other than as bargained for.

Indemnities

The buyer may seek further contractual protection in the form of indemnities included in the acquisition agreement (or sometimes in a separate deed). An indemnity is essentially a promise to reimburse the buyer in respect of a designated type of liability, should it arise in the future. The purpose of an indemnity is to provide a guaranteed remedy for the buyer, where a breach of warranty may not give rise to a claim in damages, or to provide a specific remedy that might not otherwise be available at law.

Stamp Duty

Stamp duty is the tax payable when property or shares are transferred. Stamp duty land tax is payable when real property or land is bought, and either stamp duty or stamp duty reserve tax is payable when shares are transferred.

On an acquisition of shares, the buyer pays stamp duty at the rate of 0.5 per cent. of the purchase price, although no stamp duty is payable if the purchase price is not more than £1,000. On an acquisition of a business, the buyer pays stamp duty only on those assets that are taxable (essentially land and shares). On the purchase of commercial land, no stamp duty is payable if the value of the property does not exceed £150,000. Stamp duty on the purchase of real estate above this value is payable at varying rates up to four per cent. of the value.

Schemes of Arrangement

A scheme of arrangement is a statutory procedure for business combinations effected under Part 26 of the Companies Act 2006, whereby a company may make a compromise or arrangement with its members or creditors. A company can effect virtually any kind of internal reorganisation, merger or de-merger restructuring under this section as long as the necessary approvals have been obtained, including the relevant shareholder approval and court approval.

PUBLIC COMPANY ACQUISITIONS

The Takeover Market

The UK has a long history of takeover activity. Takeover activity has increased significantly since the Takeover Panel commenced work in 1968, and approximately three-quarters of all public takeover offers in the European Union (EU) occur in the UK. There are several reasons for this overall growth, including the fact that corporate balance sheets appear to be healthier and corporate earning expectations remain positive. In addition, the rising popularity of the AIM Market (the London Stock Exchange's international market for smaller growing companies) has continued and has generated significant takeover activity as companies on the market mature and consolidation of businesses becomes an attractive opportunity.

Regulation of Takeovers

Transactions involving the acquisition of control of a public company (takeovers), and those involving the sale and purchase of public companies whose shares are listed on the London Stock Exchange, are subject to considerable additional regulation:

- The City Code on Takeovers and Mergers (the Takeover Code) is a set of rules developed by the Panel on Takeovers and Mergers (the Takeover Panel) and regulates takeovers in the UK. The Takeover Code applies to offers for public companies resident in the UK, the Channel Islands and the Isle of Man, irrespective of where their shares are listed or publicly marketed.
- The Listing, Prospectus and Disclosure Rules are made by the Financial Conduct Authority and regulate the process by which a company listed on the London Stock Exchange can enter into certain transactions, including making acquisitions or disposals.
- The Criminal Justice Act 1993 together with the Listing Rules, Disclosure Rules and Takeover Code, regulates insider dealings.
- The Financial Services Act 2012 governs misleading statements and misleading impressions.
- The Companies Act 2006 contains the main legislation governing the formation and administration of companies.
- The Financial Services and Markets Act 2000 regulates the conduct of investment business and makes provision for the official listing of securities, public offers of securities and investment advertisement.
- Merger control provisions regulate the takeover of a UK company, which may require approval from the competition authorities of the EU or the UK.

Outline of a Takeover

Takeovers are public transactions, and the Takeover Code prescribes a strict timetable to be adhered to. Unlike a private acquisition, it is not possible to simply announce the completion of a takeover. Under the Takeover Code, a takeover must be carried out publicly, and any takeover offer has to be held open for a fixed period of time. This in turn means that a potential rival bidder may make a competing offer to the target's shareholders.

In a "recommended bid", target shareholders are recommended to accept the offer by the target's directors. A "hostile bid", however, is an offer not supported by the target.

JOINT VENTURES

A joint venture describes a commercial arrangement between two or more economically independent entities for the purpose of pursuing an agreed commercial goal, in which the joint venturers share in agreed proportions the financing and control of the enterprise, as well as the profits and losses it makes.

Joint ventures may be structured through limited partnerships, limited liability partnerships, common unincorporated associations or simply by a contractual agreement. However, the most common joint venture vehicle is a limited company.

International Joint Ventures

Joint ventures are vital to the development of international business, and an alliance with a local partner can provide an inward investor with:

- An important means of business expansion;
- Access to new markets;
- Distribution networks;
- Greater resources; and
- The sharing of risks with a partner.

International joint ventures (where an overseas party combines with a local party to undertake joint business in that local jurisdiction) will require consideration of a number of issues, including choosing the type of legal structure most appropriate to the joint venture vehicle, tax considerations, restrictions on foreign participation, licensing issues and the requirement for governmental consents.

Contributions and Funding

Initial finance may be injected into a joint venture company in a number of ways. One of these would be a straightforward subscription by the partners for shares in the joint venture company in consideration for a contribution of cash or non-cash assets.

Alternatively, capital may be injected by way of loan, either from the joint venture partners or from third-party lenders. The parties will also need to consider in advance how future finance is to be provided to the joint venture company.

Management
It is common for the partners to retain some level of control and influence in the joint venture's decision-making process, either through representation on the board of directors or through requiring certain key decisions to be referred to shareholders. The level of each party's control will depend on their respective shareholdings. The management structure should be reflected clearly in the joint venture agreement.

The Joint Venture Agreement
The written agreement between partners should set out the precise terms and conditions agreed between them, and provide a framework for the ongoing alliance. It should specifically cover:

- the structure of the joint venture;
- the objectives of the joint venture;
- how the business of the joint venture is to be operated;
- the financial contributions that each partner is to make;
- the management and control of the joint venture (e.g. the right to appoint directors and each partner's voting rights);
- how profits, losses and liabilities are to be shared;
- how any disputes between the partners will be resolved; and
- how the joint venture can be terminated.

MERGER CONTROL

Merger control provisions exist under both UK and European law. Inward investors merging with, acquiring or entering into a joint venture with a UK company should be aware that the transaction may require notification to the Competition and Markets Authority (CMA) to assess its effect on competition in the relevant markets. Although notification to the CMA is voluntary, the parties to mergers that meet or exceed the qualifying threshold criteria (see below) are well advised to notify their merger to eliminate the risk of investigation and possible sanctions.

A merger will be considered as "qualifying" for investigation in the UK where:

- two or more companies, at least one of which carries on business in the UK, cease to be distinct (brought under common ownership or control);
- the merging companies supply or consume goods or services that form part of the same market, and after the merger takes place, they will supply or acquire

25 per cent. or more of those goods or services in the UK as a whole or in a substantial part of it; or

- the annual UK turnover of the business being taken over exceeds £70 million.

Larger mergers that have a "community dimension" will be reviewed by the European Commission under the EU Merger Regulation ("EUMR") (Council Regulation (EC) No. 139/2004). For more details about merger control, please refer to chapter 2.1 on competition law.

6.3 MERGER AND ACQUISITION TRANSACTION PROCESSES

Adrian Alexander, Mazars LLP

The terminology used in a merger/acquisition transaction has been covered in the previous sections by the lawyers and this provides a platform for us to focus on the transaction processes involved in merging with, or, more likely, acquiring another entity.

The following graphic (Figure 6.3.1) provides details of the stages in an acquisition process. We go into further detail about these processes in the following sections.

Figure 6.3.1

M&A transaction approach

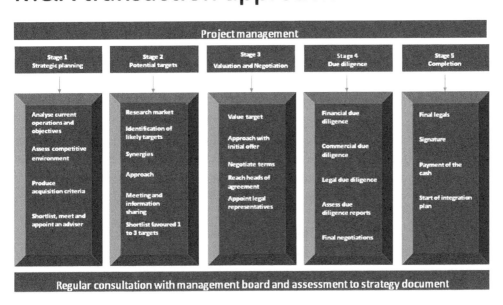

WHERE TO START

The essential starting point for a transaction, or indeed series of transactions, is to develop and document a strategy. This will help to drive the acquisition process towards pre-determined objectives and minimise the risks involved in acquiring companies. The strategy document should:

- Analyse your company's current operations and assess what the aims of the shareholders, management and other stakeholders are and what they are seeking to achieve.
- Consider the current and future competitive environment, the threat of new entrants and the impact acquisitions would have on this dynamic. This may be more challenging when analysing markets to which the company has no exposure, and formal market research should be considered to formulate a view.
- Thoughtfully consider the alternatives – acquisitions should be compared to a 'cold start' and the investment required under all the different options.
- Detail the desired characteristics of the target company, the funds available for transactions and the time scales involved.
- Provide consideration for the management time required for integration and the costs/cost savings that would be possible. This is particularly important in cross-border transactions.
- Budget for the legal, regulatory and accounting costs of a successful acquisition search process.

To ensure that an acquisition achieves long-term objectives and manages to meet or exceed shareholder expectations it is essential that this planning is carried out before a search process is undertaken. Similarly, if an unexpected acquisition opportunity arises, this should be compared back to the strategy document.

FINDING THE TARGETS

Once a strategy document has been written the process of defining the search criteria for prospective targets is considerably easier.

Depending on the results of the analysis undertaken into the market place, the targets could be easily identified from competitors. Alternatively, vertical integration opportunities may lead to subsequent cost savings or securing of necessary resources. A diversification strategy may be adopted if the market place is saturated and alternative revenue streams are required.

Whilst it would be relatively straightforward to identify targets that operate in a company's market place, in a lot of cases it is normal that a corporate finance agent/broker would be engaged to undertake the search process. This enables the management of the company to continue driving the operations and organic growth strategy forward and not to become distracted with another project. Similarly, when targets are being sourced from a diversified market place or vertical integration an advisor's breadth of connections and research capability can prove invaluable. However, the support and extensive network of contacts held by a corporate finance agent/broker shouldn't be underestimated when looking for a strategic acquisition in a foreign market, especially if considering a new international market for the first time..

These criteria used for a search process are typically a mix of financial and non-financial indicators. The acquirer may be looking to achieve critical mass which would require turnover, head count, office locations or operations in key sectors. Alternatively they may be looking at adding value to their bottom line; so synergistic savings and strong profitability would be important. The strategy document would help to guide the advisor on these criteria, whilst an awareness of "left-field" opportunities would help to supplement the target shortlist.

THE ROLE OF THE ADVISOR

The advisor would be tasked with planning and executing the search and approach process within an agreed timescale and to a set of criteria which has been agreed with the company. The advisor would keep the key individuals at the company informed of progress and provide the benefit of their experience with respect to communications, negotiations and routes to targets.

There are a number of different sources which the advisor would use to identify potential targets including public companies' accounts, trade press, corporate finance websites, specialist market research providers and, increasingly, social media sites. The company would benefit by working with a UK advisor who understands the local laws, practices and forums available for corporate financiers.

The advisor would then feed his findings and thoughts back to the company, highlighting the potential targets and rating their suitability as high, medium and low for their consideration. The ranking would be dependent upon the fit with the company's acquisition criteria.

The advisor would also be able to help with preparing internal board reports that may be needed to inform the key decision makers.

EXPRESSING AN INTEREST AND OPENING DIALOGUE

Once the targets have been identified the company, usually through their advisor, would open dialogue with the target to understand their interest in a transaction. This can be done anonymously to protect the market from knowing that a particular company is acquisitive, or it can be done openly to demonstrate their strength and growth intentions. The approach is likely to differ depending on market sector and the competitiveness of the market place.

The expression of interest is typically made through a letter (or in the modern day an email) addressed to the main shareholder at their home/personal address. The advisor will use their experience and any connections to try to obtain a warm introduction, which has a greater chance of generating a conversation, and will always agree the targets' names with their client before communicating.

The expression of interest letter may also need to include details of the acquiring company, especially if they do not have a strong brand name in the UK marketplace.

Once communication commences it is important that the company is briefed by their advisor on the process that is being undertaken, just in case any direct responses are directed to the company. It is typical for all communications to go through the advisor which ensures that the acquiring company is insulated from any difficult responses and that a professional and considered approach is given to the process.

It is this professional approach that adds credibility and distinguishes genuine acquirers from those canvassing the market for competitor information.

CONFIDENTIALITY AND INITIAL INFORMATION SHARING

The area of confidentiality, especially amongst competitors, is often a major sticking point in progressing discussions.

The purchaser will often be asked, at a very early stage in the process, to sign a Non Disclosure Agreement ("NDA") before discussions progress and certainly before the sharing of information. The NDA needs to be carefully checked to ensure that the details contained within it, with respect to time limits, the scope of information which is deemed confidential and, the "reasonable endeavours required maintaining confidentiality" are not onerous.

Once an NDA has been agreed the target will then be able to provide the purchaser any information not within the public domain which they have requested. The target may not be willing to divulge all information before a deal is agreed, especially if they are a competitor, but it is important at this stage of the transaction process that the company is able to develop a better understanding of their target. Typical initial information requested includes:

- Top 10 customers by turnover
- A breakdown of turnover by department/service line/product line
- Detailed profit and loss account for the last 3 years
- Latest management accounts and forecasts for the next one to three years
- Information on the client contracts, length, rate of churn etc
- Brief information on key employees and management structure
- Diagram and details of the corporate structure and ownership percentages of any subsidiaries

- Pension commitments
- Any claims or law suits which are pending
- Any unusual or one-off expenditure
- Details of any financial implications that would be triggered by a change of ownership

Whilst financial and operational questions typically form the bulk of the information requests, it is important at meetings with the target to understand their operational culture and how an acquisition would be received by key employees. The integration process should remain firmly in management's and the advisor's thoughts when they are assessing the culture of the two companies.

VALUATION AND NEGOTIATION

Where an advisor is in place they would project manage the transaction and handle the collection of information and analysis of this information to assist with a valuation for the target (if you choose to continue the process once the further information is provided).

The process of valuation is as much an art as it is a science. An understanding of the market sector which the target operates in, and knowledge of past deal multiples is essential whilst understanding possible cost savings, an interrogation of the validity of forecasts and the likelihood of customer retention will all affect the valuation. Valuing a business is only part of the requirement with the structuring of the deal through the use of 'earn-outs' (additional consideration conditional on future results of the company) and deferred consideration (consideration that is outstanding at completion but not conditional on future events) essential tools to help mitigate the risk of the transaction.

When grasping cross-border transactions an understanding of the local market place and local valuation techniques, compared to an acquirer's own country, is vital to pricing an opportunity correctly. This valuation should then be compared to the potential time and financial cost of setting up a new operation in the UK as opposed to acquiring.

Once the company has valued the target, the negotiation process will commence. Typically, the purchaser will provide instructions to the advisor but leave them to handle the communications. By staying removed from the process the purchaser is able to maintain a positive relationship with the target and ensure they are not viewed as the "bad guy" through the negotiation stages.

The level of negotiation required and timescale can be affected by a number of factors, although one of the key drivers would be if the target identified is an "on-market" (listed for sale with an advisor or in trade publications) or "off-market" opportunity. On-market opportunities are easier to identify as they would be professionally marketed and they are more likely to conclude a transaction as the owners were pro-actively looking to exit. However, they are likely to be subject to multiple expressions of interest which creates competition and potentially drives a higher price being paid for the target. Those which are "off-market" opportunities should not be seen as highly unlikely to complete since companies are much more open to such approaches then they have ever been before.

HEADS OF AGREEMENT

The heads of agreement is a document which outlines the broad terms of the transaction. The main part of the document is not legally binding, but intended to cover:

- The consideration proposed for the transaction and the structure of the payments
- The approach which the purchaser will take to due diligence
- Restrictive covenants by which the purchaser will want any departing shareholders to abide
- The documentation required to finalise the deal
- A brief approach to the warranties and indemnities which will be required

There are often a number of legally binding requirements and these are with respect to:
- Confidentiality and deal announcement protocols
- A commitment to a deal timetable and deadline as well as an exclusivity period
- Who pays what costs
- Which international territories law will govern the transaction. In the UK, it is accepted practice for deals to be under English law irrespective of the jurisdiction of the acquiring company.

The heads of agreement document is normally signed by both parties before detailed due diligence is undertaken and provides the basis for legal teams to create the share and purchase agreement.

It is important to keep this document simple but as complete as possible to provide a clear starting point for the drafting of the legal documents and avoid confusion and the need for too much further negotiations as the deal progresses.

DUE DILIGENCE

The objective of due diligence is to investigate the target company, develop a level of comfort with the target's existing financial and commercial position and to validate, as much as possible, its forecast performance.

Purchasers typically select an accountancy firm to undertake the financial due diligence on their behalf. There are some standard areas which are investigated. The scope and scale of work is agreed with the purchaser before the engagement commences.

The due diligence will not only assess the financial statements but also delve deeper into the targets' accounting and operational systems; for example assessing the stock value and its saleability, supplier and customer contracts (length, terms and break clauses), fixed assets, accounting policies and contingent liabilities.

The scope of the due diligence which the accountants and the lawyers (under separate engagements) will perform needs to be wide enough to provide confidence that the target being acquired is free from material errors and risks but not so wide as to place undue financial costs on the transaction. A balance between the deal size and depth of due diligence is something which needs to be found.

Commercial due diligence is often performed in-house and will be undertaken either formally or informally when assessing the target prior to making an offer. Once the heads of agreement have been reached, and especially in instances of larger deal sizes, further commercial due diligence may be undertaken which could involve specialist market research consultants, property and environmental consultants or an in-house project team. Other areas that are also often considered include looking into the target management team's and other key employees' personal history.

REACHING COMPLETION

When purchasing a target who has maintained excellent management information, clear employment contracts, has a good stock control process and up to date property, fixed asset, environmental and data protection policies the transition between due diligence and completion can be relatively simple.

In most M&A transactions however there will be issues found in either financial, commercial or legal due diligence that were not highlighted in the information memorandum or disclosed during subsequent meetings. The nature and size of these findings will have a varying impact on the transaction, from a warranty/indemnity being included (see previous chapter for further details) through to a re-negotiation of the price or deal structure, and in the most extreme case, collapse of the deal.

It is in situations like these that the advisor really proves his worth, often using any findings from due diligence as leverage to achieve a more competitive price or structuring the deal or legal wording in such a way that mitigates the risk to the purchaser.

The use of a good corporate lawyer with experience of completing transactions in the UK market place but also cross-border experience is also essential to ensure that the wording of the share and purchase agreement is favourable.

POST COMPLETION

Once the company has agreed the contracts, developed the necessary level of comfort with the target's financial, commercial and legal positions it will then be in a position to sign the share and purchase agreement and complete the transaction.

Whilst the due diligence and legal process is underway the purchaser's board or leadership team will be working on a post deal integration plan to include aspects of human resources, operations, financial, legal and other commercial requirements. This integration plan would be more detailed for an overseas acquisition as further research and consideration would need to be given to future accounting standards (recent introduction of FRS102), the reporting currency adopted and local human resources considerations including, in the UK, minimum wage and TUPE arrangements (Transfer of undertakings, protection of employment regulations 2014).

The key factor in the success of any transaction is integration; whilst on paper a target may look like the perfect bolt-on to existing operations and have numerous synergies the deal is only successful once these have been realised. Successfully managing the newly acquired company from another country will be fundamental to achieving this result. So, once the deal is complete the real work must begin.

6.4 THE AIM MARKET OF THE LONDON STOCK EXCHANGE

Christina Howard and Sarah Williamson,
Watson Farley & Williams LLP

INTRODUCTION

The global financial crisis has had a significant and well-publicised effect on the world's equity markets. The AIM Market (AIM) is no exception and the past few years have not been easy for London's junior market. However, 2015 marks the twentieth anniversary of AIM, and there are signs of improvement as companies and investors are returning to AIM.

AIM

The London Stock Exchange (LSE) launched AIM in 1995, as an alternative market for smaller growing companies, targeting businesses that either did not yet qualify for listing on London's main market or were otherwise not ready for this step. The LSE wished to provide a route to capital markets for companies that were at a relatively early stage in their development and smaller in size and resources than companies on the LSE's main market. Consequently, they required a more balanced and less burdensome regulatory environment in which to operate than was available on other markets. AIM was therefore structured with a measured level of regulation and with limited entry criteria.

The intention was to create an infrastructure that would enable companies to focus on growing their businesses rather than having to devote an inappropriate amount of management time and resources to regulatory compliance. This had to be balanced with the need to ensure the continued integrity of the market and the maintenance and enhancement of its reputation as a safe and effective place to do business. The result has been a highly successful capital raising market that now enjoys a global reputation.

The Growth of AIM

From its modest beginnings, AIM grew steadily and, notwithstanding continuing global economic uncertainty, there were 99 admissions in 2013, and 118 admissions in 2014. So far there have been 37 admissions to AIM this year (as of July 2015). As of July 2015, 1,066 companies were listed on AIM, with a combined market capitalisation of £74.84 billion.

AIM has matured significantly in recent years. Companies from all sectors are now represented on the market and the number of international (i.e. non-UK) companies admitted to AIM has grown strongly. The increasing maturity of the market has also been demonstrated by the amount of funds raised by AIM companies.

The ongoing effects of the global financial difficulties have seen fundraising remain steady, albeit at a more moderate level, namely £5.9 billion in 2014 and £3.3 billion so far this year (as of July 2015).

Figure 6.4.1 shows the number of admissions and Figure 6.4.2 shows the amount raised by AIM companies, since the launch of the market in 1995 to July 2015.

Figure 6.4.1

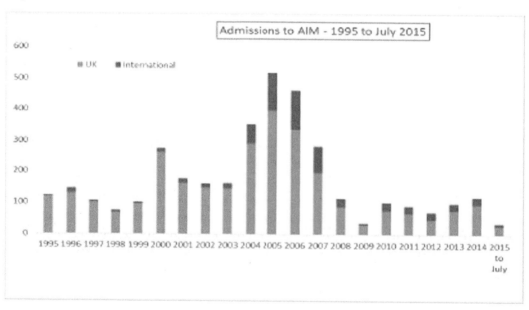

Figure 6.4.2
Source: London Stock Exchange Statistics

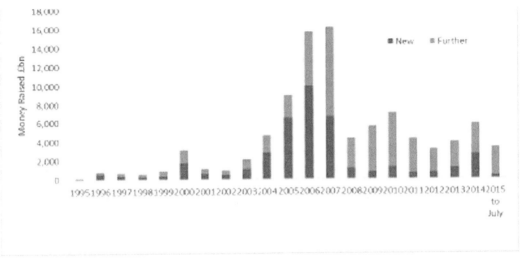

INTERNATIONAL COMPANIES

A significant development for AIM in recent years has been the growth in international admissions. As of July 2015, there were 208 international companies on AIM from some 25 or so jurisdictions, representing just over 20 per cent of the market. However, this does not take account of businesses that have incorporated a UK holding company into their group structure – a strategy adopted by many companies in view of certain benefits in doing so. Taking these companies into account, the proportion of international businesses on AIM is much higher – the number of non-UK companies listed on AIM, as per main country of operation[1], is 421 (approximately 40% of the market). Much of this growth in international business has been driven by companies from Western Europe, Africa, the US, China and South East Asia.

As of July 2015, there were 45 companies with the US as their main country of operation listed on AIM, a substantial increase from around seven years previously when just a handful were listed. The US Sarbanes-Oxley Act 2002 has acted as a catalyst for this development, but it is rarely the principal or only reason for a business to choose AIM in preference to US markets; AIM is a market more suited to a smaller growing business than other exchanges.

AIM is attuned to the needs of these companies. Besides its appropriate level

---

[1] Main country of operation is deemed to be the geographical location from which an AIM company derives, or intends to derive, the largest proportion of its revenues or where the largest proportion of its assets are, or will be, located.

of regulation and relative ease of entry, AIM has a highly developed infrastructure of advisory firms focused on the market, specialising in this area. These include nominated advisers ("nomads") that:

- provide the corporate advisory function needed for such companies;
- assess the suitability of companies wishing to join AIM under delegated authority from the LSE; and
- in many cases, also provide broking and fundraising services for their corporate clients.

MARKET CAPITALISATION

AIM is home to companies with a broad range of market capitalisations. Many AIM companies have a market capitalisation of £5 million or less; however, most AIM companies have market capitalisations of between £5 million and £50 million. As of July 2015, 64 AIM companies had a market capitalisation of £250 million or more, with 20 of these having a market capitalisation of £500 million or more. The distribution of market capitalisation across the value range is illustrated in Figure 6.4.3.

Figure 6.4.3

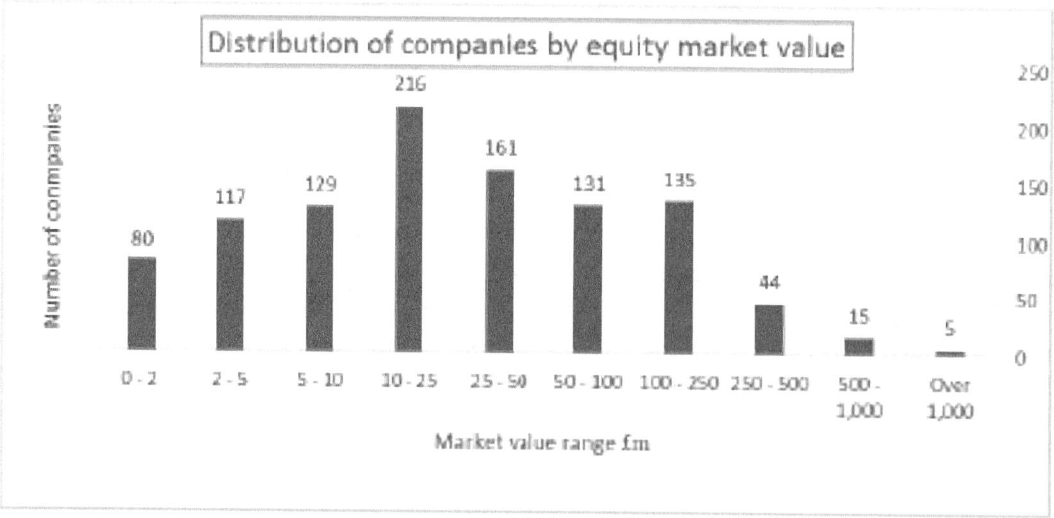

Source: London Stock Exchange Statistics
As of July 2015, the average market capitalisation of a company listed on AIM is £70.20 million.

REASONS TO SEEK A PUBLIC LISTING

There are a number of reasons for a company to seek a public listing. These include the following:

- Accessing capital for growth;
- Creating a market for its shares;
- Obtaining an objective market valuation of its business;
- Raising its profile;
- Creating the ability to fund acquisitions with share capital; and

providing incentives to employees through share ownership.

AIM provides all of the above benefits to a public company. In addition, AIM may be contrasted with other exchanges by virtue of the following:

- Absence of onerous admission criteria;
- More straightforward admission process;
- Simple secondary fundraising procedure;
- Easier acquisition rules; and
- A more balanced regulatory environment.

AIM Admission Criteria

AIM imposes few eligibility criteria on companies wishing to join the market:

- There is no minimum requirement for a particular percentage of shares to be held in public hands.
- No trading record is required.
- Admission documents do not require pre-vetting by a regulatory authority.
- There is no minimum market capitalisation requirement (save where the company is an investment company, in which case the minimum capitalisation requirement is £3 million).

Most other established exchanges require a particular length of audited trading history, a minimum market capitalisation and a certain percentage of shares to be held in public hands. In most cases, a prospectus or registration statement must be submitted to, and approved by, a regulatory authority in advance of listing, which can be onerous in terms of both timing and costs.

Although there are relatively few regulatory criteria for a company to qualify for admission to AIM, one of the essential foundations of AIM is the position occupied by the nomads, which act as the gatekeepers of the market.

ADVISERS

Nomads

Nomads are corporate finance advisers approved by the LSE. Their functions are to assist with the admission process and thereafter to advise on, and ensure compliance with, the ongoing requirements of AIM. The nomad's principal role in the admission process is to confirm that the company and its securities are suitable for admission.

Following admission, the nomad is responsible for advising the directors of the company as to their ongoing obligations, and for reviewing the company's actual trading performance and financial conditions against any profit forecast, estimate or projection included in admission documents or published elsewhere.

In view of their responsibilities to the LSE, nomads are required to carry out extensive due diligence on their clients in advance of admission. In February 2007, the LSE introduced a new rule book for nomads, The AIM Rules for Nominated Advisers, which codified the role and responsibilities of nomads based on existing best market practice. While most nomad firms conduct their businesses in accordance with best market practice in any event, the LSE was keen to ensure that all firms adopted the same standards in their review of prospective AIM companies.

The system of delegated authority from the LSE to the nomads forms one of the bedrocks of the balanced regulatory environment upon which AIM is based. It is a system that has been accepted by investors and has worked extremely well. Investor confidence in the system is reflected in the amount of funds invested in AIM securities, and the moderate additional rules that AIM has introduced are likely to enhance investor confidence further.

Brokers

Every AIM company is also required to appoint and retain a broker at all times. Brokers are approved by the LSE. The function of these firms is to provide market support for trading in the company's securities and to undertake fundraising activities for the company. The broker will also generally provide research and institutional sales support for the company, and provide information about the company to the market.

In many cases, the nomad and broker functions are combined within the same firm, although in separate divisions. There is no requirement for a single firm to adopt both roles, and some companies prefer for their nomad to be independent of their broker.

Other Advisers

In addition to a nomad and a broker, a company wishing to be admitted to AIM will need to engage legal counsel, reporting accountants and, in most cases, a public relations firm.

The role of legal counsel will be to advise the company on the legal and regulatory requirements for admission to AIM and on applicable securities laws, and to play a principal role in the preparation and finalisation of the admission documents, working closely with the nomad in this regard. The lawyers will also advise on:

- Any required corporate reorganisation;
- Any required amendments to the company's constitutional documents;
- The terms of directors' service contracts; and
- The duties and responsibilities of the directors under applicable UK law.

They will also undertake a legal due diligence review covering matters such as the company's contractual arrangements, employment agreements, and legal and regulatory compliance and litigation, as well as any other matters required by the nomad in order to satisfy itself that the company is suitable for admission to AIM.

The nomad and broker will also engage their own legal counsel to provide independent advice on legal matters in relation to the negotiation of the placing (or underwriting) agreement.

The reporting accountants, who are distinct from the company's own auditors, will:

- Undertake a review of the company's financial position and financial reporting procedures;
- Generally produce a report containing the results of its financial due diligence review; and
- Prepare with the directors a working capital report to demonstrate that the company will have sufficient working capital for at least 12 months following admission.

The role of the financial public relations firm will be to generate press and investor interest in the initial and any subsequent fundraisings, and to raise the profile of the company generally. The public relations firm will also work with the nomad, the company and its other advisers in agreeing the content of public statements.

Admission Process

Under the standard admission procedure, a company wishing to be admitted to AIM will be required to produce a formal admission document or prospectus that will include all relevant information on the company and its business. The content of the admission document is governed by The AIM Rules for Companies and is otherwise determined by reference to the UK's securities laws. Most AIM admission transactions are accompanied by a fundraising to institutional investors. If the fundraising constitutes a public offer of securities, is made to more than 150 persons in any member state of the European Union (EU) and is not otherwise exempted, a full prospectus under the EU Prospectus Directive (as amended) will be required. Such a document will require the pre-vetting and approval of the UK Listing Authority (UKLA) prior to the admission of the company to trading on AIM. For this reason, it is rare for a company being admitted to AIM to seek to raise funds through a public offer, and the vast majority of transactions are undertaken by way of an institutional placing exempt from the full prospectus and UKLA approval requirements.

The admission document will provide the basis upon which investors subscribe for shares. The broker will undertake a fundraising exercise, generally based on a marketing presentation and a near-final version of the admission documents. An AIM transaction is broadly similar to any other listing event, the principal difference being the absence of a regulatory approval process.

AIM has also introduced a streamlined secondary listing procedure, which is available to companies already listed on certain designated international stock markets. In such cases, companies can benefit from a streamlined regime under which the requirement to produce an admission document is replaced by an obligation to issue an expanded pre-admission announcement. The exchanges falling within the scope of the streamlined secondary listing procedure include the following:

- the Australian Securities Exchange;
- Deutsche Börse;
- NYSE Euronext (a European stock exchange based in Paris, France);
- Johannesburg Stock Exchange;
- NASDAQ;
- the New York Stock Exchange;
- NASDAQ OMX Stockholm;
- the UKLA's Official List;
- Swiss Exchange; and
- the TMX Group.

Cost and Timing

Although every AIM admission transaction is different, and while issues of both timing and cost will depend upon a number of factors, in most cases the admission process can be expected to take three to four months to complete. Some transactions are implemented in a shorter timescale, while others take longer, but this is a fairly reliable guide.

Similar variables apply in relation to the cost of an AIM admission. The largest single element of cost for an AIM admission with a fundraising is the commission payable to the broker or investment bank. This will generally be around five per cent of funds raised, but may be higher depending on market conditions. Other costs include the cost of the nomad, legal counsel, the reporting accountants and, for certain sectors such as natural resources, competent persons who are required to produce reports. As a guide, companies would commonly expect the total cost of an IPO on AIM to be approximately seven to 10 per cent of funds raised. This does, of course, depend upon the size of the fundraising and market conditions.

POST-ADMISSION REQUIREMENTS

Once admitted to AIM, companies must comply with the AIM rules, as well as with applicable securities law. The AIM rules are written in plain English and are less prescriptively detailed than the rules on other major markets. AIM companies must provide certain information to the market on a regular basis and specifically upon the occurrence of certain events. To ensure that the market is kept fully informed, AIM companies are obliged to make similar ongoing disclosures to those required by companies on the other major exchanges, to ensure that the market is aware of the financial position of the company and its prospects.

Each AIM company is also required to publish accounts, usually prepared in accordance with International Financial Reporting Standards (IFRS) as adopted by the EU, as well as six-monthly interim results. Each AIM company is also required to notify the market of any changes in shareholdings of directors and to provide information to the market concerning substantial or related party transactions.

It should be noted that shareholder approval is generally not required for substantial transactions, which contrasts AIM with other markets. The only exception to this is in the case of a reverse takeover or a disposal resulting in a fundamental change of business, which requires the approval of shareholders in advance of the transaction.

Corporate Governance

The UK has high standards of corporate governance applicable to public companies. The UK Corporate Governance Code is mandatory for companies with a premium listing on the Official List, regardless of whether they are incorporated in the UK or elsewhere. Although the UK Corporate Governance Code does not apply to companies trading on AIM, most AIM companies have sought to adhere to the provisions of the Code so far as is practicable, including ensuring that the roles of chairman and chief executive are exercised by separate individuals and that there is a balance between executive and non-executive directors on a board. The Quoted Companies Alliance (QCA) has issued the Corporate Governance Guidelines for Smaller Quoted Companies, and although this guidance has no formal regulatory status, it does reflect a consensus position of the AIM advisory and investing community, as well as the key provisions of the UK Corporate Governance Code. The National Association of Pension Funds has also published corporate governance and voting guidelines for AIM companies and these are generally consistent with the guidelines published by the QCA.

Tax Benefits

For individual UK taxpaying investors, certain tax reliefs may be available following an investment in shares traded on AIM. Amongst other things, the availability of such reliefs will depend on how the investment in the AIM company is structured. Broadly, such tax reliefs may include:

- relief through the Enterprise Investment Scheme;
- relief where the investment forms part of a Venture Capital Trust;
- up to 100% relief from Inheritance Tax where the investment qualifies for business property relief;
- subject to satisfying a number of conditions, entrepreneurs' relief may be available to reduce the rate of capital gains tax payable on the disposal of an investment in shares in an AIM company from 28% to 10%; and
- subject to various conditions, capital gains tax gift relief may be available to enable an individual to "hold over" the capital gains tax due on a disposal of shares in an AIM company, where the shares are transferred for a consideration other than at "arm's length".

There is an exemption from stamp duty and stamp duty reserve tax on transactions in securities admitted to trading on AIM, provided that the securities are not also listed on a recognised stock exchange.

It should also be noted that by investing in AIM companies and placing the shares in an Individual Savings Account (ISA), individuals will pay no tax on the income (including dividends) received from the shares and capital gains tax will not arise following a disposal of the investment.

Some of the above tax benefits and reliefs have been designed to encourage investment in AIM companies in the early stages of their development.

CONCLUSION

The global financial crisis has affected all international stock markets. As governments continue their work to rejuvenate markets across the world, AIM on its twentieth anniversary, with its balanced level of regulation and history of past success should be well placed to maintain its position as a leading international IPO market.

6.5 A GUIDE TO INVESTMENT IN UK COMMERCIAL PROPERTY

Gary Ritter and Charlotte Williams,
Watson Farley & Williams LLP

Historically the UK has had one of the most dynamic and transparent property markets in Europe, with a broad variety of property options, stable rents and flexible short term lease structures.

Commenting on the UK property investment market in May 2015, the London office of Cushman & Wakefield, one of the world's leading commercial property consultants, states that:

"The UK property market delivered its strongest performance for 9 years in 2014, with total annual returns reaching 19.5%, according to the IPD UK Monthly Property Index. Following a steady improvement in rental growth in H2 2014 and sustained downward pressure on yields, the industrial sector has emerged as the strongest performer of the three main commercial property sectors, with total annualised returns of 24.4% –a 20 year high – fractionally ahead of the office sector, which returned 24.3%. Central London office occupational and investment volumes are back to pre-crisis levels, with demand intense and supply constraints unlikely to ease in the short term. For retail, occupational sentiment is improving, but leasing activity is still largely confined to prime high streets and shopping centres in London and other key regional locations. The hotel investment market was vibrant in 2014, with volumes just under £5 billion, the strongest performance since the beginning of the recession.

Investment activity in all markets is being aided by the greater depth and liquidity in the financing market, with lenders increasingly moving towards new origination, as opposed to refinancing, and targeting opportunities across a wide range of UK markets and sectors. Banks, which have seen their market share eroded by non-bank lenders in recent years, are now making a strong return to the market and are increasingly competitive.

Looking ahead, prospects for the UK investment market remain bullish, with the sheer weight of capital targeting UK property expected to continue driving increases in transaction volumes and capital values in 2015. The economy is on a solid footing and while there may be some uncertainty on policy following the election and ahead of a potential referendum on EU membership, occupier markets are starting to reflect firmer business confidence, with demand strengthening across all sectors and evidence of rental growth becoming more widespread for the best property."

This chapter seeks to provide a legal background for overseas entities or individuals considering investing in or leasing UK commercial property (whether industrial, retail, offices, hotel/serviced apartments), either for occupation or for investment purposes. Importantly, there are no restrictions on foreign nationals or overseas companies buying or leasing property in the UK, subject only to tax implications.

As well as acquiring the property directly, there are a number of structures through which to invest in property including:

- Property companies;
- Partnerships;
- Joint venture vehicles; or
- Real Estate Investment Trusts ("REITs"): A REIT is a quoted company that owns and manages income-producing property, either commercial or residential which complies with certain conditions and may achieve certain taxation benefits.

OWNERSHIP OF LAND

The form of ownership and legal rights over a property can be very significant to an owner and/or occupier. Statute has established two forms of legal estate in land, with a relatively recent addition, namely:

Freehold Estate – Where the property (both land and structures) is effectively owned by the freeholder in perpetuity. An investor may prefer to own a freehold as this gives the most control, has a capital value and enables the grant of leases to secure an income stream. Nevertheless, freehold ownership may be subject to certain covenants (e.g. restricting the use of the property) and/or may be subject to the rights of others (e.g. rights of way for third parties across the property).

Leasehold Estate (i.e. taking a lease or renting the property) – Where the leaseholder's ownership of the land is contractually limited in time to the length of the term of the lease. The lease will be granted out of a freehold or superior leasehold estate.

Commonhold – This relatively new form of freehold tenure has existed since 2004. Commonhold is similar to the "strata title" and "condominium" systems that exist in Australia and the United States. Essentially, this is where each owner of a unit in a development (e.g. a flat, office or shop) owns the freehold of their unit and is also a member of a commonhold association which owns and manages the common parts of the development.

The English system enables the "legal" interest in the property to be split from the "beneficial" interest, should this be desired. The legal title holder will be the registered proprietor at the Land Registry or the legal owner of the title deeds, while the beneficial owner will be entitled to the pecuniary interest in the property and will receive the income. This would be of relevance in establishing structures for tax and accounting purposes.

As regards the beneficial interest, land can be held by more than one person in one of two ways: either as a joint tenancy or a tenancy in common. A joint tenancy

is a form of ownership where, normally, should one owner die, the property will automatically vest in the surviving owner(s), regardless of the terms of the deceased's will. A tenancy in common, however, is a form of ownership where on the death of one of the joint owners, the relevant share in the property will form part of the deceased's estate and will pass to their beneficiaries by their will or, where there is no will, in accordance with the law on intestacy.

LEASEHOLD

Key Elements
A lease is a contract between a landlord and tenant which creates a leasehold estate.

It is characterised by the landlord granting the tenant exclusive possession of the property for a fixed time (i.e. for a specified term or a period that is capable of being brought to an end by notice).

If these criteria are not met, a personal licence may be created instead of a leasehold estate. This is significant in terms of whether third parties will be obliged to recognise the occupier's rights and also because statute contains substantial protection for tenants, but not licensees, for example, security of tenure for certain residential and business tenancies.

Main Types of Lease
The ground lease: this is a (normally residential) long lease often granted for more than 99 years usually for a one-off sum, called a "premium", with a nominal rent payable (sometimes called a 'peppercorn') throughout the rest of the term. A ground lease may be perceived to be closer in nature to a freehold owing to its capital value. Residential apartments/flats are normally sold or held on a long lease.

The rack rent lease: this is the most prevalent form of commercial occupational lease usually granted for around 5-10 years. The tenant will pay a full-market rent, normally quarterly, and, usually, no premium is payable.

Short term residential occupational leases: these generally take the form of an "Assured Shorthold Tenancy" which, at the end of the lease term, entitles the landlord to possession of the premises.

COMMERCIAL LEASES

Pre-lets
Companies can take a lease of premises that are already available or may be entitled to enter into a "pre-let" agreement with a developer to lease premises prior to the carrying out or completion of construction work, enabling the future tenant to specify the design, layout and fittings of the building.

Security of Tenure
In most cases where a tenant occupies premises for business purposes, statute grants them the right to renew their lease on largely identical terms (subject to a review of rent and length of term) at the end of the term, the intention being to protect the tenant's goodwill at the premises established whilst in occupation.

Certain rights to compensation may also be available in the event that the landlord is able to rely on one or more of seven grounds to refuse to renew the lease (e.g. if it requires occupation of the premises for its own use or wishes to redevelop the property).

Nevertheless it is common for the parties to agree to exclude the tenant's right to security of tenure and right to compensation by "contracting out". A contracting out agreement will only be valid where the parties have followed a statutory process before the parties are contractually bound to enter the lease. This process requires the landlord to serve a prescribed notice on the tenant and the tenant to make a declaration that they have received the notice.

If the lease is contracted out, then the tenant must vacate the premises when the lease expires, with no right to renew and no right to compensation.

Restrictions on Use
Leases usually restrict how the premises can be used. This is often linked to planning permission but sometimes, for example, with leases of commercial units in shopping centres, the use stated may be very specific so as to ensure that the landlord has a variety of businesses within the development.

Rent Review
Where leases are granted for more than five years, it is standard to provide for a rent re-calculation ("rent review") every fifth year. These reviews can be based on the open market rent which would be payable for a lease of the property on similar terms, may be linked to the Retail Prices Index or (less commonly) on fixed increases. Such provisions generally provide for "upwards only" reviews.

Full Repairing and Insuring Lease

The majority of leases of commercial premises in the UK are on a full repairing and insuring basis ("FRI lease") which means that the tenant is liable for the upkeep and decoration of the property and for the costs of the landlord in insuring the building.

Service Charge

Where a property is let to several different tenants, the landlord will retain responsibility in relation to the structure and the common parts of the building. The landlord will recover these costs from the tenant through charging a fee called a "service charge". The amount of service charge paid is generally proportionate to the size of the tenant's individual unit in relation to the lettable space in the whole building.

Break Rights

Some leases include break rights giving the landlord and/or the tenant the option to end the lease before its expiry date. These provisions specify how much notice has to be given and may have financial implications.

Privity of Contract

Where a lease is transferred to a new party, the original tenant will be subject to different liabilities dependent on the date of the lease.

For leases signed before 1 January 1996, the original tenant remains legally responsible for the rent and other lease commitments for the duration of the lease, regardless of whether they transfer the leasehold interest to a third party.

For leases signed after this date, subject to certain exceptions, the tenant will not remain liable after lawfully transferring the lease unless the landlord requests the tenant to sign a guarantee ("AGA"). In this situation, the tenant will remain liable during the period of ownership of the lease by the new tenant, but not beyond.

PLANNING

Prior to making certain alterations, erecting new buildings or changing the use of an existing building, businesses must contact their local authority's planning department in order to obtain planning permission. Most UK planning applications are administered by the local authority covering the area in which the particular building or site is located (contact details are available on most council websites).

The UK system is set out in statute and guidance published by the Government and by local authorities. The statutory timeframe for a planning application to a local authority to be decided is between eight and 16 weeks from the formal application, depending on whether it is treated as a major application, and whether an environmental impact assessment is required. If this timeframe is not adhered to by the local authority, the applicant may appeal. Additionally, if the application is refused, the applicant may also appeal. The appeals system in the UK also follows a statutory process.

REGISTERED LAND V UNREGISTERED LAND

Registered Land

The majority of land in England and Wales is registered at the Land Registry. The register is a matter of public record and the title is guaranteed. It contains information concerning the type of estate (e.g. freehold or leasehold), the property description (through reference to a filed plan), the current owner (known as the "registered proprietor") and details of all third party rights which have been registered against the estate or protected by notice (e.g. mortgages).

Not all information relating to the property will be displayed on the register. Certain third party rights ("overriding interests") will bind a purchaser of registered land regardless of whether they are recorded on the register, or whether a purchaser has any knowledge of them.

Unregistered Land

Alternatively, where land has remained in the same hands for many years, there may not have been a trigger event requiring registration at the Land Registry and the land may still be unregistered. In the absence of a register entry, a landowner can only deduce title by proving an unbroken chain of ownership by reference to the title deeds and documents relating to the property. In practice, for a landowner to prove a good root of title, the chain of deeds must go back at least 15 years.

HOW IS LAND TRANSFERRED?

A typical sale and purchase transaction is a two-stage process involving an exchange of contracts between the buyer and the seller, followed by completion of the legal transfer. A seller's solicitor will issue a draft sale contract which will be negotiated and then exchanged with a deposit usually being paid. This is the point of no return, when both parties commit themselves to complete on a certain date. Up to this point, either party can withdraw without any liability to the other side.

Following exchange of contracts, the transfer of the property from the seller to the buyer is effected by completing the transfer deed and by complying with Land Registry registration requirements. Completion is, in effect, moving day, when the money is paid to the seller's solicitors and the keys to the property are handed over to the buyer.

Principle of "Caveat Emptor"

In UK conveyancing, the principle of "caveat emptor" ("let the buyer beware") is key and places the responsibility for due diligence and searches relating to a property on the buyer. It is normally the task of a lawyer to consider and negotiate the legal documentation and discover as much information as possible about the property through a variety of searches and enquiries, including, but not limited to:

Local search - list of enquiries about property sent to the local authority which includes questions about planning, highways, drainage etc.

Environmental search – historical information about previous uses of the land.

Preliminary enquiries - questions about the property which are sent to the seller's or landlord's solicitors requesting information about issues such as disputes with neighbours and the use of the property.

Survey and Valuation

Any property investor (whether using their own funds or funding through bank debt or sale and leaseback arrangements) should take the precaution of ensuring they have a physical survey and valuation of the property carried out by a surveyor.

Whilst not strictly property contracts, some types of real estate may be encumbered by virtue of arrangements the seller has entered into, e.g. a management agreement or operating agreement may be in place which, according to the circumstances may affect value. Any investor contemplating UK real estate investment in a specific sector will benefit from advice at an early stage to ensure that issues that may affect their investment decision are identified early in the process (e.g. any issues that go to value or may inhibit its yield, such as large scale adjoining development).

TAX IMPLICATIONS OF ACQUIRING AN INTEREST IN PROPERTY

Value Added Tax ("VAT")

Commercial property transactions may be subject to VAT. Whether a commercial property transaction is subject to VAT will depend on several factors, mainly being whether it is regarded as a "new" property or whether the seller has opted to tax the property. VAT is currently charged at 20%.

Stamp Duty Land Tax ("SDLT")

This is a mandatory tax chargeable on the purchase of property situated in England, Wales and Northern Ireland. A similar tax called "Land and Buildings Transaction Tax" is payable in Scotland. SDLT is payable by the buyer on the purchase price, on completion or substantial performance of the contract (which generally means occupation or a payment of at least 90% of the price), whichever is earlier.

The rate of SDLT payable depends on the purchase price. For residential property, SDLT is currently chargeable at a rate of up to 15% of the purchase price. In contrast, the maximum rate of SDLT on acquisitions of UK commercial property is only 4% of the purchase price. Current rates are available on the website of HMRC[1].

---

[1] http://www.hmrc.gov.uk/sdlt/intro/rates-thresholds.htm

SDLT is also payable on the grant of a lease upon both the premium (if any) and the "net present value" of the rent payable, which is based on the value of the total rent over the life of the lease. For more information on calculating SDLT please see the HMRC website.[1]

There are a number of transactions which may be exempt from SDLT, such as intra-group transfers within the same group of companies.

Business Rates

Business rates are a property tax that business occupiers pay towards the costs of local government services. They typically range from £20 to £130 per square metre (approximately £2 to £13 per square foot).

Details of business rates can be found at:

England and Wales - *http://www.2010.voa.gov.uk/rli/*
Northern Ireland – *http://www.dfpni.gov.uk/lps/index/property_rating.htm*
Scotland - *http://www.scotland.gov.uk/Topics/Government/local-government/17999/11199*

This chapter gives a brief summary of the legal issues relating to investment in UK commercial real estate. It is not intended to give any specific legal advice or take the place of advice from property experts.

---

[1] http://www.hmrc.gov.uk/sdlt/calculate/calculators.htm

Part Seven

Emergent UK Investment Opportunities

7.1 THE UK – A LAUNCHPAD FOR STARTING AND SCALING UP TO BECOME A GLOBAL BUSINESS

Alessio Bortone and Mark Bell,PA Consulting Group

As an entrepreneur you must think global from day one – from the very moment you conceive your business idea and start executing it. Even local businesses and microenterprises cannot overlook global aspects when they setup shop. Payments, communications, logistics, operations, finance, supply chain and most importantly, customers – all these vital elements of business function on a global dimension.

The UK provides the ideal launchpad to meet your global aspirations. The supporting environment in the UK is internationally renowned for providing the key parts of a vibrant business start-up and scale-up community to execute your brilliant ideas. Academic literature and our successful entrepreneurs all tell us the same things. The UK is consistently rated as number #1 in Europe for starting and doing business globally:

- The UK is international in outlook - The UK is a great Launchpad to conquer international markets.
- You keep more of what you earn - Taxation is low and business-oriented.
- You can find money to help you - There are multiple possibilities for financing the growth of the company, from start-up to scale-up phase, across all the life of the company.
- The people are brilliant - The Human Capital available is rich, diverse, flexible, innovative, highly educated – and open to positive influx from all over the world.

Starting a business is a journey. In particular, a learning journey. We don't learn in a linear way – we all learn in an organic way, using the resources that are most readily available to us, adopting solutions that are obtainable at hand, and creating value as we go along. In a strong business region, entrepreneurs can access *markets*, raise *finance* and seek talented *human capital* more easily, while benefiting from business friendly *policies*, *culture* and *supports* accessible locally.

That's why your decision on where to start a company is such a vital one. Entrepreneurs today often have the opportunity to choose where to start. This is a relatively new freedom. A few decades ago, most entrepreneurs would have been limited to starting their company in the city or country in which they were based. *Today's entrepreneurs are nomads.* You are better informed on opportunities and policies available in countries far from your own ones, you have better tools for doing research, and you are more mobile. You should always consider the UK as an option to set up their company, at least as a reference point. Let's see why:

1. The UK is consistently rated as #1 in Europe for ease of doing business, which means:
*   It's easy to set up (and close) a company. It costs around £20 to register with the Government authorities, and the process can be completed in 20 minutes online;
*   The Corporate Governance process is straightforward, as it's based on principles rather than regulations;
*   Red tape and bureaucracy are kept to the bare minimum. The Government regularly reviews procedures and regulations, making sure they do not constitute impediment to business. This continuous improvement has saved British businesses £916m last year.

2. The UK is a great Launchpad to conquer international markets, because
*   It's at the centre of two major networks of nations, the European Union (500 million consumers) and the Commonwealth of Nations (2 billion consumers);
*   Its company law is considered international standard for transparency, accountability and fairness. Most major companies around the world understand English law and contracts subjected to it;
*   There's excellent support from the Government, provided via different Departments, including advice on market entry and expansion, or the provision of finance that SMEs often need when venturing overseas;
*   The world works on London time. A Company operating in multiple countries can contact customers and managers in the Far East in the morning and customers in the West Coast of the US or in Latin America in the afternoon. UK's major cities are globally connected.

3. Taxation is low and business-oriented:
*   Indeed, the Corporate Tax and Value Added Tax rates are both 20%;
*   Tax breaks are geared towards innovation and growth. Examples here are Tax breaks for R&D - which allows recovering up to 125% of R&D expenses – or

the Patent Box, which reduces corporate tax rate to 10%, for profits stemming from patents. Both schemes have proved to be powerful tools for attracting highly innovative entrepreneurs from other countries.

4. There are multiple possibilities for financing the growth of the company, from startup to scale up phase, across all the life of the company:
- The UK has the largest Venture Capital industry in Europe.
- The UK has the largest and most active community of Business Angels in Europe, with 18,000 Angels backing companies in different stages and sectors. The volume of investment by Business Angels has greatly increased thanks to the Seed Enterprise Investment Scheme (SEIS), a policy which allows investors to recover up to 40% of the investment in tax breaks;
- The Government backed Startup Loan Company provides small loans to launch a company and mentoring to support the entrepreneur along the journey. It has funded over 28,000 entrepreneurs, of which 46% were previously unemployed;
- There are over 600 different public grants available for funding companies at different stage of life;
- Other schemes available include the Regional Growth Fund (RGF) and European Funds
- The size of crowdfunding and crowdlending investment is growing fast. Platforms such as CrowdCube, Seedrs, FundingCircle are gaining ever more importance in the scene of innovative finance.

The British Business Bank has published a comprehensive "Business Finance Guide" that provides all the possible alternatives for debt and equity financing.

5. The Human Capital available is rich, diverse, flexible, innovative, highly educated – and open to positive influx from all over the world:
- UK Universities are considered among the top in the world, with four Academic Institutions ranking among the top ten globally. UK Universities play a massive role in the production of a highly educated workforce;
- Labour laws are geared towards flexibility, so companies can employ staff in a way that suits business needs. Labour costs are lower than in many countries of continental Europe;
- Human capital is enriched by the arrival of ambitious entrepreneurs from all over the world. This influx is regulated by several types of Visas, such as Graduate Entrepreneur, Entrepreneur and Prospective Entrepreneur Visas. It is also actively encouraged by Government initiatives such as the Sirius Programme and the Global Entrepreneur Programme.

In addition to the excellent environment outlined above the UK also has that intangible asset. *The culture.* The UK is a society where ambition, positive emulation, entrepreneurship and competition are encouraged and fostered. This is often forgotten or taken for granted, especially by British people themselves! In Britain, even young children are encouraged to develop entrepreneurial skills (think of Young Enterprise in primary schools), and educators pay particular attention to positive role models who can inspire the youth, and instil a hunger for achievement. This creates a breeding ground for the next generation of entrepreneurs. This positive environment will help you make the most of your ambition.

The ease of starting up is important. So too is the ease of scaling up. Entrepreneurs from around the world don't set up in the UK to remain stagnant. They want to grow quickly, from 10 to 100 employees, from 5 million to 50 million turnover. Of course that level of growth is not easy to achieve. It never is. There are well known "growing pains" to be overcome in the process.

Companies typically need to abandon the startup mindset and adopt new processes, hire staff more adapt to structured organizations, expand to other markets and geographies, access finance within complex deals (M&A, IPOs, listing on AIM or other specialized markets and so on), and most importantly, transform their leadership teams (or even change them when needed: not many entrepreneurs and managers can perform at their best across all the stages of a company).

Through all of this change the UK continues to offer a fully supportive environment. This is because the UK recognises that economic growth can be accelerated by businesses in scale-up mode as much as businesses in start-up mode. As per the "ScaleUp report" by Sherry Coutu, "Six per cent of UK businesses with the highest growth rates generated *half of the new jobs* created by existing businesses between 2002 and 2008."

In recognition of your importance as you scale up and realise your global ambition a number of support mechanisms are in place, including For example, the British Business Bank (BBB) and the British Growth Fund (BGF) have been created with the aim of providing finance for fuelling growth – fast growing companies require capital to support their expansion.

The Elite Programme (within the London Stock Exchange) helps scale ups with turnover of 5M+ to prepare and structure for their next stage of growth. It facilitates engagement between top growth companies and the corporate advisory and investor community, so that companies can get ready for possible IPOs at the end of the process.

Similarly, Tech City has started "FutureFifty" to identify top scale ups in the digital world. The first cohort of 50 Companies, many of which are set to become household names and brands, is now receiving full support from top tier advisors. In Cambridge, the Cambridge Cluster Map has identified another set of top 50 Companies for growth rate.

The most important aspect to underline though is that companies in the UK are supported by a large portfolio of activities throughout their journey, not just at the beginning of it.

Create a new company here, or transfer the HQ from other countries makes perfect business sense. Entrepreneurs and business owners are moving fast to pursue the opportunity in the UK, and the country welcomes them here. One Company in 7 in the UK is owned by a foreign national (according to the Centre for Entrepreneurship). Famous companies and brands like Tesco, Ribena, Cobra Beer, Easyjet, Marks&Spencer, WPP, Selfridges, and many more, were created by foreign entrepreneurs who came to the UK with nothing but a dream. Their founders came here last century and built economic empires. More recently, a flurry of startups and scaleups has moved to the UK in order to go global. Transferwise and Nutmeg are two famous examples, but hundreds could be quoted. The UK has always been, and continues to be, open for international business.

If you want to join an elite band of entrepreneurs coming here from all over the world, then the UK is a great place to start...and scale.

7.2 THE UK AS AN EXPORT HUB FOR INWARD INVESTORS

Rodney Berkley, UKTI Investment Group

In the late 1990s and early 2000s, globalisation saw more companies relocating parts of their business to low-cost locations around the world where it made increased business sense. This was driven mainly by the need to reduce costs and make efficiency savings. This offshoring process saw a shift of manufacturing and services jobs from developed to developing countries.

In recent years, developing markets have evolved and their economies have grown. At the same time, the initial competitive advantages that developing markets had are starting to erode as wages rise.

When the hidden costs of offshoring are factored in, such as the difficulties involved with managing complex supply chains, dealing with transport costs, long lead times and concerns about quality and counterfeiting, the price advantage can become marginal.

At the same time, changing market drivers and new technologies mean more businesses are looking to move parts of their businesses closer to European consumer markets and increase the proportion of goods and services sourced locally. This not only provides greater supply chain security but also enables businesses to react more quickly and flexibly to changing consumer tastes as well as exploit new technologies to deliver more customisation.

The UK offers a strong proposition for businesses reappraising their global location and sourcing strategies in the wake of these shifting dynamics. It provides excellent availability in terms of trained staff, a stable and transparent legal regime, close proximity to customers, a stable tax and regulatory regime and a competitive corporate tax regime. Since 2012, it is estimated that over £1bn worth of parts purchases have been reshored by UK vehicle makers.

A recent EY report "Building a tax manifesto for Manufacturing" says that "recent developments suggest a global trend towards reshoring, with companies deciding to locate manufacturing projects closer to home markets, which will create new opportunities for the UK." It is estimated that in the right conditions reshoring could bring £15.3bn of GDP to the UK economy equating to 315,000 jobs over the next ten years.

The UK Government has been quick to recognise this opportunity and the Prime Minister established Reshore UK just over a year ago to spearhead a reshoring campaign.

Reshore UK brings together UK Trade & Investment, the Manufacturing Advisory Service (now part of the Business Growth Service) and BIS working with partner bodies in Scotland, Wales and Northern Ireland in a "one-stop shop" to take a strategic approach to capturing reshoring investment and strengthening supply chains in the UK. The service is accessible for both UK and international firms providing advice and support from industry experts with deep sectorial knowledge and experience.

For international businesses, Reshore UK can:

- work with you to match UK supplier capability and capacity to your needs, to ensure you have the confidence of a local supply chain;
- work with the supply chain companies to ensure they can meet your requirements;
- support you to understand the business case for reshoring work to the UK.

Reshoring supports increased Foreign Direct Investment, bringing back high skill and high quality jobs, creating opportunities in supply chains, driving innovation and creating positive cluster effects covering both manufacturing and services industries. In addition to the aforementioned economic benefits, reshoring can play a strong role in rebalancing the UK economy between regions and sectors.

UK CONFIRMED AS THE TOP DESTINATION FOR FDI IN EUROPE

As stated in UKTI's Inward Investment Report for 2014 to 2015, the UK produced the highest growth among G7 countries at 2.8% and continues to be a major player in the global FDI arena despite the many challenges and uncertainties across world markets. All major independent sources confirm the UK as the number 1 destination in Europe for FDI in 2014 across the three main measures of success: financial value of FDI inflows; value of FDI stock (cumulative inflows); and number of individual investment decisions (FDI projects).

EXPORT READY FDI

The UK Government sees a clear link between reshoring and increasing Exports. The UK has a target to double exports by 2020 and to do so it will require industry to use the UK as a springboard for trade. A good example of this is seen in the offshore wind industry in the UK.

Last year German steel supplier EEW and Danish steel contractor Bladt formed a joint venture to create Offshore Structures (Britain) ("OSB") which now has a facility on Teesside that will manufacture the transition piece that connects the offshore wind foundation with the turbine tower.

OSB are aiming for this facility to become a specialised and world leading centre for fabrication and having secured their first order for these relatively complex structures they have taken on 75 staff. As they continue their optimisation programme and win further orders they plan on scaling up to have around 350 people on site to make around 150 units a year, supplying to the offshore wind farms across the UK and EU. This investment in the UK reflects the confidence in the quality of the UK offer, both in terms of the UK market and as a location service to deliver exports to the rest of the EU.

Over the last 18 months alone the UK has seen two further significant investments in offshore wind. Siemens has started building a wind turbine blade factory at Greenport, Hull on the Humber which, when fully operational in 2017 will grow to support around 1000 direct jobs. This facility will be set to deliver the wind turbine blades for projects across the UK, EU and potentially beyond.

June 2015 saw the first wind turbine blade completed for the Mitsubishi Heavy Industries and Vestas joint venture (MVOW) in offshore wind. The V164 blade has been made on the Isle of Wight facility and will be delivered to the Danish utility Dong Energy's Burbo Bank offshore windfarm. The Isle of Wight facility currently employees 200 people, and with further order successes will be MVOW's global blade production centre.

The UK has also seen existing facilities managed by external investors use the UK offshore wind market to prove their capability and competitiveness to then expand into the export market. JDR Cables, with an inter array cable factory in Hartlepool docks, is a strong example. Having proved their capabilities by first delivering to the RWE/SEE Greater Gabbard project, they have gone on to secure orders in excess of £100m having now won contracts to supply three German offshore windfarms.

Whilst these investments have significantly increased the UK's ability to deliver offshore wind projects in the UK, they have also reshaped the wider EU offer. The presence of ideally located and optimised industrial facilities (close to the UK and wider EU markets) has reduced costs as well as the risks in the supply chain. Furthermore, they have also resulted in improved quality and performance.

7.3 THE UK ECONOMY OFFERS THE RIGHT MIX FOR LONG-TERM SUCCESS IN DIGITAL HEALTHCARE

Chike Eupata, PA Consulting Group

The digital revolution across the world continues to transform and drive reforms especially in the healthcare industry. Today, investors are seizing opportunities to invest in digital products that aim to solve unmet needs that healthcare systems face. Today, the pace and scale of this revolution has created a gap between early adopters and organisations that are slow to change. Signs of value of digital health solutions are already being realised but we are still far away from realising the full potential of the digital revolution.

The global digital health market was valued at 60.8 billion U.S. dollars in 2013 and is expected to increase to 233.3 billion U.S. dollars by 2020. During this time, the mobile health segment of the industry is expected to generate the second largest revenue share, reaching 55.9 billion U.S. dollars in 2020 *(Source: Statista, 2015)*.

Sustainable private and government investment are critical enablers to sew up the gap in adoption and spread of digital technologies. Investment in digital infrastructure – from data and research, digital talent and advanced technology manufacturing as well as a long term commitment from the Government will create the right environment that allows innovation to thrive and solutions developed. We will continue to see an expansion of the digital revolution and now is the ripe moment to adapt our investment portfolios to reflect this trend.

HEALTHCARE SYSTEM

Healthcare systems are in flux as they struggle to strike the right balance of efficient provision of quality healthcare services to patients and manage the cost of provision. People are also living longer and have an improved ability to manage multiple chronic conditions thanks to advances in science and research, the drug technologies available, diagnostics and medical devices. Healthcare providers operate in a more competitive market with the increased ability for patients to choose where they receive their care and the growth of medical tourism. Innovation in healthcare is being fostered by new models of funding and a realignment of incentives directed to foster innovation and change.

The UK National Health Service (NHS) is internationally recognised for delivering excellent healthcare. The Commonwealth in 2014 rated the NHS as the best overall healthcare system in the world across a range of criteria including providing effective care, safe care, co-ordinated care and patient-centred care. The NHS continues to provide quality services to people for nearly 70 years supported by Government and private investment and partnerships with industry and academia. The NHS's achievements are at risk of pressures that threaten the high-quality care. The very foundations are being challenged by a combination of rising patient demand, staff shortages and falling funding. The UK Government has made long term commitments to transform the way healthcare services are delivered. Prevention and early detection of illnesses, empowering patients to take charge and become active participants in the management of their care and system efficiency gains in the way services are provided are part of this commitment. Digital solutions and the widespread use of health information technology will play a significant role to make this happen.

The UK Government has set forth ambitions for the use of digital technologies in healthcare and has a critical role to play in encouraging foreign direct investments to realise such ambitions. We will take a look at some of the policy ambitions, funding initiatives and infrastructure opportunities linked to digital health and consider some recommendations for investors considering investing in the UK.

Policies and Service Ambitions

The Government's vision is for a patient-led, transparent and safer NHS. The Department of Health (DH) aims to lead a digital first health and care system. DH together with the NHS National Information Board in the 2014 policy document *'Personalised healthcare 2020'* set out a framework for action to improve people's health and services using digital technology. Successes of the last 12 months have seen 97% of GP practices offering patients online access to book appointments, order repeat prescriptions and view a summary of their GP records. The policy focuses upon data access; transparency and trust to enable patients and care professionals make the right health and care choices, bring forward life-saving treatments and support innovation.

FUNDING INITIATIVES

Fiscal Incentives

The investment climate in the UK is supported by fiscal incentives for businesses. Incentives such as the low corporation tax, patent box and R&D tax credits confer tax stability and promote innovation.

The Corporation tax main rate currently set at 20% and is planned to reduce to 18% by 2020. This provides a competitive corporate tax and future certainty in the tax system creating the right conditions for business investment and growth.

R&D tax credits are another example of the Government's objective for strong and sustainable private sector-led growth. This measure ensures that incentives target business R&D investment.

Government Funds

UK Government provides various funding schemes for enable businesses to grow. Such funds made available to entrepreneurs, small and medium enterprises, healthcare providers, local Government and businesses. Investors can work in partnership with the Government to bolster the size and impact of funding digital health programmes.

The Prime Minister's challenge fund, now in its second wave provides £100million for 2015/16 period to GP practices who can demonstrate how they would use the money to improve and extend patient access to services.

The £5.3billion Better Care Fund in England is a joint fund reallocated from the NHS and local Government to enable localities – Local Governments, Clinical Commissioning Groups and Health and Well-being Boards support commissioning of services that meet the needs of the local population for example, better data sharing between health and social care.

The Technology Strategy Board in conjunction with Research Councils provides funding to help set up initiatives like the Small Business Research Initiative, Digital Catapults, and Biomedical catalysts.

UK MARKET INFRASTRUCTURE

Research and Development Institutes

Existing research networks and institutes are refocusing their objectives to include digital elements. New Institutes have also sprung up that focus on developing data science and analytical capabilities to extract value from the vast databases of health information and provide smarter insights for better services management and prediction. Academics and clinicians from world-renowned institutions work with policy makers and dynamic private sector technology companies. These partnerships can access the vast resources of the National Health Service (NHS), the largest unified healthcare system in the world.

Imperial Data Science Institute launched in 2014 works in partnership with academia and health providers to support the data economy and enable personal medicine through advanced analytics and big data management. The Institute is developing the European Translational Knowledge Management and Service (eTRIKS) platform as the gold standard personalised medicine big data research platform for the European medical research community.

Scotland's dedicated Digital health and care institute co-creates economic growth through new products, services and systems developed together with businesses, academics, healthcare specialists and citizens.

The Scottish Informatics Programme (SHIP) is a Scotland-wide research platform for the collation, management, dissemination and analysis of Electronic Patient Records. The programme is a partnership of Universities of Dundee, Edinburgh, Glasgow and St Andrews with the Information Services Division (ISD) of NHS Scotland.

Real world data studies and large scale genome sequencing show the value of big data applied in healthcare. The 100,000 genome project by Genomics England powered by sequencing and analytics technology positions the UK at the forefront of science and makes the NHS the most scientifically advanced healthcare system in the world.

The Honest Broker Service in Northern Ireland enables anonymised, aggregated and pseudonymised health and social care data to be shared to the Department of Health, Social Services and Public Safety and Health and Social Care organisations and anonymised data to ethically approved health and social care related research institutes.

Developing Digital Talent

There is a significant opportunity for investors to tackle the growing demand for digital talent. In the UK and across the world, companies face a shortage of people with desired skills in data science, analytics, social network, web and mobile development to name a few and this presents a major hurdle to digital transformation. The advent of online learning platforms, gamification of the recruitment process and incubating start-ups create the setting for continual learning and sharing of new ideas. The UK has 1.46m people in digital employment across the country with 21 thriving clusters from Norwich to Northern Ireland, all of which possess great variation in key capabilities (Tech City, 2015). Scotland's Skills Investment Plan aims to attract and retain talent and widen the pool of talent through an industry-led talent academy.

World-leading universities in the UK are what many other countries aspire to emulate. Our academics are world renowned in research and innovation and UK graduates are in demand worldwide. The UK ranks second in the world for research-based university-business collaboration. The UK has one of the best talent pools in Europe, with four of the world's top six universities. Universities are the UK's hubs that support business research and innovation through a range of knowledge transfer activities. 170 UK universities and other higher education institutions create the highest number of graduates in Western Europe.

Broadband and Mobile Connectivity

By 2017, superfast coverage will have reached 95% of premises, and we expect mobile operators to have achieved 4G coverage to 98%. A competitive private market, a strong independent regulator and targeted Government intervention have played a key role to achieving such coverage.

The Government's ambition is that ultrafast broadband of at least 100Mbps should become available to nearly all UK premises. Realising this ambition will ensure that the UK remains among the best connected nations in the world. Internet connectivity is an important enabler for digital technologies, mobile and cloud-based solutions.

Looking ahead, the market is mobilising to deliver ultrafast services, including gigabit services on demand and ensure the UK is a world leader in the development of 5G. Government is keen to work with industry to highlight barriers to private investment and explore with network providers how these might be overcome, perhaps through innovative financial and commercial models.

Regulation

The two main regulators that overlap with digital health technologies in the UK are Ofcom and Medicines and Healthcare products Regulatory Agency (MHRA). There is also an EU-wide directive on Data Protection.

Ofcom's strategic review of digital communications currently underway is examining competition, investment, and innovation.

Medicines and Healthcare products Regulatory Agency (MHRA) is an internationally highly-respected regulator. The MHRA's Innovation Office is set up to help companies, small and medium-sized enterprises (SMEs), academics and individuals who have developed a novel medicine or device, or a novel approach to the development or manufacture of a product, in their regulation.

Standards and Interoperability

The Health and Social Care Information Centre (HSCIC) is the national body responsible for collecting information about treatments and care from across health and social care. HSCIC established the NHS Interoperability framework to define standards on the transfer of health data. The result, an Interoperability Toolkit sets a national standard defining requirements and rules for the creation and transport of electronic information.

RECOMMENDATIONS

Investors will need to work closer with Government and the NHS to build a better understanding of unmet needs in digital health today and identify opportunities for investment. The Government has a role to ensure the digital health market is open to investors by improving adoption and diffusion of technologies across the NHS. Innovative business models are required that combine elements of collaboration with academia and healthcare providers, co-creating solutions and sharing intellectual property.

Investors need to work more closely with Government to provide funding directed towards supporting digital health entrepreneurs and promote innovation adoption and diffusion across the health system.

To conclude, digital transformation is happening at a fast pace and is only set to continue growing. Success in this economy will be determined by our ability to fully embed new digital technologies into the core fabric of the healthcare system and society at large. This requires multiple stakeholders bought into the change effort and belief in the potential benefits of digital technology. The Government is fully committed to digital transformation across all facets of care. Investors should take a long term view and provide sustainable investments in digital infrastructure to reap the larger benefits. Now is the time to start investing and support growth of the UK digital health economy.

RECOMMENDATIONS

Investors will need to work closer with Government and the NHS to build a better understanding of unmet needs in digital health today and identify opportunities for investment. The Government has a role to ensure the digital health market is open to investors by improving adoption and diffusion of technologies across the NHS.

Innovative business models are required that combine elements of collaboration with academia and healthcare providers, co-creating solutions and sharing intellectual property.

Investors need to work more closely with Government to provide funding directed towards supporting digital health entrepreneurs and promote innovation adoption and diffusion across the health system.

To conclude, digital transformation is happening at a fast pace and is only set to continue growing. Success in this economy will be determined by our ability to fully embed new digital technologies into the core fabric of the healthcare system and society at large. This requires multiple stakeholders bought into the change effort and belief in the potential benefits of digital technology. The Government is fully committed to digital transformation across all facets of care. Investors should take a long term view and provide sustainable investments in digital infrastructure to reap the larger benefits. Now is the time to start investing and support growth of the UK digital health economy.

Appendix

CONTRIBUTORS' CONTACTS

Carter Jonas LLP
6-8 Hills Road
Cambridge CB2 1NH
Tel: +44 (0) 1223 348 607
Contact: Nick Hood
e-mail: Nick.Hood@carterjonas.co.uk

Legend Business Books Ltd
175-185 Gray's Inn Road
London WC1X 8OE
Tel: +44 (0) 20 7812 0642
Contact: Tom Chalmers
Direct line: +44 (0) 20 7812 0643
e-mail: tomchalmers@legend-paperbooks.co.uk
Jonathan Reuvid
Direct line: +44 (0) 1295 738 070
e-mail: jreuvidembooks@aol.com

Mazars LLP
Tower Bridge House
St Katharine's Way
London E1W 1DD
Contact: Toby Stanbrook
Tel: (0) 20 7063 4000
e-mail: toby.stanbrook@mazars.co.uk

PA Consulting Services Limited
123 Buckingham Palace Road
London SW1W 9SR
Contact: Khalil Souki
Tel: (0) 20 7323 5254
e-mail: Khalil.Souki@paconsulting.com

PNO Consultants Limited
Dunham House Brooke Court
Lower Meadow Road
Wilmslow
Cheshire SK9 3ND
Tel: +44 (0) 161 488 3488
Contact: Olaf Swanzy
e-mail: olaf.swanzy@pnoconsultants.com

UK Trade & Investment
Deputy Director, Investment
1, Victoria Street
London SW1H 0ET
Contact:
David McLean
Tel: +44 (0) 207 215 8775
e-mail: david.mclean@ukti.gsi.gov.uk

UKTI Team Support
Contact by e-mail: enquiries@ukti-invest.com

Watson Farley & Williams LLP
15 Appold Street
London EC2A 2HB
Tel: +44 (0) 20 7814 8000
Contact: Asha Kumar
Direct line: +44 (0) 20 7814 8182
e-mail: AKumar@wfw.com